New Waves in Philosophy

Series Editors: **Vincent F. Hendricks** and

Titles include:

Jesús H. Aguilar, Andrei A. Buckareff and Keiт
NEW WAVES IN PHILOSOPHY OF ACTION

Michael Brady (*editor*)
NEW WAVES IN METAETHICS

Otavio Bueno and Oystein Linnebo (*editors*)
NEW WAVES IN PHILOSOPHY OF MATHEMATICS

Boudewijn DeBruin and Christopher F. Zurn (*editors*)
NEW WAVES IN POLITICAL PHILOSOPHY

Allan Hazlett (*editor*)
NEW WAVES IN METAPHYSICS

Vincent F. Hendricks and Duncan Pritchard (*editors*)
NEW WAVES IN EPISTEMOLOGY

P.D. Magnus and Jacob Busch (*editors*)
NEW WAVES IN PHILOSOPHY OF SCIENCE

Yujin Nagasawa and Erik J. Wielenberg (*editors*)
NEW WAVES IN PHILOSOPHY OF RELIGION

Jan Kyrre Berg Olsen, Evan Selinger and Søren Riis (*editors*)
NEW WAVES IN PHILOSOPHY OF TECHNOLOGY

Thomas S. Petersen, Jesper Ryberg and Clark Wolf (*editors*)
NEW WAVES IN APPLIED ETHICS

Sarah Sawyer (*editor*)
NEW WAVES IN PHILOSOPHY OF LANGUAGE

Kathleen Stock and Katherine Thomson-Jones (*editors*)
NEW WAVES IN AESTHETICS

Nikolaj J. L. L. Pedersen and Cory D. Wright (*editors*)
NEW WAVES IN TRUTH

Forthcoming:

Thom Brooks (*editor*)
NEW WAVES IN ETHICS

Maksymilian Del Mar (*editor*)
NEW WAVES IN PHILOSOPHY OF LAW

Greg Restall and Gillian Russell (*editors*)
NEW WAVES IN PHILOSOPHICAL LOGIC

Future Volumes:

NEW WAVES IN PHILOSOPHY OF MIND
NEW WAVES IN FORMAL PHILOSOPHY

New Waves in Philosophy
Series Standing Order ISBN 978–0–230–53797–2 (hardcover)
Series Standing Order ISBN 978–0–230–53798–9 (paperback)
(*outside North America only*)

You can receive future titles in this series as they are published by placing a standing order. Please contact your bookseller or, in case of difficulty, write to us at the address below with your name and address, the title of the series and one of the ISBNs quoted above.

Customer Services Department, Macmillan Distribution Ltd, Houndmills, Basingstoke, Hampshire RG21 6XS, England

New Waves in Metaethics

Edited by

Michael Brady
University of Glasgow, UK

First published 2011 by
PALGRAVE MACMILLAN

Palgrave Macmillan in the UK is an imprint of Macmillan Publishers Limited,
registered in England, company number 785998, of Houndmills, Basingstoke,
Hampshire RG21 6XS.

Palgrave Macmillan in the US is a division of St Martin's Press LLC,
175 Fifth Avenue, New York, NY 10010.

Palgrave Macmillan is the global academic imprint of the above companies
and has companies and representatives throughout the world.

Palgrave® and Macmillan® are registered trademarks in the United States,
the United Kingdom, Europe and other countries.

ISBN: 978-0-230-25161-8 hardback
ISBN: 978-0-230-25162-5 paperback

This book is printed on paper suitable for recycling and made from fully
managed and sustained forest sources. Logging, pulping and manufacturing
processes are expected to conform to the environmental regulations of the
country of origin.

A catalogue record for this book is available from the British Library.

Library of Congress Cataloging-in-Publication Data

New waves in metaethics / [edited by] Michael Brady.
    p. cm.—(New waves in philosophy)
    ISBN 978-0-230-25162-5 (pbk.)
    1. Ethics. I. Brady, Michael, 1965–

BJ1012.N486 2011
170'.42—dc22   2010032358

10 9 8 7 6 5 4 3 2 1
20 19 18 17 16 15 14 13 12 11

Printed and bound in Great Britain by
CPI Antony Rowe, Chippenham and Eastbourne

Contents

Notes on Contributors   vii

Series Editors' Preface   x

Introduction   1
Michael Brady

1   Ethical Non-Naturalism and Normative Properties   7
    William J. FitzPatrick

2   Naturalistic Metaethics at Half Price   36
    Joshua Gert

3   In Defense of Moral Error Theory   62
    Jonas Olson

4   The Myth of Moral Fictionalism   85
    Terence Cuneo and Sean Christy

5   Expressivism, Inferentialism and the
    Theory of Meaning   103
    Matthew Chrisman

6   How Not to Avoid Wishful Thinking   126
    Mark Schroeder

7   Internal Reasons and the Motivating Intuition   141
    Julia Markovits

8   Beyond Wrong Reasons: The Buck-Passing
    Account of Value   166
    Ulrike Heuer

9   A Wrong Turn to Reasons?   185
    Pekka Väyrynen

10 Shmagency Revisited   208
    David Enoch

11 The Authority of Social Norms   234
    Nicholas Southwood

12 Moral Epistemology   249
    Alison Hills

13   Aesthetics and Particularism   264
     Sean McKeever and Michael Ridge

Bibliography   286

Index   299

Contributors

Michael Brady is Senior Lecturer at the University of Glasgow. His main research interests are in metaethics, philosophy of emotion, and epistemology. He is editor, with Duncan Pritchard, of *Moral and Epistemic Virtues* (Blackwell, 2003), and has published articles in such journals as *Philosophical Studies, Philosophical Quarterly*, and *American Philosophical Quarterly*.

Matthew Chrisman is Lecturer at the University of Edinburgh working on ethics (especially metaethics), epistemology (especially epistemic normativity), philosophy of language, and philosophy of action. He has published articles in *The Journal of Philosophy, Philosophy and Phenomenological Research, Oxford Studies in Metaethics, Philosophers' Imprint*, and *Philosophical Studies*.

Sean Christy is a recent graduate of Calvin College in Grand Rapids, Michigan, where he received a BA in Philosophy. He currently works in the financial services industry.

Terence Cuneo is Associate Professor at the University of Vermont. He works primarily in the areas of metaethics and history of modern philosophy. He is the author of *The Normative Web: An Argument for Moral Realism* (Oxford University Press, 2007) and the editor of six volumes, including *The Cambridge Companion to Thomas Reid* (with Rene Van Woudenberg) (Cambridge University Press, 2004) and *Foundations of Ethics: An Anthology* (with Russ Shafer-Landau) (Blackwell, 2007).

David Enoch is Associate Professor of Philosophy and Jacob I. Berman Associate Professor of Law at the Hebrew University of Jerusalem. He works primarily in moral, political, and legal philosophy. His papers have been published in such journals as *Ethics, Philosophical Review, Mind, Noûs, Philosophy and Phenomenological Research, Philosophical Studies, Oxford Studies in Metaethics, Philosopher's Imprint, Law and Philosophy, Legal Theory*, and *Oxford Studies in the Philosophy of Law*. His book *Taking Morality Seriously: A Defense of Robust Realism* is forthcoming from Oxford University Press.

William J. FitzPatrick is Associate Professor in the Department of Philosophy at the University of Rochester. His work in metaethics focuses on defending a robust ethical realism involving a non-naturalistic metaphysics of ethical facts and properties and an external reasons theory that allows for the categoricity of moral requirements. In addition to critiquing neo-Kantian constructivism, neo-Humean theories of reasons, and naturalistic forms of realism, he has also worked on critiques of appeals to natural teleology and/

or evolution in metaethical or ethical arguments. Recent publications in metaethics appear in *Oxford Studies in Metaethics, Ethics,* and *Mind.*

Joshua Gert is Professor of Philosophy at the College of William and Mary. His primary research interests are in practical rationality and reasons for action, ethical theory, and philosophy of color, generally informed by a Wittgensteinian perspective in philosophy of language. He has published one book, *Brute Rationality: Normativity and Human Action* (Cambridge University Press, 2004), and numerous articles on color and value in such journals as *The Philosophical Review, Journal of Philosophy, Noûs, Ethics* and *Philosophy and Phenomenological Research.*

Ulrike Heuer is Lecturer in Philosophy at the University of Leeds. Her main interests are in theories of practical reasons, metaethics, and normative ethics. Her recent publications appear in *Oxford Studies in Normative Ethics, Ethical Theory and Moral Practice,* and *Philosophical Studies.*

Alison Hills is Lecturer in Philosophy at the University of Oxford and a Fellow and Tutor of St John's College. She is interested in all aspects of moral philosophy. She is the author of *The Beloved Self,* forthcoming from Oxford University Press.

Julia Markovits joined the MIT philosophy faculty as an Assistant Professor in 2009, after spending three years as a Junior Fellow at the Harvard Society of Fellows. Her research focuses on ethics and, more specifically, on questions concerning the nature of moral reasons. She has published articles in *The Philosophical Review* and *Oxford Studies in Metaethics,* and is currently writing a book providing an internalist defense of universally shared moral reasons, which will be published by Oxford University Press.

Sean McKeever is Associate Professor of Philosophy at Davidson College. He works on contemporary moral theory and is co-author, with Michael Ridge, of *Principled Ethics: Generalism as a Regulative Ideal* (Oxford University Press, 2006).

Jonas Olson is a Research Fellow and Lecturer at Stockholm University. His main interests are metaethics, value theory, and history of moral philosophy. He has contributed to several collections and has published articles in journals such as *Australasian Journal of Philosophy, Philosophical Quarterly, Philosophy and Phenomenological Research, Mind, Utilitas, Theoria, Ethical Theory and Moral Practice, Inquiry,* and *Ratio.*

Michael Ridge is Professor of Moral Philosophy at the University of Edinburgh. His research interests include metaethics, especially issues surrounding expressivism and the debate over particularism and generalism. He has co-authored (with Sean McKeever) several articles and a book, *Principled Ethics: Generalism as a Regulative Ideal* (Oxford University Press, 2007), on the latter topic.

Mark Schroeder is Associate Professor of Philosophy at the University of Southern California and author of *Slaves of the Passions* (Oxford University Press, 2007), *Being For: Evaluating the Semantic Program of Expressivism* (Oxford University Press, 2008), and *Noncognitivism in Ethics* (Routledge, 2010). His articles on metaethics have appeared in *Ethics, Noûs, Philosophical Studies, Philosophers' Imprint, Philosophy and Phenomenological Research, Oxford Studies in Metaethics*, and other journals.

Nicholas Southwood is currently a Junior Research Fellow at Jesus College, Oxford University, and an assistant professor in the Philosophy Program of the Research School of Social Sciences at the Australian National University. He works mainly in moral and political philosophy, with a particular interest in questions concerning practical reason and normativity. He has published widely in these areas in journals including *Ethics, Noûs, Philosophical Studies*, and *Politics, Philosophy and Economics*. His book, *Contractualism and the Foundations of Morality* (Oxford University Press, 2010), defends a distinctively deliberative model of contractualism as an account of ultimate grounds of our moral duties.

Pekka Väyrynen is Senior Lecturer in Philosophy at the University of Leeds. He works primarily in metaethics and has published widely in this area in journals and collections including *Ethics, Philosophy and Phenomenological Research*, and *Oxford Studies in Metaethics*.

Series Editors' Preface

New Waves in Philosophy Series

The aim of this series is to gather the young and up-and-coming scholars in philosophy to give their view of the subject now and in the years to come, and to serve a documentary purpose: that is, 'this is what they said then, and this is what happened.' It will also provide a snapshot of cutting-edge research that will be of vital interest to researchers and students working in all subject areas of philosophy.

The goal of the series is to have a New Waves volume in every one of the main areas of philosophy. We would like to thank Palgrave Macmillan for taking on this project in particular, and the entire *New Waves in Philosophy* series in general.

Vincent F. Hendricks and Duncan Pritchard
Editors

Editor's Acknowledgements

I would like to thank Vincent Hendricks and Duncan Pritchard for the invitation to edit this volume; Melanie Blair, Sue Clements, Priyanka Gibbons at Palgrave Macmillan and Vidhya Jayaprakash and her team at Newgen for their sterling work throughout the editorial and production process; Simon Prosser, for permission to use his photograph for the front cover; and the authors for their help, patience, and of course their contributions.

Introduction

Michael Brady

The plan for this volume was simple: to invite some of the best young philosophers working in metaethics to write on topics they found most interesting. The resulting collection represents something of the state of play in this core area of analytic philosophy, and provides an indication of the directions that metaethical thinking might take in the future. In addition, the contributions also provide coverage of a suitably broad range of metaethical issues: included here are questions about naturalism and non-naturalism, about expressivism and cognitivism, about the nature of reasons and values, about particularism, aesthetics, moral epistemology, and social normativity. So I hope that this volume not only presents an insight into the distinctive research of individual thinkers, but also stands as an introduction to the contours of the general subject.

There are certain subsidiary themes that can play an organizational role. The first four papers are focused on broadly metaphysical issues. The opening paper, William J. FitzPatrick's 'Ethical Non-Naturalism and Normative Properties,' defends and then expands on the view that moral or ethical properties or facts are not natural properties or facts, where these are traditionally understood as being the proper subject of scientific inquiry. Moral facts and properties are, instead, *sui generis* or *irreducibly normative*. FitzPatrick is concerned to counter Allan Gibbard's recent claims that a form of expressivism can capture everything the non-naturalist wants, without being committed to any mysterious or extravagant metaphysics. (Expressivism is, roughly, the view that moral language serves the function of expressing 'non-cognitive' mental states like desire or approval.) FitzPatrick argues, *contra* Gibbard, that any such 'quasi-realist' expressivism is in fact at a significant disadvantage when compared with non-naturalism. The case for non-naturalism does not stop here, however: FitzPatrick goes on to argue that (i) ethical naturalism faces a number of serious problems of its own, and that (ii) non-naturalism has the means to avoid other objections.

Joshua Gert seeks to make a *positive* case for a metaethical naturalism in his 'Naturalistic Metaethics at Half Price.' In particular, Gert wishes to develop a form of 'linguistic naturalism' that appeals to facts about human behavior and linguistic capacities to explain why we shouldn't worry about the metaphysical status of things – such as numbers or normative reasons – that might initially appear problematic from a naturalistic standpoint. Gert's account – which he terms 'Global Expressivist Response-Dependence' or GERD – involves combining and modifying the naturalistic metaethical views developed by Huw Price and Philip Pettit. Gert proceeds to defend GERD against a number of criticisms, and deploys GERD to undermine views of practical reasons and moral language learning put forward by Michael Smith and Michael Ridge, respectively.

The focus then shifts to metaethical positions that might be attractive for naturalists, but which have more of a revisionary outlook. While non-naturalist and naturalist proposals maintain that some moral or evaluative statements are true, moral error theory defends the skeptical possibility that all such claims are false. In particular, error theorists usually hold that (i) moral judgments involve claims about categorical reasons, and that (ii) there are no such reasons, in which case moral judgments are false. Jonas Olson's contribution to the volume, 'In Defense of Moral Error Theory,' considers a number of problems for an error-theoretical approach, and shows how the error theorist can solve them. Olson first formulates moral error theory so that it is not itself committed to any first-order moral claims (which would, by the theory's own lights, be false). He then responds to recent criticisms due to Stephen Finlay, according to which ordinary speakers do not make the error of which they are accused, and finally responds to the challenge that error theory casts doubt upon the existence of hypothetical reasons and therefore proves too much. Olson argues that the error theorist can provide an account of hypothetical reasons – in terms of non-normative relations between means and ends – that is metaphysically unproblematic.

A position closely related to error theory is that of moral fictionalism. Whereas error theory encompasses claims about language and ontology, moral fictionalism is more centrally a theory about moral language, and in particular maintains that such language is 'fictive.' Terence Cuneo and Sean Christy argue against this theory in 'The Myth of Moral Fictionalism.' According to fictionalism, moral discourse is (or should be) a 'mode of pretense,' and we are (or should be) 'fictioneers' about moral facts and entities. A fictioneer is someone who performs speech acts that appear to commit her to the belief in the existence of moral facts and entities, but who isn't, in fact, committed to their existence. Cuneo and Christy argue against both the 'hermeneutic' version of fictionalism of Mark Kalderon, according to which ordinary subjects are in fact fictioneers when engaging in moral discourse, and the 'revolutionary' version, due to Richard Joyce, according to which ordinary subjects ought to take up the fictive stance. Cuneo and Christy raise doubts about the claim that ordinary people engaged in moral discourse are actually moral fictioneers; and they maintain that any benefits revolutionary fictionalism brings can be generated by naturalistic theories that don't have the costs of fictionalism.

The next two papers in the collection focus on different issues raised by non-cognitive approaches to moral thought and judgment, which maintain (again, roughly) that moral claims or statements are not capable of being true or false. Matthew Chrisman's paper 'Expressivism, Inferentialism and the Theory of Meaning,' starts with the question of how an expressivist account of the meaning of ethical sentences fits in with a more general account of sentence meaning. Chrisman argues that this question poses a serious problem for expressivism, but not for his preferred sort of non-representationalist account, namely *inferentialism*. Inferentialist (or conceptual-role) theories of meaning maintain that a sentence means what it does, not in virtue of what it represents or in virtue of the thought it expresses, but in virtue of its inferential relations – and, in particular, its inferential commitments, entitlements, and obligations. Chrisman's main aim is to show that inferentialism is a viable option in metaethics, and one that fits much better than expressivism with a general account of the meaning of sentences.

Mark Schroeder is also concerned with presenting problems for non-cognitivism in his paper 'How Not to Avoid Wishful Thinking.' Schroeder takes his lead from Cian Dorr's 2002 challenge to non-cognitivism, which has become known as the 'wishful thinking problem.' The challenge is that non-cognitivist expressivist approaches seem committed to the claim that it is sometimes rational to form beliefs on the basis of one's desires. But then, *contra* common sense, expressivism is committed to thinking that wishful thinking is a rational method of acquiring beliefs. Schroeder aims to assess the current state of play with respect to this problem, by focusing on the attempted solutions offered by David Enoch and James Lenman. Schroeder argues that neither is particularly plausible, and suggests that any solution will require that the non-cognitivist develops a better understanding of epistemological notions of evidence and justification.

The next three papers mark a shift from a focus on moral facts and ethical language to a consideration of two more central themes in metaethics, namely (the nature of) practical reasons, and the relation between reason, agency and value. Julia Markovits's paper, 'Internal Reasons and the Motivating Intuition,' addresses Bernard Williams's seminal paper 'Internal and External Reasons,' and in particular looks at the 'motivating intuition' that drives Williams's argument. This is the thought that reasons must be capable of explaining action: a reason for an agent to act must be a possible source of motivation for her to act, at least in so far as she is rational. Markovits argues that, despite its initial air of plausibility, there are a host of counterexamples that force us to reject the motivating intuition. Some of these are examples where reasons we have for acting would no longer apply to us if we were fully rational. Other examples show that reasons that do apply to us when fully rational are nevertheless incapable of motivating us.

This does not, however, mean that we should reject an internalist account of reasons; instead Markovits explains that there are good grounds to think that there is a necessary connection between our reasons and our motives.

Ulrike Heuer's paper, 'Beyond Wrong Reasons: The Buck-Passing Account of Value,' investigates the prospects for explaining or understanding goodness in terms of reasons for certain responses or behaviors. Heuer is concerned, in particular, with the 'metaphysical' version of buck-passing, which holds that the fact that something is valuable consists in the fact that it has some other property which constitutes a reason to respond favorably or to behave in certain ways towards it. Heuer argues that, in so far as buck-passing accounts incorporate a 'fitting attitude' analysis of value, they are susceptible to a familiar problem termed the 'wrong kind of reasons problem.' Although Heuer thinks that there are solutions to this problem, she also holds that they are unavailable to the buck-passer, and so concludes that those who favor buck-passing should reject fitting attitude analyses of value. In the final section of her paper Heuer assesses the prospects for such a buck-passing account.

In 'A Wrong Turn to Reasons?' Pekka Väyrynen addresses attempts to explain normative and evaluative phenomena – such as right, wrong, admirable, required, just, terrifying, etc. – by appealing to reasons. (Väyrynen considers the buck-passing account of goodness as a 'local' instance of a 'turn to reasons;' but this explanatory strategy can take a 'global' form and seek to accommodate a broader range of normative notions.) In particular, Väyrynen wishes to investigate whether an appeal to reasons – for acting, thinking and feeling – is a better way for us to account for normative and evaluative phenomena than appealing to value or any other concept. Väyrynen is skeptical about this claim of priority on behalf of reasons. He argues that reasons relations *themselves* require explanation, and it is difficult to see how such demands can be met in a way that is compatible with the claim that reasons are fundamental. If so, we can doubt whether the turn to reasons offers any explanatory advantages with respect to normative and evaluative notions.

Questions concerning the nature of normativity are prominent in the two papers that follow Väyrynen's contribution. David Enoch's 'Shmagency Revisited' focuses on the claims of *constitutivism*, which maintains that normativity is grounded in norms or standards or motives or aims that are constitutive of agency. Despite its intuitive appeal, constitutivism faces a serious problem, which is that agents need not care about being agents, or care about their behavior being action. They might, instead, be happy to be 'shmagents,' who lack that which is constitutive of agency but are in other respects very similar to agents. Enoch initially raised this challenge to constitutivism in 2006, and here responds to constitutivist responses – focusing on David Velleman's discussion – in order to assess the current state of play with regard to this particular objection, and (more broadly) to promote a better understanding of what constitutivism is and of the motivations behind it.

In 'The Authority of Social Norms,' Nicholas Southwood considers the question of how we should understand social normativity. A central problem with any such attempt is that social norms are both normative *and* a matter of custom or convention, and these aspects can seem to be in conflict. Attempts to capture the customary nature of such norms run the risk of failing to capture the fact that they are genuine *requirements*; but proposals that focus on the normativity of social norms can fail to capture their customary aspect. After criticizing standard accounts of social normativity, Southwood explains an approach that promises to accommodate both the customary and the normative nature of social norms. On this view, social norms are collections of normative judgments that are, nonetheless, different from other normative judgments of morality and prudence because they are grounded in social practices. This allows social norms to have a particular kind of social authority.

The final two papers address metaethical questions raised by issues in epistemology and aesthetics. The topic of 'Moral Epistemology' by Alison Hills is an epistemic puzzle that generates a problem for certain metaethical views: in particular, for versions of moral realism that insist that there are mind-independent, objective moral facts and properties, and for versions of non-cognitivism maintaining that moral claims have an expressive rather than a representational function. The puzzle is that *moral* epistemology has certain central features that appear to be in tension. Thus, we think that there is something suspect about forming moral beliefs purely on the basis of testimony; that deferring to the beliefs of others in moral matters is illegitimate; that we tend not to give weight to the opinions of others in moral matters, whereas we are happy to in non-moral affairs; and, finally, that taking *advice* from others about moral issues is often a good idea. Hills argues that standard forms of moral realism and of non-cognitivism will struggle to accommodate all four features of moral epistemology. Nevertheless, all four features can be captured, Hills proposes, provided we recognize that the target of moral thinking and inquiry is (and should be) moral understanding rather than moral knowledge.

In 'Aesthetics and Particularism,' Sean McKeever and Michael Ridge consider a challenge to a generalist position in ethics that is raised by a particularist approach in aesthetics. Generalism maintains, roughly, that there are sound and informative principles governing some domain; particularism about some domain denies this. McKeever and Ridge are concerned because they regard particularism about aesthetics and aesthetic judgment as *true*, but wish to defend a generalist approach in ethics. Their worry, then, is that their defense of generalism in ethics might prove too much if it rules out a plausible view in aesthetics. The authors seek to address this worry by first recapping their arguments for generalism in ethics, and by then proceeding to show why such arguments do not apply with respect to aesthetics. Central to their argument is the idea that aesthetic knowledge requires a kind of 'direct engagement' with the art work – a kind of non-conceptual, non-inferential, and global apprehension of the object of appreciation – that is not essential in ethics, and that this requirement makes particularism in aesthetics a good deal more plausible than its ethical cousin. There is thus sufficient asymmetry between ethical and aesthetic evaluation to undermine the challenge to generalism in ethics.

Although the papers have been grouped together according to broad themes, this is, in a sense, rather artificial. For another of the notable features of the contributions is the extent to which they show how metaethical questions and issues are interrelated and interlinked. So we see discussions of categorical reasons informing claims about moral language, accounts of linguistic capacities having a bearing on theories about moral facts, issues in (moral) epistemology generating views about the plausibility of expressivism, statements about (internal) reasons leading to theses about the nature of normativity, thoughts about normativity in the social and aesthetic realms grounding arguments about normativity in other areas, and so on. The papers in this collection thus stand as testimony to the very high quality of research in metaethics being produced by younger philosophers, and also to the rich, complex, and holistic character of this vibrant area of analytic philosophy.

1
Ethical Non-Naturalism and Normative Properties

William J. FitzPatrick

Ethical non-naturalism, as I shall understand it, is the view that there are real ethical properties and facts that are not among the natural properties and facts of the world. This is to say that ethical properties (such as moral rightness or goodness) and facts (such as the fact that an act is wrong, or that a certain consideration is a reason for acting) are neither among the properties and facts that are the proper subject of scientific inquiry, nor constructible from those that are. They are instead *sui generis*. Ethical non-naturalists are thus ethical realists who reject naturalistic construals of ethical properties and facts.

It is no secret that many theorists find ethical non-naturalism intolerably mysterious and extravagant. Allan Gibbard, an expressivist who rejects both ethical non-naturalism and ethical realism, describes non-natural properties as 'strange and incredible things' (Gibbard, 2008, p. 20). He finds it puzzling 'why [one] should think that the universe contains properties that are non-natural, or how a primitive, non-naturalistic concept could be a legitimate part of our thinking'; and he wonders how anyone 'could have learned of a non-naturalistic subject matter' (Gibbard, 2010, p. 2). Indeed, the latter may seem especially problematic given that we are evolved creatures with epistemic faculties forged by natural selection in ancestral environments.

Instead of embracing non-naturalism, Gibbard argues that we can capture everything attractive about non-naturalist realism within a quasi-realist expressivism that 'exactly mimics a [non-naturalist] normative realism' (Gibbard, 2010, p. 9).[1] My aim here is to take some steps toward answering Gibbard's questions, and in the process (i) to clarify non-naturalism as contrasted with both quasi-realist expressivism and non-reductionist ethical naturalism, (ii) to explore the significant shortcomings of quasi-realist expressivism as an alternative to non-naturalism (focusing on Gibbard's current view), while also raising problems for some forms of ethical naturalism, and (iii) to address some further objections to non-naturalism.

1. Irreducible normativity and non-naturalism: concepts and properties

To begin with Gibbard's first question, the reason why some of us posit non-natural properties and facts is that this seems to us necessary in order to accommodate a conviction that ethics contains an element of *irreducible normativity*.[2] There is in fact a point of commonality here between the non-naturalist and an expressivist such as Gibbard in that both agree that (at least some) normative claims – claims about what is good or bad, right or wrong, or ought to be done or avoided – cannot be captured in non-normative or purely descriptive terms. The question, however, is why this is and what follows from it. Gibbard's view is that whatever apparently irreducible normativity there is in ethics can be isolated to the realm of our ethical *thinking*, and so can be accounted for without positing non-natural *properties* (Gibbard, 2003, section III; 2006). The non-naturalist, by contrast, holds that irreducible normativity is a feature of real ethical properties and facts, which requires that they themselves be understood as non-natural.

For Gibbard, normativity is a feature only of normative concepts and thoughts – not of properties, facts or states of affairs in the world – and it is simply a matter of the essential *practicality* of normative concepts. Such concepts are 'directive' or 'plan-laden' in that thoughts employing them have a certain practical function involving planning what to do. In this way, normative concepts and thoughts may be said to be 'non-naturalistic' in so far as they are not in the business of expressing propositions with naturalistic representational content, but instead have an essentially practical role to play.[3] But this non-naturalism about directive concepts and thoughts clearly doesn't imply ethical non-naturalism as defined earlier. In particular, it doesn't imply that normative claims express any *irreducibly normative representational content*, purporting to describe irreducibly normative facts, the grasping of which might in turn explain our corresponding normative beliefs. Gibbard rejects any such account. For him, the irreducible normativity consists just in the practicality of the *role* played by directive concepts and thoughts. As far as properties, facts, or states of affairs are concerned, they are all perfectly natural or 'prosaic,' and any explanatory work they do is likewise fully naturalistic (Gibbard, 2003, p. 181; 2006).[4]

By contrast, ethical non-naturalists maintain that an account such as Gibbard's fails to capture the irreducible normativity found in ethics. Instead, they will argue, in so far as ethical concepts and thoughts are irreducibly normative, this is precisely because they have *irreducibly normative representational content*. Ethical claims purport to state irreducibly normative facts, ascribing irreducibly normative properties to things – 'irreducibly normative' in the sense that they are *properties for which we can have only normative concepts*, due to the normative nature of these properties themselves. (This contrasts with Gibbard's natural properties for which we can have *both* normative and non-normative concepts, to be discussed later.) Of course, even an error theorist, who believes all positive ethical claims to be false, might agree with this much: indeed, he may hold that it is precisely because ethical claims have this rich content that they are all false, the world being devoid of irreducibly normative properties. So the non-naturalist, by contrast, crucially holds that there *are* such properties and facts, and that at least in some cases it is just such irreducibly normative facts that *explain* our ethical beliefs, in so far as we have the beliefs we do because we have grasped such facts.[5] On this view, then, the irreducible normativity of the concepts and thoughts is derivative, pointing to the more fundamental irreducible normativity of the ethical properties and facts that are the proper subject matter of ethical inquiry.

This clarifies the differences between the non-naturalist and the expressivist. While Gibbard agrees that normative concepts are in a sense non-natural (they are not used to express propositions with naturalistic representational content), he does not ultimately believe in irreducible normativity, but in effect *reduces* normativity to the *practicality* of directive, plan-laden concepts and of the mental states associated with them.[6] The non-naturalist, by contrast, insists that irreducible normativity is just that: a feature of certain properties and facts themselves that cannot be cashed out or understood in terms of anything other than normativity itself. This is the crucial difference between them and will figure importantly in elucidating the non-naturalist's dissatisfaction with Gibbard's proposal for capturing normativity.

The other part of the non-naturalist's claim is that this irreducible normativity cannot be accommodated within ethical naturalism any more than it can within expressivism. As with Gibbard, however, many ethical naturalists will likewise offer something that purports to capture a kind of irreducible normativity in ethics. A non-reductionist naturalist, for example, might claim that normative terms such as 'good' and 'right' cannot be replaced by any non-normative terms such as 'pleasant' or 'optimific,' because, although the former terms pick out fully natural properties, constructible from scientific ones, the properties in question are unique complexes that are not the referents of any *other*, non-normative terms we possess. Indeed, this will be cited as part of the explanation for the 'open questions' Moore repeatedly encountered in connection with the naturalistic identifications he considered (for example, the fact that the question 'is X good?' seems to remain open even after granting that X is pleasant). He found open questions in part because all such identifications (such as goodness = pleasure) were simply inapt: the natural property to which 'goodness' refers, which we attribute to things in our ethical judgments, is far more complex than the natural properties picked out by terms such as 'pleasant'. Such open questions, therefore, tell not against ethical naturalism itself but only against the crude identifications imagined by Moore (see Sturgeon, 2003; 2006; and, for a good discussion of this 'one-term naturalism', Dancy, 2006a).

Sophisticated naturalists might thus claim that they can accommodate something like irreducible normativity in this sense: although all properties and facts are natural, ethical ones are 'irreducibly normative', at least in the weak sense that no non-normative concepts in fact track them, so that normative vocabulary is indispensable. This is indeed a weak sense, however, and is importantly different from the non-naturalist's notion of irreducible normativity, as there is no claim here that ethical properties possess any special normative nature. Non-normative concepts fail to track these properties *only because of the complex constitution and organization* of these properties, the patterns of which make sense only from the perspective of ethical inquiry and concern, within which they also play useful roles in historical and sociological explanations (Boyd, 1988; Brink, 1989; Sturgeon, 1988; 2006). But again, there is nothing special about the nature of these properties themselves: they are just specially grouped clusters of prosaic natural properties.

Alternatively, an ethical naturalist might adopt part of Gibbard's expressivist strategy for capturing the apparent element of irreducible normativity by appeal to moral semantics and pragmatics. David Copp, for example, has argued for a naturalistic 'realist expressivism' according to which ethical terms have a 'coloring' as part of their meaning, such that sincere assertions of ethical claims express not only ethical beliefs (which have objective truth conditions, and so can be straightforwardly true) but also – through conventional implicature – a conative state of mind consisting roughly in an endorsement of the standards relevant to the claim and an intention to comply with those standards (Copp, 2007). Ethical assertions are thus unlike assertions in non-normative terms in that the former carry the implication of these attitudinal and motivational elements while the latter do not. This again can be used to help answer Moore's open question objections to naturalism: the gaps Moore found are real, but instead of telling against naturalism they merely reflect the fact that ethical terms have a special coloring whereby they are used to express conative states as well as beliefs; this is why ethical claims cannot be fully captured using merely descriptive terms (Copp, 2007, p. 199). An ethical naturalist might thus argue that he can capture a kind of irreducibly normative element in ethics in much the same way as Gibbard does: ethical *terms* and *assertions* are irreducibly normative in the sense that they serve in part to express special, practical mental states that are not expressed by assertions employing merely descriptive terms.

As before, the crucial question is whether these naturalistic moves succeed in adequately capturing whatever irreducible normativity there may be in ethics. Where one finds oneself in this debate, therefore, depends on whether one agrees that there is some kind of irreducible normativity in ethics, and, if so, whether it can be fully accommodated in terms of moral semantics or pragmatics of one kind or another, or instead requires locating irreducible normativity more deeply in the nature of ethical properties and facts themselves, committing one to ethical non-naturalism.

2. Ethical realism vs. quasi-realist expressivism

I have elsewhere explored the motivations for non-naturalism (as part of a robust ethical realism) in contrast to various forms of ethical naturalism, and sketched the form that a robust non-naturalism might plausibly take (FitzPatrick, 2008a).[7] One response to that discussion, however, might be that much of what is said there to motivate non-naturalism is fully consistent with expressivism. Indeed, this is precisely Gibbard's line about non-naturalism: 'pretty much everything non-naturalists say in elucidating their position is right, properly understood,' where this last qualification means: understood as applied only to normative *concepts*, not to properties, and given an *expressivist* construal (Gibbard, 2010, p. 2). In fact, however, the quasi-realism he offers the non-naturalist – and the realist more generally – falls far short of allaying the concerns of people with even moderate leanings in these directions, failing to provide an account of normativity that we should find attractive or tempting. Gibbard's version of quasi-realist expressivism is especially useful to explore in this connection because, in addition to seeking to accommodate non-naturalism in his treatment of normative concepts, Gibbard seeks to accommodate ethical realism by incorporating a central *metaphysical* claim of ethical naturalism, thus speaking simultaneously to the concerns of realism, non-naturalism, *and* ethical naturalism, all without leaving an expressivist framework. In bringing out the unsatisfactory aspects of Gibbard's approach, we will thus have occasion to examine not only the limits of expressivism in accounting for normativity in terms of the practicality of concepts, but also the problems with forms of ethical naturalism that overlap partly with his metaphysical view of the properties picked out by normative concepts.

To begin, then: realists and expressivists have traditionally squared off precisely over the question whether or not there are real properties along the lines of *being what one ought to do*, with realists affirming and expressivists denying that there are. No longer. Gibbard has changed all that by accommodating just such properties within his expressivist view, thus purporting to take much of the wind out of the realist's sails. His claim is that 'some broadly natural property constitutes being what one ought to do' (Gibbard, 2006, p. 324). This *sounds* a lot like an embrace of ethical naturalism, but it's not.

First, while he does grant the existence of such properties, he doesn't take them to be *ethical* or *normative properties* (recall that he rejects the idea of normative properties): they are just prosaic natural properties, for which we can have both normative and non-normative *concepts* – where the concept of 'being that which one ought to do' is an example of the former. So he would not endorse the typical ethical naturalist claim that *ethical* or *normative properties* are natural properties; he merely says that certain properties for which we have normative concepts (as well as non-normative ones) are real, natural properties. Second, and more importantly, unlike the ethical naturalist, Gibbard denies that the function of normative concepts in normative judgment is to attribute such properties to things: to judge that a person in a burning building ought to leave it is *not* to attribute to this act the natural property of being what one ought to do, but to engage in an act of contingency planning (Gibbard, 2006, p. 324; 2003, pp. 102–3).[8] So there are some metaphysical similarities and also important semantic differences between Gibbard's expressivism and ethical naturalism, and Gibbard takes this to allow him both to capture attractive elements of naturalist ethical realism and to retain a distinctive expressivism that better captures normative thinking.

How does Gibbard deliver the metaphysical result that is supposed to speak to the concerns of naturalist ethical realists? He begins, in typical expressivist fashion, by focusing on the mental states involved in normative judgment, and proposes that *what it is* to *think* that a person *ought* to do A in circumstances C is to *plan* for a contingency: that is, to plan to do A in the event of ever finding oneself in C. Without getting distracted by the (impressively developed) details, we can sketch the basic move to the naturalistic property as follows. Imagine someone with a 'hyperplan,' that is, a plan covering every possible contingency, naturalistically described: if in C1, do A1; if in C2, do A2, and so on. If normative judgment consists in contingency planning, then for such a person there is a naturalistic property that constitutes *being what one ought to do*, namely, the following massively disjunctive property an act may have: being {A1 in C1, *or* A2 in C2, *or* A3 in C3, and so on}. If, for example, an act has the property of being A2 in C2 (leaving the building when it is on fire and one is not engaged in a life or death matter), then it satisfies that disjunct and so has the property of being what one ought to do, relative to the hyperplan in question (Gibbard, 2006, pp. 324–7).

Now, although not even the most hyper planners among us actually possess anything approaching a hyperplan, Gibbard claims that, in having the incomplete plans we do have, we are similarly committed to the existence of some such disjunctive property that is consistent with all our actual plans as far as they go. That is, in having the incomplete contingency plans I have, involving acts A1–An for circumstances C1–Cn, I am thereby committed to performing precisely those acts that possess the disjunctive property in question by satisfying one of the disjuncts (and this commitment holds regardless of how I might go on to fill out my plan more fully, as long as I don't change my mind). So, if such contingency planning captures normative judgment – if to think one *ought* to do A1 in C1 just is to *plan* to do A1 if ever in C1 – then an act's having the disjunctive property in question (which is a natural, if contrived, property), must just *be* what it is for the act to be *what one ought to do*, according to the person with the plan in question. Thus, Gibbard argues that every agent, in so far as she engages in planning, is committed to the 'natural constitution claim,' the idea that there is some natural property that constitutes being what one ought to do (Gibbard, 2006, pp. 325, 328).

Now this move may seem to deliver something attractive to naturalist ethical realists, inasmuch as it gives us a real, natural property that constitutes being what one ought to do, which acts can straightforwardly possess or fail to possess. But the reduction of normative judgment to contingency planning, which underlies Gibbard's derivation of the natural property in question, is problematic in its own right as well as leading to a view with little to tempt anyone with even mildly realist leanings. Indeed, the proposed naturalistic property identification fails in any case, and the nearest more plausible candidate is far from the sort of property that might be interesting to a realist, failing to accommodate much of real concern (as quasi-realism is supposed to do). Let me take these up in turn.

2.1. Normative judgment and planning

Even in the simplest first-personal cases, where thoughts about what I ought to do are at least clearly related in some way to my own planning activity (as in thinking about what I ought to do in the event of a fire in my building), there are puzzles to raise about the proposed reduction of normative judgment to contingency planning. But set this aside for a moment. A more striking worry is that for a variety of other cases such a reduction will be so plainly contrived as to be a non-starter. Someone worried about the problem of evil, for example, who opines that God *ought* to have prevented the earthquake in Haiti, is surely not thereby making hypothetical plans (just in case), in the event of finding himself to be God on 12 January 2010, to prevent an earthquake from happening in Haiti. The problem with such a construal is not that thinking about such far-removed 'oughts' is useless and impractical, being disconnected from actual decision-making. Gibbard is quite right to point out that even highly fanciful normative thinking and conversation serves many important purposes in clarifying, refining and communicating our normative beliefs and commitments (Gibbard, 2003, p. 52). The problem is just that, as useful as it may be to think or to talk about what God, Caesar, or the Cat in the Hat ought to have done, it is plainly not a matter of *planning* for such wild contingencies. Planning in such a context ('what *will* I do if I ever find myself, *per impossibile*, in the circumstance of being God prior to the earthquake?'), where there is a total disconnect from actual decision-making, would be a transparently bizarre undertaking. We do need some way of making sense of such exercises of normative thinking divorced from actual decision-making, but planning is rather clearly not the key to understanding this (Brink, 2007, pp. 270–1).

To be sure, we might well think imaginatively about what we *would* do in such circumstances, were we to find ourselves occupying the role of deity, say; this needn't be bizarre and again may serve important reflective and social purposes. But it is not planning: it is simply and irreducibly an exercise in normative thinking, where the 'would' functions as it does in the question 'what would you do?' asked of someone presented with a moral quandary. What is sought here is not a weirdly dislocated plan ('what *will* you do in the event of your being in such circumstances?') or a psychological prediction ('what do you expect you would in fact do if in such circumstances?'), but just thoughts about *what one should do* in the imagined circumstances. And, importantly, proposed answers will depend for their very *intelligibility* on being backed up with appeals to the relevant kind of normative factors or values at play in the situation – a condition that doesn't similarly apply to planning what one *will* do as such. (We can easily understand *that* someone plans to do something stupid, eccentric or evil, even if we fail to understand why, but we cannot similarly understand his claim that one *should* so act without being supplied with the right kind of story to make the claim at least intelligible. See Foot, 1978.)

If we must put everything in terms of planning (and it is unclear why we must), we may say that we're imagining how we *ought* to plan were we, say, to find ourselves being God. But the construal of *this* thought as itself being a form of planning here and now has no plausibility. Perhaps Gibbard will say that these cases of normative thinking about circumstances we know we will never face aren't themselves cases of planning but only of *pretending* to plan (Gibbard, 2003, pp. 50 f.). But, while it is certainly possible to pretend to plan – as one might, for example, pretend to plan for a trip to Italy as part of fantasizing about a dream vacation one is in no position actually to plan for – there is no reason to think that this is what is going on whenever we make normative judgments about people in circumstances we'll never be in. Is it really plausible to claim that, while my judging that I ought to work to reduce my debt consists in planning to do so, my judging that Congress ought similarly to work to reduce the national debt consists in *pretending to make plans* to do so (in the event of finding myself to be Congress?), just like pretending to plan for a trip I'd take if I were rich? Making such judgments about Congress, or God, or historical or fictional characters doesn't feel remotely like fantasy planning an itinerary for a trip to Tuscany: it feels simply like employing normative concepts and citing relevant considerations to support them, exactly as we do in realistic first-person cases.

I suggest, then, that the plan-based expressivist account fails for the wide range of normative judgments we've been considering, where construals in terms of planning are implausible and the move to pretend planning is contrived and ad hoc. But if so, this in itself casts doubt on the appropriateness of Gibbard's account even for the more central first-personal cases: for it would be quite surprising if we needed completely different basic accounts of normative judgment for different contents; surely it would be better to have a unified basic account of normative judgment, whether the content involves God's preventing earthquakes, Caesar's crossing the Rubicon, or people leaving burning buildings or balancing their budgets. Independently of this, however, the reduction of normative thinking to planning is implausible even in first-personal cases.

This is because, while normative thinking is certainly *related* to planning, the relation seems to be simply that normative thinking *should* (and typically does) *inform* our planning, and when it does it partly *explains* our planning, rather than normative thinking itself just *consisting in* planning (Brink, 2007, p. 271). A normatively unreflective, purely opportunistic schemer, for example, is appropriately criticized precisely for failing to inform her planning with general normative reflection and judgment, and a piece of immoral planning will be criticized by saying that it should have been informed by better normative reflection and judgment. Moreover, people often knowingly make plans against their own better normative judgment: an akratic adulterer, for example, might make elaborate contingency plans to do things he well knows he shouldn't be doing. All of this suggests that judging that something ought to be done is not just the same thing as planning or deciding to do it, but is instead something that ought to inform planning or deciding.[9]

Gibbard, of course, recognizes this obvious line of objection, but he is wary of drawing any such distinction because he thinks it opens up a problematic gap between settling what we *ought* to do and settling 'what to do' (Gibbard, 2003, pp. 9–17, 55).[10] But it doesn't follow from the fact that settling what we ought to do is not itself *identical* to deciding what to do that there is some problematic practical gap between the two, such that the very relevance of normative judgment for decision-making becomes mysterious. There is in fact no gap here, because, while normative judgment isn't identical to decision-making, it is intimately related to it, and the relation is itself an *irreducibly normative* one: our decision-making *ought* to be properly informed by adequate normative reflection and judgment (such as 'ought' judgments); that is just part of what it is to be a rational agent (cf. Wedgwood, 2004, 406 f.; 2007). Settling what we ought to do isn't itself deciding or planning to do it (recall the akratic agent), but it is nonetheless the *appropriate way of reaching decisions or settling what to do* (at least in cases where there is something one ought to do), and this is the link between 'ought' judgments and decision: we don't need identity to forge the necessary tie.[11]

It is, of course, easy to generate a misleading sense of a deep gap if we simply posit some meaningless placeholder property – as Gibbard does by positing some mystery property referred to by the term 'exnat' – and then try to imagine reaching a decision on what to do simply on the basis of attributing this dummy property to an act; and surely Gibbard is right that merely going on to stipulate that this property is 'non-natural' doesn't help one bit (Gibbard, 2003, p. 16). But this is a misguided objection to both realism and non-naturalism. The property we're talking about isn't just some random property that would require some special magical connection to action, having no more internal connection with action than color or mass to begin with. It is rather a property such as *being best to do*, or *being what ought to be done*, and we shouldn't pretend that settling *this* would still leave us completely in the dark when trying to decide what to do, as if we'd merely been told that an act was 'exnat'. And, as for this property's being non-natural, it is just a misrepresentation of the dialectic to portray the non-naturalist as proposing that *agents* have to *believe that* normative properties are non-natural in order to move from normative judgment to decision (Gibbard, 2003, pp. 9, 55). The non-naturalist makes no such claim, which would indeed be 'a little fantastic,' as Gibbard puts it.

Whether normative properties are non-natural or not is of concern only to philosophers, and the reasons for thinking them to be non-natural will be philosophical ones having to do with doubts (such as the ones raised in this chapter) about whether natural properties could ever do the work needed to make sense of normativity. Ordinary agents needn't be concerned with this issue at all, and they certainly needn't take a stand on such metaphysical issues in order to have preferences and make decisions. For that matter, neither do they have to succeed in grasping non-natural properties (without necessarily knowing they are doing so) in order to have preferences and make decisions or plans. The non-naturalist's claim is just that there are normative properties such as being what ought to be done, that these are in fact non-natural properties, and that they are what agents ought to be trying to discover (though they needn't conceive of them as non-natural) in the course of deciding what to do, because grasping such properties is typically important to planning and deciding *well*.

2.2. Normative properties and resultance base natural properties

Gibbard further wonders, though, why any such non-natural property should matter – what role it could play in settling what to do, over and above the ordinary natural properties and facts we cite when giving our reasons for a decision (Gibbard, 2003, p. 16). For example, Gibbard claims that a universal hedonist should understand his normative view as implying (roughly) that the property of *being pleasant* is identical to the property of *being what one ought to do* (just as the property of being water is identical to the property of being H_2O, though the concepts are different). If we ask 'why eat chocolate?' the answer will be: 'because it is pleasant,' and that will be the end of that story; so doesn't that show that being pleasant *just is* being what one ought to do, according to the hedonist? How could the latter be a *distinct* property with any real role (Gibbard, 2006, pp. 328–30)?

Gibbard is, of course, correct in claiming that 'because it is pleasant' is the end of a certain line of explanation, that is, the one that answers the question: 'why eat chocolate?' It would indeed be a mistake to suppose that we need to add some non-natural property *alongside pleasantness* within this same line of explanation ('we ought to eat chocolate because it is pleasant and furthermore it has the non-natural property of being something we ought to do'). But this does not imply that (according to the hedonist) to be pleasant *just is what it is to be* what ought to be done – and this is true despite its being the case, according to the hedonist, that all and only pleasant things are things that ought to be done. To see why the normative property remains distinct from the natural properties that realize it and provide a complete explanation in answer to a certain line of questioning, it is useful to consider a simple parallel involving artifacts.

If asked why a given computer is a good one, a proper answer will cite certain natural properties: it has a certain clock speed, memory capacity, parallel processing capabilities, and so on. These are its good-making properties, the ones *by virtue of* which it qualifies as a good computer. And, if asked for reasons for attributing goodness (the 'resultant' evaluative property) to it, we simply cite those properties (the 'resultance base' properties).[12] It doesn't follow, however, that its being a good computer just *consists in* its having these properties. The evaluative fact that it is a good computer, after all, consists not simply in the fact that it has these properties considered in themselves, but in the more complex fact that it has these properties *and* that by virtue of having these properties it satisfies the standards of excellence appropriate for this kind of computer, enabling it to carry out the function of such a computer successfully.

As a general point, two objects may share many of the same base properties but differ in their resultant evaluative properties precisely because in one case those properties count as good-making while in the other they do not (as sharpness is a good-making property in a knife but not in a bookmark). This shows that it is a mistake simply to identify the evaluative property with the base properties by virtue of which the evaluative property is realized in a given case. This is true even though we typically needn't mention anything other than the base properties themselves in answering the question 'why is this a good computer?' We still need to look beyond the base properties and facts themselves in order properly to identify the resultant evaluative properties and facts, which consist also in relations to relevant standards of goodness for the kind of thing in question, which they stand in by virtue of possessing the base properties in question.[13]

This does not, of course, show that the evaluative properties of artifacts are *non-natural*, nor do I wish to claim that they are; they are plausibly natural, grounded in natural facts about the intentions and practices of designers and users. If ethical properties (such as the moral goodness of people) are non-natural, that will be a further point – one that we come to by concluding that in the case of ethics, unlike that of artifacts, the facts about appropriate standards (the standards of goodness for human action as such) cannot ultimately be derived from natural facts, as standards for artifacts can. I'll return to this. What the parallel with artifacts does illustrate, however, is that having an answer to a normative 'why?' question in terms of resultance base properties – an answer that is complete within that particular line of explanation – does not imply that the normative or evaluative resultant property is *identical* to the resultance base properties in question.

To return, then, to Gibbard's example: although 'it's pleasant' is a sufficient and complete answer to 'why ought one to eat chocolate?', it is a mistake to suppose, even on simple hedonist assumptions, that this means that the property of being pleasant is identical to the property of being what one ought to do. Even if all and only pleasant things are things one ought to do, the fact that one ought to do something does not consist simply in the fact that it is pleasant, as such, any more than the fact that a computer is good consists simply in the fact that it has certain descriptive features such as speed. The fact that one ought to do something would instead consist (roughly) in the fact that that it is pleasant *and* that by virtue of being pleasant it satisfies relevant standards of goodness or practical rationality appropriate to human action. The property of being what one ought to do is similarly complex, rather than being simply identical to the property of being pleasant – even though it is sufficient to cite the latter in answering the question why something ought to be done, as in the case of eating chocolate.

Likewise, if we go on to argue substantively with the hedonist, we are not disagreeing over whether the property of being pleasant is really identical to the property of being what one ought to do (on the model of arguing over whether water is really H_2O, as Gibbard claims). Rather, we are arguing about whether the standards of goodness or practical rationality for human action are really such that the only base property relevant for satisfying those standards is pleasantness. The analogue would be arguing with someone who claims that the only thing that matters to goodness in computers is memory capacity, our suspicion being that he has an overly simplistic understanding of what matters to being a good computer.

If Gibbard is mistaken, then, in just identifying resultant properties (such as being what one ought to do) with the resultance base properties by virtue of which the resultant properties are attributed, then we may unapologetically see the resultant property as a *distinct, normative property*. What role does it play, then? Not, as we've said, providing something to tack on to the natural resultance base properties in an explanation of why one ought to do something ('one ought to eat chocolate because it is not only pleasant but also possesses a nifty, distinct normative property!'). Instead, the role played by the distinct normative property is the one mentioned earlier: for a rational agent, planning or decision-making ought to be informed by responsible normative reflection and judgment, which means seeking to determine what there is genuine reason to do, or sometimes what there is most reason or decisive reason to do, or what one ought to do. The normative concepts function to focus our deliberation on the normative properties our acts must have to be choice-worthy, which in turn is what focuses and gives point to our practical thinking about the various potential natural resultance base properties.

We think about these various natural properties, after all, not simply in their own right *as* various particular natural properties, but *as good-making*, say, and thus contributing to an act's having the normative property – being something one has reason or ought to do – that we should be treating in our deliberations as the *gateway to decision*. If pleasantness matters, for example, it matters not simply *qua* pleasantness, but in so far as being pleasant, in the given circumstantial context, is a good-making property, making the action something good to do or something that ought to be done, which in turn is what we should be trying to determine as we responsibly make plans and decisions.

If this is right, then we have an answer to Gibbard's challenge. Normative properties are distinct from the base properties by virtue of which they are attributed to things, both in the simple case of artifacts (where the normative properties are plausibly natural) and in the case of ethics (where the normative properties may instead be non-natural). Our normative views (such as hedonism, in the simple illustration above) do not commit us to identifying these properties, and so do not commit us to regarding normative properties as not really normative properties at all but just natural properties for which we can also have normative concepts (as Gibbard holds, arguing that on hedonist assumptions, for example, the property of being what one ought to do is just identical to the property of being pleasant, as water is identical to H_2O, though we here refer to it using a normative concept). Moreover, we can explain the role of both normative concepts and normative properties in rational deliberation: far from being superfluous to the process of deciding what to do, they play – or ought to play – an *organizing and guiding role* in thinking about natural properties in the way we ought to think about them in deliberation, namely, in so far as they are significant in helping to make an action good or rational to perform in the given circumstances, all things considered, which in turn *ought to inform* our planning or decision-making.

2.3. Normative properties and coextensive disjunctive natural properties

Beyond answering Gibbard's challenge, however, we are also now in a position to see why Gibbard's earlier identification of the natural property he takes to constitute being what one ought to do is dubious. The identification that would actually follow from the rest of his view is different, and bringing this out reveals just how little such a metaphysical claim about 'ought' properties really speaks to the concerns of anyone sympathetic to ethical realism – which quasi-realism is supposed to do, showing us that we can have everything worth having within an expressivist framework.

Recall that Gibbard's general claim is that the property of being what one ought to do is constituted by some natural property, D, understood as a disjunction of circumstance–act pairs specified by a complete plan (that is, being A1 in C1, or A2 in C2, or A3 in C3, and so on); as planners, he argues, we are each committed to the existence of some such natural property that constitutes being what one ought to do, since it is coextensive with it: all and only acts that have the property of being what one ought to do are acts that have D. But coextension does not imply constitution, for reasons already brought out in connection with artifacts. The property of being a good computer may be coextensive with the property, N, of having N1, or N2, or N3 (where each of these is some combination of resultance base properties sufficient to qualify for goodness as a computer); but being a good computer is not simply a matter of having N as such, but rather something more complex: namely, having N together with N's being such as to make a computer satisfy the standards of excellence S for computers. It is this metaphysical *structure* of facts about goodness or of the property of being good that explains, after all, why we aren't in a position to know whether or not an unfamiliar object is good just by knowing its various descriptive properties: if we don't also know relevant facts about what it is and the standards of goodness appropriate to such things, we won't know whether, for example, its sharp edges make it a good knife or a lousy bookmark. This also shows that merely attributing ordinary descriptive properties to something, which we can do without knowing anything about the evaluative standards for such things, does not amount to *evaluation*, a point I'll return to later.

Now the very same lessons apply to Gibbard's natural property D above. We can grant that on Gibbard's approach there is a contrived, disjunctive natural property D that is coextensive with the property of being what one ought to do: all and only acts that have D are acts one ought to do. But this doesn't imply that *what it is to be something one ought to do* is simply *having property D*. The identification actually implied by Gibbard's plan-based view is instead a more complex one: what it is to be something one ought to do is to have the property of *being consistent with a given plan P by having D, which an act does by being A1 in C1, or A2 in C2, or A3 in C3*, and so on. This relation of *consistency with a given plan* is the analogue here of the relation of *satisfying a relevant set of standards of goodness* in the artifact case (and, I've suggested, in the case of ethics too, on a realist view, though I haven't said anything here about what those standards are grounded in for ethical evaluation, beyond noting the non-naturalist's skepticism that they can be fully accounted for by appeal only to natural properties and facts).[14]

So, for example, according to the plan in question the answer to 'what ought to be done in C2 (when the building is on fire and one is not engaged in a life or death matter)?' is simply 'A2! (leave the building)'; but such an evacuation's *being what one ought to do* consists not simply in its *being A2 in C2* and thereby being D (by satisfying that disjunct of it), but in its *thereby being consistent with plan P*. This makes explicit the *plan-relative* nature of the property in question. D is relevant at all only because possessing it makes an act consistent with plan P; it is not relevant in its own right simply as a strange objective natural property. So we cannot use plan P to define this property D as being relevant to what one ought to do and then forget P and focus simply on D in itself as constituting the property of being one what ought to do.

Gibbard has not, therefore, shown that his view implies that there is some objective natural disjunctive property such as D that constitutes being what one ought to do (or, more precisely, that as planners we are committed to there being some such objective natural property that constitutes being what one ought to do). Being what one ought to do, on his plan-based account, is instead properly identified as *being consistent with a given plan P*; and a particular act's being something one ought to do is *constituted* by its being consistent with a given plan P by virtue of possessing D, which it does in turn by satisfying one of the disjuncts. The focus on D in itself, then, is misleading: the relevant natural property is essentially a relational one involving some plan or other, and it will vary from person to person, each of us being committed to a different such property depending on the content of our contingent, particular plans. It is still a natural property, but it is a *radically relativized* one, much like the sort of property posited by a subjectivist naturalist. And for this reason it falls far short of capturing any idea of real normative properties that might be attractive to anyone with even moderate realist inclinations. As quasi-realism goes it is far more *quasi* than realist: the promise of giving us a real, natural property that constitutes being what one ought to do has turned out to be a hollow one, at least from a realist perspective.

To take stock, then: we have seen two main reasons why Gibbard's attempt to capture normativity in a way that speaks to the basic concerns of realists, all the while remaining within an expressivist framework, does not deliver on that promise. First, the reduction of normative judgment to planning does not seem to succeed in capturing the nature or role of normative judgment in practical reasoning, which suggests that the attempt to account for normativity simply in terms of the *practicality* of normative *concepts* is inadequate (at least for a plan-based approach such as Gibbard's). Second, the identification of a property such as being what one ought to do with a coextensive, objective, disjunctive natural property is erroneous, and the more accurate identification (given Gibbard's plan-based approach) turns out to be a radically relativized property – relative to the contingent plans each person makes for her life (cf. Brink, 2007, p. 270). That sort of property is no closer to capturing what a realist might find plausible for normative properties than are the natural properties proposed by subjectivists.

2.4. Plan-relativism and normative relativism

Gibbard has recently addressed this last issue of relativism, denying that his view is problematically relativist. His strategy is the same one Blackburn has long employed in arguing that expressivism can avoid relativism and give us all the mind-independence and objectivity we could legitimately want: when accused of relativism, simply shift from metaethical theorizing to first-order normative claims and build non-relativistic elements into the content of those claims (Blackburn, 1993; 1998). For example, Gibbard considers a practice among the Hopi he calls 'chicken pull' (described in the 1940s by Richard Brandt), where young men try to pull a mostly buried chicken out of the ground by its neck as they ride by on horses (Gibbard, 2010, pp. 3 f.). Now, many of us would like to say, non-relativistically, that this cruel sport is wrong by virtue of the unnecessary suffering it causes the animals, and that it is wrong not merely for us to engage in but equally for the Hopi, despite the fact that they do not believe it to be wrong (as they do not take animal suffering to be a sufficient reason for refraining from the sport). How can Gibbard accommodate this in a quasi-realist fashion? Like Blackburn, he notes that, as a moral agent himself, engaging in first-order normative judgment, he can say everything above and even make claims of mind-independence in the same vein: chicken pulling is wrong, he'll say, and he doesn't make his normative judgment here contingent on anyone's beliefs or attitudes, but comes to it based simply on the unnecessary suffering caused to the chickens for sport; so the wrongness is in this sense independent of contingent moral beliefs or attitudes and the practice thus remains wrong even when done by the Hopi.[15]

Gibbard's construal, however, of what he is doing when he says such realist-sounding things is that he is *planning* for how he is to treat chickens under various circumstances: in claiming that, despite the pleasure it brings young Hopi men, it is wrong for them to engage in chicken pulling given the suffering it causes, he is *planning* 'for how to weigh considerations for the case of being...a Hopi' – that is, planning that if he finds himself a Hopi and his buddies suggest a bracing game of chicken pull, he'll weigh the suffering of the chicken more heavily than the pleasure of the game and decide against it. I will not repeat the earlier worries about the conversion of what seems to be a straightforward normative judgment into a markedly peculiar act of planning for an impossible situation.[16] The present point is that, if this is all the realist-sounding normative judgments amount to, then we have not, after all, eliminated the relativistic elements but have only papered them over at the first-order level with personal commitments. No doubt Gibbard and Blackburn can make the content of their first-order commitments as non-relativistic as they like: there is nothing in the structure of expressivism to force the content of first-order commitments in a relativist direction. But that was never the objection.

The real worry is this: while Gibbard can make humane plans that rule out chicken pulling, and express these plans in first-order judgments that sound realist, his metaethical view entails that any number of other people can make any number of different plans, including inhumane ones, and likewise express these plans in first-order judgments endorsing such things as chicken pulling (perhaps just as non-relativistically as Gibbard condemns it) and condemning efforts to constrain sports in the name of animal welfare (again, just as non-relativistically as Gibbard endorses them). Here lies the deep and abiding relativism in the expressivist approach: at the end of the day, there are just various agents with various plans, making conflicting normative judgments and committed to different, plan-relative natural properties as constituting what one ought to do. Each can say, in a plan-laden way from within his own plan-based first-order perspectives, that the others are mistaken, and there are *no objective normative facts* by appeal to which such disputes could even in principle be adjudicated.

Now, the way I have just put this point might make it sound like a merely methodological or epistemic one: how could we ever be in a position reliably to trust, and to show to everyone's satisfaction, that our perspective on a normative issue such as chicken pulling is correct and the others are mistaken, thus settling such normative disputes? But that is not the problem realists have with expressivism. Indeed, this *epistemic* challenge is one that realists themselves must wrestle with, as Gibbard points out, and it is in fact especially pressing for non-naturalists (like myself) who reject any derivation of ethical standards from some ethically neutral foundation (such as an ethically prior theory of human nature or societal needs) in principle available to all parties to substantive ethical debates – some Archimedean point that would allow us to escape reliance on our own ethical lights in ethical inquiry. I have addressed this issue elsewhere and fully acknowledge the limitations in our ability to demonstrate the correctness of our views to others with very different views, though without conceding that this should by itself undermine our confidence in the reliability or correctness of our views (FitzPatrick, 2008a).[17] But to repeat: the realist objection to expressivism is not one about methodological or epistemic limitations. It is rather that on the expressivist view there are simply *no normative facts that make it objectively the case (not merely relative to one contingent plan or another) that one normative view is correct while another is mistaken* (never mind whether or how we could know or demonstrate this difference). At the end of the day, it's all just plan-relative, each plan denouncing the others, but all ultimately on a par with one another apart from such defects as internal inconsistencies, non-moral factual errors, or lack of reflection; each has no greater claim on us (except trivially from within its own plan-laden perspective) than any other.

Once again, the quasi-realist ambition has not been achieved: merely pointing out that a given person can say realist-sounding things in expressing *his own* plans (while others can with equal legitimacy say the opposite in expressing theirs) does not mitigate the deep normative relativism and mind-dependence built into expressivism. Plan-relativism, and quasi-realist expressivism more generally, saddles us with an unattractive normative relativism after all, and it is precisely in order to avoid this result that realists posit not merely normative *concepts* understood in terms of practicality, but *objective normative properties and facts* that can properly ground deeply non-relativistic normative claims.[18]

3. Jackson's disjunctive descriptive properties

The contrived natural property Gibbard cites as constituting being what one ought to do is metaphysically very similar to the 'possibly infinite disjunctive descriptive properties' Frank Jackson claims to be identical to ethical properties (Jackson, 1998, p. 124). Jackson does not derive his natural properties via the idea of hyperplans, so his account is not plan-relative like Gibbard's and he is not similarly vulnerable to objections concerning relativism. Moreover, he uses these disjunctive properties to pose a challenge to non-naturalists: for whatever view the non-naturalist puts forward for a given ethical property E, as long as acts possess E *by virtue of* possessing various relevant natural properties (the resultance base properties we cite in explaining why acts have E), Jackson's method allows him to define a disjunctive natural property D that is *necessarily coextensive* with E, such that all and only acts that possess that disjunctive natural property will also possess E; and Jackson argues that necessary coextension entails identity, thus resulting in ethical naturalism after all.[19]

I believe there are compelling arguments against the inference from necessary coextension to identity, as already suggested. Alvin Plantinga has also recently pressed this case forcefully (Plantinga, 2010). For example, consider divine command theory – the view that an act's being morally obligatory consists in its being commanded by God. Suppose it is essential to God to command people to treat each other in ways that satisfy certain conditions C involving honesty, kindness, respect, and so on, and not to issue other commands beyond these. Since conditions C are naturalistic ones (ruling out lying, cheating, coercion, etc.), it turns out that there is a naturalistic property equivalent to moral obligation: necessarily, all and only acts that possess property D (where an act possesses D by satisfying conditions C, in whatever way) are morally obligatory. Yet, as Plantinga points out, D is plainly not identical to the property of being morally obligatory according to divine command theory: for D does not entail God's existence, whereas the property of being morally obligatory does, since (according to divine command theory) the latter is the property of *being commanded by God* (Plantinga, 2010, p. 20).[20]

Whatever one thinks of divine command theory (and I am not suggesting it has any plausibility), this clearly illustrates the problem with Jackson's inference from necessary coextension to identity: merely identifying a necessarily coextensive property does not suffice to establish property identity; if it did, it would make divine command theory simply incoherent in a way that it is not. And this criticism is very much in line with the argument I made earlier against Gibbard's identification, using the parallel case of artifacts and their evaluative properties. A given computer's being a good computer consists not simply in its possessing certain natural properties in themselves, but in *its satisfying the standards of goodness for computers* by virtue of possessing natural properties that make it meet those standards; likewise, an act's being what one ought to do, given Gibbard's approach, should be understood not simply as its possessing the disjunctive natural property he identifies, but as *its being consistent with a given plan P*, by virtue of possessing the naturalistic property in question, which is relevantly related to P. (In both cases, the italicized descriptions correspond, in Plantinga's example, to an act's *being required by God's commands*, which property it will have by virtue of having natural properties relevantly related to those commands.) The argument against Jackson's identification is therefore similar: an act's possessing ethical property E (for example, being right) does not consist simply in its possessing natural property D, but in something more complex, such as the act's *satisfying the standards of rightness for human action* (whatever exactly those are, and however exactly they are grounded) by virtue of possessing natural properties that make it meet those standards (which latter will be equivalent to possessing D).

Just as attributing sharpness to some object is not, in itself, to evaluate it (*even if* the object happens to be a knife and sharpness is precisely what makes a knife a good one), so too merely attributing a natural property such as D to an act is not to *evaluate* it at all – and neither is merely attributing a set of ordinary natural properties of the sort we cite in explaining *why* an act is good or ought to be done (that is, the resultance base properties, parallel to sharpness in a knife). On this, I agree entirely with Gibbard, but for a very different reason. Gibbard denies that attributing a natural property to something is in itself to make a normative judgment because making a normative judgment is a matter of *planning*, using special, plan-laden concepts. This, I claim, is the wrong explanation: the reason why merely attributing such properties as D or various resultance base properties falls short of evaluative or normative judgment is simply that *these aren't evaluative or normative properties*, though they're importantly related to them.

This doesn't show, of course, that *no* natural properties are evaluative properties. As noted earlier, I grant that some natural properties are evaluative properties, as in the case of artifacts, where it seems plausible that the property of *being a good computer* can be fully cashed out in terms of natural properties involving functional standards that can in turn be understood in terms of facts about design, intention, use and so on. But the evaluative property isn't identical to or exhaustively constituted simply by the resultance base properties we cite in explaining why a certain computer is a good one. It is, rather, the natural property of satisfying the relevant standards of goodness by virtue of its particular base properties and their relation to those standards – natural because the standards are all a matter of natural facts in this case. To attribute that property to a computer is both to attribute a natural property to it and to evaluate it (which is, of course, what the ethical naturalist says also about *ethical* judgment).

While it is true, then, that we ought to reject forms of ethical naturalism that identify ethical properties with properties such as Jackson's D, or that take ethical properties to be exhaustively constituted by the resultance base properties by virtue of which they are ascribed in a given case, this doesn't yet show that ethical naturalism must be rejected altogether. For, if a fully naturalistic account could be provided of the facts about ethical standards of goodness for human action, which avoided excessive relativism and succeeded in capturing the normative authority of such standards for reflective human agents, showing them to be appropriately binding on us, then this might allow a form of ethical naturalism that a fairly robust ethical realist could be happy with: ethical properties could be complex natural properties on the standard-based model of other evaluative properties.

I am a non-naturalist because I don't think this can be done. One can certainly take some plausible steps in that direction, as Copp has done, for example, in his society-centered moral naturalism (Copp, 1995). On that view, a set of moral standards M is justified relative to a given society S in terms of its being instrumentally rational for S to adopt and live according to M in so far as that will allow S to meet its basic societal needs (such as continued existence, stable cooperation among members, internal harmony, and peaceful relations with other societies), where these needs and their relevant weightings and priorities can all be specified in a naturalistic way. I have argued elsewhere (FitzPatrick, 2008a) that there are a variety of difficulties with any such naturalistic approach, at least if we aim to preserve several central elements of a fairly robust ethical realism. Space permits only a brief summary of some of those considerations here.

The claims advanced about basic social needs and their relative weightings, first of all, are themselves matters of evaluative judgment about what constitutes the sort of social flourishing we have most reason to care about; and while some needs may seem obvious (such as the need for survival), there will be lots of substantive and controversial questions about lots of other claims of need and how they should be prioritized in order for a society to be relevantly succeeding. To take a currently salient example: has a society best 'met its needs' when its people live under significant economic constraints but enjoy universal health care coverage, or when they are less encumbered by taxes but a significant portion lack access to health care? Which is more important? It is hard to see how to answer such questions without already appealing to evaluative standards. And if one proposes to derive such standards in turn from purely natural facts, such as facts about human biology or psychology, it is far from clear that this will result in standards that would be genuinely binding on us as reflective agents, having the kind of normative authority for us that moral requirements seem (to many of us) to have.

Why accept the deliverances of some ethically prior psychological theory about human needs and priorities, when our own ethical reflection may suggest other alternatives that seem like better ways to live? How could any purely natural facts here amount to the fact *that these naturalistically grounded standards are the ones we have most reason to live by* – even for people who may not happen to care about the sort of societal flourishing in question?[21] There will also be worries about whether such an instrumental approach can adequately explain moral facts such as the wrongness of slavery, which seem to require a different sort of explanation than one in terms of the failure of moral codes permitting slavery to meet distinct societal needs such as long-term social stability. If the wrongness of slavery is instead primarily to be explained directly in terms of its violation of human dignity, giving everyone decisive reason to avoid it, the question is again how such facts can plausibly be made out to be natural ones.

These brief remarks are not intended as a sufficient critique of naturalist approaches, which is not my purpose here. They should, however, at least illuminate the motivation for non-naturalism in opposition to ethical naturalism. Certain forms of naturalism, such as Jackson's, miss evaluation altogether by misidentifying evaluative properties – a misidentification very similar to Gibbard's own identification of (what most of us would call) normative properties with certain disjunctive natural properties. Other forms of naturalism may get closer, but the non-naturalist remains skeptical that they can account for all the necessary facts about unqualified standards for human action in a purely naturalist way. If there are to be robustly realist facts about normatively authoritative and non-relative ethical standards, those of us sympathetic to non-naturalism suspect, they are going to have to be non-natural facts. I have suggested, for example, that they are rooted in irreducibly evaluative or normative features of an essentially value-laden world; facts about basic human rights, for example, may be rooted in an irreducibly normative property of basic dignity or inviolability attaching to persons as such (FitzPatrick, 2008a).[22]

4. Evolution, normative concepts and normative properties

Let me conclude by considering one last worry Gibbard has raised about non-naturalism. As we have seen, he agrees that our ethical concepts are non-naturalistic, but he does not take them to be primitive: they can be further explained in terms of the role they play in planning, which is their evolved 'biological function' inasmuch as 'we evolved to have directive concepts' because 'we evolved to act and to be intelligent about it' (Gibbard, 2010, p. 2). By contrast, the non-naturalist rejects the reduction of the normativity of ethical concepts to anything like planning; instead, ethical concepts are taken to be irreducibly normative because they have irreducibly normative representational content and so are used to attribute irreducibly normative properties to acts or persons (properties for which there can be *only* normative concepts), thus stating irreducibly normative facts, as in claiming that a certain act is wrong. It is this primitiveness of normative concepts that Gibbard finds mysterious. How could we have acquired such concepts? And how could they be a legitimate part of our practical thinking (Gibbard, 2010)?

The first point to emphasize here is that, while Gibbard's treatment of the normativity of normative concepts is quite general, by understanding their normativity to consist in their plan-ladenness across the board, the non-naturalist's position is structurally different. The claim is not about normative concepts themselves, but only about certain employments of them. I have not claimed that all employments of normative or evaluative concepts involve attributions of irreducibly normative or evaluative properties, but only that this is true of *ethical* employments of normative or evaluative concepts. When we employ the concept of goodness to computers, the evaluative property we are attributing is plausibly a (complex) natural one, as I've said, which means that this employment of the concept of goodness does not involve using that concept in a non-naturalistic way. Similarly, we can grant that there are employments of normative concepts such as 'ought' that involve no non-naturalistic commitments, as when it is clear from the context that we are using it purely instrumentally relative to a presumed end, in which case its content can plausibly be cashed out naturalistically simply in terms of an act's instrumentality to an end. Such restricted uses of evaluative or normative terms do not require non-naturalistic claims about either the attributed properties or the concepts themselves – which is precisely why Mackie was happy to allow for them as falling outside the scope of his skeptical attack on 'objective values' (Mackie, 1977, pp. 25–7).

The non-naturalist is not, then, claiming that a whole class of concepts – evaluative or normative ones – are primitively non-naturalistic. The concepts themselves admit of all sorts of mundane uses, where they attribute properties no more mysterious or non-natural than the goodness of a computer or of a spearhead, or than the 'oughtness' of avoiding dropping one's computer or eating a poisonous plant. This means that there is no mystery as to how we could have come to possess such evaluative or normative concepts themselves: we came to possess them because it has always been important in countless ways to be able to evaluate things and to recommend or discourage actions, even for our distant ancestors (the point of the reference to spearheads and poisonous plants). There is simply nothing surprising in the development of evaluative or normative language used, at least initially, in these obviously practical ways. So, if there is any question here about etiology, it will be not about how we could have come to have certain special concepts, but about how we could have come to *employ* these concepts in *ethical* contexts in a way that *does* involve non-naturalistic commitments.

That is a legitimate question, but not one that should leave us shaking our heads in disbelief that it has even been asked. My suggestion has been that ethical employments of evaluative and normative concepts are *structurally* similar to others, involving judgments about (for example) an act's relations to appropriate standards, such as standards of goodness for human action as such, by virtue of the act's natural properties, so that it meets or fails to meet those standards. So there is, so far, no special problem for ethical employments of such concepts. The only difference is in the nature and grounding of the standards: the non-naturalist I've been considering maintains that these standards cannot be derived from natural facts alone, whether objective facts about basic needs and the conditions of meeting them, or about biology or psychology, or subjective facts about what we would approve of, or want, or be motivated by under various ethically neutrally specifiable idealizing conditions involving empirical information and deliberation. The facts embodied in the non-relativistically correct set of standards for evaluating human action, we claim, cannot be fully accounted for in terms of natural facts alone, and neither can the very fact that a given set of standards is a non-relativistically correct one. So our question becomes: how could human beings have come to employ evaluative or normative concepts in their ethical thinking in a way that at least seeks to be accountable to such non-naturalistic standards?

Though I cannot here develop a complete answer to this important question, a sketch of the answer goes as follows. Human evolutionary history has provided human beings with large brains equipped not only with 'domain-specific' modules for solving particular adaptive problems, but also with an evident capacity for reflection and reasoning that follows autonomous standards appropriate to various subjects of inquiry, such as mathematics, philosophy, or the sciences; our thinking in these areas is not compelled to proceed slavishly in the service of evolutionarily given instincts merely filtered through cultural forms or applied in novel environments. Such reflection, reasoning, and judgment are *autonomous* in the sense that they involve *exercises of thought that are not themselves significantly shaped by specific evolutionarily given tendencies, but instead follow independent norms appropriate to the pursuits in question* (Nagel, 1979). It would be hard to deny the existence of such mental capacity in the face of such abstract pursuits as algebraic topology, quantum field theory, population biology, or modal metaphysics, all of which plainly involve precisely such autonomous applications of human intelligence. And, while there are undoubtedly complications regarding the extent to which we possess and exercise this capacity for autonomous reflection and reasoning in *ethics*, and the extent to which specific evolutionary influences on emotional dispositions may interfere with it, there have been no good, non-question-begging arguments – whether scientific or philosophical – to show that we do not possess and at least often exercise this capacity to a significant degree in the realm of ethical thought (FitzPatrick, 2008b).

My proposal, then, is that it is precisely through the emergence of such autonomous reflection and reasoning in the sphere of ethics that human beings came to employ evaluative and normative concepts in relation to standards of human conduct that resist purely naturalistic construals. It is precisely because our ethical inquiry is autonomous in this way that our ethical questions are not settled for us by appeals to standards grounded in ethically neutrally specifiable facts about biology, psychology, or even our own hypothetical attitudes, desires or motivation: whenever we are presented with claims underwritten by such standards, there is always a kind of 'open question' about why we should take those standards as being normatively authoritative for us, allowing them to govern our lives. Again, inasmuch as our own ethical experience might suggest alternative ways of living that seem ethically better upon reflection, why should we defer to the deliverances of some such ethically prior theory of human needs or flour-ishing, for example? Or, if the appeal is to a theory rooted in our own ideal-ized psychological responses (in what we ourselves would desire to desire, say, if we were fully empirically informed and deliberated rationally), why should we defer even to that, as opposed to thinking that perhaps even our own 'idealized' responses may be distorted by ethically impoverished starting points given our own limited experience and imperfect character development (Rosati, 1995; 2003)?

Now if, despite all this, there remains a fact of the matter as to what the correct standards are, and that fact is to have normative authority for us, it will not be a natural fact but a non-natural one, because it will have to be irreducibly evaluative or normative, rooted simply in facts about the objec-tive values we are at least seeking to discern in our autonomous ethical reflection. It will not, for example, consist in the natural fact that these are the standards that, if followed, would bring us most satisfaction as meas-ured by an ethically neutral psychological metric, or in the natural fact that if we deliberated consistently with full empirical information we would approve of these standards: for these are precisely the kinds of fact that fail to carry normative authority for autonomous ethical agents, always leaving open questions. Instead, the fact in question will simply be the evaluative or normative fact that the objective values there are entail a certain set of standards S for human action. Nothing, of course, guarantees that we will correctly grasp this fact in our autonomous ethical reflection, but it will in any case be S that we are seeking in our ethical reflection, as we try to get our ethical judgments right; and, while we can always wonder whether or not we have things right, there is no open question of the sort that arises for standards based in natural facts, as long as we avoid trying to ground S in some non-evaluative, non-normative way.[23] So we learn to apply evaluative or normative concepts in a non-naturalistic, irreducibly evaluative or normative way by learning to think ethically in an autonomous way, where the standards on which we strive to base our judgments are not naturalistically given, but are rooted in irreducibly evaluative or normative features of the world (at least according to a robust version of non-naturalism).

While this is only a sketch of an answer to Gibbard's question about how we could come to employ normative concepts in a way that involves irreducibly normative, non-naturalistic content, it is enough to make some progress. The story does not, after all, require an etiology for a whole special class of concepts, but only an account of how familiar normative concepts might come to be employed in ways that go beyond more restricted employments, to make unqualified evaluative or normative judgments about human actions in connection with standards that, if they exist at all, will not be naturalistically given but will be grounded in irreducibly evaluative or normative features of the world (such as human dignity, to take the example mentioned earlier). This is not a surprising step for beings with autonomous mental capacities to make in the course of reflectively employing evaluative or normative concepts in their practical thinking.

The more difficult question, which Gibbard also raises, is how we could actually have come to *know* about a non-naturalistic subject matter: how do we, to the extent that we do, actually grasp non-natural facts about reasons and values? This is an important and difficult question for the non-naturalist: an epistemology for non-naturalist ethical realism is certainly owed and remains the most difficult challenge for such a view. It is especially difficult in connection with a robust non-naturalist view such as the one I favor, which posits irreducibly evaluative or normative aspects of certain features of the world (for example, dignity as an irreducibly normative feature of human beings). We have to have something to say about how it is that we are capable of employing our epistemic faculties, which we possess largely as a result of human natural selection history, in such a way as reliably to discover and track such features of the world, given that these features have nothing as such to do with the story of how these basic faculties evolved in the first place (Gibbard, 2010, pp. 9, 13; Street, 2006).

There are indeed things to say here: for example, we can note that we are evidently able to employ our evolved mental faculties to discover all kinds of facts that are equally irrelevant to the story of how and why our mental faculties evolved, such as facts about metaphysical necessity (water is necessarily H_2O, and so on) or higher mathematics or quantum field theory (FitzPatrick, 2008b). It is just a mistake to suppose that we *need* evolution to have shaped our faculties specifically to detect truths of a certain kind in order for us now to be able to use our evolved faculties reliably to do so; we need no evolutionary 'vindication' for the thinking we do in philosophy (backing up claims we make about metaphysical necessity, personal identity, universals, and so on), and we need none for the thinking we do in ethics: all we need is good reason to think that, despite some evolutionary influences on our thinking, we are also able to exercise our intelligence reasonably autonomously in ethics just as in other spheres, and that our methods of ethical reasoning are sound enough that we needn't fall into wholesale doubt about them.

Deep challenges remain, however, especially if we have to posit, in the ethical case, direct acquaintance with non-natural evaluative or normative properties, such as another person's inherent value and dignity. I do not want to downplay the work needed here, which will require epistemic models going well beyond familiar pictures involving nothing but naturalistic causal mechanisms, and so will likely strike some as extravagant and 'spooky' for that reason alone. What I hope to have shown is that there is better motivation for carefully exploring this non-naturalist alternative than many who are quick to dismiss it appreciate, both (i) because many of the common objections can in fact be answered, and (ii) because the alternatives – such as Gibbard's quasi-realist expressivist attempt to accommodate everything plausible about non-naturalist realism simply in terms of directive concepts, planning, and contrived, disjunctive natural properties – actually do a far from satisfactory job of really speaking to the concerns that have led some of us in the direction of non-naturalist realism to begin with.

Notes

1. More precisely, quasi-realism is intended to mimic claims made by realists that are 'in line with common sense' and admit of interpretation within an expressivist framework, such as the claim that many facts about wrongness are independent of our moral beliefs or attitudes, as discussed later. Obviously the very claims that are definitive of realism and distinguish it from expressivism cannot themselves be accommodated by expressivism without losing the very terms of the metaethical debate. (On this problem, see Dreier, 2004.) For example, Gibbard does *not* take quasi-realism to seek to mimic 'the claim that understanding normative properties and relations as objective matters of fact is basic to explaining how judgments of wrongness work', which is a claim he just takes to be mistaken, and for which he substitutes an expressivist explanatory account (Gibbard, 2010, p. 11).
2. This is an important theme developed in Parfit (2010).
3. While Gibbard concedes that ethical concepts are non-naturalistic in this sense, he does not hold that they are *primitively* so: he takes himself to have much more to say about them than ethical non-naturalists claim is possible. On his view, for example, we can explain the normative concept of warrant in terms of planning (2010, pp. 2, 5).
4. For Gibbard, insofar as normative concepts pick out properties, the properties they pick out are natural ones, for which we can *also* have non-normative, naturalistic concepts (2006, p. 323). This is denied by the ethical non-naturalist, as noted just below.

5. Dreier (2004) appeals to this sort of difference in explanatory accounts as the key to distinguishing realism from sophisticated quasi-realist expressivism. Cf. the quote from Gibbard about explanation in note 1 above.

6. This amounts to an expressivist analogue of the neo-Kantian constructivist reduction of normativity to *practical necessity* associated with the conditions of agency. For critiques of the latter approach, see FitzPatrick (2005) and Enoch (2006). I will not explore neo-Kantian constructivist views here.

7. By a *robust* non-naturalism I mean one that has significant metaphysical implications: the world turns out to have non-natural features along with its familiar natural ones (FitzPatrick, 2008a). Some non-naturalists instead adopt a non-metaphysical alternative, holding that non-natural properties and facts – in particular, facts about reasons – do not strictly 'belong to the world' in a way that would require a metaphysical account, being perhaps more like mathematical properties and facts than natural ones (Parfit, 2010; Scanlon, 1998).

8. Given Gibbard's understanding of what the natural property in question is, as discussed below, one could attribute that same property using *non*-normative concepts, yet such an attribution would clearly not be a normative judgment; two people, for example, could agree on this property attribution and yet disagree about whether the action is 'the thing to do,' since they are committed to different plans.

9. For simplicity, I am here focusing on 'ought' judgments as representative normative judgments, but there are in fact lots of normative judgments that cannot plausibly be treated in terms of 'ought' judgments, such as judgments about contributory reasons, as Jonathan Dancy argues (Dancy, 2006b). Nothing I say here is meant to deny the subtleties and complexities of normative judgment that Dancy helpfully explores.

10. There is again an interesting parallel here between Gibbard's worries about a gap between realist normative judgment and decision-making and Korsgaard's attack on realism as involving a deep gap between the grasping of independent normative truths and exercising the will.

11. A closely related point about normativity and motivation: non-naturalists reject any reduction of facts about normative reasons to facts about motivation (actual or hypothetical), but this doesn't mean we deny the intimate relation between reasons and motivation: there is undoubtedly such a relation, but it is itself an *irreducibly normative* one. If R is a decisive reason for me to do A, then, while nothing is guaranteed about my actual motivations or even my hypothetical motivations under ethically neutrally specifiable idealizing conditions (such as full empirical information and consistent deliberation), it remains true that in light of R I *ought* to be *motivated* to do A, and that is the only connection we need to grant. I defend this position in FitzPatrick (2004). Cf. also Scanlon (1998, p. 58).

12. I am here adopting Dancy's helpful terminology (Dancy, 1993, pp. 73–7; 2004c).

13. I develop these points more fully in FitzPatrick (2008a, pp. 186 f.).

14. Again, I explore the motivations for non-naturalism about basic ethical standards, and sketch the beginnings of a non-naturalist account of ethical standards, in FitzPatrick (2008a).

15. This exactly parallels Blackburn's earlier discussion of 'bear baiting' in Blackburn (1993, p. 153).

16. It's worth noting, though, that the considerable strain of reducing all normative judgment to *planning* shows up even more clearly here: for the planning in question is planning here and now for the case of being a Hopi who *doesn't* care

about animal suffering, to refrain from playing the game simply on the grounds that it hurts the chicken (Gibbard, 2010, p. 7). One would thus be planning now to do something that under the circumstances wouldn't make any sense to oneself. This is, to say the least, not merely a different notion of planning from the ordinary one (which Gibbard acknowledges), but a highly peculiar notion in its own right, and one might again wonder whether this much stretching is really worth it just to avoid positing non-natural properties and facts, which are not obviously any 'stranger' or more 'incredible' than such strained construals of simple normative judgments.

17. On my (partly Aristotelian) view, we should not *expect* to be able to convince others with very different moral upbringings of our ethical views simply through argument, but this casts doubt neither on the existence of ethical truths nor on the possibility of being justified in thinking we are (sometimes) grasping such truths that others are missing. The latter will depend on the quality of our support for our views (Nagel, 1979) together with the plausibility of our theories of error for rival views, such as those of Hopi youth, who accord no normative significance to animal suffering. There have in fact been many plausible responses to the 'argument from disagreement' that Gibbard finds so compelling against realism, and he gives up far too easily on the possibility of good explanations for fundamental disagreement in moving from (i) the thought that if we had been raised Hopi we would believe the same things they believe to (ii) the concession that their normative views are no less justified than ours, and (iii) the idea that the only legitimate condemnation of their views as mistaken is therefore the plan-laden judgment we make from within our own first-order commitments (while they can, of course, say the same with regard to our views). That is, however, an issue to explore elsewhere.

18. Horgan and Timmons (2006) have recently offered what is perhaps the most thorough defense of expressivism against the relativism objection. They show that, in so far as expressivism allows ascriptions of truth or falsity to moral claims, it is not committed to any objectionably relativistic uses of 'true' or 'false': in morally engaged contexts, 'true' can be used in a minimalist fashion simply to endorse the non-relativistic moral content expressed in first-order moral judgments (p. 88); in morally detached contexts, expressivism denies any role for positive ascriptions of truth or falsity to moral judgments (except as embedded in descriptive reports of others' moral beliefs, as in saying that Jones believes it is true that stealing is okay, and such uses obviously do not involve any endorsement and so do not imply moral relativism; pp. 89–90). While their points are very well taken, however, and complicate the project of articulating the relativism objection properly, they do not get to the heart of the real worry underlying accusations of relativism – a point they seem to recognize in the final section of the article (pp. 95–6). The real objection is what I have tried to bring out in the text above, and, while they might resist framing this in terms of relativism, I think the problem in question is very naturally described as a form of relativism (though we can always give up the word if it proves distracting). For a similar line of objection to expressivism, though put in terms of an inappropriate *dependence* relation rather than in terms of relativism, see Enoch (2010, pp. 133–6).

19. The idea is roughly to string together disjunctively all the various sets of natural properties possessed by any possible acts that also possess E. That disjunctive property D is then one which will be possessed by *every* act that possesses E (since that act's natural properties will be included as one of the disjuncts in D) and

only by acts that possess E (given that the disjuncts in D are just sets of natural properties possessed by acts that are E).

20. Plantinga offers much further argument to cast doubt on the move from necessary coextension to identity, but this is enough to indicate the basic problem for present purposes.

21. Here a naturalist might appeal to idealized subjective approaches to account for normative reasons in terms of facts about motivation under various hypothetical conditions specified in an ethically neutral way. I critique such approaches in FitzPatrick (2004) and (2008a), and will return to this briefly in the next section.

22. One objection Gibbard has to a robust realism is that he takes it to posit basic normative facts beyond our power to grasp them, and it seems dubious that there could be such facts (Gibbard, 2010, p. 10). But a robust realist needn't be committed to such facts at all. Denying that ethical facts are a function of our beliefs, desires, attitudes, or decisions – whether actual or idealized via ethically neutrally specifiable idealizing conditions – does not entail that ethical facts could outrun our ability, even in principle, to discover them. They may, for example, still be functions of evaluative or normative aspects of human life that are in principle accessible to us, at least if we have the right kind of upbringing and experience and engage in sufficient ethical reflection. Indeed, this seems most plausible if these are really going to be ethical facts about human life, providing norms *for human beings*. If they were rooted in something inaccessible to us, how could they constitute normative facts about how we should live and against which we could fairly be judged? Gibbard's skepticism about this is warranted, but it is equally shared by plausible forms of even robust ethical realism.

23. That is, there is no open question of the form: 'Granted, S is the set of standards entailed by the objective values there are, which anyone would recognize as appropriate who was properly sensitive to the full range of genuine values, through proper upbringing, suitable experience, and sound reflection, but is S really the appropriate set of standards to live by?' Open questions arise when S is characterized in natural terms, and they could equally arise if S were characterized somehow in non-natural terms that were *also* non-evaluative or non-normative, such as facts about Gibbard's 'exnat' mentioned earlier. But they don't arise if S is characterized in irreducibly evaluative or normative terms, as above, which again is why the appeal to the non-natural is necessary (though again we can always worry about whether or not we've got S right, which isn't the same kind of problematic open question as a question about the normative authority of a non-normatively grounded candidate for S). See FitzPatrick (2008a) for more on this.

2
Naturalistic Metaethics at Half Price

Joshua Gert

Let us call the world of facts studied by science 'the naturalistic world.' And let us call 'naturalism' the view that all facts have to fit neatly into the naturalistic world. The relevant notion of 'fitting into' is meant to be quite broad, but one obvious way in which a fact could fit into the naturalistic world would be for that fact simply to be a fact about the naturalistic world.[1] On this interpretation, naturalism amounts to the view that all facts are naturalistic facts. One can make this view more or less controversial by having a more or less restricted view of what counts as science, and therefore as the naturalistic world. But a problem for anyone who wishes to defend a version of this simple sort of naturalism is that certain kinds of facts have seemed difficult to understand as a part the naturalistic world, even quite liberally conceived: facts about evaluative matters, facts about the meanings of words, facts about conscious experiences, and about mathematics and logic, to name just a few. One promising strategy for dealing with these threats to naturalism is to move to a more sophisticated understanding of 'fitting into' the naturalistic world. This strategy begins by appealing to the kinds of facts that do not seem problematic, even on the simpler understanding of what it is to fit into the naturalistic world: facts about human behavior and about our linguistic capacities. It then seeks to show that our ways of thinking and talking about the problematic topics – including in many cases our regarding them as being factual – are completely unproblematic and unsurprising. This is the strategy I will pursue in the present paper, and I will call it 'linguistic naturalism.' It is important to keep linguistic naturalism distinct from other strategies that place language at the center of philosophy, since it is possible to think of language in another way: as our best evidence for the structure of thought, and so also as the starting-point for philosophy.[2] A danger associated with this second kind of linguistic strategy is that there are strong non-naturalistic temptations once we begin to focus our attention on the nature of thought, and the relation of thought to the world. As a result of these temptations, interesting discoveries in the structure of language can easily lead to extravagant metaphysical pictures of the nature of the world.[3]

There are, I think, two importantly distinct, though compatible, forms of linguistic naturalism. One focuses primarily on whole domains of discourse: normative or moral talk, mathematics, psychological talk and so on. The other focuses on particular words: 'red,' 'good' and 'wrong' have been very popular choices. One of the most ardent and eloquent contemporary defenders of the first form is Huw Price.[4] And one of the ablest contemporary defenders of the second form is Philip Pettit.[5] I do not think it is a coincidence that both Price's view and Pettit's can be seen as global versions of strategies that have been employed more frequently as local solutions to more specific philosophical problems. It is no coincidence because both Price and Pettit explicitly find the seeds of their accounts in the philosophy of the later Wittgenstein, who had no reluctance to follow his insights out to their furthest reaches. I find very much to admire in both Price's and Pettit's views. The present paper is an attempt to combine them and put the result to work in defense of some metaethical claims I have made elsewhere.

1. Price's pragmatism

Perhaps the best way to explain Price's view is to begin with a local version. Consider moral discourse. For those with naturalistic impulses and a certain view of the paradigmatic function of descriptive discourse, moral discourse presents a problem to be solved. The view of the paradigmatic function of descriptive discourse is that it is used to represent the way things are; property-words pick out properties, object-words pick out objects, and the claim 'Object O has property P' represents the fact that O does indeed have property P. In this explanation the words 'pick out' and 'represent' are intended to be understood in a substantive way. What precisely this means is not clear, as various attempts to clarify them have shown.[6] But let this pass for the moment; all that is required is that they are more robust, in an important way, than the minimal deflationary sense soon to be explained. Now, moral discourse seems to ascribe moral properties to actions. But these properties have seemed to many philosophers to be properties that cannot be understood as naturalistic. For example, some have thought that a clear perception of the moral wrongness of an action has some kind of necessary link to an unwillingness to perform it. For present purposes, it does not matter what this link is understood to involve, or indeed whether or not a 'naturalistically respectable' property could somehow manage to do the job. What is important is that many philosophers have thought that no naturalistic property could in fact do the job, and have therefore claimed that the surface grammar of moral assertions is misleading. Rather than representing facts, or expressing beliefs, moral claims, according to these philosophers, serve a different function: they give expression to non-cognitive attitudes. But the view cannot stop here; it must also explain why it is that moral discourse exhibits all the syntactical trappings of descriptive discourse. That is, it must explain why we say that moral claims are true or false, why they function in inferential contexts in the same way as descriptive claims, why we speak of moral facts and beliefs, and so on.

Now, for the view just explained – ethical expressivism – to remain a *local* view, it must mark a clear and coherent distinction between ethical claims and those for which the surface grammar is *not* misleading. And for the ethical expressivist to mark this distinction he will need to give a clear sense to expressions such as 'is true' or 'expresses a belief,' taken as *literal* or *robust*. But, given the success of the non-cognitivist, and given the well known philosophical difficulties involved in providing robust accounts of truth and the related notions of reference, assertion, and belief, it should start to seem doubtful that there is a clear contrast between moral discourse and the kind of discourse that has seemed less problematic to naturalists. The problem here is not with the ethical expressivist's claim that moral claims express motivational attitudes, or with his explanation of our talk of moral properties, facts, and beliefs. Rather, the problem is with the assumption that there is a clear distinction between moral talk and other kinds of talk – a distinction that we can draw in terms of truth, reference, and related semantic notions. And this assumption – excusable in someone who has not considered the view that all the characteristic behavior of semantic terms such as 'true' and 'refers' can be explained without assuming that they are substantive – is strangely persistent even among those who have not only considered this view, but have taken great pains to demonstrate it.

There are a number of candidate accounts of the notions of truth and reference that are sufficiently insubstantial that they cannot be used to distinguish evaluative talk from talk about tables or elementary particles. One is the disquotational view, according to which '... is true' serves to construct a sentence with the same content as the sentence mentioned in the truth claim. On this view, the usefulness of talk about truth comes from the ability to use '... is true' to construct claims, the content of which one is not in a position to express explicitly, as in 'whatever Victoria told you is true.'[7] Use of the term 'refers' and its cognates can also be understood in similar ways.[8] Now, one problem with this kind of theory of truth and reference is that it calls out for an explanation as to why it is only *assertions*, and not, say, *questions* or *commands*, that are liable to be constructed via a disquotational device. In providing an explanation for this fact, Price makes what may be his most distinctive contribution to linguistic naturalism: an explanation for the fact that we have, in human languages, utterances that function as assertions do, and words such as 'true' and 'false' with which we voice our agreement or disagreement with the utterance of someone else. Here is not the place to present Price's view in detail.[9] But a central point is that for some psychological states – ones that we do not antecedently have to think of as representational, which would commit us to a prior understanding of truth and reference – it turns out that a linguistic community does better, in the long run, if there is pressure towards uniformity. One way of applying such pressure is for people to be disposed to confront anyone whose utterances express psychological states that are in conflict with their own, and to try to eliminate the conflict. Now, this kind of story requires us to understand the relevant notion of conflict without appeal to semantic notions. It will not do to gloss 'in conflict' as 'incapable of simultaneous truth.' Price has something to say about this as well, in terms of signaling, and the need to distinguish significant failures to signal from what we might call *mere* failures to signal (say, because one has died). Although Price does not say it, his story here actually seems applicable to plants and non-verbal animals as much as to human beings, which supports his claim that it need not rely on any semantic notions.[10]

On Price's view, we have a uniform explanation of some central features of descriptive talk, whether that talk is about mathematics, evaluative matters, or the world of middle-sized dry goods. All that the explanation requires is that the psychological states to which assertions in these various domains give voice be such that it is advantageous in the long run that there is pressure towards uniformity, and that there are ways, in cases of conflict, of applying that pressure. That explanation doesn't require that all such talk be representational in any robust sense; indeed it is consistent with the view, which Price also defends, that different domains of descriptive talk perform very different functions. Blackburn's quasi-realism about normative talk can be seen as a local version of this view. Price simply recognizes that Blackburn's project can be pushed further – and that, indeed, there is no principled stopping-point, unless one can provide a plausible substantive account of truth and reference: a daunting task.

Price's view suggests that there is a *prima facie* case against attempts to reduce the objects and properties of any given domain to those of science – much less to those of physics in particular. As he and John Hawthorne put it:

Once we have an adequate explanation for the fact that the folk *talk* of Xs and Ys and Zs, an explanation which distinguishes these activities from what the folk are doing when they do physics, why should we try to reduce the Xs and Ys and Zs to what is talked about in physics?[11]

Although Price and Hawthorne intend this question to be rhetorical, in fact it need not always lack an answer. In some cases – for example the case of water and H_2O – it might well be appropriate to reduce one kind to another. But in other domains – the normative, the mathematical, the modal – there is no particularly compelling way to challenge the *prima facie* case against reduction.

Now, the passage quoted above most directly concerns *explanation*. And certainly there can be explanations of talk of Xs and Ys that show that such talk is deeply confused or incoherent or in error in some other ways. A good candidate for a domain of discourse that has these defects might be astrology. It is not very mysterious that we human beings go in for astrology. But it is not very controversial amongst philosophers that astrology is simply bogus: that our best philosophical theory of astrology would be an error theory. There is a danger that the view I am defending in this paper will be taken to commit me to the idea that there is no more to be said against astrology than against talk of normative reasons for action. I will address this worry later. For the moment I only want to signal my awareness of it. The worry might be put in the following way: the project I am engaged in seems to want to vindicate certain domains that have historically been hard to square with naturalism, but all I actually offer is naturalistic explanations for their existence.[12]

As Price has been remarking with increasing poignancy for twenty years, the view just explained is surprisingly invisible in contemporary philosophy. There are many possible explanations for this invisibility, some of which Price himself explores. I would like to mention a number of other possible explanations. The first is a kind of exasperated impatience on the part of those to whom it is presented, when it is presented as the basis for a rival account of a common subject. The exasperation stems from a desire to talk about the subject itself, and not about language. But, of course, in talking about anything one must use language, and it is naïve to suppose that we can take for granted that language is related to the world in a sufficiently simple way that we can mentally 'subtract' the linguistic medium in which we are discussing, for example, value, or color, or desire, and then, with this subtraction completed, hold the remainder – the objects and properties themselves, as it were – clearly in mind. This is obvious when one considers domains of philosophical theorizing that have seemed appropriate for local versions of expressivism or deflationism. A philosopher who exhibited impatience with a theory of the function of words such as 'true' and 'false,' and who said that he simply wanted to talk about the properties of truth and falsity, would be overlooking an eminently plausible view of what is going on when we make assertions about the truth or falsity of propositions. But why think that anything is importantly different when one is offering a theory of color, or value, or desire?

Another reason some philosophers are averse to linguistic naturalism is that they are quick to take its focus on language to imply that it is simply ordinary language philosophy of the sort that attempts to systematize the platitudes to which competent speakers of the language would immediately assent. The messiness of what actual speakers tend to say, and the ease with which they can be brought to paradox, do seem to count against this form of philosophy. As a result, one sees the following sort of claim:

> From the point of view of the biologist, the word 'food' is applied by ordinary people in a somewhat arbitrary way. According to them, the

synthetic cooking oil Olestra, which has no nutritional value at all, is a food, but vitamin tablets and beer are not. An investigation of how ordinary people use the word 'food' is not particularly relevant to biology. What is relevant is an investigation into the sorts of substances human beings can digest, whether or not the biological category of the digestible lines up exactly with the folk category of food. *The problem of color realism is like the investigation of what humans can digest, not the investigation of the folk category of food.* The enquiry concerns certain properties that objects visually appear to have, not how ordinary people use color words, or how they conceptualize color categories.[13]

These reflections are offered by Alex Byrne and David Hilbert as a reason for pursuing the question of color realism by focusing exclusively on 'various especially salient properties that objects visually appear to have,' and paying no attention to the issue of how it is human beings acquire and use color language. This seems to me to be a crucial mistake.[14]

A related reason for the invisibility of linguistic naturalism is a strong and understandable resistance to the idea that philosophy, properly done, is essentially the construction of plausible stories regarding the evolutionary history of human linguistic behavior. That would constitute a discipline-wide change of subject, and it is not surprising that many philosophers do not want to leave off their investigations into, say, the nature of color or value, and sign up for anthropology instead. One response to this worry is to assure such philosophers that there is still room, within the linguistic practices that the linguistic naturalist seeks to explain, to make illuminating claims. Indeed, there is room within linguistic naturalism for the idea that whole domains of discourse are systematically mistaken in their ontological presuppositions, just as astrology is. There is much philosophical work to be done in determining whether or not a domain is like this – indeed, much contemporary metaphysics does not need much modification to be seen as engaged in precisely this work. At its most modest, linguistic naturalism can be seen simply as an argument that the default status for domains that seem to be working pretty well – such as the domains of practical rationality, probability, mathematics – should be 'unproblematic,' even if the objects and properties that figure in those domains are not understood as the objects of scientific investigation. A second response is to point to the work of Wittgenstein, Price, Pettit, and others, as examples of the obviously philosophical nature that the relevant form of 'speculative linguistic anthropology' can take.

2. Pettit's response-dependence

Philip Pettit is another contemporary philosopher whose views are clearly inspired by those of the later Wittgenstein. In particular, his global response-dependence is offered as an interpretation of Wittgenstein's views on rule-following. The picture of rule-following that Wittgenstein was trying to combat was one that required that the grasp of a rule – paradigmatically a rule for the use of a word – involved something like the presence in one's mind of a representation of the rule that would guarantee correct applications. Wittgenstein's point was that any such representation – a picture, say – simply could not fulfill that role. For imagine that it really was a picture that we had in our heads, or minds, when we applied a rule; still we would need to have some rule to follow in order to apply the picture, and from this point the regress is obvious. Of course, if there were only one way in which a picture (or whatever) could be applied, then there would be no problem. But it is characteristic of rules that they apply to an open-ended number of instances, and that there are any number of ways of extrapolating from a finite set of initial instances.

Pettit's solution to the problem of rule-following is clearly inspired by Wittgenstein's own claims about forms of life. Pettit begins by noting that we human beings are, as a matter of contingent fact, set up to extrapolate in more or less the same ways from a finite stock of initial examples. That does not mean that we cannot see that other ways are logically consistent with that same initial stock. But it does mean that we can teach each other how to use words, and that those who learn those words will tend to go on as we ourselves do. Pettit also notes that within a linguistic community there is a disposition to note discrepancies in the application of words, and to seek explanations for these discrepancies. While not explicitly noted by Pettit himself, this claim is correct whether or not the 'application' of the word is a naming or describing of something, since the same story goes for *all* words. In some cases a discrepancy in application is explained by appeal to the fact that one speaker was in what both speakers can come to regard as distorting conditions. For the application of a color term, this might involve the presence of a strong after-image. In other cases neither speaker need have been in any such distorting condition, but one speaker might nevertheless have what both can come to regard as an advantage: for example, a superabundance of relevant additional information. For simplicity, let us ignore this distinction and focus only on the fact that there can be differences in how well placed two speakers can be, and that these differences can explain why they apply a common term in different ways. We can then give a functional characterization of the 'favorable conditions' that figure in response-dependent biconditionals such as

X is red $\leftrightarrow$ X would appear red under favorable conditions.

That functional characterization is something like the following. Consider cases of conflict in the application of some term – cases that are explained by differences in the conditions of the two speakers. In such cases the speakers can select one set of conditions and decide that the application of the term in those conditions is to be preferred over the application of the term in the other set. Some ways of selecting which conditions to prefer will be better than others in terms of producing long-term convergence in the application of the term. Favorable conditions are those that are *best* in this way: appealing to them in order to resolve discrepancies in the application of a term would *maximize* expected long-term convergence in the application of that term. Obviously the favorable conditions of relevance for the biconditional that is true of color terms will be different from the favorable conditions of relevance for the biconditional that is true of terms like 'living,' 'bad,' and so on.

What is to some degree surprising in Pettit, especially given his Wittgensteinian inspiration, is his almost exclusive focus on what he takes to be referential words. Here is a characteristic remark:

> The favourable conditions that interest me are those conditions that are favourable for the detection of how things are: those conditions that serve to connect what is with what seems and what seems with what is. [...] The conditions that interest me are favourable-for-detection in a serious and literal sense of 'detection'.[15]

But, clearly, a contingent uniformity in human extrapolative capacities also helps to explain how it is that we learn to use such words as 'ouch,' 'goodbye' and 'unless' in consistent ways. Similarly, it can explain how we learn to use such words as 'true' and 'false,' even if deflationists are correct about their non-representational function. One point Price makes that Pettit should certainly take on is that it is better not to rely on robust semantic notions such as reference if one can help it, and that in theorizing about language one can often help it. That is, the global response-dependence of Pettit – whether Pettit appreciates it or not – need not take 'going on in the same way' to mean 'referring to things of the same kind.' Pettit's story about our coming to master the rules for the use of words in public languages is the same whether (a) we take such words to be robustly referential or (b) we take them to be verbal pieces in the various functionally characterized language-games that Price, and Wittgenstein, describe: pieces that can only be said to refer unmysteriously if we take reference to be understood in some non-substantive way.

Pettit seems to rely heavily on substantive semantic vocabulary. For example, in introducing his response-dependent story, he writes:

> Consider how we are each capable of being directed to a certain property – and therefore to the semantic value that is to attach to a corresponding term – by means of a finite list of examples.[16]
>
> ...mastery of [...] basic terms, and possession of the corresponding concepts, is dependent on that person's being responsive in a certain way to the referents of those terms: say, to the properties picked out by them.[17]

These claims certainly *suggest* reliance on a robust view of semantic relations. It is possible that this suggestion is misleading. After all, even Price, who is explicit in his repudiation of a substantially representationalist view of the function of descriptive language, will not complain about a story about our acquisition of the concept of 'red' that makes mention of red objects; that is, objects that have the property of redness; that is, objects that have the property referred to by 'red;' that is, the semantic value of 'red.' Price might regard the latter formulations as excessively technical and dangerously liable to robust readings, but, given the availability of deflationary views of 'property,' 'reference' and even 'semantic value,' he cannot say that they are simply false. I suspect that Pettit does subscribe to a more robust metaphysical picture than Price. But the fact that his language need not actually *commit* him to such a picture is an interesting one, and it means that it need not be so difficult to combine Price and Pettit into a Wittgensteinian unified view.

3. Wittgensteinian superglobalism

I have been trying to suggest that Price's and Pettit's distinct global views can be seen as filling out two different levels of a unified Wittgensteinian view: a view that sees language as a collection of heterogeneous and partially overlapping language-games. Price asks 'Why have a game with this form?' and Pettit asks 'How do we learn the rules?' It is true that, for Pettit's view to be fully consistent with Price's, Pettit should make explicit that his reliance on semantic vocabulary is not to be taken robustly, and that he endorses Price's views regarding the pluralistic nature of assertion and belief.[18] I do not expect that he would be willing to do this. But my concern is not to show that he would, or even that he should: it is to construct a unified Wittgensteinian account that has all the advantages of both views.

Since I see myself as closer to Price than to Pettit in many ways, my strategy in this section will first be to offer a few relatively minor emendations to Price's views, in order to establish my starting point. From there I will modify and incorporate Pettit's view. Once Pettit has been made more congenial to the global expressivist, I will appeal to some of Pettit's insights to make a number of further points regarding the nature of assertion, fact, and property.

3.1. Modifying Price

One point that can seem obvious to a critic of Price is that it is impossible to begin theorizing about language without making some ontological assumptions. If so, Price himself cannot avoid commitment to a 'real world' of basic entities and properties, and this commitment will entail a clear contrast between these 'genuine' entities and properties and the 'quasi' entities and 'quasi' properties that are referred to – in a deflationary way – by the relevant terms in the language-games he is at such pains to explain.[19] Price himself confronts this objection by appeal to something like Carnap's point that there are internal and external existence questions that we can raise regarding any domain. Within the domain of mathematics, for example, we can ask whether there exists an irrational number which, when raised to an irrational power, yields a rational number. From outside the domain, it can seem that we can ask a superficially similar question: do numbers exist? But, unlike the internal answer, for which there can be a clear justification for an affirmative or negative answer, the external question – like all such external existence questions – is simply ill-posed. Now, when we theorize about the origins of linguistic practices, we are operating within a certain kind of scientific domain. Within that domain our explanatory ontology includes human beings and the kinds of objects with which they interact: stones, trees, other animals. But within that domain we need not appeal to values or – perhaps – to numbers or possibilities. For Price this means that, within the project of linguistic naturalism, we can say such things as ' "human beings" refers to human beings' and this will be true for disquotational reasons. But we need not talk about values at all. It is thus an artifact of the project we are engaged in – scientific explanation – that we must accept a certain (scientific) ontology, but need not accept another (say, the ontology of values).[20] This can seem to favor the scientific ontology, but in fact merely reflects the commitments of one domain amongst many.

Perhaps Price's explanation is correct. My own response to the challenge, however, is (I think) different. I do not think we should concede robust reference to any ontology at all to the scientific realist. Rather, we should simply start with the assumption that our language is in perfect working order as it is, and that most of us know how to use it quite well.[21] This does not even commit us to robust reference to an entity referred to by 'our language' (or, therefore, by 'it'), since we have not yet theorized in any way about what we are doing with the sentence 'our language is in perfect working order as it is.' Of course, the idea that our language is in perfect working order is consistent with our using it to make false claims on occasion – even with our using it to make systematically false claims (say, about witches or phlogiston). But if we rely only on claims that no one would ever dream of disputing, and claim that language is working unproblematically when we make these claims, we need not go beyond this and say anything at all about what this unproblematic functioning consists in. In particular, we need not claim that the property words we use in providing our explanations for the emergence and structure of, say, evaluative talk are referring words in any other sense than the deflationary sense. I think this response to the scientific realist avoids Price's potentially problematic idea of 'the scientific perspective.'

3.2. Modifying Pettit

We have seen that Pettit at least seems to appeal to semantic notions in his explanation of our acquisition of words for properties. For example, in the following passages he is explaining our tendency to look for an explanation when there is a discrepancy in the application of a term as between two speakers of the same language:

> It is not surprising that we look for an explanation of such discrepancy. Given *the assumption that the term has constant semantic value* across the discrepant sides and that it is introduced ostensively, say *to designate a property* that is allegedly salient from examples, we could not comfortably treat the discrepancy as inexplicable.

> The constancy of the *semantic value* means that we have to think of one and the same property – or the absence of that property – as *registering* with one side and not with the other.

> [T]heir practices commit people to supposing, that *there is a property* or other entity there for a term like 'red' or 'regular' to *designate*.

> [I am offering a] theory of how the relevant terms come to be *semantically attached* to corresponding *properties or other entities*.[22]

What is surprising in these explanatory remarks is the apparent appeal to a clear understanding of what a *property* is, and that such a thing might be the *semantic value* of a term: an understanding that language-learners evidently have prior to acquiring any particular property-words. Instead of making this problematic claim, Pettit would have done better to adopt something similar to Price's explanation for the emergence of such a thing as assertion, but directed instead at the existence of property-words. I am not sure precisely how such an explanation would go; it would have to say something about the usefulness of the subject/predicate form of a class of basic sentences, and about what it is that distinguishes subject words from predicate words. And it would have to do this without relying on substantive representational relations. I expect that the seeds of such an explanation could be found in the work of Ruth Millikan, but I do not have space to explore this issue here.

Another surprising omission by Pettit is his failure to note that his own examples of response-dependent terms span a range of property-words that are extremely variable in their apparent degree of what we might call 'objectivity.' For example, he remarks that his response-dependent story of concept acquisition goes as well for 'funny' as it does for 'straight' or 'smooth.'[23] In this case he does note that 'funny' is more dependent on culture. But he does not note the existence, in the case of 'funny,' of a much more extensive class of no-fault disagreements – which puts pressure on the idea that an objective property is picked out by the term. Similarly, in illustrating the practice of looking for explanations of discrepancies in the application of some term, one of Pettit's examples is the originality of a painting or building or piece of music.[24] But surely even lay people may respond to a question such as 'Which of these two buildings is more original?' with a dismissive wave of the hand. Still, it is true that we *sometimes* do try to persuade each other that a failure to agree is the result of prejudice or some other distorting fact. A plausible Wittgensteinian view should make room for these phenomena, which include the idea that some property-words do not seem to pick out genuine or objective properties.

In attempting to avoid the conclusion that response-dependence involves infallibility, Pettit points out that there is no effective procedure for determining when we are in favorable conditions.[25] This is both correct and important. But, given the unavailability of any such effective procedure, there is no real pressure to assume that there is a unique but unknowable set of favorable conditions. We can simply say that in the case of certain words we have a practice of noting discrepancies and seeking to resolve them. When we engage in this practice we sometimes find that there is a *further* discrepancy: a discrepancy in the application of such terms as 'distortion.' When this happens we can either seek to explain this further discrepancy, or not. And so on. As Pettit should be the first to admit, language use is at bottom a matter of the manifestation of dispositions – dispositions that tend to overlap imperfectly but extensively within a linguistic community.[26] How much agreement must there be in the application of some term, and how successful must our efforts to resolve disagreements be, in order to vindicate the claim that the word picks out a property? The answer to this question is, of course, a matter of the correct application of the word 'property.' One important point, with which Pettit is in agreement, is that the existence of *some* ineliminable disputes does not undermine the appropriateness of such claims as 'redness is a property.'[27]

3.3. Price again

As we have seen, Price offers more than a merely disquotational account of truth. One advantage of his view is that it helps to explain why there is a term that functions disquotationally only within the domain of assertion. Again, the reason is that assertion itself is explained in terms of the usefulness of a form of expression that invites dispute in cases of conflicting behavioral dispositions. And talk of truth need only function disquotationally in order to make an important contribution to this sort of conflict resolution. But those who are sympathetic to more local versions of this sort of view (ethical expressivists, for example) might well feel unsatisfied if we stop at this point. After all, there remains a strong intuition that some claims that take the form of assertion are, as we might say, *literally* truth-apt, while others merely *function as if* they were truth-apt. I think that Price is generally correct in the particular arguments that he offers against those who express this worry, and who either offer no account of the distinction or offer an account that relies on unexplained semantic notions or some other philosophically vexed criteria. But I also think that someone sympathetic to Pettit's form of global response-dependence has the materials to hand for an explanation of intuitions of robust truth that both Price and (some of) those with whom he is arguing could accept. And similar arguments may also allow for intuitions that some property-words refer to *genuine* properties, while others only *function as if* they do.

In fact, Price does not object to the idea that some assertions are, as we might say, less truth-apt than others. And, given the link between the truth of an assertion and the ascription of properties to entities, he should not object to the idea that some property-words are less objective (or genuine or robust or whatever) than others. In *Facts and the Function of Truth* Price spends a fair amount of energy showing that, in the domains of probability and morality, some disagreements simply evaporate when more information comes to light – and not always because the parties come to agree. This is because no long-term advantage is to be had from treating the disagreement as factual in such situations. These disagreements do not fit what Price calls the 'factual pattern' of disagreement, the crucial feature of which is that 'it requires us to say that of any pair of conflicting judgments, at least one must be false.'[28] Given a range of explanations for these kinds of non-factual disagreements, he therefore thinks that he can capture many of the intuitions that lead philosophers to adopt local versions of anti-realism. Although he might not put it this way, Price *could* say that disagreements that stray sufficiently far from the factual pattern involve assertions that are less truth-apt than those involved in disagreements that fit the pattern more strictly.[29]

There is a further reason why Price should be open to the idea that some kinds of assertion are not to be regarded as genuinely fact-stating. His perspective on language is evolutionary and anthropological. This kind of perspective immediately opens up space for what we might call 'exaptive' uses of various linguistic devices. That is, just as an organ that evolved to perform one particular function can be co-opted by evolution to perform other *distinct* functions, so too might the assertoric form be co-opted in such a way that we can distinguish relatively sharply between a number of distinct functions that it serves. For Price the primary function is one that brings along with it the appropriateness of talk of truth and falsity. My point is that, even if this *is* the primary function, it need not be the only one. If so, we may be able to understand the assertoric form as applicable to ethical and evaluative claims without *having to say* that they express belief in facts. This would allow us to stop the 'creep' of minimalism that threatens to obliterate the distinction between realism and anti-realism in various domains.[30]

I think that Pettit's response-dependence can help us draw some limits around the notion of a robust fact. Some sorts of claims – ones that take the form of assertions, and that we can endorse or disagree with by making use of 'true' and 'false' in their minimal senses – might lack so many of the features of paradigmatic fact-stating assertions that they simply are not seen in the same way as we see such claims as 'grass is green.' Price identifies the existence of a large class of no-fault disagreements within a certain domain of indicative sentences as one way in which utterances in that domain can differ from paradigmatic assertions. But there are others. One idea, appealed to by many non-cognitivists about evaluative issues, is that the mere possession of a belief cannot by itself provide motivation to a particular action; for that some desire is also required. Non-cognitivists who hold this view may be latching onto a sort of proto-theory that resonates with lay people, and running with it in a characteristically philosophical way (that is, in a way that is both overly simple and incredibly sophisticated). But the proto-theory may resonate with people not because it is true, but because directly motivating action is sufficiently uncharacteristic of belief to *count against* that belief's being a belief in a *fact* (or against its being a *robust* or *genuine* belief). Recognition of the direct motivational role of the state so expressed might be part of what is latched onto by our mechanisms of response-dependent concept-acquisition, and it might help to classify such utterances as non-factual, when it is present in conjunction with other departures from the factual pattern. These reflections on the nature of evaluative discourse are, importantly, consistent with Price's pluralism about factual domains. That is, it does not undermine the factual nature of probabilistic discourse, mathematical discourse, or color discourse, since in those domains no particular assertion by itself tells us how someone will act, unless we posit some other independent motivational state. Moreover, it is also consistent with these reflections that some evaluative talk will still be rightly regarded as factual. Perhaps only in combination with a sufficiently high proportion of evaporative or no-fault disagreements does the link to motivation push an assertion out of the privileged circle of the robustly factual.

There is something especially nice about providing a response-dependent account of such concepts as those that correspond to the terms 'fact' and 'property,' or perhaps to those that correspond to the terms 'real,' 'robust,' or 'genuine' as applied to 'fact' and 'property.' This move allows Price's account to avoid representing itself as a *rival* of various forms of non-cognitivism – even those that operate with a commitment, explicit or otherwise, to 'genuine' assertoric discourse. Rather, it can represent itself simply as a more general theory that gives some sense to the distinction between genuine assertion and something else. Of course the notion of 'the genuine' here will disappoint non-cognitivists of a certain temperament. But disappointment need not amount to disagreement. Moreover, given a large class of no-fault disagreements in the application of terms such as 'robust,' it may well be that robustness itself is a non-robust property, much like, perhaps, funniness. This may initially sound paradoxical, but in fact it involves nothing objectionable. This strategy also helps combat the worry that, on the

Wittgensteinian view, any term that functions grammatically as a predicate will count as a property-word. For, even without a set of necessary and sufficient conditions, it may not be very difficult to show that the rules of use of some predicates (say, 'true' and 'false,' if the disquotationalist is correct) differ so wildly from the rules of use of paradigmatic property-words as to make it unmysterious that we spontaneously and correctly regard them as failing to correspond to any real, robust, or genuine property.

4. Wittgensteinian metaethics

The view I have so far tried to make clear combines the global expressivism of Price with the global response-dependence of Pettit. I have been referring to it as a Wittgensteinian view, but in order to acknowledge my debt to Price and Pettit we might also call it 'Global Expressivist Response-Dependence,' or GERD for short. One problem with this label is that the term 'expressivism' in Price's phrase 'global expressivism' may misleadingly suggest a view on which all our assertions express motivational or conative attitudes, as metaethical versions of expressivism typically do. Worse, it may suggest a view on which our assertions do *not* express beliefs. But that is no part of the view. Indeed, one of the virtues of Price's view, as I see it, is that it allows (some) evaluative assertions to express beliefs in as robust a sense as mathematical assertions or assertions about the shapes of objects. But, as long as one keeps these points in mind, the label should not confuse anyone.

In order to combine Price and Pettit into a unified view, Pettit's view needs to be understood as avoiding, initially, any reliance on theoretically significant interpretations of semantic notions. Given the heavy use he makes of such notions, this may seem to involve a radical rereading (but, interestingly, little if any rewriting) of Pettit, and perhaps it does go against his intentions.[31] But it also seems perfectly possible. Price's view is not in need of modification as much as supplementation. In particular, Price should acknowledge that there is some point to a distinction between genuine fact-stating assertions and other kinds of assertions. Of course, this distinction is not metaphysically freighted: rather, it can be underwritten by a response-dependent account of the notion of the genuine, or of the robustly factual. This distinction may go beyond a mere matter of degree, even if it is underwritten by little more than differences in degree. As Price remarks elsewhere, there seems to be a real difference between the behavior of 'red' and of 'bitter' – a difference that may have its origins in the extent of the overlap in response shared by normal human beings, but that is reflected in more than merely quantitative ways.[32] In the case of 'red,' those who fail to have the appropriate response are classified as color-blind, and are convicted of error. But the corresponding notion of taste-blindness does not really seem useful, and there is typically no term for such a sensory defect.

GERD makes it easy to see that when one approaches any philosophical issue there are two kinds of questions that one should ask. The first is: why do we – human beings in general – have the category of discourse in which the issue arises? Why, for example, do we have normative discourse? Or if, as is likely, that is too broad a question, perhaps we can ask why we have specifically moral discourse, or the practice of giving and asking for practical reasons. The second kind of question is: how do we – particular human beings – come to master the discourse? An answer to the first question will give us an account of the origins of the practice as a whole, while the second will give us an account of how someone can be inducted into the ongoing practice. Let us call these two questions 'the question of origins' and 'the question of inheritance,' respectively. Just as a working knowledge of physiology can help even a sculptor with a very good eye for external shapes, answers to the origin and inheritance questions can yield a greater insight into the actual shape of our linguistic practices than can be achieved by the most careful 'external' observation.

I hope it will relieve some skeptical readers to know that one consequence of a plausible answer to the question of origins might well be an equally plausible conviction that the discourse is deeply flawed, and that it centrally involves commitments that ought to be discarded. To repeat my stock example, astrology is like this. It is not really surprising that there are systems like those of astrology, giving people various things that they want: explanations for misfortune, hope for the future, and so on. So we may well be able to explain the origins of astrology. But astrology, unlike many of the domains that make trouble for philosophical naturalists, does seem to make causal claims, and these causal claims compete with (and lose badly to) other causal claims. The fact that astrology makes causal claims means that it is not autonomous in a certain way; we must obey rules that do not belong merely to astrology when we are doing astrology.[33] Wittgensteinian views are sometimes wrongly thought to suggest (and sometimes wrongly do suggest) that we cannot call whole domains of discourse into question: that, if they function for us and serve their purposes, they cannot be taken to be making systematically false claims. But that is no part of GERD. Instead, GERD holds that for some discourses – those of probability, mathematics, and practical reason, for instance – it is quite plausible to hold that they *are* autonomous in the sense of not essentially involving claims that are put in doubt by uncontroversial claims in other domains. In particular, I do not think that probability or mathematics or practical reason need be taken to commit us to any substantive empirical claims. Probably the same can be said of morality as well. But I do not want to make any of these claims *a priori*. Indeed, I want to suggest that at least *some* of those who argue for error theories or eliminativist views in these areas are best understood as having a straightforward disagreement with me about what it is that mathematical or normative talk commits us to. That is another reason why acceptance of the Wittgensteinian picture does not spell the end of philosophy as we know it. The important point to take from GERD is not that every domain is in good working order. Rather, it is that *if* a domain is in good working order, then the fact that it involves talk of properties and entities that cannot be reduced to the physical is no reason to deny that those properties and entities are *as real as* those that can be so reduced. Of course they are not physical properties and entities. But it simply begs the question against GERD to take this admission as equivalent to the admission that they are not real properties and entities.

I believe that I have been operating with something like GERD in the background for many years without explicitly formulating it, and therefore without really understanding it. But I did understand enough of it to see that both the question of origins and the question of inheritance needed to be addressed by any adequate account of any philosophical issue, and to see that once the question of an explanation for our use of a term was satisfactorily answered – and it was shown that such use committed us to no false claims – no metaphysical questions could linger. In this section I want to show how attention to the two questions about linguistic practice, and GERD's way of answering them, can undermine views that fail to take them sufficiently into account, and can lend support to rival views that I have tried to support. It may be worth noting that not all of the commitments of GERD are required to motivate the points in sections 4.1 and 4.2 below. In particular, the criticisms of Michael Smith and Michael Ridge that I am about to present probably go through with the same force even if we take it that there is a metaphysically basic 'real' ontology of the sort I tried to argue against in section 3.1 above. But I take GERD to be independently motivated, so it does not matter to me that my criticisms need not appeal to every aspect of GERD. By taking on the full account, however, one can apply the techniques of the following subsections to many more domains than merely those of rationality, reasons, and moral discourse.

4.1. Rationality and the first-person perspective

In order to see the importance of the question of origins, it will be useful to take a look at the views of Michael Smith on practical reasons. Smith offers us an analysis of the notion of a *pro tanto* normative reason for action. One way of expressing the view is the following:

> An agent has a normative reason to perform a certain action if and only if an ideally rational version of that agent would have some desire that she – the unidealized agent – perform that action.[34]

Since Smith also thinks that it is part of our idea of a normative reason that such reasons are objective in a certain way, he also holds that, if there are to be normative reasons, there must be convergence in the hypothetical desires of idealized agents. That is, if there is a normative reason to perform a certain action in a certain situation, this is because the idealized version of *any* agent would have the relevant desire that her unidealized self perform the action.

Smith understands rationality in terms of coherence of desires and beliefs, and he also takes it that there are automatic rational mechanisms that serve to push our beliefs and desires in the direction of coherence.[35] There are many questions and worries about Smith's view. But, in order to illustrate the virtues of GERD, I want to focus on the following question: why should we human beings have developed a convenient linguistic means for talking about the desires of ideal versions of ourselves for our own, unidealized selves?

One might suggest the following answer to the above question: we have the concept of a practical reason because it is so useful to become clear about such reasons by being able to talk and think about them. After all, if we are clear about them, then we will tend to act rationally. And surely that is a desirable thing. But a problem with this answer is that we are, according to Smith, *already* set up to move towards coherence in our beliefs and desires. Allowing higher-order beliefs about the desires of our idealized selves to enter the mix does not seem a very promising way to augment the functioning of our automatic rational mechanisms. Indeed, they represent a real danger. On the basis of claims by one's friends or other people whose opinion one respects, one could become convinced that one's idealized self would have certain desires without having any conception of *why* she would have them. If we allow these higher-order beliefs to exert motivational force we open ourselves up to manipulation by people we regard – perhaps rightly, perhaps wrongly – as smarter and more insightful than ourselves. Better if rational persuasion had to appeal to genuine substantive reasons – facts of the following sort: that one will be burnt or imprisoned or made unhappy in some other way, or that someone else will suffer some such consequence. And, indeed, these are the considerations that are typically offered in arguments.

In my view, Smith commits an error that one sees in almost every corner of ethics: theorizing about normative notions from the first-person point of view, and trying to explain their functioning without asking why a *group of language users* would end up having a certain form of discourse. This is the ethical version of a standard problem that Wittgenstein identifies most famously when talking about sensation language. From the first-person point of view, it certainly seems possible simply to refer to one's own private sensations. And it is unlikely that someone who takes the simple referential model of sensation language to be correct will ask 'why do we have sensation language?' After all, isn't the point of language to give us the means to name things and talk and think about them? And isn't this as useful to an isolated individual as to an individual considered as a member of a group? Returning to Smith, the first-personal point of view regarding reasons seems plausible because reasons do indeed seem easily accessible to us in deliberation. Moreover, from that perspective they seem intimately connected with motivation. After all, one tends to take into account only those considerations that one antecedently cares about. But, in the case of sensation language, the Wittgensteinian perspective allows us to see that sensation language serves a *social* function, and that, from an exclusively first-personal perspective, such language doesn't seem very useful (indeed, it may not even be possible, but that point is distinct). Similarly, we should be looking for a social explanation for the emergence of the forms of language we use to talk about reasons and rationality.[36]

What are the social origins of the notions of practical rationality and reasons for action? In 'Response-Dependence and Normative Bedrock' I tried to suggest that rationality is a response-dependent notion, and that the response of relevance is a failure of an automatic first-pass interpretive mechanism that presents the behavior of other human beings as intentional.[37] It is easy to see why we might have developed a way of picking out, describing, and discussing such actions. When people's actions fail to make immediate sense, one of two things may be true. First, they may actually not make sense. That is, they may be irrational actions, caused by various mental malfunctions. On the other hand, they may make sense if we understand more about the context in which they are performed. In either case, it is useful to know what is going on. For it is always useful to know why the people with whom one interacts are acting as they are, and it is also useful to know if someone is in fact irrational in some way. This story explains in a very simple way why 'irrational' functions as a dissuasive term: those of us who are rational are, of course, disposed to avoid irrational action. As a result, if we are convinced that some proposed course of action is irrational, it will tend to dissuade us from pursuing it.

On the basis of the above response-dependent account of practical rationality, we can also understand why there would be a notion of a practical reason. At least, this is true on the assumption that there are certain kinds of considerations that make systematic contributions to the rational status of an action. To me this seems extremely plausible; risk of death or injury to the agent, for example, seem to place an action in need of some rational justification (that is, they seem to yield *prima facie* requirements that we avoid certain actions), and the promise of pleasure, or knowledge, or longer life, for example, seem to provide that justification. GERD makes it much easier to see that practical reasons can play these two roles (requiring and justifying), and thus that they are appropriately characterized in terms of two sorts of normative strength. Once one sees this a whole vista opens up – one that I have explored in a number of other papers.[38]

4.2. Ethical expressivism and language-learning

In order to see the importance of the question of inheritance, let us turn our attention to a problem it poses for ethical expressivists. I will be using 'ethical expressivism' here as a name for a local doctrine according to which ethical claims function primarily to express pro- and con-attitudes of various sorts, in contrast to claims that express beliefs. In 'Expressivism and Language Learning' I argued that, even if ethical expressivism provides a good account of some normative terms, it should not be taken to be a monolithic account of all normative terms.[39] Rather, any proposed account of any normative term – indeed, of any term whatsoever – must meet the following condition:

(C) Given the actual way in which human beings learn language, the appropriateness of the proposal must be preserved from one generation of language-speakers to the next.

I then suggested that, when we are evaluating the plausibility of an expressivist account of a particular normative term, the task of determining whether or not the expressivist proposal meets (C) requires us to ask the following question:

(Q) Is the presence of the purportedly essential attitude *in the language-learner* part of the criteria by which the language-learner's own utterances are judged to be acceptable?

Since for some normative terms the answer to (Q) is 'Yes,' while for others it is 'No', my conclusion was that some normative terms should receive expressivist analyses, and others should not. As an example of a normative term that failed to meet condition (C) – because the answer to (Q) was 'No' – I offered 'morally wrong.' My paper was first, therefore, a challenge to moral expressivists to show how their semantics met condition (C), and, second, an effort to show that their prospects for doing so were not good.[40]

Michael Ridge responded to my challenge on behalf of moral expressivists, accepting (C), but calling the importance of (Q) into question.[41] My argument for the importance of (Q) depended on the assumption that children would not be able to pick up an expressivist usage for a normative term merely by observing adults, even if those adults were (consciously or not) using the term in accord with such a usage. Rather, those children would have to be *taught* how to use the terms correctly, and such teaching would have to involve correcting the child when that child's use of the term wasn't accompanied by the appropriate attitude. I put this assumption in terms of the rejection of a neo-Augustinian view of language learning, in favor of a more Wittgensteinian view. Ridge's strategy for meeting my challenge was to question that assumption. He argued that, in the case of 'morally wrong' at least, there is plenty of reason to think that the neo-Augustinian view is close enough to correct to allow (C) to be met even when the answer to (Q) is 'No.'

In his response to my paper, Ridge admitted that it is 'almost certainly true…in the majority of cases' that 'children will…learn to associate a particular descriptive meaning with "morally wrong" on the basis of their parents' correcting them when they call something morally wrong that the parents take not to be morally wrong.'[42] But he held that this descriptive meaning would be secondary, while the expressivist meaning would be primary. For, as children grow up, they note that people whose usage of 'morally wrong' does not match their own, or that of their parents, are not accused of linguistic confusion. But, unless we are to suppose that non-philosophers are in the habit of distinguishing linguistic from substantive error, it will be very hard to draw any conclusions from this piece of data. When two people disagree about some moral matter, the assumption may be that they actually could resolve the problem if they just came to agreement on the non-moral facts and eliminated various distorting influences on their judgment. Moral argument very often consists in a back-and-forth about the consequences and antecedents of a certain action. And, as Pettit's view suggests, this kind of argument is characteristic of normal property-words, and with the idea that in favorable circumstances there would indeed be agreement. If, on the other hand, it becomes clear that there is *complete agreement* on all the relevant facts, and moral disagreement persists, it would not be surprising to hear one or both participants express themselves in the following way: 'if you think that's [not] wrong, I just don't understand what you mean by "wrong".' I do not mean to suggest, with this, that the participants *would certainly* regard each other as linguistically confused. I only mean to point out that the data Ridge appeals to here are not transparent in their implications, and are certainly consistent with the idea that moral wrongness is a univocal property.

If expressivism about moral wrongness is to be plausible, it is necessary that there be some specification of the *particular* non-cognitive attitude that 'morally wrong' and its cognates serve essentially to express. Blanket disapproval will not do, for we disapprove of many things that we would not wish to call 'morally wrong.' Thus, correct usage of 'morally wrong,' according to the expressivist, requires that we call an action 'morally wrong' only in circumstances in which we disapprove of the action *in the relevant way*. In order to bolster the neo-Augustinian view, Ridge explains why there is ample data available to a child regarding the expressivist function of moral language. Such data result from the fact that the frustrating work of raising children means that parents 'are prone to transparent displays of emotion.' Because of this, 'even the most self-controlled parents sometimes become exasperated enough to display not merely stern firmness but anger, disappointment and frustration.'[43] But is the child then to learn that 'morally wrong' serves to express stern firmness, anger, disappointment, or frustration? In fact, it can be none of these, for the attitude that makes it appropriate to call an action 'morally wrong' must be one that is appropriate in all and only circumstances in which it would be appropriate to call an action morally wrong. Since neither stern firmness, nor anger, nor disappointment, nor frustration have this feature, the child will have to note the underlying attitudinal regularity *not only* in the face of the misleading descriptively centered correction by its elders, *but also* in the face of a host of very salient negative attitudes that also obscure the issue. This is why, in anticipating a worry about my reliance on a contentious view of language learning, and when I pointed out that a neo-Augustinian view would be attractive to expressivists, I added that 'it would have to be supplemented by the claim that we have extremely acute perception of extremely subtle attitudes.'[44]

Ridge's head-on response to my argument forced him to link the use of moral vocabulary to attitudes such as anger, frustration and disappointment. As I have just remarked, it does not seem to me that any of these attitudes are capable of sufficient nuance to serve the moral expressivist's purposes. Nor, as I have also just argued, does the existence of moral disagreement seem by itself to provide any very powerful argument that a child's understanding of moral terms could be refined in the way that Ridge's view requires. But let us put all of this aside for the moment. What is much more interesting and important is that Ridge seems to have forgotten all about the question of inheritance as soon as he turned his attention towards constructing his own preferred version of ethical expressivism: a view he calls 'ecumenical expressivism.'

According to ecumenical expressivism, a moral utterance expresses both a belief and a pro-attitude. The pro-attitude expressed is one that the speaker holds towards actions in so far as they would be approved of by a certain sort of advisor – an advisor whose nature varies from speaker to speaker. And the belief expressed is that the action one is judging to be morally wrong would be approved of by that kind of advisor. The reference to the advisor is achieved by an anaphoric mechanism; that is, we can usefully think of the belief as including an actual indexical such as 'that' in the phrase 'that kind of advisor.' As a result we need not assume that the speaker even has a very detailed conception of the advisor. This view requires us to have a conceptual item available to play the role of the initiator of an anaphoric chain. This means, at a minimum, that there must be an element of the speaker's psychology that refers to a kind of advisor. Now, it may be that part of our conceptual endowment as human beings is a psychological architecture that includes such an item. But as an empirical hypothesis the claim that there is such an item is wildly speculative. Moreover, Ridge has given us no plausible (or implausible) mechanism by which initial instruction in moral discourse, coupled with subsequent exposure to people with other moral outlooks, could train speakers in such a way that his ecumenical expressivist semantics would accurately capture the application conditions for their moral vocabulary. What Ridge has done is precisely what I claimed too many philosophers do: he has constructed a semantics for moral discourse that very cleverly explains a number of features of that discourse, but that is thought of only in terms of a timeless community of speakers who pop into the world already having mastered the use of the relevant vocabulary. No attention at all has been paid to the problem of explaining how it is that, given the mechanisms of language transmission, these semantics could also plausibly characterize the moral discourse of the next generation of language speakers. I am not saying that Ridge could not come up with such an explanation; the question is largely empirical. But I am saying that no attention has been paid to this important issue, and that the problem it presents is formidable. One avenue for Ridge to explore might first point to religious discourse, in which moral injunctions are transparently connected with approval by God, and might then try to interpret secular morality as somehow inheriting and obscuring this appeal to a moral authority. Another avenue might exploit data about actual moral development, and our initial understanding of rules as backed by the force of our elders. But I am not optimistic on Ridge's behalf, since GERD suggests an alternate picture of moral discourse quite generally: one in which the expression of conative attitudes is not essential to sincere moral utterances.

GERD urges us to think of the origins of moral discourse in terms of the social functions it performs – allowing certain kinds of sanctions, perhaps, that help to inculcate certain behavioral tendencies in each new generation: tendencies that help to coordinate behavior and solve prisoners' dilemmas. Surely *something* like this is extremely plausible. If this general picture is correct, then there will be certain kinds of considerations that it makes sense to urge in arguments about what is morally correct. Individual speakers will learn both the general extension of moral terms, and also the kinds of considerations that can be brought to bear in justifying moral claims. An important consequence of this explanation is that it does not imply anything at all about what an *individual* need be doing with a moral assertion. It will not matter if a certain proportion of people fail to have their motivations engaged by moral norms. These people will still be able to learn all there is to learn about the use – and therefore the meaning – of moral vocabulary. There is a tendency for philosophers – especially ethical expressivists – to think that such people will only be using moral terms in an 'inverted comma' sense. But what pressure is there to say this, once the social function of moral discourse is acknowledged? Surely we have words such as 'food,' 'poison,' and so on, partly because of the importance to human beings of eating food and avoiding poison. But there is no reason at all to suppose that someone who wants to starve to death, or who wants to poison herself, is using these words in any but their standard senses.

5. Conclusion

GERD is, of course, more of a program for the construction of various theories than a theory itself. One part of that program consists of clearing the ground where the new theory will be built. In the case of theories of rationality, GERD provides some useful machinery for clearing that ground. In particular, it provides reasons to doubt any theory that takes a primarily first-personal perspective on practical reasons, and ignores or downplays the use of our talk of rationality and reasons from a third-person perspective. Given that language is essentially social, the third-person perspective should really be the default perspective from which any initial attempts at a theory – of anything – begin. Most versions of internalism about reasons do not recognize this. Similarly, GERD provides reasons to doubt the adequacy of any theory that posits a semantics that it would be hard to teach to people. Virtually all expressivist accounts of moral language need to include more or less ingenious complications in order to account for the surface grammar of moral claims. But these very complications make them an easy target for GERD-inspired criticism.[45]

Notes

1. Timothy Williamson (forthcoming) takes this view of naturalism, claiming that 'naturalists hold that everything is part of the natural world, and should be studied as such.' I agree with Daniel Callcut that naturalists really ought to include claims such as 'There is a table in the living room' as unproblematic. I am less sure whether this requires changing the formulation of naturalism, or understanding science in a sufficiently broad way.
2. See Dummett (1978, p. 458) for this characterization of Frege.
3. I am thinking of Wittgenstein (1922) and Russell (1986).
4. Price (1988, chapter 8; 1992; 1997). Of course Price also focuses on some particular words: 'true,' 'assertion,' and 'belief,' for example. But part of the reason for this focus is to reconcile their uniform use with his pluralism about discourses. Earlier defenders of related views include Carnap and Quine, and the later Wittgenstein.
5. Pettit (2002), essays 1–5. Pettit's view has some connection with that of Johnston (1989), McDowell (1985) and Wiggins (1998) and the later Wittgenstein.
6. Wiggins (1980).
7. Quine (1970).
8. Brandom (1984).
9. See Price (1988; 1992; 1997; 2003). See also Wright (1993), pp. 66–7.
10. In fact, much signaling can be understood in terms of opponency: a signal that is not merely an on/off condition, but is a positive/negative condition that can be greater or lesser in degree. This makes cases in which there could be a confusion between no signal and a significant but neutral signal extremely rare.
11. O'Leary-Hawthorne & Price (1996, pp. 291–2). See also Price (2009), pp. 122–3.
12. Korsgaard (1996).
13. Byrne & Hilbert (2003), p. 4.
14. One reason it seems to be a mistake is that it makes the naïve assumption that we can think, talk and write about 'properties that objects visually appear to

have' without making use of concepts that we have learned as we learned the language.

15. Pettit (1999), pp. 22–3.
16. Pettit (1999), p. 29.
17. Pettit (1998), p. 113.
18. Pettit (1991, p. 593) makes it clear that he is understanding truth disquotationally, and gives a structural description of assertion. His later use of semantic vocabulary – say, in Pettit (1999) – might be forced into this same mold, or might be seen as backsliding.
19. I am not sure, but this objection may be at the root of Simon Blackburn's (2009) remarks on Price.
20. Price (1997), p. 259.
21. Compare Wittgenstein (1953, §124); Kripke (1982, p. 146).
22. These passages (my italics) are from Pettit (1999), pp. 31, 31, 34 and 39, respectively.
23. Pettit (1999), p. 29.
24. Pettit (1999), p. 32.
25. Pettit (1999), pp. 41–2.
26. In fact, Pettit (1990, p. 16) makes remarks that are much more congenial to the present suggestion, when he is pointing out that he has not offered a reductive account of rule-following.
27. Pettit (1991), 618–19.
28. Price (1988), p. 161.
29. Compare Gert (2007b).
30. See Dreier (2004), p. 29.
31. See Wright (1993), p. 69.
32. Price (1988), p. 196.
33. Compare Shafer-Landau (2007), pp. 322–3.
34. Smith's most extensive presentation of this view can be found in Smith (1994a). But he still adheres to it in its essentials. See, for example, Smith (2007).
35. It may be worth noting that coherence does not obviously push towards convergence; coherence may be a formal matter, for which different 'input' beliefs and desires yield different 'output' beliefs and desires. Smith does not try to argue that this might not be true – only that, if it is true, then there will sometimes be no fact of the matter as to what reasons an agent has.
36. A dim awareness of this point may be behind a move away from what might be called 'individual internalism' to what might be called 'community internalism.' See Dreier (1990), pp. 10–11. But, once one sees the practice-based reason for the move to the level of community, then even the claim that most people must be motivated by their beliefs about reasons should seem too simple. Why couldn't normative language have arisen even without this empirical fact being true? Couldn't normative language perform an important function without relying on a background in which most people, or even most 'normal' people, are motivated by their beliefs about reasons and rationality, let alone morality?
37. Gert (2009).
38. Most of these are collected in Gert (2004). But see also Gert (2007a) and, for an argument that Smith himself should accept my account, see Gert (2008).
39. Gert (2002).
40. For the purposes of this paper, 'moral expressivism' can be taken to mean 'ethical expressivism about terms that are more-or-less synonymous with "morally wrong".'
41. Ridge (2004).

42. Ridge (2004), p. 309. Here the Wittgensteinian should understand 'descriptive meaning' as something like 'meaning characterized by the marks Pettit picks out as characterizing property-words.'
43. Ridge (2004), pp. 307–8.
44. Gert (2002), p. 307.
45. Thanks to Bernard Gert, Heather Gert, Cei Maslen, Huw Price, participants in the Evolution, Emotion and Metaethics Workshop in Sydney, audiences at Otago, Wellington, and Auckland, and especially to Daniel Callcut for comments on an earlier version of this paper.

3
In Defense of Moral Error Theory

Jonas Olson

1. Introduction

My aim in this essay is largely defensive. I aim to discuss some problems for moral error theory and to offer plausible solutions. A full positive defense of moral error theory would require substantial investigations of rival meta-ethical views, but that is beyond the scope of this essay. I will, however, try to motivate moral error theory and to clarify its commitments.

Moral error theorists typically accept two claims – one conceptual and one ontological – about moral facts. The *conceptual claim* is that moral facts are or entail facts about categorical reasons (and correspondingly that moral claims are or entail claims about categorical reasons); the *ontological* claim is that there are no categorical reasons – and consequently no moral facts – in reality. I accept this version of moral error theory and I try to unpack what it amounts to in Section 2.[1] In the course of doing so I consider two preliminary objections: that moral error theory is (probably) false because its implications are intuitively unacceptable (what I call the Moorean objection) and that the general motivation for moral error theory is self-undermining in that it rests on a hidden appeal to norms.

The above characterization seems to entail the standard formulation of moral error theory, according to which first-order moral claims are uniformly false. Critics have argued that the standard formulation is incoherent since – by the law of excluded middle – the negation of a false claim is true. Hence if 'Torture is wrong' is false, 'Torture is not wrong' is true. Contrary to what moral error theorists contend, then, moral error theory seems to carry first-order moral implications that by the theory's own lights are uniformly false. In Section 3 I suggest a formulation that is consistent with the standard formulation of moral error theory, free of first-order moral implications, and subject to no logical difficulties.

In Section 4 I consider and rebut Stephen Finlay's recent attack on moral error theory. According to Finlay the conceptual claim is false because all moral claims – and indeed all normative claims – are, or should be understood as, relativized to some moral standard or system of ends. Moral error theorists thus attribute to ordinary speakers an error that simply isn't there. I argue that Finlay's view has some very implausible implications and that it does not avoid commitment to various forms of error theory. This becomes especially clear when we focus on fundamental moral claims.

In Section 5 I consider the worry that error theorists' rejection of categorical reasons proves too much; in particular, the worry that error theorists' qualms about categorical reasons apply equally to claims about *hypothetical reasons*, that is, claims to the effect that there is reason to take the means to one's ends. In my view error theorists such as Mackie and Joyce have failed to pay due consideration to this problem. What the challenge establishes, I submit, is that error theorists cannot just take for granted that hypothetical reasons are metaphysically unproblematic; they must offer an account of hypothetical reasons that shows that they are. I argue that the only plausible account available to error theorists is one according to which claims about hypothetical reasons reduce to non-normative claims about relations between means and ends.

2. Motivating moral error theory

Ever since John Mackie's seminal discussion, standard arguments for moral error theory are routinely lumped together under the label 'arguments from queerness' (Mackie, 1977: ch. 1). In my view some of these arguments have considerably more force than others. The most acute of Mackie's queerness worries about moral facts is not that moral facts – that is, facts to the effect that some agent morally ought to do or not to do some action; that there are moral reasons for some agent to do or not to do some action; that some action is morally permissible; that some institution, character trait, or what have you, is morally good or bad; and the like – would be intrinsically motivating in the sense of exerting a motivational pull on anyone who takes herself to be aware of them. This worry presupposes a version of *motivational internalism*.[2] But, as many critics have pointed out, motivational internalism is after all a highly controversial view (e.g. Brink, 1984; Dworkin, 1996). In other words, it is far from clear that it is part of ordinary speakers' conceptions of moral facts that they exert a motivational pull on anyone who takes oneself to be aware of them.[3]

Richard Garner and other commentators have noted that the most acute of Mackie's queerness worries is, rather, that moral facts would have to be, as Mackie said, *objectively prescriptive*. What makes moral facts queer is that they make demands from which we cannot escape (Finlay, 2008; Garner, 1990; Joyce, 2001; Robertson, 2008).[4]

Ronald Dworkin has complained that Mackie's talk about the objective prescriptivity or 'inbuilt to-be-pursuedness' of moral facts is overly metaphorical (1996: 114). I agree that Mackie's discussion is sometimes opaque, and I will therefore try to unpack what it is that Mackie and other moral error theorists object to.[5]

As Mackie and other error theorists have noted, there is a sense in which we are all familiar with objective prescriptivity as instantiated in the real world.[6] For instance, it is a familiar fact that chess players ought not to move the rook diagonally and that there are reasons for soccer players not to play the ball to their own goalkeeper when under pressure. But these are not examples of the kind of objective prescriptivity Mackie objected to. Mackie did not deny that there are rules and standards according to which certain agents in certain situations ought or have reason to behave in certain ways (Mackie, 1977, pp. 25–7).

The kind of objective prescriptivity Mackie did object to is one that involves *categorical* reasons. To say that there are categorical reasons for some agent, A, to behave in some way, Φ, is to say that there is reason for A to Φ irrespective of whether A's Φing would promote satisfaction or realization of some of A's desires or aims, or promote fulfillment of some role A occupies, or comply with the rules of some activity A is engaged in. Suppose, for instance, that torturing animals for fun is morally wrong and that donating 20 per cent of one's income to charity is morally required. It seems commonsensical that there would then be reasons for any agent not to torture animals for fun and to donate 20 per cent of her income to charity, even if doing so would not satisfy or realize one of her desires or aims, or promote fulfillment of some role she occupies, or comply with the rules of some activity she is engaged in. In other words, moral facts entail facts about categorical reasons and moral claims entail claims about categorical reasons.

Elsewhere I have distinguished between *transcendent* and *immanent norms* (Olson, forthcoming). The former apply to agents categorically; their reason-giving force transcends particular aims, activities, or roles. Immanent norms, by contrast, are those whose reason-giving force depends on agents' engagement in certain goal-oriented or rule-governed activities or their occupation of certain roles, such as institutional or professional roles; the reason-giving force of immanent norms does not transcend goal-oriented or rule-governed activities or roles, which is why immanent norms imply merely *non-categorical* reasons.[7] Another way of putting it is to say that, while immanent norms determine correct behavior according to rules or fixed standards, it does not follow that there are *categorical reasons* to comply with these norms. For transcendent norms, it does follow that there are categorical reasons for compliance.

As mentioned above, it is a plausible conjecture that on the commonsense conception of moral norms these are examples of transcendent norms, whereas the norms of, for instance, chess, soccer, grammar, and etiquette are prime examples of immanent norms. To say that a norm is a moral norm is to say that there are reasons for any agent to comply with that norm, irrespective of her desires, ends, or roles.[8] To say that some norm is a norm of etiquette or grammar, by contrast, is not to say that there are categorical reasons to comply with it, but rather to say that some sort of behavior would be incorrect relative to a certain standard of etiquette or relative to the rules of grammar.[9] In my terminology, *norms* are transcendent or immanent and *reasons* are categorical or non-categorical.

Error theorists do not object to the existence of immanent norms and non-categorical reasons. There is nothing metaphysically queer about the fact that there is (conclusive) non-categorical reason for chess players not to move the rook diagonally, since this is just the fact that moving the rook diagonally is incorrect according to the rules of chess; there is nothing metaphysically queer about the fact that there is (non-conclusive) reason for soccer players not to play the ball to their own goalkeeper when under pressure, since this is just the fact that such play tends to give the opposing team opportunities to score (and preventing the opposing team from scoring is one of the goals in soccer). Similarly, there is nothing metaphysically queer about the fact that there is non-categorical reason for a soldier to comply with the orders of a general, since this is just the fact that complying with the orders of those superior in military rank is part of the role of being a soldier. Note that a soldier might not *desire* to comply with the general's order, and he might have no ends that would be served by his compliance. The same goes for chess players and soccer players; they might not desire to play by the rules and they need not even desire to win. That is why I add that error theorists can recognize non-categorical reasons that depend on agents' *roles* and goal-oriented or rule-governed *activities*. Agents can occupy roles they have no desire to fulfill and engage in activities they have no desire to succeed in.

Moral norms and moral reasons, as we have seen, are a different a matter. The reason-giving force of moral norms transcends agents' desires, aims, and roles. One way of unpacking the popular view that moral facts are *non-natural* is in terms of categorical reasons. On this interpretation, what non-naturalist realists mean to capture in claiming that moral facts are non-natural is precisely that these facts are or entail categorical reasons.[10] By contrast, facts about, for example, etiquette and rules of grammar are natural since they do not entail categorical reasons.

Following others (e.g. Miller, 2003; Smith, 1994a), we can call the claim that moral facts are or entail categorical reasons (and correspondingly that moral claims are or entail claims about categorical reasons) *the conceptual claim*. Moral error theorists accept the conceptual claim, but they also accept *the ontological claim* that there are no such reasons in reality. Some naturalist realists aim to demystify moral facts by denying the conceptual claim (e.g. Brink, 1984). I shall consider and reject one such recent attempt in Section 4 below.

Other realist critics of moral error theory accept the conceptual claim but deny the error theorist's ontological claim.[11] The problem for these realists is precisely to explain how there can be facts that *in themselves*, that is, irre-spectively of the desires, aims, roles, or activities of human beings and other agents, require, or *count in favor of,* certain forms of behavior.[12] A popular realist rejoinder is to adopt a 'partners in guilt (or innocence)' strategy and claim that moral facts are not metaphysically queerer than, for example, mathematical and logical facts, or facts about set theory (cf. Scanlon, 1998: 62–4).[13] The latter kinds of facts about abstracta may be metaphysically problematic in a number of ways, but they do not display the feature that moral error theorists find especially queer about purported moral facts – they do not entail categorical reasons.

Someone might object that, for example, logical facts do entail categori-cal reasons for belief. An example might be that the fact that *p* and *if p then q* entail *q* entails that, if one believes *p* and *if p then q*, there is reason to believe *q* or give up at least one of the prior beliefs. The error theorist's response is that the reason here is non-categorical, since the claim that, if one believes *p* and *if p then q*, there is reason to believe *q*, or give up at least one of the prior beliefs, simply amounts to the claim that, according to the *modus ponens* rule, if one believes *p* and *if p then q*, it is correct to believe *q*, or give up at least one of the prior beliefs (cf. Olson, forthcoming). The *modus ponens* rule is an example of a rule that tells agents what there is reason to do *qua* (occupying the roles of) reasoners, or *qua* engaging in the activity of reasoning. But such rules do not give categorical reasons to comply with them. By contrast, when we make moral claims we do not merely mean to state or express correct moral rules for behavior; we mean to say that there are categorical reasons to comply with these rules.

2.1. Two initial objections: the Moorean argument and the hidden appeal to norms

At this point one might object that metaphysical doubts about transcend-ent norms and categorical reasons are based on pretty advanced, or at least controversial, philosophical theorizing. And are we not comparatively more certain that some actions – for example, torturing animals or children for fun – really are morally wrong than we are that reality harbors no categori-cal reasons and consequently no moral truths? Since it marshals common-sense against philosophical theorizing, let us call this argument *the Moorean argument* against moral error theory.[14]

But metaphysical qualms about categorical reasons are not the sole cor-nerstone of the case for moral error theory. Moral error theorists often give debunking explanations of why we humans tend to believe that there are moral facts (Joyce, 2001; 2006; Mackie, 1977, pp. 105–24). One important ingredient in these debunking explanations is the evolutionary advantages of moral beliefs. For instance, moral norms against stealing, harming, cheat-ing, and so on tend to promote senses of trust and security, which facilitate cooperation, which in turn raise prospects of survival. As Mackie said, in human evolutionary history morality serves as a 'device for counteracting limited sympathies' (1977, p. 107).[15]

Belief in transcendent norms and correlative categorical reasons is useful in other respects too: it puts pressure on individual agents and makes them less likely to succumb to temptations to maximize expected short-term egoistic or parochial benefits. In short, morality persists in the world of human thinking partly because of its socially useful coordinating and regulative functions.

In addition, there are plausible hypotheses, which are congenial to moral error theory, as to how and why belief in moral facts originates in the individual human mind. Shaun Nichols (2004) argues that belief in moral norms originates partly because of the linkage to affect. Witnessing suffering in others tends to give rise to intense distress in most human beings, and this is at least part of the explanation for why most people are strongly motivated to enforce and comply with norms against harming innocents, such as animals and children. Reactive distress causally explains beliefs to the effect that violations of norms against harming are generalizably wrong (Nichols, 2004, p. 180). This clearly echoes Hume's famous dictum that moral judgement stems from a 'productive faculty, [that] gilding or staining all natural objects with the colours, borrowed from internal sentiment, raises, in a manner, a new creation' (1998, p. 163).

These are rough sketches of attempts at debunking explanations of moral beliefs. Other writers have offered highly impressive and detailed elaborations, and I won't delve deeper into the matter here (see, e.g., Joyce, 2006; Nichols, 2004). Suffice it to say that these elaborations have enough plausibility to undermine the Moorean argument. For, once we take these debunking explanations into consideration, it is far from clear that we are more certain that some actions – such as torturing animals or children for fun – really are morally wrong than we are that there are no categorical reasons and consequently no moral truths (Joyce, 2010; Mackie, 1977, p. 42). Proponents of the Moorean argument might protest that we *are* comparatively more certain that certain actions really are morally wrong than we are about the correctness of debunking explanations of these beliefs. But proponents of debunking theories à la Mackie, Joyce, and Nichols have the upper hand here, since these theories predict that certain moral beliefs will be held with a high degree of certainty, and also explain why this is so. The explanation is simply that the regulative and coordinating functions they facilitate are of such vital importance to us.

It is fairly obvious that the argument against categorical reasons that proceeds via Mackie's queerness worry and debunking explanations of moral beliefs is based on an appeal to Occam's Razor. The gist of the argument, after all, is that error theory offers a *theoretically simpler* and hence *preferable* explanation of the phenomena to be explained (i.e. moral thought and talk) than do competing realist explanations.[16] But appeals to Occam's Razor and considerations of theoretical simplicity seem to be appeals to *norms*. And consequently the moral error theorist's argument against the existence of some norms, such as moral norms, seems to involve a hidden appeal to other norms, which makes it smack of self-defeat (cf. Sayre-McCord, 1988, p. 277f.).

In response, the moral error theorist should concede that appeals to Occam's Razor and considerations of theoretical simplicity are indeed appeals to norms. But these are immanent rather than transcendent norms. To say that a theory T offers a theoretically simpler explanation of some phenomenon than a distinct theory T' is not to say that the comparative simplicity of T is a *categorical* reason to prefer T to T'. It is just to say that T is in one respect preferable to T' according to a standard of theory assessment commonly accepted by many philosophers, naturalists and non-naturalists alike, and commonly adopted in many natural and social sciences, to wit, that T is preferable to T' if T makes fewer problematic assumptions without loss of explanatory power. This is the case with moral error theory as compared with realism. The greater theoretical simplicity of the former as compared with the latter is therefore a non-categorical reason to prefer moral error theory to realism. Appeals to norms such as Occam's Razor are hence unproblematic from the moral error theorist's naturalist perspective.

I hope that what has been said so far makes moral error theory seem, if not a promising theory, then at least not a dead end in metaethics. That much suffices as a rationale for my defensive project in the remainder of the essay. I shall consider three challenges to moral error theory, starting with the most basic one, according to which the standard formulation of moral error theory is incoherent.

3. Formulating moral error theory

It is routinely said that, according to moral error theory, first-order moral claims are uniformly false. A first-order moral claim is a claim that entails that some agent morally ought to do or not to do some action; that there are moral reasons for some agent to do or not to do some action; that some action is morally permissible; that some institution, character trait, or what have you, is morally good or bad; and the like. But this raises the question of what to say about the truth-values of negated first-order moral claims, which leads to two worries: Is the standard formulation of moral error theory coherent?[17] Can it be maintained that moral error theory lacks first-order moral implications?

Mackie insisted that his error theory is purely a second-order view and as such logically independent of any first-order moral view (1977, pp. 15–17). But this can be doubted. According to the standard interpretation of Mackie's error theory, a first-order moral claim like 'Torture is morally wrong' is false. According to the law of excluded middle it follows that its negation, 'Torture is not morally wrong', is true. That torture is not morally wrong would seem to imply that torture is morally permissible. More generally, then, the apparent upshot is that, contrary to Mackie's contention, moral error theory does have first-order moral implications. And rather vulgar ones at that; if moral error theory is true, any action turns out to be morally permissible!

But it seems that we can also derive an opposite conclusion. According to moral error theory, 'Torture is morally permissible' is false. According to the law of excluded middle it follows that torture is not morally permissible, which seems to entail that torture is morally impermissible. More generally, then, the apparent upshot is that any action is morally impermissible! This may not be a vulgar first-order moral implication, but it is surely absurd. It also transpires that the standard formulation of moral error theory leads to a straightforward logical contradiction, since we have derived that it is true that, for instance, torture is morally permissible (since any action is morally permissible) and that it is false that torture is morally permissible (since any action is morally impermissible). Ronald Dworkin has argued that this demonstrates the impossibility, indeed the incoherence, of being 'sceptical about value [...] all the way down' (1996, p. 91).

Walter Sinnott-Armstrong has suggested the following way out of the predicament: the scope of moral error theory is to be restricted, to the effect that only *positive* first-order moral claims are deemed uniformly false (2006, pp. 34–6). A positive first-order moral claim is defined as a claim that entails something about what some agent morally ought to do or not to do, what there are moral reasons for some agent to do or not to do, and so on and so forth; or what would be morally good or bad, or morally desirable or undesirable, and so on. It says nothing about mere permissibility.

Restricting moral error theory to positive first-order moral claims only rids moral error theory from incoherence and from the absurd implication that anything is morally impermissible. But one may object that it remains the case that a negative first-order moral claim such as 'Torture is not morally wrong' entails 'Torture is morally permissible,' since it seems to be a platitude that any action that is not morally wrong is morally permissible. In other words, moral error theory would still imply vulgar first-order moral nihilism, according to which anything is morally permissible. But Mackie's contention that his error theory is purely a second-order view and as such logically independent of any first-order moral view must be taken to include the first-order moral view that anything is morally permissible. In other words, Mackie's moral error theory holds that no first-order moral claims are true, and claims about moral permissibility are no exception.[18]

A better way out is to deny that the implications from 'not wrong' to 'permissible' and from 'not permissible' to 'wrong' are conceptual, and maintain instead that they are instances of conversational implicature. To illustrate, 'not wrong' conversationally implicates 'permissible,' because normally when we claim that something is not wrong we speak from within a system of moral norms, or moral standards for short. According to most moral standards, any action that is not wrong according to that standard is permissible according to that standard.[19] General compliance with Gricean maxims that bid us to make our statements relevant and not overly informative (Grice, 1989, p. 26ff.) ensures that we do not normally state explicitly that we speak from within some moral standard when we claim that something is not wrong. But the implicature from 'not wrong' to 'permissible' is cancellable. The error theorist can declare that torture is not wrong and go on to signal that she is not speaking from within a moral standard. She might say something like the following: 'Torture is not wrong. But neither is it permissible. There are no moral properties and facts and consequently no action has moral status.' This would cancel the implicature from 'not wrong' to 'permissible.' (Analogous reasoning, of course, demonstrates why the error theorist's claim that torture is not morally permissible does not commit him to the view that torture is morally impermissible and hence morally wrong.) On this view, error theory has neither the vulgar implication that anything is permissible nor the absurd implication that anything is impermissible.

But one might object that the problems remain. The law of excluded middle entails that if 'Torture is wrong' is false, then 'Torture is not wrong' is true. If the latter claim is a first-order moral claim, the standard formulation of moral error theory still has first-order moral implications, that is, implications that by its own lights are false.

In response, recall that, according to our above definition, first-order moral claims are claims that entail that some agent morally ought to do or not to do some action; that some action is morally permissible; that some institution, character trait, or what have you, is morally good or bad; and so on. Now, according to the view on offer, a negated claim like 'Torture is not wrong' does not *entail* that torture is permissible; it merely conversationally implicates that it is, since the implicature from 'not wrong' to 'permissible' is cancellable. Likewise, 'Torture is not morally permissible' does not entail that torture is impermissible and hence wrong; it merely conversationally implicates that torture is impermissible and hence wrong. Thus negated atomic claims involving moral terms are not strictly speaking first-order moral claims, but some such claims conversationally implicate first-order moral claims.[20] Since claims like 'Torture is not wrong' are true, we cannot derive that their negations (such as 'Torture is wrong') are true. This saves the standard formulation of moral error theory from the threat of incoherence and from implausible first-order moral implications. I shall continue to say, then, that according to moral error theory first-order moral claims are uniformly false.[21]

Having defended moral error theory against the most basic challenge, I turn in the next section to the challenge that the theory is ill motivated, since the error it claims to identify in ordinary moral discourse is a chimera.

4. Defending the conceptual claim: the error in 'The error in the error theory'[22]

Although many philosophers accept the conceptual claim, it hasn't gone unchallenged.[23] In his recent article 'The Error in the Error Theory' (2008), Stephen Finlay argues that moral claims – and indeed all normative claims – are, or should be understood as, relativized to some (contextually implicit) end or system of ends.[24] According to this view, for a fact, F, to be a reason to Φ, relative to an end, E, is for F to explain why Φing would be conducive to E (2006, p. 8). Whether some fact is a reason is thus independent of agents' aims, desires, and roles. It appears, then, that Finlay's view does not rule out the notion of categorical reasons as characterized in Section 2 above. But Finlay adds that whether a reason *matters* to an agent does depend on the agent's attitudes, in particular her cares or concerns (2006, p. 17). There might be moral reasons for an agent to donate 20 per cent of her income to charity irrespective of her attitudes, but these reasons will matter to her just in case her donating 20 per cent of her income to charity would conduce to satisfaction of her cares and concerns.

I want to resist the distinction between a fact being a categorical reason and that fact mattering normatively.[25] I believe it is of the essence of a categorical reason to matter normatively (i.e. to count in favor of, to demand), irrespective of agents' attitudes. If F is a categorical reason for some agent, A, to Φ, then F matters normatively to A irrespective of whether A has the relevant cares or concerns, because even if she does not have them she *ought* to have them. So let me add explicitly to the characterization in Section 2 that to say that F is a categorical reason is to say that F matters normatively, irrespective of agents' desires, aims, or roles. With this addition in place, it is clear that Finlay rejects the notion of categorical reasons. As Finlay sometimes puts it, moral claims lack 'absolute authority' (2008, p. 351f.). According to Finlay, then, the error in the error theory is that it attributes to ordinary moral discourse an error that simply isn't there; ordinary moral claims are not and do not entail claims about categorical reasons, so the error theorists' conceptual claim is false.

I shall argue that the view that all moral claims are relativized to some end has some very implausible implications and that it does not avoid commitment to various forms of error theory. This becomes especially clear when we focus on fundamental moral claims.

4.1. On the disputation evidence for the conceptual claim

Finlay seeks to undermine various sources of evidence for the conceptual claim (2008, pp. 352–60). I shall comment on one such source, since this ties in with my arguments against Finlay's relativistic view to be offered in Section 4.2. We tend to pursue moral arguments even with people whom we take not to share our fundamental moral views, and we do so with the objective of convincing them that we are right and they are wrong. This suggests that we do take moral judgements to be absolutist rather than relativistic. Following Finlay (2008, p. 355), we can call this 'disputation evidence' for the conceptual claim.

Finlay makes two points in response. First, he claims, 'most moral discourse takes place between people who share their fundamental moral values, and assume that they share these values' (p. 356). Second, Finlay claims that, to the extent that disputation between speakers who do not share fundamental moral values does occur, withholding relativizations of moral judgements is to be seen as a pragmatic device to win the opponent over. Withholding the moral standards or system of ends to which one's moral judgements are relativized 'is a rhetorical way of expressing the *expectation* (demand) that the audience subscribes to the speaker's ends or standards' (p. 357, Finlay's italics).[26]

Finlay's first point underestimates the prevalence of fundamental moral disagreement in many current societies. Even a cursory glance at public political debate in many countries will reveal fundamental moral disagreements between conservatives and feminists; socialists and neoliberals; cosmopolitans and nationalists; and so on. Moreover, fundamental moral disagreement between, for example, 'ethical vegetarians' (who believe that animal suffering is on a par morally with human suffering) and speciesists (who believe that humans are especially valuable *qua* being humans), and between 'pro-choice' and 'pro-life' activists regarding abortion, are not uncommon in everyday conversations.[27] In fact, we need not step outside the confines of academic moral philosophy to find many cases of fundamental moral disagreement between utilitarians and deontologists; Rawlsians and Nozickians; anarchists and communitarians; and so on. Finlay asks us to 'survey the moral judgements made on television or radio talk shows and news broadcasts, and try to recall the last time [we] engaged in moral discourse with someone like Charles Manson or a neo-Nazi' (2008, p. 356). But why assume that the person with whom you have a fundamental moral disagreement is such a depraved character? She might, rather, be a utilitarian, a Nozickian, a liberal, a conservative, a socialist, a nationalist, an ethical vegetarian, or a 'pro-life' activist.[28]

Finlay's second point backfires. The idea that moral judgements are partly rhetorical devices used to put pressure on people to behave in certain ways is congenial to both moral error theory and Finlay's relativist theory, but it fits better with the former. First, it fits well with the already mentioned hypothesis that part of the reason why moral thought and talk evolved is that their coordinating and regulative functions are highly useful from an evolutionary perspective (recall Mackie's view of morality as 'a device for counteracting limited sympathies'). It is a plausible conjecture that moral discourse fulfills these functions better if moral claims entail claims about categorical reasons than if they are reduced to claims about what would conduce to some end (cf. Joyce, 2006; Olson, 2010).[29]

Second, the most straightforward explanation of why moral claims have the kind of rhetorical force that demand certain behavior is that the conceptual claim is true: moral claims have rhetorical force *because* they are or entail claims about categorical reasons. Compare the following two claims:

(1) 'It is bad manners to eat peas with a spoon.'
(2) 'It is morally wrong to cheat on your tax declaration.'

In both (1) and (2) the standard or end to which the claims are supposedly relativized are withheld. But (1) and (2) differ in that (2) has a lot more rhetorical force than (1). Finlay's proffered explanation is that '[m]oral standards or ends are of pressing concern to [us], [and this explains] why we are much more serious and intransigent about our moral appraisals than we are about our appraisals of manners' (2008, p. 354). But one would expect the difference in seriousness and intransigence between moral claims and etiquette claims to be reflected in the concepts we use to make them. The conceptual claim makes good on this expectation: the fact that moral standards or ends are of especially pressing concern to us explains why moral claims entail claims about categorical reasons.

Furthermore, if moral claims and etiquette claims were of the same status, in so far as both kinds of claims reduce to claims about what would conduce to some end or accord with some standard, it is hard to see how moral claims could *maintain* their greater rhetorical force – someone who does not care about the relevant standard or end could waive (2) just as easily as someone who does not care about table manners could waive (1). The conceptual claim provides a straightforward explanation of why moral claims maintain greater rhetorical force than etiquette claims. It also explains straightforwardly why (2) cannot be waived as easily as (1).[30] This is simply because, unlike etiquette claims, moral claims entail claims about categorical reasons.

4.2. Against Finlay's relativist theory

Finlay holds that the *essential application conditions* for moral terms, that is, 'the criteria on which a [moral] concept or term is applied', are relational, even in the use of those who avowedly accept the conceptual claim: 'An action is judged to be *morally wrong* if and only if it is supposed that it frustrates certain ends or violates certain standards' (Finlay, 2008, p. 365).

Taken in one sense, Finlay's claim about essential application conditions for *moral wrongness* is entirely innocuous. Any ordinary moralizer who judges, for example, a particular action wrong will agree that that particular action violates the moral standard she endorses at the time of her utterance.[31] To cut any ice, then, Finlay's contention must be that *all* moral claims, and not just moral claims about particular actions, are relativized to standards.

It is a plain fact that we make moral judgements not only about particular actions but also about other things, including persons, institutions, societies, and *moral standards*. For instance, one might judge that some utilitarian moral standard is correct and that deontological moral standards are incorrect, or that some utilitarian moral standard is more likely to be correct than deontological moral standards. But on Finlay's relativist theory such claims become problematic.

Consider the following claim, which many utilitarians endorse:

(3) Utilitarian standard U – according to which an action is right if and only if it would bring about at least as great a balance of happiness over unhappiness as any other available alternative, and wrong otherwise – is the correct moral standard.

It should be uncontentious that (3) is a moral claim.[32] But utilitarians who utter (3) certainly don't mean to say that U is correct relative to some distinct moral standard or ends; they mean to say that U is the correct fundamental moral standard.

At this point there are two main options for relativists such as Finlay. One is to take fundamental moral claims like (3) to deviate from the general pattern of analysis in that they are not to be relativized to ends. Perhaps fundamental moral claims could be given an expressivist analysis, or perhaps they could be analyzed along the lines of error theory or fictionalism (cf. Finlay, 2009, p. 334f.). The drawback of this option is that it leads to an unhappily *disunified* metaethical theory. If expressivism, error theory, fictionalism, or some other non-relativist account gives a plausible analysis of fundamental moral claims one would expect that account to give an equally plausible analysis of non-fundamental moral claims, such as claims about the moral status of particular actions. Moreover, disunified theories are unattractive in that they invite a double load of critique. For example, a disunified theory that gives an expressivist analysis of fundamental moral claims and a relativist analysis of non-fundamental moral claims is vulnerable both to standard objections to expressivism and to relativism. These may not be conclusive criticisms, but they place a heavy burden of proof on defenders of disunified metaethical theories.

The second main option is to hold that fundamental moral claims do not deviate from the general pattern of analysis and maintain that they be relativized to themselves. An advantage of this option is that it leads to a unified metaethical theory. Finlay has recently made a suggestion along these lines (2009, p. 334).[33] The thought is that fundamental moral claims express tautologies. More specifically, any normative claim is implicitly or explicitly prefixed by an 'In order that *e*' clause, where *e* is some end. 'In order that *e*, it ought to be the case that one perform Φ' expresses the claim that, if one performs Φ, the likelihood that *e* be realized is greater than it would be if some alternative to Φ were performed. The utilitarian fundamental moral claim that one ought not to perform actions that fail to maximize happiness is thus to be understood as the following tautological claim: 'In order that one does not perform actions that fail to maximize happiness, it ought to be the case that one not perform actions that fail to maximize happiness.' It is, of course, trivially true that if one does not perform actions that fail to maximize happiness the likelihood that one does not perform actions that fail to maximize happiness is greater than it would be if some alternative actions were performed. Let us call this suggested analysis of fundamental moral claims the 'tautology approach.'

The tautology approach has many troublesome implications. Here I shall briefly highlight four interrelated problems.[34]

(i) *No absolutely correct fundamental moral standard.* I said above that utilitarians who endorse (3) do not mean to say that U is correct relative to some *distinct* moral standard. Neither do they mean to say that U is correct relative to itself. It is trivially true that any fundamental moral standard is correct relative to itself, but utilitarians who endorse (3) mean to say something that is not trivially true, namely that U is correct in a non-relativized way, that is, that U is the *absolutely* correct fundamental moral standard.[35] But, according to the tautology approach, there is no absolutely correct fundamental moral standard. Hence the approach vindicates error theory about absolutely correct fundamental moral standards.

(ii) *No incorrect fundamental moral standard.* Ordinary speakers normally assume that it is possible to be mistaken about which fundamental moral standard is correct. They normally deem incorrect any fundamental moral standard that appears incompatible with the ones they endorse. For instance, an ethical vegetarian might believe that any fundamental moral standard that sanctions eating meat is incorrect; a 'pro-life' activist might believe that any fundamental moral standard that sanctions abortion is incorrect. But, according to the tautology approach, these beliefs are false.[36] As we saw in (i), any claim to the effect that some fundamental moral standard is correct is trivially true, so there is no such thing as an incorrect fundamental moral standard. Hence the tautology approach implies an error theory according to which claims to the effect that some fundamental moral standard is incorrect are uniformly false.

(iii) *No disagreement in asserted content.* What has been said in (ii) illustrates that speakers who apparently disagree about fundamental moral standards, such as utilitarians and deontologists or ethical vegetarians and speciesists, disagree at most 'in attitude' but not in what is asserted. This means that the common belief – that when speakers make incompatible fundamental moral claims they disagree in what they assert – is false.[37]

(iv) *No informative fundamental moral claims.* Many moral philosophers, as well as many ordinary speakers, believe that their fundamental moral claims are informative, often unobviously true, and perhaps even highly controversial. But the tautology approach implies that these beliefs too are false.

Finlay might retort that attributing false beliefs about fundamental moral standards to ordinary speakers is not a big cost, since fundamental moral claims rarely appear in ordinary moral discourse. When they do, they function as conversation stoppers, the point of which is to demand motivation and action, rather than to convey semantic content (Finlay, 2009, p. 334).[38]

But this is unconvincing. First, as has already been indicated, it is not uncommon for ordinary speakers to appeal to fundamental moral standards in, for example, debates about ideology, vegetarianism, or abortion. It is, of course, debatable how frequently cases of fundamental moral disagreements occur. (Finlay suspects they occur a lot less frequently than I do.) But, irrespective of this empirical issue, it is clear that fundamental moral beliefs and disagreements are of crucial importance to many people. Many people take very seriously their doubts about whether the fundamental moral standard they accept is really correct. In asking such questions they do not doubt or ponder trivial truths. The tautology approach, then, implies error theory about possibly large, and definitely crucial, parts of ordinary moral discourse.

Second, and relatedly, I agree that fundamental moral claims often function to demand motivation and action, but it is implausible that they do not normally also function to convey semantic content. After all, many ordinary speakers, not just moral philosophers, are willing to engage in debates about fundamental moral standards. It is implausible that fundamental moral claims function merely as conversation stoppers in such debates. Open-minded participants typically hold their views about fundamental moral standards open to scrutiny and revision. As points (i)–(iv) have already suggested, they do not normally take them to be trivially true.[39]

Let us sum up. The tautology approach agrees with moral error theory in taking claims to the effect that some fundamental moral standard is absolutely correct to be uniformly false, and even goes beyond it in taking claims to the effect that some fundamental moral standard is incorrect also to be uniformly false. Furthermore, it attributes to most moral philosophers and users of ordinary moral discourse false beliefs about disagreement over fundamental moral standards and over the logical and epistemic status of fundamental moral claims – while they are normally taken to be informative, often unobvious, sometimes highly controversial and mutually inconsistent, they are all trivially true. Attributing all these errors to ordinary moral discourse seems more far-fetched than attributing error about moral metaphysics.

Relativists such as Finlay might, of course, attempt an alternative to the tautology approach to fundamental moral claims. But it seems that any such alternative view leads to a disunified metaethical theory. And, as suggested above, defenders of disunified theories must accept a heavy burden of proof. Until relativists such as Finlay have elaborated a plausible analysis of fundamental moral claims, the case against the conceptual claim remains unconvincing. I conclude that Mackie's theory fits better than Finlay's with ordinary moral thought and talk.

5. Does the rejection of categorical reasons prove too much?

It was argued in Section 2 above that the most powerful argument from queerness targets categorical reasons. It is easy to see that the argument generalizes: those who accept it are committed to error theory not just about moral discourse but about any discourse that involves commitment to categorical reasons. Some critics have argued that this is an embarrassment for moral error theory. For instance, it has been argued that epistemic reasons should be – from the error theorist's perspective – equally problematic as moral reasons (Cuneo, 2007; Stratton-Lake, 2000). I discuss this issue elsewhere (Olson, forthcoming) and won't pursue it further here.[40]

It has also been argued that moral error theorists' argument against categorical reasons apply to claims about *hypothetical reasons*, that is, claims to the effect that there is reason to take the means to one's ends. This is a potential problem for many moral error theorists, who have wanted to accept hypothetical reasons. Consider Mackie:

> 'If you want X, do Y' (or 'You ought to do Y') will be a hypothetical imperative if it is *based on* the supposed fact that Y is, in the circumstances, the only (or the best) available means to X, that is, on a causal relation between Y and X. The reason for doing Y *lies in* its causal connection with the desired end, X. (1977, pp. 27–8, emphases added)

Later on, Mackie says that 'the reason for doing Y is *contingent upon* the desire for X by way of Y's being a means to X' (p. 29, emphasis added), and later still that the desire for X '*creates* the reason for doing Y.' (p. 75, emphasis added)[41]

One might ask what exactly it means to say that hypothetical reasons are 'contingent upon' desires (Hampton, 1998). That is a fair question. And it is not answered by Mackie's claims that hypothetical reasons are 'based on' or 'created by' desires, or that they 'lie in' desires. Clearly, error theorists cannot hold that there is a transcendent norm to the effect that agents take (what they believe to be) the means to their ends, for that would mean that error theorists are committed to there being categorical reasons after all.

I said above that error theorists find it puzzling how there can be facts that count in favor of certain courses of behavior. But why would it be any the less puzzling for facts about desires, and facts about what would bring about satisfaction of those desires, to count in favor of certain courses of behavior? In other words, if categorical reasons are metaphysically puzzling, why believe that hypothetical reasons are any the less metaphysically puzzling (Bedke, 2010)?

This is yet another fair question. In response, error theorists should deny that hypothetical reasons are properly understood in terms of the counting-in-favor-of relation. According to error theory, claims about hypothetical reasons are true only if they reduce to empirical claims about agents' desires and (actual or believed) efficient means of bringing about the satisfaction of these desires. So, for instance, the claim that there is hypothetical reason for some agent to Y can be true if and only if it reduces to the claim that doing Y will or is likely to bring about the satisfaction of some of the agent's desires.[42] Such claims are clearly dependent for their truth on agents' desires and ends. Hence hypothetical reasons, thus understood, are instances of what I called non-categorical reasons in Section 2 above. Note, however, that error theorists need not claim that all hypothetical reasons claims are reducible to empirical claims. Those that are not so reducible are false, just as categorical reasons claims are uniformly false.

It might be objected that reducing claims about hypothetical reasons to empirical claims about agents' desires and means to bringing about their satisfaction removes the normativity of claims about hypothetical reasons, since no mention is made of facts counting in favor of certain courses of behavior. That is true, but from the error theorists' perspective it is just as it should be; reducing claims about hypothetical reasons to empirical claims is the only way of saving them from being uniformly false.

A related objection is that, since claims to the effect that some action will or is likely to bring about the satisfaction of some desire are empirical and not normative, it is a violation of ordinary language to say that such claims are claims about *reasons* in any sense of the term. But this objection can be safely dismissed. 'Reason' is notoriously ambiguous and there is clearly a sense of the term that fits the proposed understanding of hypothetical reasons. For instance, we might say that there is reason for Sleepy to have an extra cup of black coffee this evening, meaning by this nothing more than that Sleepy desires to stay up late and were he to have an extra cup of black coffee he would be less likely to fall asleep early. To make it even clearer that such claims need not be normative, consider the fact that we might say that there was reason for Hitler to invade Britain during World War II, meaning by this nothing more than that Hitler wanted to win the war and had he invaded Britain he would have been more likely to do so. Thus there clearly is a usage of 'reason' in ordinary language according to which the term merely signifies connections between agents' desires and means to bringing about their satisfaction.

I conclude that moral error theory can meet the challenges considered in this paper.[43]

Notes

1. There are other ways of arriving at moral error theory, some of which are discussed in Joyce (forthcoming). They won't be considered here.
2. According to this version, when one judges that an action has a moral property one judges that it has a property that exerts motivational pull. This allows for the possibility of judging that an action has a moral property without being motivated to act (since the judgement might be mistaken, as it necessarily is, according to moral error theory), though it would be incoherent to judge that an action has a moral property and to judge simultaneously that one is not motivated to act. Thus Mackie's version of motivational internalism does not postulate a necessary connection between making a moral judgement and being motivated to act accordingly (cf. the next footnote).
3. Recently, critics have argued that Mackie made the mistake of mislocating this kind of queerness. Mackie claimed that moral *properties* and *facts* are queer because intrinsically motivating, but motivational internalism is often taken to be a view about a necessary connection between making (sincere) moral *judgements* and being motivated to act. In other words, Mackie should have located the queerness in moral *judgements* rather than in what they are about (Dreier, 2010; cf. Copp, 2010, p. 146). He should then have concluded either that there are no moral judgements or that moral judgements are not beliefs, but rather some kind of non-cognitive attitude. The former conclusion is wildly implausible, while the latter vindicates non-cognitivism. To Jamie Dreier, Mackie's 'mistake of mislocation' 'seems very strange' (2010, p. 82). But, on a plausible reading of Mackie, there is no mistake. When Mackie presents his queerness arguments (1977, pp. 38–42) he takes himself to have established already that that moral judgements are beliefs and hence that non-cognitivism is false (1977, p. 32f.). Now, Mackie obviously thought that some version of motivational internalism (see the previous footnote) is a conceptual truth, but, since he had already argued that moral judgements are beliefs and since beliefs are not necessarily motivating, where could he locate the motivational force, if not in the subject matter of moral beliefs, that is, in moral properties and facts? In other words, I take Mackie's idea to have been that our ordinary conception of a moral property is a conception of a property that 'makes [one] pursue' what one correctly judges to possess it (Mackie, 1977, p. 40). Given Mackie's dialectic, I fail to see that he mislocated queerness in the way Dreier and Copp suggest. However, as noted in the main text above, I agree with Mackie's critics that it is highly disputable whether intrinsic motivational pull is a feature of ordinary speakers' conceptions of moral facts and properties. *This* kind of queerness might well be a chimera.
4. Two clarifications: first, moral facts may be facts about moral permissibility. Such facts would not be objectively prescriptive but rather, as we might say, objectively *permissive*. Second, the fact that an agent ought morally to Φ would not necessarily entail that there are conclusive reasons for that agent to Φ. It is a common view that morality does not exhaust normativity; there are other normative reasons besides moral reasons, and the former may trump the latter. But see Tännsjö (2010) for a dissenting view.
5. One example of opacity in Mackie's discussion has already been mentioned: his failure to distinguish clearly between the claim that moral facts would be queer because intrinsically motivating and the claim that they would be queer because objectively prescriptive. Another example is the overly compressed discussion of why moral supervenience is troublesome for realists (1977, p. 40). I won't expand

on this point here; see, for instance, Sobel (2001) for a clarifying discussion of metaphysical qualms about moral supervenience.

6. Mackie (1977, pp. 25–27, 79–82); Joyce (2001, pp. 30–41). Joyce distinguishes between 'strong' and 'weak' categorical imperatives, and his version of error theory denies the existence of the former but grants the existence of the latter (p. 36). Joyce's strong categorical imperatives correspond to what I will call categorical reasons, while weak categorical imperatives correspond to what I will call non-categorical reasons. I prefer my terminology because, first, Joyce's terminology suggests, implausibly, that categoricity comes in degrees; secondly, it is not clear why weak categoricity would be less metaphysically queer.

7. To clarify: I take *norms* to be facts expressible by universally quantified sentences that imply that there are, for some class of agents in some set of circumstances, reasons to behave in a certain way, or that, for some class of agents in some set of circumstances, some form of behavior would be (in)correct or (im)permissible. *Reasons* I take to be facts that explain why some agent ought (*pro tanto*) to behave in certain ways, or why some form of behavior would be (in)correct or (im)permissible. I allow for the possibility that some norms are self-explaining – that some norm holds might itself be a reason to behave in certain ways. See also Olson (forthcoming).

8. As mentioned in footnote 2 above, some moral norms are norms of *permissibility*. Norms of moral permissibility are transcendent too. For instance, to say that homosexual activity is morally permissible is to say that one *may* engage in homosexual activity, irrespective of agents' aims, desires, or roles. Note also that some claims about moral permissibility entail claims about categorical reasons. The claim that homosexual activity is morally permissible entails the claim that there are categorical reasons not to prevent people from engaging in homosexual activity. Thanks to Christian Coons and Jussi Suikkanen for discussions here.

9. It is possible, of course, that some transcendent (e.g. moral) norms require compliance with some immanent (e.g. etiquette) norms.

10. A common charge against naturalistic realism is that it cannot account for the *normativity* of moral claims (e.g. Dancy, 2006a, pp. 132–8; Parfit, forthcoming). This is often taken to mean that moral naturalism cannot account for the fact that moral claims are or entail claims about categorical reasons. Cf. Mackie: '[Naturalism] leaves out the categorical quality of moral requirements' (1977, p. 33).

11. Among them are Nagel (1986), Scanlon (1998), and Shafer-Landau (2003; 2009). Dworkin (1996) spends a fair bit of time criticizing Mackie's claim that moral facts are queer because they would be intrinsically motivating. As I note above, this queerness worry is not particularly forceful. Dworkin is much swifter about Mackie's claim that moral facts are queer because they would be or entail non-categorical reasons. Dworkin says: 'There is nothing bizarre in the idea that a moral duty necessarily supplies a moral reason for action, however. That can be true only in virtue of what "duty" and "reason" mean' (p. 115). It is easy to see that Dworkin simply restates the conceptual claim. He does not attempt to answer the question of how there can be facts that in themselves, that is, independently of desires, aims, roles, or activities, of human beings and other agents, count in favor of certain behavior.

12. The 'counting in favor of' locution is currently the most popular way of spelling out the notion of a normative reason. See, for example, Scanlon (1998) and Parfit (2001).

13. For a thorough critique of using 'partners in guilt (innocence)' strategies in defense of normative realism, see Lillehammer (2007).

14. An early proponent of the Moorean argument against moral error theory was A.C. Ewing (1947, pp. 30–3). For recent versions, see Huemer (2005, pp. 115–17) and Shafer-Landau (2009).
15. Mackie cites Protagoras, Thomas Hobbes, David Hume, and G.J. Warnock as sources of inspiration.
16. A full positive defense of moral error theory would, of course, have to specify what is wrong with expressivist and naturalistic accounts of moral thought and talk. I cannot offer such a defense here. But I am inclined to believe that there are several aspects of ordinary moral discourse that even the most sophisticated versions of expressivism and naturalism cannot account for. This means that these views will have to be put forward as revisionary rather than descriptive metaethical theories, or they will be committed to some form of error theory. For recent critiques of expressivism along these lines, see Cuneo (2006), Bykvist & Olson (2009) and Olson (2010). For critiques of naturalism, see Timmons (1999, ch. 3), and Horgan and Timmons (2009).
17. This problem has been discussed by, for example, Pigden (2007), Sinnott-Armstrong (2006), Sobel (MS) and Tännsjö (2010).
18. Joyce (2001, pp. 6–9) suggests a version of moral error theory according to which moral claims are neither true nor false because they rest on false presuppositions (though he does not do so in the context of attempting to solve the error theorist's problem with negated moral claims). But Joyce gives no principled argument for why moral claims would be neither true nor false, rather than false. In general, I take claims that predicate non-instantiated properties of some individual or individuals to be false. For instance, a claim to the effect that some person is a witch (where being a witch involves being a woman with magical powers) is false. (Joyce, in fact, seems to admit this; 2001, p. 96.) The same, as another example, goes for a claim to the effect that acts of torture are morally wrong. This latter claim too is false, because it predicates a non-instantiated property of an action type. I assume a liberal account of properties, according to which there is a property P if there is in some natural language a predicate that purports to pick out P and P gives rise to no Russellian paradoxes. The predicate 'morally wrong' fits this description, so there is a property of moral wrongness, but error theorists maintain that it is metaphysically impossible for this property to be instantiated.
19. Some moral standards allow for moral dilemmas, in which one and the same action token is simultaneously not wrong and impermissible, or simultaneously not wrong and wrong.
20. Some, but not all. For instance, the claim that it is not the case that Dick believes torture is wrong does not conversationally implicate a first-order moral claim.
21. Pigden (2007) calls the problem of formulating moral error theory the *Doppelganger Problem*. My solution is similar to Pigden's (p. 453f.), barring some differences. Pigden does not appeal to conversational implicatures, and in the summary of his article he states that moral error theory should be formulated as the view that '*non-negative atomic moral judgements* are all false' (p. 455, Pigden's italics). On my view, however, 'non-negative' is a superfluous proviso since, as I say above, negated atomic claims involving moral terms are not strictly speaking first-order moral claims, but they may conversationally implicate first-order moral claims.
22. 'The Error in "The Error in the Error Theory"' is also the title of Joyce's forthcoming response to Finlay. I note with satisfaction that Joyce acknowledges that I 'beat him to the punch' in using this title (Joyce, forthcoming).
23. Foot (1972) delivered an early attack on the conceptual claim. Joyce (2001) responds to Foot; Finlay's 2008 article is largely a rejoinder to Joyce.

24. By an 'end' Finlay means 'a possible aim for action or object of desire' (2006, p. 8). He also makes clear that his view amounts to 'a naturalistic reduction of the relation of "counting in favour of" to a relation specifiable in only nonnormative terms' (p. 8). But, as I argue in the main text above, I believe that the 'counting in favor of' relation cannot be reduced to a naturalistic relation. To say that F counts in favor of Φing is to say not merely that F explains why Φing would be conducive to some end, but also that F matters normatively.

25. Here I side with Shafer-Landau (2009) and Parfit (forthcoming) on what it is for a fact to be a categorical reason. Unlike Shafer-Landau and Parfit, however, I do not believe that there are any categorical reasons.

26. It's a familiar fact that we sometimes withhold relativizations to standards or ends for rhetorical purposes and in cases where the relativizations are obvious to the involved parties. Finlay points out that it would be strange for a rugby captain to prefix his advices about rugby tactics with an 'in order to win the game', or 'in order to score a try' (2008, p. 353). But a crucial disanalogy is that it *would not* be strange for a moralizer to make moral claims such as 'Irrespective of your desires, aims, roles, or activities, you ought not to torture animals for fun.' By contrast, it *would* be strange for a rugby captain to express his advice about tactics by saying something like 'Irrespective of the aim to win or score, and irrespective of your role as teammate, you ought to play so and so.' Were the moralizer to prefix his claim that one ought not to torture animals for fun with an 'in order to fulfill your desires', or 'in order to fulfill a certain role or comply with the rules of certain activities', the claim would likely change its character or lose a good deal of its rhetorical force (as I argue in the main text). Were the rugby captain to prefix his advice about rugby tactics with an 'in order to win the game', or 'in order to score a try', he would at most be unnecessarily explicit. Cf. Joyce (forthcoming).

27. It is a familiar fact that seemingly fundamental moral disagreement sometimes stems from non-moral, such as empirical or theological, disagreement (Finlay, 2008: pp. 356–8). But it would be implausible and uncharitable to consider all, or even most, cases of seemingly fundamental moral disagreement as stemming from non-moral disagreement. Furthermore, people sometimes doubt or wonder whether the fundamental moral standard they accept is correct. When people ask such questions they are not merely doubting or wondering whether some courses of behavior conduce to some end. (I get back to this in Section 4.2 below.)

28. Finlay argues that it is not enough merely to locate fundamental moral disagreement between speakers. In order to count as evidence, it must also be established that speakers recognize that they are involved in fundamental moral disagreement (2008, p. 356f.). I believe it is not uncommon for people to recognize that they are involved in fundamental moral disagreements. This often happens in ideological debates, for example.

29. There is the possibility that ordinary speakers believe falsely that moral claims do entail claims about categorical reasons when in fact they reduce to claims about what would conduce to some end. In other words, there is the possibility that ordinary speakers are systematically mistaken about the meaning of moral terms. But this view seems considerably less likely to be true than the view that ordinary speakers are systematically mistaken about moral metaphysics. (See, further, Section 4.2 below.)

30. Cf. Joyce's response to C.L. Stevenson's claim that moral claims are imperatives disguised as assertions (2001, pp. 14–15).

31. Even moral particularists will agree. They will add only that the standard in question is irreducibly situation-specific.
32. Might Finlay avoid the problem by denying that (3) is a moral claim? In addition to being blatantly ad hoc, this move would allow moral conclusions to be derived from non-moral premises. For instance, it follows from (3) that, if some possible action, Φ, would bring about a greater balance of happiness over unhappiness than some distinct alternative, ψ, then ψ is wrong. The claim that ψ is wrong, and that it is wrong because it would be suboptimal in this way, seems a clear example of a moral claim. But then Finlay's theory would violate Hume's Law, in that it would entail that some moral claims – for example, the claim that ψ is wrong – are entailed by some non-moral claims – for example, (3) in conjunction with some further non-moral premises.
33. Finlay acknowledges that this analysis of fundamental moral claims is 'preliminary' and 'speculative' (2009, p. 334).
34. Finlay himself considers some of them (2009, p. 334).
35. Similarly, as Matt Bedke pointed out, those who reject (3) do not mean to deny a trivial truth. They normally mean to deny that U is the absolutely correct fundamental moral standard.
36. A speciesist moral standard, S, is of course incorrect relative to a non-speciesist moral standard, NS. But the claim that S is incorrect relative to NS is not a claim to the effect that S is an incorrect *fundamental* moral standard. To maintain that S is an incorrect fundamental moral standard, the ethical vegetarian must make the false claim that S is incorrect relative to itself.
37. The tautology approach, of course, shares this problem with expressivism. Unlike the former, however, expressivism is not committed to the implausible view that any fundamental moral claim is trivially true.
38. Finlay takes this conversational function of fundamental moral claims to be 'quite compatible with their being tautologous' (2009, p. 334). Cf. 2009, p. 334, note 41.
39. Finlay acknowledges in a footnote that it is a 'serious objection' that 'since people don't ordinarily take themselves to be asserting end-relational propositions when they utter ought-sentences, it is most unlikely that they are' (2009, p. 335, note 41). The serious objection I press above is that, since people don't ordinarily take themselves to be asserting tautologies when they make fundamental moral claims, it is most unlikely that they are. Finlay postpones a full response to these objections to a future occasion, but advertises that his response will rely on 'distinguishing sharply between what we mean by our words and what we think we mean' (2009, p. 335, note 41). This amounts to an error theory according to which ordinary speakers are systematically mistaken about what they mean by (some of) their words.
40. Let me just comment on one such line of criticism. It is sometimes suggested that error theory is self-undermining because it offers reasons to believe that there are no reasons (see, e.g., Stratton-Lake, 2000). In response, it should be borne in mind that consistent versions of error theory offer arguments to the effect that error theory is true (i.e. that there are no categorical reasons); they do not offer offer arguments to the effect that there are reasons to believe that error theory is true. See Olson (2009, 177f.; forthcoming) for further discussion.
41. Mackie thinks that once we have dispensed with categorical reasons it will be of no particular consequence whether Y actually is a means to X, or whether the agent knows or merely believes (truly or falsely) that it is: 'In each of these cases, the statement that [the agent] has a reason, and ought to [Y], is a thoroughly intelligible implementation of the general meanings of the terms' (p. 77).

42. Note that doing *Y* need not *cause* the satisfaction of the relevant desire. Suppose Romeo desires to embrace Juliet. Romeo's embracing Juliet does not cause the satisfaction of Romeo's desire; it is rather that Romeo's embracing Juliet *brings it about* that his desire is satisfied. Another example is that omissions sometimes bring about satisfaction of desires. But omissions do not cause anything.

43. Earlier versions of this paper were presented at a seminar at Stockholm University; at *Filosofidagarna* in Lund, June 2009; at the *RoME* congress in Boulder, Colorado, August 2009; and at a workshop on naturalism in ethics and metaphysics at Leeds University, September 2009. I thank the participants, in particular Selim Berker, Ross Cameron, Christian Coons, David Copp, Daniel Elstein, Ulrike Heuer, Jonathan Ichikawa, Gerald Lang, Daniel Nolan, Jan Österberg, Karl Pettersson, Wlodek Rabinowicz, Ted Sider, Jussi Suikkanen, Pekka Väyrynen, and Ralph Wedgwood, for helpful discussions. I am especially grateful to Matt Bedke, Stephen Finlay, Jens Johansson, Niklas Möller, and the editor of this volume, for their generous feedback.

4
The Myth of Moral Fictionalism

Terence Cuneo and Sean Christy

Naturalists wonder whether there is a place in the world for moral facts. Some believe not, advocating either a view according to which moral discourse is massively in error or one in which it fails to express moral propositions altogether. Other naturalists believe there is a place for moral facts, but only if they are identical with (or perhaps constituted by) natural facts. According to these philosophers, moral discourse embodies no fundamental error and is straightforwardly assertoric. For some time, many philosophers believed that these positions exhausted the options for naturalists. Recently, however, a new position has emerged as an alternative. This position, dubbed *moral fictionalism* by its advocates, maintains that moral thought and discourse either are or should become modes of pretense, wherein we pretend that there are moral facts.

In this paper, we explore the issue of whether moral naturalists should accept moral fictionalism. We argue that they should not. Understood as a view about actual moral discourse, we claim that the position is false. Understood as a position about how we ought to revise such discourse, we claim that it is unfeasible. We do not deny that moral fictionalism has its allure, especially for those of an anti-realist bent. But naturalists, we contend, should resist its attractions.

1. Fictionalism: two elements

Fictionalism is a type of view that comes in multiple, incompatible varieties. This raises the question of whether there is a common core to the various positions that are called fictionalist. About this issue we remain agnostic; we do not know whether there is such a common core. We do, however, believe that there are two claims that any plausible fictionalist position will incorporate.[1] In this section, our task is to identify them.

To identify these claims, it will be helpful to have some terminology at hand. Suppose we stipulate that the expression 'the Fs' can stand for entities of any type whatsoever – possible worlds, material objects, gods, moral facts,

85

or the like. Suppose, further, that we say that an *existential proposition with respect to the Fs* is a proposition such that, were it true, it would imply that there are Fs. Fundamental to fictionalism of any variety with respect to the Fs is the claim that an agent can take up the *fictive stance* toward them.[2] An agent S takes up the fictive stance toward the Fs, we shall assume, just in case the following three conditions are satisfied.

First, S performs speech acts in a range of circumstances C that appear to imply that she believes that there are Fs. That is, in C she performs speech acts the awareness of which would, were one not 'in the know,' naturally lead one to believe that she had thereby committed herself to the truth of some existential proposition with respect to the Fs. Second, in performing these speech acts S does not genuinely express any commitment to there being Fs. In these circumstances, she doesn't (intentionally) commit herself to the truth of any existential propositions with respect to the Fs. Third, when performing these speech acts, S does something else with regard to the existential propositions regarding the Fs: she plays the role of the believer, pretending to accept them.[3] It may bear emphasizing that the person who takes up such a stance might do so in such a way that she offers no clues to her audience that she is doing so. That she takes up the fictive stance, then, may be something of which her audience is entirely unaware.

For ease of reference, let us say that a *fictioneer* with respect to the Fs is a (mentally competent) adult agent who takes up the fictive stance with regard to the Fs in a range of circumstances C. (We should add that the fictioneer with respect to the Fs is not to be identified with the *fictionalist* with regard to the Fs. The latter, in our terminology, is someone who accepts a fictionalist *theory* regarding the Fs. We assume, however, that the fictioneer may have no views about a fictionalist theory and, so, needn't be a fictionalist.) The fictioneer with respect to the gods, for example, is someone who in a given range of circumstances takes up the fictive stance with respect to the gods, performing speech acts that would appear to commit her to belief in the existence of the gods but in fact do not.

We can now identify the two claims that we take to be common to any plausible version of fictionalism with respect to the Fs. The first claim is what we shall call:

> **No Commitment**: The agent who is a fictioneer with respect to the Fs needn't (*qua* agent) take up one type of doxastic stance toward the Fs rather than another.

Philosophers typically maintain that an agent can take up any of three doxastic stances toward a proposition at a time: she can believe that it is true, she can withhold judgment about its truth, or she can believe that it is not true. No Commitment tells us that the fictioneer with regard to the Fs can maintain any of these stances toward the Fs when she takes up the fictive stance toward them.

To illustrate, consider once again the subject of the gods. The fictioneer with regard to the gods may believe that there are no gods. That would give her excellent reason to take up the fictive stance toward the gods, especially if she believes that there are good practical reasons to be part of a community most of whose members believe in the gods. Somewhat differently, the fictioneer might simply be unsure about whether the gods exist. In this case, she might take up the fictive stance toward the gods for similar practical reasons. Finally, the fictioneer might firmly believe in the gods, but she might find it beneficial to strike the fictional stance with regard to them in some circumstances, as she might find that projecting fictions about them is helpful for teaching others about the gods. To which it is worth adding an additional point: it is, we assume, epistemically possible that either the atheist or the theist is correct about the gods. If this is right, a plausible fictionalism with regard to the Fs can remain noncommittal about whether the Fs exist. Fictionalism with respect to the Fs needn't have any particular ontological commitments with respect to them.[4]

The second claim that is central to fictionalism we term:

> **Back-off**: In critical contexts, the fictioneer with respect to the Fs disavows (*qua* fictioneer) any commitment to there being Fs, all else being equal.

There are several types of critical context in which the fictioneer with respect to the Fs disavows any commitment to there being Fs. On this occasion, we limit our attention to only one.

The type of critical context we have in mind is one that carries a strong presumption of truth-telling, such as the court room or the philosophy seminar room. Suppose that, after having sworn to tell the truth and nothing but the truth, Fred, who is a fictioneer with respect to the gods, takes the witness stand. Fred is asked whether he believes that the gods have recently meddled in human affairs. If Fred is sincere and an atheist, he will disavow any commitment to such claims. His answer will be: 'I believe in no gods and, hence, no recent activity on their part.' Likewise, if Fred is a believer he will say something like this: 'Yes, I do believe in the gods. But when I was speaking of their recent exploits, I didn't express any such belief. I was simply telling an edifying story.' Or, somewhat differently, if Fred is an atheist and a trained philosopher, then (all else being equal) when he enters the philosophy seminar room he will shed any pretense regarding belief about the gods that he may exhibit in religiously infused contexts. Among other things, when in the seminar room, he will not spin edifying stories about divine exploits. For, if fictionalists about morality, such as Richard Joyce, are correct, the philosophy seminar room is a critical context. It is a place where philosophical reflection and the pursuit of truth are held in high regard and pretense held in low regard (Joyce, 2001, ch. 7, section 4). Or, to put it more guardedly, it is so under suitably idealized conditions.

2. Moral fictionalism: two types

Let us now turn our attention from fictionalism broadly understood to moral fictionalism. If our discussion has been on the mark, we know that any plausible version of moral fictionalism will accept both No Commitment and Back-off. What, however, renders a position a species of moral fictionalism?

If recent philosophical discussion is any guide, it is the acceptance of one of two claims. According to hermeneutic moral fictionalists, such as Mark Eli Kalderon, sufficient for being a fictionalist about morality is accepting the claim that 'actual moral practice is best described in fictionalist terms' (Kalderon, 2005, p. 140). In our terminology, hermeneutic moral fictionalism is the view that, when engaging in ordinary moral discourse, ordinary agents are fictioneers regarding the moral domain. By contrast, according to revolutionary moral fictionalists, such as Richard Joyce, sufficient for being a moral fictionalist is accepting a thesis about the character of ordinary moral thought and discourse and a recommendation for how they should be revised. Proponents of revolutionary moral fictionalism maintain that ordinary moral thought and discourse are massively mistaken, for they purport to represent moral facts, which do not exist. However, philosophers such as Joyce also claim that the folk needn't be mired in their commitment to moral falsehoods. There is an exit strategy, which is that the folk collectively take up the fictive stance toward moral propositions. This is the revolutionary aspect of the position. The revolutionary moral fictionalist recommends a radical revision of our moral practices.

Moral fictionalism, then, is the view that either ordinary thought and moral discourse are fictive or that they should be. Kalderon offers various reasons to accept the former view, while Joyce furnishes reasons to embrace the latter position. In what follows, we shall largely pass over the reasons offered for accepting either of these positions, opting instead to engage with the views themselves. Our central contention is that neither of these views should be accepted. Hermeneutic moral fictionalism offers us an incorrect account of the character of ordinary moral discourse, while revolutionary moral fictionalism fails to offer compelling reasons to believe that it is the best response to the recognition that the moral beliefs of the folk are in massive error.

3. Against hermeneutic moral fictionalism

Hermeneutic and revolutionary moral fictionalism offer us strikingly different accounts of the nature of ordinary moral discourse. Proponents of the former view maintain that it is fictional in character, while defenders of the latter view do not. Do we have reason to prefer one of these views to the other? We believe so. To make our case, let us begin by working with an example in which we compare the moral domain with one in which we are clearly fictioneers.

Many of us were reared by adults who were fictioneers about 'creatures of the holidays.' Among other things, these adults told us about Santa Claus and his holiday doings. As children, many of us accepted this testimony at face value, believing for some time all sorts of things about Santa and his activities. Then some of us figured out that there couldn't be such a man. We subsequently had our suspicions confirmed by peers, parents, teachers, and the like. Others of us, who didn't figure this out for ourselves, were told by adults the (often jarring) truth. The adults we knew disavowed any commitment to the existence of Santa and other creatures of the holidays, teaching us how properly to employ language that expresses fictional concepts.

Do we find any parallel to this in the moral domain? As best we can tell, no. Most of us were reared by adults who taught us that there are moral principles which are to be followed. Many of us accepted this testimony at face value. We accepted that stealing really is wrong, honesty is required, and so forth. This teaching was reinforced by an elaborate program of social conditioning in school, church, synagogue, youth camps, and the like. Perhaps some of us harbored doubts about whether there really is such a moral code or whether there is any reason to follow it. Still, in our youth, if we raised doubts about the reality of morality, our doubts were not by and large confirmed by peers, parents, priests, and teachers. Few of us had any parallel in the moral domain to the experience of being told there is no Santa. Few of us discovered that our parents or priests were fictioneers about morality; they never backed off the claim that, when they said that stealing is wrong, they were committing themselves to the wrongness of stealing.

Earlier we said that an important mark of fictional discourse is that, in critical contexts, fictioneers with respect to the Fs disavow any commitment to the Fs. We have drawn attention to a type of pedagogical context in which children are taught the proper application of paradigmatic fictional and moral concepts, noting the differences between them. If pedagogical contexts are a type of critical context (in our sense of this term), then we have identified evidence that the folk are not fictioneers about morality.

Let us now round out the case for this claim. Following Joyce, we suggested that the philosophy seminar room is a critical context (under suitably idealized conditions), where truth is held in high regard and pretense held in low regard. If hermeneutic fictionalism were true, then one would expect to hear philosophers in the seminar room disavowing the claim that their ordinary moral discourse commits them to moral truths, admitting to one another that they, with the rest of the folk, are moral fictioneers. As most readers will know, this is not what one in fact hears when one steps into a philosophy seminar room. Rather, one hears philosophers defending all manner of metaethical views, ranging from Platonism to constructivism to expressivism. In their defenses of these views, some philosophers hazard generalizations about the character of ordinary moral discourse, maintaining that ordinary moral discourse is best viewed as being assertoric (or expressive, as the case may be). Conspicuously lacking, however, is any indication that these philosophers have 'come clean' about the fact that they, along with the rest of the folk, are engaged in pretense when they participate in ordinary moral discourse outside the seminar room.

We could go on in this vein for some time, pointing out that it is rare to find ordinary people disavowing their commitment to morality in other critical contexts, such as the courtroom or in situations in which there is a high welfare cost to being committed to moral principles. To be sure, furnishing additional cases of these types would strengthen the case against hermeneutic moral fictionalism, providing us with additional reasons to believe that hermeneutic moral fictionalism falls afoul of Back-off. Arguably, however, adducing more cases of this variety would make little headway against hermeneutic moral fictionalism. Why? Because hermeneutic moral fictionalists such as Kalderon hold that the folk *unwittingly* take up the fictive stance toward morality. In Kalderon's view, it is no surprise that the folk fail to back off any apparent commitment toward morality in critical contexts. They do not do so because they do not understand that, when they engage in moral discourse, they are taking up the fictive stance at all (2005, p. 153).

The claim that ordinary people are massively and unwittingly in error about what they are doing when they engage in actual moral discourse offends Davidsonian sensibilities: it is an uncharitable view of the folk. Kalderon is sensitive to this worry. He contends, however, that it can be addressed satisfactorily, offering several reasons to believe that it is not implausible to think that the folk are in the dark about the character of ordinary moral discourse. After all, our attitudes and actions, Kalderon points out, are often not transparent to us. We sometimes don't know what we really believe or want. Furthermore, we cannot discern the character of moral discourse simply by looking more closely at the 'content of moral vocabulary' (2005, p. 154). Accordingly, if one is not already 'in the know' about how such discourse is being used, it is impossible to discern genuinely assertoric from fictional discourse. Finally, Kalderon claims, our 'representational idioms' are ambiguous. 'Sometimes', Kalderon writes, 'by "representing o as F" we mean that the proposition that o is F is being put forward as true. Sometimes by "representing o as F" we mean that the proposition that o is F is expressed whether or not that proposition is being put forward as true' (2005, p. 155). The folk cannot be expected to mark the difference.

Is Kalderon's response adequate? Well, suppose we focus for the moment on the character not of moral thought but of moral discourse. And suppose we assume that, unusual cases aside, such as slips of the tongue, performing a speech act of a given type is an intentional or deliberate action. Asserting a proposition is not something that happens to us; it is an action that we deliberately perform. Suppose, further, that expressing a fictive stance is a speech act of a given kind (or something very similar thereto) and, hence, one that is usually intentionally performed.[5] Given these assumptions, is it plausible to believe that we are entirely in the dark about our speech act intentions when we engage in moral discourse?

We think not. We human beings, after all, are story-telling animals. Competent adults know well the difference between spinning fictions and telling the sober truth about some matter. We navigate the distinction all the time. Admittedly, here and there we may unintentionally 'fall into' taking up the fictive stance. But, highly unusual cases aside, we are capable of discerning when we have done so. If this is right, then we can concede that our representational idioms are sometimes ambiguous. And we can concede that we cannot grasp the character of moral discourse simply by examining moral vocabulary. And we can concede that we can be mistaken about our attitudes and intentions. It is, however, one thing to concede all this and another to maintain that nearly all of us all of the time are mistaken about what we are doing when we engage in moral discourse – that, for some reason, when it comes to the moral domain in particular, we are unable to draw a distinction that we naturally and easily make in other domains, namely, between believing a proposition and taking up the fictive stance toward it. In our judgment, to attribute this mistake to the folk would require an extraordinary justification. The justification, as best we can tell, is not available. Given certain assumptions about meaning, we can imagine that ordinary people do not know what some of their claims *mean*. But we do not see how the folk would fail to have any inkling about what types of speech act they intend to perform when they engage in moral discourse.

Indeed, we suspect that the following, more robust claim is true: it is impossible that the folk be systematically deceived about whether they are taking up the fictive stance toward moral facts when engaging in moral discourse. For suppose it is true that performing a speech act of a given type is typically an intentional or deliberate action: unusual cases aside, an agent performs a speech act of a given type only if he intends to perform it. Suppose, furthermore, that taking up the fictive stance with respect to the Fs is to engage in pretense, pretending to commit oneself to there being Fs. Suppose, finally, that, if moral fictionalism is true, moral discourse consists in expressing the fictive stance toward moral facts (or propositions). If these three claims are true, then it is difficult to see how it could be that, when engaging in ordinary moral discourse, agents systematically and unwittingly pretend that there are moral facts. What, after all, would it be for someone systematically and unwittingly to pretend that there are things of a certain kind?

Rather than drop the matter here, let us offer a conjecture about what may have led Kalderon to the position that we are all unwitting fictioneers with regard to morality. In a fine chapter about expressivism, Kalderon notes that expressivist attempts to solve the Frege–Geach problem suffer from a failure to distinguish the state of believing from its object (2005, pp. 61–4). Leaving aside the details of Kalderon's argument for the moment, it is worth noting that the term 'fiction' is systematically ambiguous in much the same way as the term 'belief'. The word 'fiction' can be used to talk of the act of project-ing a fiction, such as when we say 'John is engaged in an elaborate fiction,' or the object of a propositional attitude, such as when we say that 'What John believes is an elaborate fiction.' In his official presentation of the view (chapter 3), Kalderon works with the first use of the term. He maintains that to be a fictioneer is not to be identified with directing one's attitude toward a fiction but to take up the fictive stance toward a proposition. In the last chap-ter of his book, however, when Kalderon furnishes examples of unwitting fictioneers, such as the members of Moore's Bloomsbury group, he employs the term 'fiction' in the second sense to denote not the fictive stance but the object of an attitude. 'Moore's *Principia*,' according to Kalderon, 'functioned as the master fiction' of the Bloomsbury group (2005, p. 162).

Note, however, that, if one uses the term in this latter sense, it is natural to think that one can unwittingly be a fictioneer. According to this under-standing, so long as the object of one's attitude is a fiction, one is thereby a fictioneer. Moore, we concede, may have been a fictioneer in this sense. Non-naturalism may, after all, be a fiction in the sense that it is a rather fan-tastic position that is false. (This is one way to interpret J.L. Mackie's argu-ment from queerness: non-naturalism is just too fantastic to be true.) If it is, then this is something of which Moore may have been entirely unaware. But, even supposing that one can unwittingly project a fiction, we find it incredible to believe that a philosopher of Moore's sophistication and his followers were unwittingly engaged in pretense when defending moral non-naturalism. Accordingly, we balk at attributing such a position to Kalderon. Hence our conjecture: what accounts for the characterization of Moore as a moral fictioneer is that Kalderon has lost sight of the difference between taking up the fictive stance toward a proposition and having a fiction as the object of one's propositional attitudes. Similarly, we conjecture that any plausibility that attaches to the claim that the folk are unwitting fictioneers is due to the fact that we are thinking of them as fictioneers only in the sense that the object of their moral attitudes is a fiction. We concede that this may be the case. But it should not lead us to believe that, when engag-ing in actual moral discourse, ordinary people are moral fictioneers in the sense we described at the outset of our discussion.

4. Against revolutionary moral fictionalism

Earlier we claimed that hermeneutic and revolutionary moral fictionalism offer very different accounts of the nature of moral discourse. Hermeneutic moral fictionalists, we said, defend the view that actual moral thought and discourse are fictional. Revolutionary moral fictionalists do not, maintaining that actual moral discourse is both straightforwardly assertoric and massively in error. Unlike other error theorists, however, revolutionary moral fictionalists do not leave it at that. They offer a proposal for responding to the discovery of this error, which is that we transform moral discourse into fictive discourse.

Let us assume, for argument's sake, that moral discourse is in error in the way that error theorists believe. Revolutionary moral fictionalists recognize that fictionalism is not the only response to the discovery of moral error. There are other options, of which Joyce identifies three. The first is *abolitionism*, which is the view that a proper response to the discovery of error is the elimination of the use of moral concepts. The second is *propagandism*, which is the view that the elites, who are those philosophically sophisticated enough to engage in metaethics, hush up the evidence of the error so that the folk can continue engaging in moral discourse and thinking in ordinary moral terms. The third option, which goes unnamed in Joyce's book, but we call *intransigentism*, says that the proper response to the discovery of error is to carry on with business as usual, refusing to entertain seriously any evidence that contradicts the claims made in moral discourse.

According to Joyce, none of these options is satisfactory. Abolitionism, says Joyce, is too extreme. If Joyce is correct, adopting it will result in a loss of the practical benefits of morality, such as its ability to provide a foundation for social cohesion. Propagandism, in contrast, is inherently unstable. To implement it is to run the risk that the folk will find out about the deception, resulting in 'a very confused group of people, unsure of what to believe, and unable to trust their normal belief-producing mechanisms' (2001, p. 214).[6] Intransigentism, finally, would merely be a temporary response to the discovery of error, for '[n]o policy that encourages the belief in falsehoods, or the promulgation of false beliefs in others, will be practically stable in the long run' (ibid.). Fictionalism is the best option among the four because it allows moral thought and discourse still to be practiced and, hence, the folk to reap their benefits.

What are the practical benefits of continuing to engage in moral thought and practice? Joyce points to two. First, engaging in moral thought and discourse, says Joyce, bolsters self-control. Moral obligation 'imbues certain desirable actions with a "must-be-doneness", which raises the likelihood of their being performed' (2001, p. 181). Likewise, moral prohibition imbues certain undesirable actions with a must-not-be-doneness, which decreases the likelihood of their being performed. Second, moral thought and discourse provide a foundation for social cohesion. Morality binds communities together and is an economical way of prescribing which actions are for the benefit or the detriment of the community. Joyce concedes that choosing fictionalism over its competitors may not result in the folk enjoying these benefits exactly as they did before the error was discovered. Still, fictionalism, Joyce claims, stands a better chance than the other three options of preserving these benefits. Because of this, Joyce recommends implementing the revolutionary program, claiming that it is the best response to the discovery of error.

Of this we are dubious. In our judgment, there are other non-fictionalist responses to the discovery of error that are at least as promising as revolutionary fictionalism. In this regard, consider propagandism once again. Recall that, according to Joyce, propagandism is the view that the elites, who are those philosophically sophisticated enough to engage in metaethics, hush up the evidence of error so that the folk can continue using moral discourse and thinking in ordinary moral terms. It is worth emphasizing, however, that this view can be understood more expansively than Joyce describes it. Let us call a more expansive version of this position *propagandism in the broad sense*. Fundamental to propagandism in the broad sense are the following three claims.

First, the error theorist's diagnosis of ordinary moral discourse is correct. Actual moral discourse is by and large in fundamental error.

Second, while those aware of the error should be prepared to cover up evidence of it were the need to arise, the need in fact rarely arises. Why not? If propagandists in the broad sense are correct, for at least the following reasons. For one, the folk generally have neither the time nor the resources to dedicate to thinking through metaethical matters. Philosophy, for most, is a luxury. Moreover, many are unable to appreciate the reasons for believing that an error has been committed. After all, to appreciate the nature of the error and the reasons for believing that it has been committed requires not only sufficient time, effort, and training, but also a level of conceptual sophistication not possessed by most people. (It may be worth reminding ourselves of the degree of sophistication required to understand, say, Blackburn's argument from supervenience or Horgan and Timmons' Moral Twin Earth argument.) Finally, appreciating the error requires being open to seriously considering of views that are opposed to deeply entrenched convictions about morality – convictions that are often grounded in religious beliefs and practices. Many of the folk do not exhibit openness of this sort. If propagandists in the broad sense are right about all this, attempting to communicate to the folk what is at stake in metaethical debates and what should be done about it is not worth the trouble. Better to let sleeping dogs lie.

Third, and finally, those aware of the error must often engage in moral deliberation with the folk. Propagandists in the broad sense maintain that the best way to do so is not to take up the fictive stance toward moral propositions in which we pretend to assert them. Rather, they recommend that the elite take up various types of non-doxastic stances toward moral propositions, employing them in ordinary speech not to pretend to assert them, but to do such things as encourage, edify, or blame their interlocutors.

Admittedly, to the uninitiated, the linguistic expression of these non-doxastic stances will often appear to be one or another species of assertion. But in reality they are not. To use the vernacular of speech act theory, when engaging in ordinary moral discourse, the elite present moral propositions not so as to assert them (or pretend to assert them) but to have various kinds of perlocutionary effects on their audience, such as their feeling encouraged or guilty.[7]

Is this view any less plausible than revolutionary moral fictionalism? Suppose we approach this question by doing a miniature cost–benefit analysis, comparing the virtues and vices of each view. It is clear that there is one sense in which revolutionary moral fictionalism appears to have a clear advantage over propagandism in both senses we distinguished earlier. All else being equal, having massive amounts of false beliefs is bad. (We assume, for the moment, that the value of truth is not merely instrumental. There is, we assume, something non-instrumentally worthwhile about getting into cognitive contact with reality.) Accordingly, if someone were to find himself with packs of false beliefs about what Locke called 'matters of maximal concernment,' such as morality and religion, then he should want to remedy this. To its credit, revolutionary moral fictionalism recognizes this. And it offers a strategy for remedying the problem, at least when it comes to morality. Propagandism, in contrast, does not.

Still, once the problem is recognized, one should like to have a strategy that has a decent chance of fixing it. The worry about the strategy that revolutionary moral fictionalists recommend is that it will not fix the problem. In what follows, we raise four difficulties with their view.

The first is that successfully implementing the revolutionary strategy requires convincing enough people that their moral views are massively in error. The problem is not so much the practical issue of how one would go about communicating this message to the world (late night infomercials?). Nor is it that it is unclear who would communicate the message. (According to our count, even among philosophers, there are rather few error theorists to communicate it.) It is rather that, according to revolutionary fictionalists such as Joyce, the reasons for believing that there is an error are philosophical arguments. The arguments themselves, moreover, are run-of-the-mill philosophical arguments. That is, they are extremely contentious; they do not command anything like widespread assent even among those who dedicate their lives to considering them.

Consider, for example, the most celebrated of these arguments, namely, Mackie's so-called argument from queerness. It purports to show that, if moral truths exist, then they would be very odd, unlike anything else we encounter in our ordinary lives. Suppose the argument is correct in its central contention. The fundamental problem with the argument, at least as far as the revolution goes, is that many philosophers are willing to believe strange things. More importantly, so also are the folk. The vast majority of the folk, after all, believe in God. To inform the folk that morality is strange in roughly the way that God is strange would hardly be to offer them a (psychologically) compelling reason to believe that their moral views are in massive error. Indeed, if we appreciate the degree to which moral views are intertwined with religious ones, we can better see how much the revolution must accomplish. Arguably, it must convince the folk not merely that moral facts do not exist, but also that God does not exist. This is a tall order. It has been tried before on a national scale (Soviet Russia comes to mind) with limited success.

So, revolutionary moral fictionalism faces the formidable problem of convincing the folk of the truth of error theory. Progagandism in the broad sense does not face any similar problem. It does not even attempt to convince ordinary people of the fact that their moral views are in massive error.

A second difficulty with the strategy that revolutionary fictionalists recommend concerns moral pedagogy. Suppose we assume that the unlikely has occurred: through a process of rational persuasion and what Richard Rorty calls 'sentimental education,' error theorists have ushered in the fictionalist eschaton. In the eschaton, most of the folk have been convinced of the error of both their moral and religious views. Moreover, they have revolutionized their moral practices in such a way that they now conduct their moral discourse as fictioneers. The fictioneers, however, now face a question: how do we ensure that this way of moral thinking and talking is passed down to and endorsed by the next generation?

Let us assume that, to reap the social and personal benefits of morality, the children must be taught that stealing is really and truly wrong, honesty is really and truly the best policy, and so on. At no point in their younger years will there be anything in their moral training analogous to being told that Santa does not exist. The risks of doing so would be too high: confusion, mistrust, and disorientation might ensue, justifications could not be communicated well enough because most lack the conceptual sophistication to understand them, and some might legitimately wonder why moral thought should be taken so seriously if it is mere pretense. In effect, then, the youth will be reared in such a way that they will be given little indication of morality's true status. This has two results worth highlighting.

First, revolutionary moral fictionalism is not so different from propagandism in the narrow sense introduced earlier. In the eschaton, those 'in the know' must engage in an extensive hushing-up of the truth to the youth. We have already noted that Joyce believes that this position is unsustainable, at least when it comes to morality. But if it is, say, because it risks the result of a confused people unsure of whom to trust and what to believe, then so also is revolutionary moral fictionalism. Admittedly, the confused and disorientated will likely not be the adult fictioneers but the youth. Still, the risk of this seems severe enough that it is very difficult to see how revolutionary moral fictionalism can be recommended as a superior option to propagandism. Both views share, if not the same problem, at least very similar ones.

Second, suppose that in the eschaton the induction into the life of being a moral fictioneer were deferred until later in life – say, until the age of maturity (Joyce, 2001, p. 229). If so, then justifications would have to be offered anew. And presumably these would be the same justifications mentioned earlier, namely, philosophical arguments of various kinds, perhaps buttressed by various manipulative techniques. But it is not a predetermined outcome that, upon engaging with them, the uninitiated would become fictioneers about morality. Consider a parallel. Imagine that most people were fictioneers about God but raised their children in a religious environment, which gave no indication that their parents, priests, and teachers did not believe that God exists. Upon being told the truth about what their parents, priests, and teachers believe about God, it would be, we think, overly optimistic to expect that the youth would become fictioneers about religion. Presumably the youth would have varied reactions to the news concerning the true views of their parents, priests, and teachers. They might continue to be theists, or become Mackie-style atheists, or embrace expressivism about religion. Similarly, when told the truth about what their parents, priests, and teachers believe about morality, we should expect similar reactions. Those made privy to the real views of their parents, priests, and teachers might continue along just as they were, embracing something like realism. Alternatively, they might become disenchanted with all the secrecy and accept abolitionism. To expect a homogeneous response would be to expect too much.

So, there is a second problem for revolutionary moral fictionalism. It is a problem that propagandism in the broad sense does not face. If propagandism of this sort were true, there would be no need to try to indoctrinate the youth in such a way that they, too, become fictioneers about morality. In a phrase, there is no problem of propagation for propagandists.

We now turn to the third problem. In various places, Joyce compares revolutionary moral fictionalism to Hume's position regarding skepticism about the external world (2001, pp. 190–94). Recall that, according to Hume, when he is in his study, he can become quite exercised about skeptical problems, finding himself deeply perplexed by the issues. But, when he steps out of his study for a game of backgammon with his friends, these skeptical worries recede. His indigenous belief-forming faculties take over and Hume finds himself unable to accept skepticism about the external world, comporting himself like an ordinary human being.

Now suppose morality were similar to skepticism of this sort. In critical contexts such as the seminar room, one finds oneself convinced by various anti-realist arguments. But, when one emerges, one finds oneself thinking and acting as if certain acts really are wrong and certain character traits really are morally admirable. One's indigenous belief-forming faculties take over and one cannot help but accept these things. The phenomenology of moral experience forces this upon us.[8] But if this were the case, then revolutionary moral fictionalism would have a problem. The point of the revolution, after all, is to extricate the folk from error. But if, in ordinary contexts, the folk were to find themselves accepting moral propositions, then the error would not have been averted. The folk would find themselves continually backsliding into their indigenous realist habits of mind (recall that, for revolutionary moral fictionalists such as Joyce, this is our natural disposition). Admittedly, if this were true, the error would not be on the same scale as it was before the revolution. In critical contexts at least, the folk would accept the truth. Still, the error would be considerable. It would be bad enough that the point of implementing the revolution would have been largely scuttled.

Let us be clear about what we are claiming. We have not claimed that, were the fictionalist eschaton to be realized, the folk would lapse into their realist habits. Rather, our claim is twofold. First, revolutionary moral fictionalists cannot lean too heavily on parallels with Humean critical contexts. Were the parallels close, their project would be jeopardized. Second, and more importantly, it is critical for the revolution to guarantee that when operating in ordinary contexts most agents do not lapse into the habit of actually accepting moral propositions. Rather, were revolutionary moral fictionalism to achieve its aim, ordinary moral agents would have to become like expert actors. They would have to become people who are capable of bracketing their ordinary beliefs, wholeheartedly immersing themselves into fictional roles, and yet not believe what they say when occupying them (Joyce, 2001, p. 219). We worry that this is to demand too much of the folk. To operate in this way requires not only that the folk reliably keep critical and ordinary contexts distinct, but also that they exercise remarkable discipline and imagination when in ordinary contexts, governing their belief-forming faculties in such a way that they do not produce moral beliefs. Perhaps this could be accomplished in some way. But we imagine that for many this will prove psychologically very difficult. We are not hopeful that the folk will want to put forward the effort.

A third difficulty for revolutionary moral fictionalism, then, is that it asks the folk reliably to accomplish something that is psychologically very difficult to do. Propagandism in the broad sense, by contrast, requires none of this. If it were implemented, ordinary people would be able to go on largely as they always have.

We have just pointed out that, even if the folk were persuaded to become moral fictioneers, there is no guarantee that they could reliably immerse themselves in this role. It may prove too challenging. Imagine, however, that this concern could be addressed satisfactorily. There is still another difficulty worth raising, and that is whether the institution of morality would survive if the folk were to become moral fictioneers.

When Joyce addresses the issue of why abolitionism is unacceptable, his eye is on the benefits of morality. He observes that engaging in moral practice has certain practical benefits: it promotes self-control and social cohesion. Let us now add that, for the institution of morality to have these benefits, certain *stability conditions* must be satisfied. Among other things, the practices that the institution recommends must be such that they can be reliably passed on from generation to generation, they must be such that there is a fairly high degree of conformance with them, and they must be such that the people think it makes sense to engage in them.

Suppose, however, that, instead of emphasizing the benefits of morality, we were to focus on its costs. We know that morality is hard. It can demand great sacrifices of us, sometimes suffering or death. Presumably, in the fictionalist eschaton, the folk would be aware of this. Not only would they be aware of this, but, as moral fictioneers, they would also realize that they can move back and forth between ordinary and critical contexts with relative ease. They will realize that, while one is in an uncritical context, a critical context in which one backs off the fictive stance is only a step away, as it were. This prompts a question: if most people realized all this, would the stability conditions that attach to the institution of morality be satisfied?

The last thing we want to do is issue dire predictions about the death of morality in the fictionalist eschaton. Perhaps morality would keep chugging along as it has for millennia. But we have our doubts. We do not doubt that, when the cost of commitment to morality is high, some fictioneers will hold fast. For example, we can imagine people becoming so attached to their role of being a moral fictioneer that they could not bear backing off morality when it calls for sacrifice. And we can imagine others being gripped by the fear that backing off would threaten to undermine the institution, which they greatly value. Still, in the eschaton we suspect that many others would find it difficult to see why they should sacrifice anything of importance for morality's sake. These people know full well that morality has its uses (although it is worth noting that the values appealed to by philosophers such as Joyce are general, impersonal ones, such as helping to secure social cohesion). But they realize that their commitment to it is at bottom pretense; they are playing the role of being a true believer. We suspect that many will rightly wonder whether maintaining the pretense is worth it when the costs of conforming to morality are high, such as when it threatens one's own well-being or that of one's loved ones.

The standard justifications for standing fast, after all, are unavailable. Moral fictioneers do not believe that moral norms are the expressions of the will of a benevolent deity who will reward the faithful for conforming to them. And they do not believe that moral norms are somehow 'magnetic', as Plato believed of the Form of the Good. Nor do they believe that these norms have rational authority in Kant's sense or hook into our deepest cares in broadly Aristotelian fashion. If any of these views were true, there would be a robust story to tell about why morality should command our allegiance, even when the cost of conforming to it is high. But none of these stories is available to the moral fictioneer. Or, more exactly, they are available, but only as mere stories, fictions alongside many others that have pragmatic uses. Revolutionary moral fictionalists maintain that moral practice will go on in much the same way as it did prior to the revolution. The worry we wish to raise is that we do not have sufficient reason to expect that it will. Fictionalism may have the paradoxical consequence that accepting it will undermine the very purpose for which it was introduced, namely, sustaining the institution of morality.

So, there is a fourth difficulty that revolutionary moral fictionalism must face, which is whether it can sustain allegiance to morality in such a way that the institution is stable. Propagandism in the broad sense, by contrast, has no similar difficulty. The folk have at their disposal all the standard justifications for believing that conforming to morality, even when the costs are high, is well worth it. On the assumption that the folk generally would be unmoved by the types of considerations that move some philosophers to become moral anti-realists, then the folk can appeal to these justifications when the price of conforming to morality is high.

When assessing his own case for revolutionary fictionalism, Joyce is modest, writing:

> I do not pretend to have firmly established the case that taking the fictive stance towards morality will definitely bring pragmatic gains. It is an empirical matter, and I have only put forward some considerations in favor of the hypothesis, not a mature theory....[M]y argument doesn't depend upon the fictive stance providing an *enormous* practical gain: if the returns are reliably just slightly higher than those of its competitors, then the case for moral fictionalism is made. (2001, p. 228; cf. pp. 230–31)

In a similar spirit, we acknowledge that the cost–benefit analysis we've provided would have to be expanded considerably to establish decisively that fictionalism is not a better option than its competitors. Still, we submit that we have furnished enough evidence to induce doubt that the returns of fictionalism are at all higher than some of its competitors. These doubts, we submit, leave us with no more reason to accept revolutionary moral fictionalism than other alternatives such as propagandism in the broad sense identified earlier.

5. Conclusion

We began our discussion by raising the following question: should naturalists be moral fictionalists? There is no denying that in some respects fictionalism should be attractive to naturalists. In its most plausible forms, fictionalism promises to sidestep thorny ontological issues. In principle, naturalists who are fictionalists could simply remain non-committal about whether there are moral facts – why not wait until science gives us reason to jump one way or the other? – while recommending a view about moral discourse according to which the folk needn't commit any mistake of the sort error theorists countenance. Moreover, the view may avoid the standard pitfalls of expressivist views, such as making sense of moral argumentation. According to fictionalism, the object of moral judgments is, or should be, moral propositions.[9] Still, identifying a plausible version of moral fictionalism has proved elusive. Fictionalism does not capture the character of ordinary moral discourse. And it is not apparent that we could revise moral discourse in the way some fictionalists recommend. We conclude that our leading question should be answered in the negative. There are better options for naturalists to embrace than moral fictionalism.

Among these options, we believe, is the view we have called propagandism in the broad sense. In our engagement with revolutionary moral fictionalism, we presented the rudiments of this rival position, suggesting that it should be attractive to naturalists of an anti-realist bent. As we presented it, propagandism in the broad sense accepts the error theorist's diagnosis of ordinary morality: large portions of ordinary moral discourse are in massive error. But it rejects the revolutionary moral fictionalist's remedy: the response to this error is not to transform moral discourse. Rather, it is to more or less leave things as they are. Of course, moral anti-realists must often engage with the folk in moral deliberation. Propagandists in the broad sense suggest that the best way to do so is to take up various types of non-doxastic stances toward the moral propositions that the folk assert. As we say, we think there is much to like about this view. But an elaboration of it will have to wait for another day.[10]

Notes

1. For those familiar with Mark Eli Kalderon's and Richard Joyce's work on moral fictionalism, the first claim is inspired by Kalderon's *Moral Fictionalism* (2005), while the second is inspired by Joyce's *The Myth of Morality* (2001).
2. Or toward the existential propositions with respect to the Fs, depending on whether one thinks of such an attitude along *de re*/predicative or *de dicto* lines. We shall slide between both ways of characterizing the fictive stance. Clearly, fictionalism must be understood in such a way that taking up the fictive stance toward the Fs does not imply that the Fs exist. There are several ways to secure this result, among which is to stipulate that the expression 'the Fs' designates a role of a certain kind that may or may not be occupied. Oddie (2005, pp. 12–13) offers a helpful discussion of this approach.
3. Kalderon (2005, pp. 119–29) canvasses several ways in which pretense of this sort can be understood.
4. Two points bear mention: first, some might wonder whether it is possible to take up the fictive stance toward a proposition that one believes is true. To see that

this is indeed possible, it is helpful to recognize, first, that a fiction needn't be a false proposition and, second, there is nothing about the concept 'the fictive stance' which implies that its object be a proposition that the fictioneer believes is false. Think of historical fiction in this regard. Presumably, when projecting a work of historical fiction, authors such as James Michener take up the fictive stance toward a wide range of propositions that they believe are true. Still, in projecting such a world, they do not *present* them as true. Second, some fictionalist positions commit themselves to the claim that fictional discourse about the Fs such as 'The Fs are P' should be glossed as 'In the fiction, the Fs are Ps.' Claims such as this, it is said, are true just in case in the fiction the Fs are P. And, on the assumption that some such claims are true, fictionalism implies that there are some fictional truths. We do not attribute this position to moral fictionalists, as neither of its main defenders, Kalderon or Joyce, explicitly embraces it. (In fact, Joyce rejects it.) For a discussion, see Kalderon (2005), p. 121 and Joyce (2001), p. 200.

5. Alston (2000) defends the view that, in the paradigmatic case, speech acts are intentional, while Wolterstorff (1980) defends the position that projecting a fiction is an illocutionary act.

6. Here Joyce quotes from Richard Garner.

7. Those familiar with the literature on fictionalism know that there are two main schools of thought regarding the character of fictive discourse. Some, such as John Searle (1979), maintain that it consists in pretending to assert propositions. Others, such as Nicholas Wolterstorff (1980), believe that it consists in taking up other non-doxastic attitudes toward them with the purpose of having some perlocutionary effect on an audience. Propagandism in the broad sense, in effect, appropriates this latter view without maintaining that it best captures the character of fictive discourse.

8. Horgan and Timmons (2007), though not themselves moral realists, maintain that moral phenomenology has many of the features that realists claim it does.

9. Although see Joyce (2001), p. 200 for a contrary view.

10. We wish to thank Dan Hooley, Don Loeb, Rik Peels, and René van Woudenberg, as well as an audience at the Vrije Universiteit, Amsterdam for their comments.

5
Expressivism, Inferentialism and the Theory of Meaning

Matthew Chrisman

1. Introduction

One's account of the meaning of ethical sentences should fit – roughly, as part to whole – with one's account of the meaning of sentences in general. When we ask, though, where one widely discussed account of the meaning of ethical sentences fits with more general accounts of meaning, the answer is frustratingly unclear. The account I have in mind is the sort of metaethical expressivism inspired by Ayer, Stevenson, and Hare, and defended and worked out in more detail recently by Blackburn, Gibbard, and others. So, my first aim (Section 1) in this paper is to pose this question about expressivism's commitments in the theory of meaning and to characterize the answer I think is most natural, given the place expressivist accounts attempt to occupy within metaethics. This involves appeal to an ideationalist account of meaning. Unfortunately for the expressivist, however, this answer generates a problem; it's my second aim (Section 2) to articulate this problem. Then, my third aim (Section 3) is to argue that this problem doesn't extend to the sort of account of the meaning of ethical claims that I favor, which is like expressivism in rejecting a representationalist order of semantic explanation but unlike expressivism in basing an alternative order of semantic explanation on inferential role rather than expressive function.

2. Expressivism and the theory of meaning

Metaethics is often taught as beginning – in a way that has any clear distinction from normative ethics – with Moore's (1903, chapter 1) discussion of the 'naturalistic fallacy' and presentation of the 'open-question argument' against the reduction of moral terms like 'good' to non-moral terms like 'what's desired.' To be sure, almost no contemporary metaethicist thinks that the 'naturalistic fallacy' really is a fallacy or that the 'open-question argument' shows everything that Moore thought that it showed. However, it is widely assumed that one's metaethical view must take a stand on

Moore's contention that moral terms cannot be analyzed in natural terms. In response, I think we see four basic kinds of theories favored by most contemporary metaethicists:

- *Non-naturalists* agree with Moore's initial proposal, at least in its spirit even if not its details. That is, they argue that the only plausible way to accept Moore's negative argument and to continue to take ethics seriously is to posit the existence of *sui generis* moral properties, which can then be seen as the referents of moral terms.[1]
- *Naturalists* balk at the ontological commitments involved in non-naturalism. So, they argue that Moorean arguments for unanalyzability either can be met or are beside the point. If they think they can be met, they propose an analysis of moral terms in non-moral terms. If they think it's beside the point, they argue that, even if we cannot analyze moral terms in non-moral terms, that doesn't show that moral properties aren't natural properties any more than the fact that we cannot analyze the term 'water' with the coextensive term 'H_2O.'[2]
- *Fictionalists* see an easier way to ontological parsimony. They argue that we can accept Moore's negative argument and agree with the non-naturalist about the ostensible referents of moral terms, but we can think of our language referring to these *sui generis* properties as a convenient fiction rather than as manifesting actual ontological commitments.[3]
- *Expressivists* propose something quite different. They argue that we can accept Moore's negative argument while avoiding commitment to *sui generis* moral properties by arguing that ethical claims have a distinctive expressive role in our discourse, which obviates any need for a theory of the referents of moral terms.[4,5]

One traditional way to think about these divisions is in terms of each view's commitments in the theory of reality. In this regard, non-naturalism and naturalism are usually seen as forms of moral realism because they are committed to the reality of moral facts alongside other sorts of facts (physical, biological, economic, etc.). By contrast, fictionalism and expressivism are usually seen as forms of moral anti-realism because they seek to avoid commitment to the reality of moral properties and correlative facts. There may be ways of talking about ethics that seem to commit one ontologically, but, if expressivists and fictionalists engage in these, they'll insist on an account of them that evades commitment in the final ontological reckoning.

Another way to think about these divisions is in terms of each view's commitments in the theory of meaning. Here, non-naturalism, naturalism, and fictionalism are allied in a 'descriptivist' (or 'factualist') order of explanation for the meaning of ethical claims. The idea is basically that ethical claims mean what they do, ultimately, in virtue of how they describe the world as being. (Of course, non-naturalists and naturalists hold that some of these descriptions are literally correct, while fictionalists deny this, but the basic style of semantic explanation is the same.) By contrast, expressivists reject the descriptivism[6] implicit in the other theories, asserting instead that ethical claims mean what they do in virtue of their distinctive expressive role in our discourse.

This rejection of descriptivism purports to have two dialectical advantages. First, it lays the foundation for a novel account of the way ethical discourse seems distinctively connected to action. If ethical claims get their meaning in virtue of their distinctive expressive role, then, as long as what they express is connected to action in a special way, it's no surprise that ethical claims are distinctively connected to action. Second, it vindicates the expressivist's stance on the theory of reality without needing to treat ethical discourse as in any way fictional or second-rate. The idea is that, because ethical claims aren't in the business of describing the world, we have no theoretical need to account for the facts other theorists think they describe.

But what do expressivists mean by 'distinctive expressive role'? Or, more pertinently, what *could* they mean by this phrase, given that their view is intended as a view about the meaning of ethical claims that undercuts a core semantic assumption of the main competitors to expressivism, while fitting with a broader view of meaning in the philosophy of language?

Let's approach the second part of this question first by considering what seems to me to be a deep theoretical choice point in the philosophy of language. In a recent survey of general developments in the theory of meaning, Loar writes, 'Twentieth-century theory of meaning is divided into two: *truth* theories, and *use* theories'[7] (2006, p. 85). I take it his idea is that, while all philosophers of language will want to have an explanation of the relationships between meaning, truth-conditions, and rules of use, some theories of meaning afford explanatory priority to truth-conditions, while others afford explanatory priority to rules of use. In order to afford explanatory priority to truth-conditions, however, one must think that truth is more than merely a device of semantic ascent and generalization.[8] Thus, a 'truth theory' of meaning will assume a non-deflationary, indeed typically a realist, notion of truth.[9] And this, I think, makes it into what Fodor and Lepore refer to as the '"Old Testament" story, according to which the meaning of an expression supervenes on the expression's relation to things in the world' (1991, p. 329). The idea, at its core, is that meaning is a matter of word-world representational purport, which is why I will refer to it as a *representationalist* account of (what constitutes) meaning.

By contrast, use theories don't depend on any particular conception of truth, but they do need an account of how use and the correlated rules of use constitute meaning. And, typically, the idea is to start with the observation that meaning (linguistic meaning, anyway) is a conventional and thus rule-governed affair. Given rules of correct use, the use theorist claims that some of these rules – the *semantic* rules – are constitutive of an expression's meaning. So far this is purposefully vague, and I'll only call it *anti-representationalism* at this stage, because I want to distinguish between two versions of the idea below. But, if we are so inclusive, then I think anti-representationalism about meaning is what Fodor and Lepore refer to as the ' "New Testament" story, according to which the meaning of an expression supervenes on the expression's role in a language' (ibid.).

So, the choice I think we should press expressivists to make at this point is between representationalism and anti-representationalism as a general theory of meaning. For, if their account of the meaning of ethical claims is to fit with a broader theory of meaning in the philosophy of language, then they'll have to find a place on one or the other side of this divide. We've already seen that the expressivist's main competitors are allied in what I referred to as a descriptivist view of the meaning of ethical claims; and I think this fits pretty clearly with representationalism, as an application of a general theory to a specific case. The anti-expressivist idea (slightly recast) is that, just like non-ethical claims, ethical claims mean what they do in virtue of how they represent the world as being, that is, in virtue of their word-world representational purport.[10] And different anti-expressivist theories will differ based on what kinds of facts they think ethical claims purport to represent. Since expressivism begins with an attempt to undercut this idea, it may seem as if the expressivist must take the other side of the divide, that is, endorse an anti-representationalist account of meaning, in general.

Although I think all contemporary expressivists do endorse a form of anti-representationalism, it's not initially as straightforward as I've just made it sound. For there is a way to be a representationalist in the theory of meaning while nonetheless endorsing what is widely thought to be a form of expressivism. This is to say that meaning can, in general, be explained representationally, but to go on to insist that, strictly speaking, ethical expressions have no meaning. In fact, this seems to be very similar to Ayer's idea that the mixed ethical–non-ethical sentence 'Your stealing that money was wrong' has as its 'factual meaning' that you stole that money, and that the correlative ethical generalization 'Stealing money is wrong,' as he puts it, 'has no factual meaning – that is, expresses no proposition which can be either true or false' (1936/1946, p. 107). This view is consistent, of course, with thinking that ethical expressions have something broader than factual meaning: call it 'linguistic significance.' It's just that this sort of expressivist will stress the fact that linguistic significance outstrips what we're accounting for in a theory of meaning as word-world representational purport.

I think this version of expressivism is appropriately dubbed the 'boo-hooray theory' of the meaning of ethical expressions. For terms like 'boo' and 'hooray' arguably do not have meaning, when that is construed as word-world representational purport, though they clearly do have linguistic significance. So, if the expressivist thinks that ethical terms function roughly like those terms, he can continue to endorse a representationalist account of meaning, while disagreeing with non-naturalists, naturalists, and fictionalists that this general theory of meaning should be applied to ethical expressions. We might thus view the expressivist's position in the theory of meaning as a version of semantic representationalism (about the non-ethical) plus semantic nihilism (about the ethical).

The problems with this way of developing the expressivist idea have become glaringly obvious over the past fifty years of metaethical debate. In the following two paragraphs, I sketch what I take to be the core of the problem.

Because of the productivity and learnability of language, it's highly plausible that meaning is compositionally systematic, in the sense that, if two sentences have the same deep grammatical form, then the meaning of each sentence can be represented as a single function on the meaning of the correlative parts. We can make the point at the level of subsentential parts, such as predicates, which compose with things like terms, quantifiers, and other predicates to form whole sentences. But the same point applies at the level of logically simpler sentences, which compose with sentential connectives and operators to form logically more complex sentences. So, for example, the meaning of a sentence such as 'Grass is green' can be represented as a function SUBJPRED from the meanings of 'Grass' and 'is green.' Likewise, the meaning of a logically complex sentence 'If grass is green, then chlorophyll is green' can be represented as a function COND from the meaning of 'Grass is green' and 'Chlorophyll is green.'

The problem this generates is that, by the normal standards of syntacticians, each ethical claim seems to have the same deep grammatical form as some non-ethical claim. If that's right, it means that we should be able to represent the meaning of a sentence such as 'Tormenting is wrong' as the (exact same) function SUBJPRED from the meanings of 'Tormenting' and 'is wrong' as before. Likewise, we should be able to represent the meaning of a logically complex sentence such as 'If tormenting is wrong, then torturing is wrong' as the (exact same) function COND from the meanings of 'Tormenting is wrong' and 'Torturing is wrong'. However, the boo-hooray version of expressivism is incompatible with this idea, since it denies that predicates such as 'is wrong' and sentences such as 'Tormenting is wrong' have meaning. Because of this, the boo-hooray expressivist is committed to defending a highly implausible presupposition of his theory, that is, that the deep grammatical form of ethical sentences such as 'Tormenting is wrong' and 'If tormenting is wrong, then torturing is wrong' is radically different from the deep grammatical form of non-ethical sentences such as 'Grass is green' and 'If grass is green, then chlorophyll is green.'[11]

This is one way of viewing Geach's (1965) and Searle's (1962) point in arguing that (early) expressivists cannot make sense of the semantic similarity between a logically unembedded occurrence of an ethical sentence, such as 'Tormenting the cat is wrong,' and a logically embedded occurrence, such as 'If tormenting the cat is wrong, then getting your little brother to torment the cat is wrong.' The problem is not – as it has sometimes been supposed – that expressivists have nothing they can say about why endorsing these two sentences licenses endorsing the sentence 'Getting your little brother to torment is wrong.' Of course, they are theoretically prevented from saying that the meaning of the unembedded sentence and the antecedent of the conditional are both a function of their representational purport, but they can tell some other story linking the linguistic significance of the unembedded sentence to the linguistic significance of the conditionalized sentence. The problem, rather, is that a commitment to the compositional systematicity of meaning puts a very heavy explanatory burden on anyone who would explain the semantic relationship between these three sentences in any way different from the explanation of the semantic relationship between the non-ethical sentences 'Tormenting the cat is loud' and 'If tormenting the cat is loud, then getting your little brother to torment the cat is loud' and 'Getting your little brother to torment the cat is loud.' In short, the meaning of conditionalized sentences – whether ethical or non-ethical – needs to be represented as a *uniform* function of the meanings of their antecedents and consequents. That is encouraged by viewing meaning as compositionally systematic across deep grammatical similarity.[12]

Although I think this problem undermines expressivism, understood as committed to semantic representationalism plus nihilism, it's not clear whether it undermines expressivism *tout court*. For, given the broader distinction between representationalist and anti-representationalist accounts of meaning in the philosophy of language, it remains open for expressivists to reject representationalism, quite generally, and go in for some form of anti-representationalism. Recall that these theories are ones that start their explanation of meaning not from a notion of representational purport but from a notion of rule-governed linguistic role. So, the expressivist who wants to avoid the problems with the boo-hooray theory will need to appeal to an account of how rule-governed linguistic role constitutes meaning, which comports with the compositional systematicity of meaning.

Here, the strategy which motivates the name 'expressivism' is, I believe, to cash out the notion of linguistic role in terms of *expressing a mental state*. For example, Gibbard writes, '[W]hat "rational" means is explained by saying what it is to call something "rational", and to call something "rational", the analysis says, is to express a state of mind' (1990, p. 84). This approach to linguistic meaning is not a new one created for the purposes of salvaging metaethical expressivism. It draws inspiration from a general theory of meaning tracing back to Locke, who wrote 'Words in their primary or immediate Signification, stand for nothing, but the Ideas in the Mind of him that uses them' (1690/2008, chapter II). Grice (1957), Schiffer (1972) and Davis

(2003) have made this idea much more plausible by distinguishing between speaker-meaning and sentence-meaning, and then arguing that a sentence's meaning could be explained in terms of mentalistic notions such as belief and intention, linguistic regularities, and conventions created and eventually ossified by the speaker-meanings in a community of language users.

The general idea is to start with the observation that people outwardly express what's going on internally in all sorts of ways (e.g. wincing, smiling, winking, giving a thumbs-up, etc.), and this can be either intentional or unintentional. One more way people express what's going on internally is by using language with the intention of indicating what's going on internally. However, for this to work, there must be tractable regularities between the use of certain sign/sound-designs and certain mental states. Thus, over time, conventional rules develop, which govern the use of these sign/sound-designs. And in light of these conventional rules we can speak not just of the mental state token expressed by some person in doing something but also of the mental state type expressed by a particular sign/sound-design. If we allow the term 'idea' to refer to mentally instantiated concepts which can be expressed in language and the term 'thought' to refer to combinations of such concepts into judgments (the mental analogues of making a claim), the core thought here is to understand meaning as constituted by what we might call word-idea/thought (conventional) expressive function. And, as a version of anti-representationalism, this general program in theory of meaning is sometimes called *ideationalism*.

How does ideationalism fit with a commitment to the compositional systematicity of meaning? It was violating this plausible commitment in the theory of meaning that undermined the boo-hooray version of expressivism. But it looks as though ideationalists can do better, since, like the representationalists, they have a generic formula for specifying the meaning of any predicate and sentence. So, for example, while the representationalist can say that the meaning of the predicate 'is green' is its purporting to represent some property, in this case greenness, the ideationalist can say that this predicate's meaning is what concept conventionally expresses, that is, the concept of greenness. And, while the representationalist says that the meaning of the sentence 'Grass is green' is its purporting – via the systematic contribution (represented above by the function SUBJPRED) of the representational purport of its parts – to represent the fact that grass is green, the ideationalist can say that the meaning of the whole sentence is its conventionally expressing – via the systematic contribution (also representable as the function SUBJPRED) of the expressive function of its parts – the thought that grass is green. This is similarly the case with logically complex sentences such as 'If grass is green, then chlorophyll is green.' Here the representationalist says that the meaning is the sentence's purporting – via the systematic contribution (representable as the function COND) of the representational purport of its parts – to represent the fact that, if grass is green, then chlorophyll is green. And the ideationalist has a parallel story: this sentence's meaning is its conventionally expressing – via the systematic contribution (also representable as the function COND) of the expressive function of its parts – the thought that, if grass is green, then chlorophyll is green. And so on.[13]

So the general strategy available to the ideationalist for capturing the systematicity of the meaning of whole claims through an isomorphism with the structure of thoughts is much like the representationalist's strategy of appealing to an isomorphism with the structure of what is represented. Given that compositional systematicity is precisely the stumbling block for any form of expressivism that signs up to a representationalist plus nihilist account of the theory of meaning, ideationalism would seem to be a very good general theory of meaning for expressivists to opt for instead. If they do so, it seems that they can provide a uniform account of the meaning of ethical and non-ethical claims by saying that all claims mean what they do by virtue of the conventional word-idea expressive function of their parts and the systematic contribution of these parts to the conventional sentence-thought expressive function of whole sentences.

3. A problem

So far, I've argued that the most natural general account of meaning for an expressivist to endorse is an ideationalist account, which explains linguistic meaning in terms of word-idea expressive function. However, those who favor representationalism in the general theory of meaning are unlikely to see the ideationalist's switch from word-world representational purport to word-idea expressive function as making much progress in accounting for meaning. For, even if it's true that sentences mean what they do in virtue of the mental states they conventionally express, the representationalist will insist that this is true only because mental states have the content that they have in virtue of how they represent the world as being. That is, from the representationalist's point of view, ideationalism will not look like a free-standing account of meaning but only a 'dogleg' through ideas/thoughts (mentalistically construed) on the way to representations of the world. And, in so far as this is correct, the representationalist will insist that it's the notion of representational purport, rather than expressive function, that is doing the fundamental explanatory work. And, moreover, whatever explanation the ideationalist has of the systematic compositionality of meaning in terms of the compositional structure of the content of thoughts it's derivative of the representationalist's explanation in terms of the compositional structure of the facts represented.

An ideationalist might argue in response that words are mere scribbles or sounds until they are *imbued* with their representational purport. Then, the ideationalist could argue that what imbues some scribbles and sounds with representational purport is, quite generally, their incorporation in a human practice via the generation of expressive conventions linking scribbles and sounds to human ideas (i.e. parts of human thoughts). The idea is that scribbles and sounds that represent parts of the world do so only because they are linked via conventional rules to ideas and thoughts, which themselves represent parts of the world. More abstractly, the claim is that the notion of word-world representational purport could not even be attached to words without first appealing to the notion of word-idea expressive function. Hence, although the former notion can attach to words, the latter notion is more explanatorily fundamental. This, I take it, is what many ideationalists in the philosophy of language would say in response to the representationalist's criticism that their theory is a mere dogleg. And, moreover, it preserves the primacy of the structure of the content of thoughts in explaining the systematic compositionality of meaning.

However, it's unclear whether this line of response can work for the expressivist who wants to give an ideationalist explanation of the systematic compositionality of meaning while underwriting the view that ethical claims and non-ethical claims play a *distinctive* expressive role. More specifically, it seems that an expressivist who endorses ideationalism as a general theory of meaning will nonetheless have to hold that, while ethical and non-ethical claims both mean what they do in virtue of the thoughts they express, ethical thoughts do not have their contents in virtue of the representational purport attached to them via human expressive practices. Otherwise, the expressivist hasn't really denied the representationalism implicit in non-naturalism, naturalism, and fictionalism. To appreciate this, notice how these anti-expressivists can, as far as their debate with the expressivist goes, accept that ethical claims mean what they do in virtue of their distinctive expressive role. They'll say that ethical claims express ethical thoughts and non-ethical claims express non-ethical thoughts. However, that's not yet a metaethically interesting contrast. For, by the same token, physical claims express physical thoughts, biological claims express biological thoughts, economic claims express economic thoughts, etc.

Thus, expressivists need an expressive contrast drawn not in terms of the differing contents of the mental states expressed but in terms of the different kinds of mental states expressed. More specifically, it seems that expressivists need to cash out their core thesis that ethical claims mean what they mean in virtue of playing a distinctive expressive role by arguing that non-ethical claims express *beliefs*, while ethical claims express something like desires, intentions, or plans. This is a familiar distinction from Humean psychology of motivation, which is often characterized in terms of a difference in direction of fit.[14] Beliefs function like *maps* in that they are meant to fit the way the world is, while desires, intentions, and plans function more like *orders* in that they're meant to get the world to fit them. However, what this makes apparent, in light of our discussion of general theories of meaning, is that the expressivist cannot endorse a standard form of ideationalism that accepts a strict isomorphism between the semantic content of sentences and the mental content of the ideas they conventionally express. For, although he's happy to say that a non-ethical sentence, such as 'Tormenting is loud,' means what it does in virtue of expressing the *belief* that tormenting is loud, he must deny the structurally isomorphic explanation of the meaning of an ethical claim, such as 'Tormenting is wrong.' This, on his view, expresses a desire, intention, or plan.[15]

However, it should now be clear that this spells trouble for the sort of expressivist I've been discussing in this section. For the main advantage of adopting ideationalism in the theory of meaning rather than the representationalism plus nihilism adopted by early expressivists was that ideationalism can explain the semantic content of whole sentences as a systematic function of the semantic content of their parts and the ways that they combine. However, if the expressivist now says that ethical and non-ethical claims both mean what they do in virtue of expressing thoughts, but the relevant way in which these thoughts differ is not directly in their contents but in their nature as beliefs or desires/intentions/plans, this undermines the ideationalist's ability to explain the meaning of whole sentences as a *systematic* function of the meaning of their parts and the deep grammar of ways they are combined.

That's all a bit abstract. Perhaps an example will help to make the point more concrete. Recall the logically complex sentences:

> 'If grass is green, then chlorophyll is green'
> 'If tormenting is wrong, then torturing is wrong.'

If we accept the expressivist's idea that non-ethical thoughts are beliefs, which aim to fit the world, then the ideationalist account of the meaning of the first sentence amounts to the following. The logically simple sentence 'Grass is green' means what it does in virtue of expressing the belief that grass is green, whose content can be viewed as a systematic function (SUBJPRED) of the combination of the ideas of grass and greenness into a thought, and similarly with the logically simple sentence 'Chlorophyll is green.' Then, the conditionalized combination of these two sentences means what it does in virtue of expressing the conditionalized belief whose content can be viewed as a systematic function (COND) of the thoughts expressed by its parts, that is, the belief that, if grass is green, then chlorophyll is green. That's compositional systematicity of meaning at its finest.

What does the expressivist say about the meaning of the second conditionalized sentence? Well, compositional systematicity encourages us to break it into its logically simple parts as before: 'Tormenting is wrong' and 'Torturing is wrong.' However, according to the expressivist these are not the conventional expression of ethical beliefs (as the anti-expressivists say); rather, they're the expression of desires, intentions, or plans.[16] The problem is that, although desires, intentions, and plans may be thought to have contents, it's clear that their contents are not isomorphic to the sentences that express them. If 'Tormenting is wrong' expresses a desire, intention, or plan, then surely it's not the desire that tormenting is wrong, or the intention that tormenting is wrong, or the plan that tormenting is wrong. Rather, it's something like the desire that people not torment, or the intention to stop people from tormenting, or the plan not to torment.

That already means that the expressivist cannot give a standard ideationalist explanation of the meaning of logically simple sentences as a systematic function of their parts determined by their deep grammar. The needed isomorphism between the contents of thoughts and the contents of sentences must break down in the ethical case, for the expressivist. The situation just gets worse when we consider logically complex ethical sentences. What thought does the second conditionalized sentence blocked out above express, according to the expressivist? Even if we agree that it does express a desire, intention, or plan, it's clear that the content of this desire, intention, or plan is not isomorphic to the content of the conditionalized sentence. It's not obviously even intelligible to desire, intend, or plan that, if tormenting is wrong, then torturing is wrong.

One way out of this problem is suggested by Blackburn's (1998, pp. 71–4; 2002) talk of 'being tied to a tree.' His idea is that logically complex claims should be seen, quite generally, as committing one to a predictable pattern of beliefs and attitudes. This would be consistent with the ideationalist idea that all sentences mean what they do in virtue of thoughts they express only if it is interpreted as the view that all logically complex claims – both ethical and non-ethical – express a complex desire-like disposition, which, depending on their combination with different claims that one endorses, leads one to have further thoughts and endorse further claims that express them. For example, on this kind of view, a claim such as 'If Grass is green, then chlorophyll is green' would be said to express not the belief that if grass is green then chlorophyll is green but something like the desire, intention, or plan that (i) if one thinks that grass is green then one thinks that chlorophyll is green and (ii) if one thinks that chlorophyll is not green, then one does not think that grass is green.

The problem I see with this way of respecting the systematicity of meaning across similar logical contexts is that it misplaces the distinction between claims that describe the world and claims that don't describe but express desires, intentions, or plans. For, on it, *any* logically complex claim comes out as non-descriptive. For example, 'Grass is green' would be said to describe the world in virtue of expressing a belief, but 'It is not the case that grass is not green' would be said to express a desire, intention, or plan that is characterizable as 'being tied to a tree.' I don't know if that is how Blackburn intends his view to be interpreted (he speaks of 'commitments' that are specifiable in terms of what other mental states it 'makes sense' to hold in combination). However, I think this is the most natural way to interpret the idea within an ideationalist account of meaning. As we'll see below, there is an inferentialist tradition in the theory of meaning that may subvert the distinction between descriptive and non-descriptive sentences, and another way to interpret Blackburn's idea is in inferentialist terms,[17] but within an ideationalist version of expressivism I think it would be quite awkward if the only sentences thought to express beliefs and so to describe the world were atomic non-ethical sentences such as 'Grass is green.'

For these reasons, it seems to me that the only way an expressivist, who is committed to ideationalism as a general theory of meaning, can avoid this problem is to return to the core ideationalist idea that all claims express the same kind of mental state, whose differing contents explain differences in meaning. However, that is inconsistent with the expressivist's aspirations in metaethics to draw an ontologically and psychologically interesting contrast between ethical and non-ethical discourse in a plausible way.[18]

4. A different way

In Section 1 I suggested that two different forms of expressivism emerge when we query the view's underlying assumptions in the theory of meaning. Early versions of expressivism seem to be committed to semantic representationalism (about the non-ethical) plus semantic nihilism (about the ethical), whereas later versions of expressivism seem to be committed to a form of anti-representationalism called ideationalism. I've pointed to the problems almost everyone agrees undermine early versions of expressivism, and I've rehearsed a related problem for the later versions of expressivism. In this section I want to argue that this is not enough to strike anti-representationalist accounts of the meaning of ethical claims off the list of theoretical options in metaethics. And I want to do so by again focusing on foundational issues in the theory of meaning that I believe should underpin the metaethical debate about the meaning of ethical claims.

Ideationalism is not the only anti-representationalist theory of meaning one finds in the philosophy of language. Indeed, in their presentation of 'Old Testament' theories of meaning, which are founded on word-world relations, it's clear that Fodor and Lepore mean to contrast these not with ideationalist theories but with *inferentialist* or *conceptual-role* theories of meaning, which are founded instead on the inferential/conceptual connections between words.[19] These 'New Testament' theories are anti-representationalist in that their most basic explanation of what constitutes the meaning of words and sentences doesn't rest on word-world representation relations. But they're not ideationalist forms of anti-representationalism, since they also don't take word-idea/thought expressive function as the most basic. Rather they focus on the inferential (and perhaps more broadly conceptual) connections between words and (more importantly) between the sentences they can be used to compose.

I think such theories of meaning are very promising, but I won't argue in general for them here, as my purpose is not to defend a general theory of meaning but to point out its near absence[20] in the metaethical debate about the meaning of ethical claims and to argue that it has some advantages over expressivism. To this end, however, it is necessary to sketch enough of an inferentialist theory of meaning to contrast it with representationalist and ideationalist theories sketched above.

Recall that representationalists hold that a declarative sentence means what it does in virtue of what fact it can be used to represent, and ideationalists hold that a declarative sentence means what it does in virtue of what thought it can be used to express. Thus, for example, the sentence 'Grass is green' would be said, by the representationalist, to mean what it does in virtue of representing the fact that grass is green, and, by the ideationalist, to mean what it does in virtue of conventionally expressing the thought that grass is green. The inferentialist position, in contrast, can be put in terms of the notion of an inferentially articulable commitment. The idea is that a sentence means what it does in virtue of what commitment it can be used to undertake.

Such commitments are not conceived ontologically, that is, as commitments to the existence of some fact in the final ontological reckoning. This is what makes the view a form of anti-representationalism. But neither are they conceived psychologically, as some part of an agent's mind. This is what makes the view a form of anti-representationalism that is different from ideationalism. There may be connections to commitments conceived ontologically or psychologically, but, in the first instance, the commitments I have in mind are conceived in terms of the inferential entitlements and obligations that undertaking them carries.[21]

The idea is that one can gain entitlement to a commitment (e.g. to grass's being green) by undertaking another commitment (e.g. to grass's being full of chlorophyll and chlorophyll's being green); and one can be obligated by one commitment (e.g. to grass's being green) to undertake another commitment (e.g. to grass's being colored). The inferentialist contends that the meaning of a claim is constituted by its place in a network of these sorts of connections. Thus, in contrast to representationalism and ideationalism, inferentialism says that the claim 'Grass is green' means what it does in virtue of the fact that it can be used to undertake a commitment to grass's being green; and this commitment is constituted by the network of inferential entitlements and obligations that commitment carries.

It's important to appreciate that this style of semantic explanation offers a completely generic formula for explaining the meaning of a claim, which extends to any degree of logical complexity. So, for instance, the inferentialist will also say that the conditionalized sentence 'If grass is green, then chlorophyll is green' means what it does in virtue of the inferentially articulable commitment it can be used to undertake. In this case, it's a commitment to chlorophyll's being green in case grass is green. But if the sentence were instead 'If grass is red, then chlorophyll is purple,' we'd get the structurally isomorphic result: it means what it does in virtue of being usable to undertake a commitment to chlorophyll's being purple in case grass is red. The general theory, then, is that a claim means what it does in virtue of the inferentially articulable commitment it can be used to undertake.

I want to flag and try to put aside two questions about this general theory of meaning before exploring the different path I think it offers in the metaethical debates about the meaning of ethical claims.

First, a representationalist might wonder: isn't the commitment to something's being a certain way best understood in representationalist terms? This question points to a vexed issue about the notions of being, fact, and representation that I won't delve into deeply here. But I do want to recognize that one way to understand the notion of a commitment to something being a certain way (e.g. a commitment to grass being green) is in terms of the notion of representing the world as containing the fact that this thing is that way (e.g. the fact that grass is green). However, either this is a trivial and ontologically neutral reformulation, or it gets one very deep into questionable ontological commitments. For instance, most philosophers are committed to its being impossible that $1 + 1 = 3$ and to its being unlikely that the sun will rise an hour later tomorrow. However, in so far as ontology goes, it's up for debate whether these commitments entail commitment to the world containing the fact that $1 + 1 = 3$ is impossible and the fact that it is unlikely that the sun will rise an hour later tomorrow. For commitment to something being impossible might plausibly be thought to be about not merely what's a fact in this world but what could and couldn't be a fact, as we sometimes say, in other unreal but possible worlds. And commitment to something being unlikely might plausibly be thought to be not about what will in fact happen but about the strength of someone's evidence for thinking that something will happen. There are, of course, realist views of impossibility and improbability, but they raise naturalist qualms even more than realist views about what's ethically right and wrong. So, I think there is considerable theoretical room to resist the idea that commitment to something being a certain way is best thought of as an ontological commitment in implicitly representationalist terms.

Second, someone impressed with truth-conditional theories of the compositional systematicity of meaning might ask: what does the inferentialist say about the meaning of subsentential parts of sentences? In the case of representationalism and ideationalism, a 'bottom-up' explanation of meaning seems to be in the offing. For example, the representationalist could say that a predicate means what it does in virtue of the property, the having of which would make the predicate true of something. And the ideationalist could say that a predicate means what it does in virtue of the concept, the falling under which would make the predicate true of something. Then facts can be viewed as built (at least partially) out of properties, while thoughts can be viewed as built (at least partially) out of concepts. Again, there are vexed issues here that I will not delve into deeply. However, I think it's important to appreciate that, although the inferentialist's explanation of meaning starts at the level of full claims, which are the proper relata of inferential/conceptual relations, this doesn't preclude a 'top-down' explanation of the meaning of subsentential parts of sentences. For example, the account could represent the meaning of predicates as sets of inferentially articulated commitments. The meaning of 'is green', for instance, could be seen as the set of inferentially articulable commitments one gets by substituting into 'x is green.' This is by no means the end of the story, but it should be clear enough that, by generalizing across claims with equivalent subsentential parts, we can represent the meaning of these subsentential parts by a process of top-down abstraction.[22]

Having flagged and put aside those two difficult questions, I now want to consider how the inferentialist theory of meaning applies to the metaethically interesting case of ethical claims. The discussion above suggests that an inferentialist will say that a sentence such as 'Tormenting is wrong' means what it does in virtue of the fact that it can be used to undertake an inferentially articulable commitment to tormenting being wrong. What it means for this commitment to be inferentially articulable is the same as before. It carries with it a network of entitlements and obligations to other commitments. So, it's ultimately the network of these inferential relations that constitutes the claim's meaning.

This style of explanation extends to logically complex ethical sentences in the expected way. So, for instance, the claim 'If tormenting is wrong, then torturing is wrong' means what it does in virtue of the inferentially articulable commitment it can be used to undertake. In this case, the commitment will be a commitment structurally isomorphic to the commitments undertaken with the conditional claims above: 'If grass is green, then chlorophyll is green' and 'If grass is red, then chlorophyll is purple.' That is, it's the commitment to torture being wrong in case tormenting is wrong.

So far, it seems that representationalism, ideationalism, and inferentialism – considered as general theories of meaning – have importantly different but parallel formulas for explaining the meaning of claims in a way that respects the compositional systematicity of meaning. They're explained in terms of the fact represented, the thought expressed, or the commitment undertaken. And, as long as there is a systematic function between the deep grammar of the claim and the structure of the fact, thought, or commitment, the explanation can respect the compositional systematicity of meaning on which early expressivists floundered.

Above, however, I argued that more recent expressivists, who assume an ideationalist order of semantic explanation, flounder in a more subtle way on the compositional systematicity of meaning. This is because their metaethical convictions force them to violate the systematic connection between the deep grammar of some claims and the structure of the thought they express. In order to fund the purported difference in expressive role between ethical and non-ethical claims, contemporary expressivists have to tell a different story about ethical claims and their logical parts from the standard story about non-ethical claims and their logical parts. For, in order to challenge the semantic assumption underlying non-naturalism, naturalism, and fictionalism, they have to defend an anti-representationalist account of the meaning of ethical claims. But, in order to do this, they draw a distinction between thoughts that are like maps in representing the world and thoughts that are like commands in guiding one through the world, which in turn leads to the idea that the thoughts expressed by ethical claims are not beliefs but, rather, something like desires, intentions, or plans. But it turned out to be implausible to think that the content of desires, intentions, or plans bears the same systematic structural relation to the deep grammar of the sentences that express them as the content of beliefs. Would similar metaethical convictions force an inferentialist to make a similarly problematic move?

I don't think so. If we conceive of the commitments that constitute a claim's meaning not in ontological or psychological terms but in inferential terms, then we already have a general theory of meaning that challenges the semantic assumption underlying non-naturalism, naturalism, and fictionalism. It seems that this cannot be undermined by an analogue of the dogleg argument against ideationalism sketched above. For inferentially articulable commitments do not have the content they do in virtue of the facts they represent the world as having. Rather, it's precisely the point of calling them 'inferentially articulable' that their content is articulated in terms of inferential/conceptual connections to other claims and not in terms of their representational connection to facts putatively in the world.

So far as that goes, however, inferentialism may seem to undermine the contrast between ethical and non-ethical claims that was supposed to carry two dialectical advantages for anti-representationalist metaethical views such as expressivism over representationalist views such as non-naturalism, naturalism, and fictionalism. In my view, that's only partially right, which we can appreciate by reconsidering these putative dialectical advantages from the point of view of inferentialism.

The first putative dialectical advantage mentioned above was that the expressivist's way of being an anti-representationalist provides the basis for a novel and compelling explanation of the distinctive connection between ethical discourse and action. So stated, this is ambiguous between the idea that ethical claims seem to be distinctively connected to their authors' being motivated to act in certain ways, and the idea that ethical claims seem to be distinctively connected to the justification or legitimization of certain actions from their authors' point of view. I think that both of these ideas can, when properly understood, be better captured by the inferentialist than by the expressivist.

Early expressivists were sometimes animated by the thought that one who sincerely makes an ethical claim will be at least somewhat motivated to act in its accord. However, this form of judgment-internalism is clearly too strong. Often ethical claims are not about anything that their author expects to have a bearing on how he or she acts (e.g. claims about the rights and wrongs of international policy or about what some historical figure did), or they are about *pro tanto* considerations that their author considers outweighed (e.g. about what would most please one's mother), or they are abstract enough to leave one cold (e.g. that one ought to act in such a way that one could will one's maxim as universal law), or they simply do leave one cold because of akrasia or some other disconnect between conviction and motivation. So, whatever form of judgment-internalism is true, it must be weak enough to allow motivations and sincere ethical claim-making to diverge. But, if that is the case, then I think the inferentialist can say two plausible things about judgment-internalism. First, perhaps sincere ethical claim-making is indeed better correlated with having the sorts of desires, intentions, and plans that explain motivation, but the exceptions to this psychological correlation indicate that it shouldn't dictate our explanation of the meaning of the relevant claims. We can recognize that certain sorts of ethical claims conventionally express desires, intentions, and/or plans without holding that they mean what they do in virtue of expressing these things. Second, if ethical commitments are inferentially connected to the core concepts deployed in practical reasoning in a way that doesn't hold for all other commitments – as I will suggest below – then it wouldn't be surprising if agents generally, though defeasibly, acquired motivation to act in ways justified by (at least some of) their ethical commitments. Perhaps the reason we expect one who claims that giving to charity is morally required to be motivated to give to charity is that this claim expresses a commitment that inferentially supports the practical commitment to give to charity; and we generally expect people to be defeasibly motivated to do what they're committed to in virtue of the commitments undertaken by their claims.

The other way to disambiguate the idea of a distinctive connection between ethical discourse and action is about justification or legitimization of action rather than directly about motivation. I think this idea is even more easily captured by the inferentialist than by the expressivist. To see this, notice that the expressivist has to say that it's something about the desire, intention, or plan expressed by ethical claims that explains why related actions are justified or legitimate, from the agent's point of view. Whether one finds that compelling will depend on whether one thinks desires, intentions, and plans can play this justifying or legitimating role. Perhaps they can, but, depending on how passively acquired such states are, one might also reasonably worry that they can't play that justificatory role until the agent endorses them. In contrast, the inferentialist can build the notion of a justifying or legitimating connection into his account of the meaning of ethical claims. The details can be worked out differently for different ethical claims depending on how tight one thinks the connection is. But, as an example, consider a claim of the following form: 'I ought, all things considered, to ɸ.' It would not be implausible to think that part of the inferential articulation of the commitment undertaken by this claim construes it as obligating its author to a further directly practical claim that we might express as 'I shall ɸ when the appropriate time comes.' And we could then capture the apparent contrast with non-ethical claims by pointing out that they do not carry similar inferential connections to the core 'I shall' type claims involved in practical reasoning.

So, I think the inferentialist can actually do better than the expressivist in capturing the apparently distinctive practicality of ethical discourse in comparison to non-ethical discourse. If right, this means that the first dialectical advantage claimed for expressivism over non-naturalism, naturalism, and fictionalism actually counts more in favor of inferentialism than expressivism. But what about the second dialectical advantage? This had to do with the expressivist's stance in the theory of reality towards ostensible ethical properties and facts. By adopting expressivism, one is able to maintain a kind of naturalist-inspired anti-realism about the ethical, which obviates the need for certain controversial sorts of explanations crucial to non-naturalism, naturalism, and fictionalism. Can an inferentialist claim the same advantage?

In one sense, the answer is clearly 'yes,' since inferentialism – at least as far as it's been sketched here – is a thoroughgoing anti-representationalist theory. Unlike the ideationalist, who says that claims mean what they do in in virtue of the thoughts they express but then goes on to grant that some thoughts (i.e. beliefs) have the content they have in virtue of how they represent the world as being, the inferentialist doesn't have to appeal to the notion of representing the world as being a certain way even as a secondary explanatory notion in his theory. This means that there is a way to be an inferentialist that generalizes the expressivist's naturalist-inspired anti-realist stance towards the ethical into a general anti-realist stance across the board.

However, I suspect that many metaethicists would view that way of validating a naturalism-inspired anti-realist stance towards the ethical as subverting the relevant debate in the theory of reality rather than capturing the anti-realist motivation for expressivism. That is to say that, if the reason ethical claims don't commit us ontologically to ethical facts is that no claims ever commit us ontologically, then the issue of ontological commitment and naturalism-inspired anti-realism is spurious.

Even if it is spurious, that still leaves inferentialism looking better than expressivism with respect to issues about the compositional systematicity of meaning and the apparently distinctive practicality of ethical discourse. And it would appear better than naturalism, non-naturalism, and fictionalism, in so far as they make supposedly spurious ontological claims. However,

I think a more subtle form of inferentialism wouldn't spurn the ontological debate, but would rather seek to reconstruct it in directly inferentialist terms. In characterizing inferentially articulable commitments above, I said that they are not conceived *in the first instance* as ontological commitments. That is to say, they are not constituted by which facts they commit one admitting into one's ontology. On this way of thinking of things, one can be committed to the impossibility that $1 + 1 = 3$, the unlikelihood that the sun will rise an hour late tomorrow, and the wrongness of torture, without being committed *ontologically* to the existence of some piece of reality that corresponds to these commitments. However, that doesn't rule out the possibility that something else would commit one ontologically, and that something else could make a difference between the types of commitments just canvassed and commitments to things like grass being green and grass being full of chlorophyll, about which we may want to be more realist.

The question of what else could commit one ontologically is a difficult question in meta-ontology, and there are vexing related issues about how best to understand the notions of nature, observation, and explanation. I won't be able to address these issues here, but I do want to explain how a historically prominent idea might serve as a placeholder for a more fully worked-out account.

What I have in mind is the idea that ontological commitment tracks with commitment, not to something being true, but to something being part of the best natural explanation of what we can observe. The rough idea is that our theory of reality is an implicit and incomplete attempt to explain our actual and potential observations of the world. If that's right, and an inferentialist wants to be a realist about a claim such as 'Grass is full of chlorophyll,' then she can say that this claim is implicitly explanatory. That is to say that part of what it obligates one to, inferentially, is a certain explanatory claim – that is, that grass's being full of chlorophyll explains why we can observe certain things about grass. What's important is that there's theoretical space to go in the other direction as well. If an inferentialist wants to be an anti-realist about a claim such as 'It's unlikely that the sun will rise an hour late tomorrow,' then she can say that this claim is not similarly explanatory in its inferential implications. Perhaps it doesn't commit its author ontologically to facts about what has the property of being unlikely, but rather commits its author practically to treating certain future contingents as settled.

Whichever way this contrast is refined, I think we can begin to see theoretical space for the inferentialist to reconstruct the realism/anti-realism debate in metaethics in directly inferentialist terms. If an inferentialist wants to be an ethical realist, then he'll argue that the commitments undertaken when one makes an ethical claim are implicitly explanatory. That is, his account of the inferential implications of this claim will be similar to the one just sketched for the claim 'Grass is full of chlorophyll.' However, if an inferentialist wants instead to be an ethical anti-realist, then he'll have to argue that the commitments undertaken when one makes an ethical claim are not implicitly explanatory in this way. That is, his account of the inferential implications of this claim will be similar to the one just sketched for the claim 'It's unlikely that the sun will rise an hour late tomorrow.'

I think something like this provides a more nuanced version of inferentialism that is able to capture not only the idea that there is a distinctive connection between ethical discourse and action, but also the prospects of a naturalism-inspired form of anti-realism about the ethical. Since these were the two dialectical advantages expressivists claim over traditional anti-expressivists, and since expressivism faces a problem with the systematicity of its form of semantic explanation that is not faced by the inferentialist, I think this means that inferentialism has better prospects than expressivism as an anti-representationalist theory in metaethics.

5. Conclusion

The guiding thought of this paper is that one's metaethical account of the meaning of ethical sentences should fit with one's account of the meaning of sentences in general. In metaethics, one finds non-naturalist, naturalist, fictionalist, and expressivist accounts of the meaning of ethical claims. And, in the theory of meaning, one finds representationalist theories, which take word-world representational purport as their fundamental explanatory notion, ideationalist theories, which take word-idea expressive function as their fundamental explanatory notion, and inferentialist theories, which take claim-claim inferential connections as their fundamental explanatory notion. So, my guiding thought led me to ask how those more specific metaethical theories fit with these more general theories of meaning. In the case of non-naturalism, naturalism, and fictionalism, the answer is relatively straightforward: they are implicitly forms of representationalism (perhaps allowing for the possibility of a 'dogleg' through mentalistic notions). However, in the case of expressivism, the answer was not so straightforward. The crux of this paper has been searching for this answer, articulating problems with it, and using those problems to motivate a kind of metaethical theory that is not on the standard maps of theoretical options in metaethics. This is the theory that fits with or is an application of a more general inferentialist theory of meaning.

I don't take myself to have defended or even articulated this theory fully. My aim here was more modest. I want inferentialism to be considered one of the viable theoretical options in metaethical debates about the meaning of ethical claims. To this end, I've tried to place it as a form of anti-representationalism that differs from expressivism in important respects. First, by appealing to the notion of *an inferentially articulable commitment undertaken* rather than to *a thought conventionally expressed* by a claim, I think inferentialism has resources to respect the compositional systematicity of meaning, which both early and later versions of expressivism lacked. Second, I think inferentialism retains old resources and brings new resources to explaining the distinctive connection between ethical discourse and action. Third, there is room in the inferentialist theory to reconstruct the realism/anti-realism distinction in a way that doesn't depend on different directions of fit with the world that different types of mental states (beliefs or desires) might be thought to have.

That being said, however, I'd like to close by voicing a worry about inferentialism in metaethics. Even if the sort of account I've pointed to does to some extent work to explain the meaning of ethical claims, one might think that it does so by merely pushing the metaethical question back a level. Inferentialism explains the meaning of ethical claims in terms of the inferentially articulable commitment they can be used to undertake, but what is its account of the meaning of claims about the entitlements and obligations involved in a commitment's inferential articulation? For instance, the claim 'One who is committed to grass's being green is committed to grass's being colored' is not an ethical claim, but it seems to be a normative claim. Doesn't it raise all of the same metaethical issues as ethical claims? It does, but I think it's already some advance if we're able to locate the metaethical issue about meaning and normative character of ethical claims within a broader meta-normative issue about normative claims more generally. However, I think there is also a deep and difficult question about the genesis and nature of these norms. Here, I think more work needs to be done to determine to what extent the metaethical debate will simply be re-engaged at a more fundamental level, or to what extent pursuing it at that level affects the relative attractiveness of the various theoretical options.[23]

Notes

1. Cf. Shafer-Landau (2003, ch. 3), Parfit (forthcoming: ch. 24). Distinguishing what is non-natural from what is natural is notoriously difficult, especially since non-naturalism is usually thought to involve the denial that moral properties are supernatural as well as the denial that they are natural. See Ridge (2008) and Sturgeon (2009) for useful discussion. Another way, then, to organize theories into the first two camps would be to distinguish between *reductionists* who see moral properties as reducing to some other sort of property, and *anti-reductionists* who deny this. The differences between these ways of organizing the kinds of metaethical views are not important for my present purposes, which are more focused on the semantic assumptions of these theories.
2. Boyd (1988), Sturgeon (1985; 2003), Brink (1986; 1989), Railton (1989), Smith (1994a, ch. 5–6).
3. Mackie (1977, ch. 1) defends a form of Error-Theory, which is the progenitor to modern fictionalism. Cf. Joyce (2001), Kalderon (2005).
4. Blackburn (1984; 1992; 1998), Gibbard (1990; 2003), Timmons (1999), Ridge (2006).

5. A view that does not show up explicitly on my list is the sort of metaethical constructivism defended by Korsgaard (2003) and Street (2008). I remain unsure of its distinctiveness, but I also don't know where to slot it in. See Fitzpatrick (2005) and Hussain and Shah (2006) for useful discussion of constructivism. Response-dependent views such as McDowell (1985) are also hard to place, but that is because it's hard to know whether or not the facts about response dependence to which he appeals are to be thought of as natural facts. In any case, the location of views such as Korsgaard's and McDowell's won't matter for the critical discussion of expressivism to follow.

6. This is consistent with a later attempt to reclaim whatever talk of description is part of ordinary ethical discourse, as the quasi-realist does (Blackburn, 1993; 1998; Gibbard, 2003). It's just that, at the more basic theoretical level, the expressivist doesn't think the idiom of description can serve in the best account of the meaning of ethical claims.

7. He is perhaps omitting the verificationist theories that were prominent at the beginning of the twentieth century, but I think he is right that *contemporary* philosophers of language are often divided into these two broad camps.

8. Admittedly, spelling out the notion of explanatory priority here is not straightforward. For all theorists of meaning will want to recognize that meaning is conventional, in the sense that it's only because of regularities of use that some arbitrary sign/sound-designs have meaning while others don't. However, the truth-theorist sees that as pragmatic background and takes the notion of a truth-condition to be semantically more basic than the notion of a rule of correct use, whereas a use-theorist thinks that we can explain why sentences have the truth-conditions that they have only via semantic rules of use.

9. It would, of course, be possible instead to endorse a non-realist but non-deflationary conception of truth, such as pragmatism or coherentism about truth. However, as theories of truth, these are quite implausible, although pragmatist and coherentist ideas have found their way into general philosophical views naturally allied with deflationist or minimalist accounts of truth. See Wright (1992), Rorty (1995) for relevant discussion.

10. This may involve, as a corollary, a connection to mental states. More specifically, the anti-expressivists mentioned above may want to say that ethical claims serve to express beliefs – but they'll want to understand the contents of these beliefs in representationalist terms. I return to this issue in Section 2.

11. Schroeder (2008, ch. 2) and Blome-Tillmann (2009) make similar points.

12. Schroeder (2008, ch. 3–5) makes a similar point.

13. Compare Schroeder (2008, ch. 4–5). The representationalist's and ideationalist's functions COND and SUBJPRED are not strictly identical but isomorphic. The important point is that, whatever one's favored order of semantic explanation, there's a uniform semantic function between parts and wholes for sentences with the same deep grammatical form.

14. See, especially, Smith (1994a, ch. 4) and citations therein.

15. Some expressivists may be happy with the ordinary practice of calling these states 'beliefs,' but they'll have to insist that their underlying nature is different from descriptive beliefs. See Gibbard (2003, pp. 181–3), Ridge (2009).

16. Again, at one level, the expressivist may insist that there is no problem in calling these 'beliefs,' of a sort. But, in order to maintain his distinctive position in metaethics, he'll have to argue that, at a deeper explanatory level, they're not on a par with descriptive beliefs but more like desires, intentions or plans.

17. See Blackburn (2006, p. 247) where he seems to interpret himself in these terms.
18. There may be *implausible* ways to draw the contrast that are inconsistent with ideationalism. One of these would be to extend recent hybrid views of ethical claims (e.g. Ridge, 2006) to claim that *all* claims express a hybrid belief–desire state. Another comes from Schroeder (2008, ch. 4–9) who argues that the best way for an expressivist to respect the compositional systematicity of meaning is to treat all claims as expressing a state he calls *being for*, which one can take towards different contents. However, Ridge agrees that it would be problematic if we had to say that a descriptive claim such as 'Grass is green' means what it does in virtue of expressing a hybrid belief–desire state (personal communication); and the remainder of Schroeder's book involves drawing out many implausible consequences for the view that all claims express states of being for.
19. See, for instance, Sellars (1969; 1974), Rosenberg (1974), Harman (1982), Block (1987; 1993), Brandom (1994; 2000; 2008).
20. Wedgwood (2001; 2007, ch. 4–5) has championed a conceptual-role account of the meaning of ethical terms. This bears some resemblance to the sort of inferentialism I will go on to sketch, except in the important respect that Wedgwood sees his theory as resolutely realist and so it is in a sense deeply representationalist. As mentioned above, Blackburn (2006) now interprets his own previous views in inferentialist terms.
21. This is consistent, I believe, with the thought that one hasn't *fully* accounted for meaning until one has explained the conventional expression relations that stand between public language and private thoughts and the representation relations that stand between language/thought and the world. It's just that the inferentialist thinks that inferential-role is most fundamental for understanding semantic content, which means that, in so far as these other notions are relevant to meaning, they must be conceived ultimately in inferential terms rather than vice versa.
22. See Brandom (2008, ch. 5) for discussion of the top-down strategy for capturing compositional systematicity in an inferentialist framework.
23. I'd like to thank Michael Ridge and the audiences at the University of Glasgow and the University of Sydney for helpful feedback on material for this paper.

6
How Not to Avoid Wishful Thinking

Mark Schroeder

In 2002, Cian Dorr offered a new challenge to metaethical non-cognitivism: the wishful thinking problem. Based on considerations from epistemology, it is quite distinct from the usual problems associated with the title 'Frege–Geach' which assail non-cognitivists in the philosophy of language, and, in contrast to the Frege-Geach Problem, it poses a challenge for non-cognitivist views in *ethics* which does not arise for similar views about, for example, probability judgments, epistemic modals, or conditionals. But, after an immediate round of attempted solutions from sympathists (James Lenman) and critics (David Enoch) of non-cognitivism alike, the ripples in the pond have somewhat quieted.

The aim of this paper is to critically assess the state of play with respect to the wishful thinking problem by putting Enoch's and Lenman's attempted solutions into context with one another, and placing them in a space of possible solutions. The morals are (1) that Enoch's solution is very unpromising, (2) that Lenman's solution takes on very strong commitments that from many points of view are problematic in themselves, and (3) that doing better than Lenman's solution may require non-cognitivists to develop better tools – in particular, acquiring a better understanding of how to think about concepts such as evidence and justification within a non-cognitivist framework.

1. The target: non-cognitivism

We may start by getting straight on a little bit of terminology. Dorr uses the term 'non-cognitivism' specifically for the class of views shared paradigmatically by Simon Blackburn (1984; 1993; 1998) and Allan Gibbard (1990; 2003), which might more properly be called 'non-cognitivist expressivism.' As a historical matter, the term 'non-cognitivism' began life as a name for metaethical theories according to which moral sentences lack truth values, and was used to describe theories such as those of Ayer (1936), Carnap (1935), Stevenson (1937), and Hare (1952). But, by the early 1990s, work by Simon Blackburn in particular made it clear that there could be a view that in many ways resembled these earlier 'non-cognitivist' theories, but held that moral sentences *do* have truth-values.

Rather than abandoning the label 'non-cognitivism,' Michael Smith (1994a, b) and others showed how it could be reclaimed as a name for views like Blackburn's, by being reinterpreted to mean that moral judgments are not beliefs, but, rather, are desire-like attitudes. The meaning of 'non-cognitivism' thus became tied to a view shared by Blackburn and Gibbard, but which was not part of the picture of Ayer, Carnap, Stevenson, or Hare, whose views were formulated primarily about language, rather than about thought. It turns out that we can raise variants of the wishful thinking problem for many of these other views, but I'll follow Dorr in this article in restricting attention to contemporary versions of non-cognitivist expressivism (henceforth, following Dorr, 'non-cognitivism'), emphasizing that it is important to appreciate the differences from these earlier views and to consider separate cases separately.

In any case, we may understand contemporary non-cognitivist expressivism, for purposes of the wishful thinking problem, as primarily a thesis about moral thoughts: that for any moral sentence, 'P', to think that P is to be in a desire-like state of mind. This state of mind may be an 'attitude' (Blackburn, 1998) or a state of 'norm-acceptance' (Gibbard, 1990) or a 'planning state' (Gibbard, 2003) or an 'ought-belief' (Horgan and Timmons, 2006a) or a 'preference' (Dreier, 2006) or a state of 'being for' (Schroeder, 2008); the important thing is that this state *is* not and moreover *does not involve* any ordinary belief about an ordinary matter of fact. This characterization is important; as Michael Ridge (2007) has rightly emphasized, any 'hybrid' theory that maintains that, where 'P' is a moral sentence, to think that P is to be in a complex state of mind which involves both a desire-like attitude and an ordinary belief about an ordinary matter of fact has the resources to escape the wishful thinking problem. The problem is thus directed solely at 'pure' non-cognitivist theories.

2. The wishful thinking problem

The idea behind the wishful thinking problem is that, intuitively, we ordinarily think that forming beliefs about what the world is like only on the basis of your desires about how you would like things to be is a kind of irrationality – it is 'wishful thinking.' But, if expressivism is right, then it should sometimes be rational to form beliefs about what the world is like, on the basis, essentially, of desires. You do this whenever you accept the conclusion of a *moral-descriptive modus ponens* argument on the basis of accepting its premises.

For example, consider the following moral-descriptive *modus ponens* argument, borrowed from Dorr's original article:

P1 If lying is wrong, the souls of liars will be punished in the afterlife.

P2 Lying is wrong.
C The souls of liars will be punished in the afterlife.

It is intuitively possible for someone (let's follow Dorr in calling him 'Edgar') to rationally come to accept the conclusion of this argument, for the very first time, on the basis of reasoning from these premises. For example, Edgar might start by accepting P1 and at the time have no other evidence for C, and then later come to accept P2 – at which point he may rationally go on to infer C on the basis of this argument.

All of this is very intuitive. But it presents expressivists with a dilemma. Either all of this is right, and Edgar really *can* rationally come to accept C on the basis of P2, having started out only by accepting P1, or it is not right, and Edgar cannot rationally come to accept C on this basis. If it is *not* right, then that is its own problem, because, on the face of it, this is a completely rational inference. So, on the first fork of the dilemma, the expressivist fails to explain the rationality of what is intuitively a perfectly rational inference. But if it *is* right, then, by expressivism's lights, it is rational for Edgar to form an ordinary descriptive belief about the world (after all, to accept C is to have an ordinary descriptive belief about what will happen to the souls of liars in the afterlife) on the basis of a desire-like attitude (after all, according to expressivists, to accept P2 is simply to have a desire-like attitude). But in that case it looks like wishful thinking. So, on the second horn of the dilemma, the expressivist is committed to allowing that wishful thinking is sometimes rational.[1]

As noted earlier, the problem as stated is a problem specifically for non-cognitivist expressivism, rather than for earlier related views, such as those of Ayer, Carnap, Stevenson, or Hare. It is contemporary non-cognitivist expressivists who think that coming to accept P2 involves coming to want something – to have a certain desire-like attitude. And the charge, on the second fork of the dilemma, is that it is *wishful thinking* to come to accept a conclusion about the world on the basis of a change in what you want. So the charge is one that applies specifically to these contemporary views.

But there *is* a related problem for these other related views. Suppose, for example, that coming to accept P2 is a matter of issuing a special sort of command or prescription, or of trying to create a special sort of influence, as other kinds of views hold. Now, someone who changes her mind about what the world is like only in order better to fit with the commands she is issuing, or only in order better to fit with the influence that she is trying to create, is not engaged in something that we would ordinarily call 'wishful thinking,' precisely. But it does not appear to be any more rational of her to do so. Moreover, *any* view on which coming to accept P2 is different from coming to have any new belief or other cognitive state would appear to have this same general property – how could that make it rational to draw a conclusion about how things are? So it seems that the wishful thinking problem generalizes to a problem for a family of related views. Nevertheless, I will continue to set these other views aside, just to fix the issues.

3. The shape of the problem

It is important to appreciate the difference between the wishful thinking problem, which invites expressivists to explain the rationality of inferring C on the basis of P1 and P2, and the problem of explaining the *inference-licensing property* of valid arguments.[2] An argument has the inference-licensing property just in case someone who accepts its premises is rationally *committed* to going on to accept its conclusion. Famously, it doesn't follow from this that it is actually rational for him to go on and accept the conclusion; it could be that the only rational course would be for him to stop accepting one of the premises. For example, if Edgar has much better evidence against C than he has for P1 or P2, then the rational thing is not to accept C, but to give up on P1 or P2. Or, alternatively, if the only reason Edgar accepts P1 is that he is confident that P2 is false (compare: 'if the moon is made of green cheese, then I'm a billy goat'), the rational response to coming to accept P2 is to stop accepting P1 – not to accept C, even in the absence of other evidence against C.

So the inference-licensing property applies to *every* case of a *modus ponens* argument – *whenever* you accept the premises, you are rationally committed to accepting the conclusion. But only in some cases is it rational for you to discharge this commitment by going on to accept the conclusion. In other cases, the only rational way of dealing with the commitment is to give up on one of the premises.

It has been a part of the traditional Frege–Geach Problem to explain the inference-licensing property, which applies to each and every case, because one of the desiderata of the Frege–Geach Problem is to explain the *validity* of moral arguments, and non-cognitivists have proposed to turn the usual order of explanation on its head, and to explain validity in terms of the inference-licensing property, rather than following the usual strategy of expecting the inference-licensing property to be explained by validity. But the wishful thinking problem concerns only the rationality of actually going on to accept the conclusion, which applies only in some cases. So the wishful thinking problem is not a problem about logic or about validity; it is a problem in epistemology – about justification.

Another way of seeing that the wishful thinking problem is distinct from the Frege–Geach Problem – a point that Dorr himself highlights – is that the Frege–Geach Problem arises in full force for expressivist theories in any domain – including theories about probability judgments, epistemic modals, or indicative conditionals. For example, an expressivist about probability judgments might hold that to think that the probability of P is 60 per cent is to have a credence of 60 per cent in P, an expressivist about epistemic modals might hold that to think that Jack might be in Seattle is to have a positive credence that Jack is in Seattle, and an expressivist about indicative conditionals might hold that to have a confidence of n that, if you ask, she'll say 'yes,' is to have a conditional credence of n in the proposition that she'll say 'yes,' conditional on the proposition that you ask.

All of these theories face the traditional Frege–Geach Problem, and need to explain how the sentences of which they seek to provide a special account can combine in complex sentences with the right semantic properties – including validating the right arguments. The Frege–Geach Problem is a *general* problem for expressivist theories. But none of these theories face the wishful thinking problem or any analogue of it, for there is nothing problematic about the idea that a subject could come to be justified in forming an ordinary descriptive belief about a matter of fact, on the basis of having a credence of 60 per cent in P, on the basis of having a positive credence that Jack is in Seattle, or on the basis of having full credence in the proposition that she'll say 'yes,' conditional on the proposition that you ask. Forming beliefs on the basis of other cognitive attitudes – such as levels of credence or conditional credence – is not intuitively problematic in the way that wishful thinking is, so there is no second fork to the dilemma.

In short, in light of these considerations it should be clear that the wishful thinking problem is not just a part of the Frege–Geach Problem, wrapped up in new trappings; it is a distinct problem that arises for non-cognitivist expressivism within epistemology, and is neither a problem about logic nor a general problem for expressivism.

4. Mapping out strategies for a solution

Because, as we noted in the last section, the wishful thinking problem focuses on a problem about justification that does not arise in the case of every valid argument or every case in which a subject entertains some valid argument whose premises she accepts, I'm going to introduce a distinction between the cases in which it *is* intuitively rational for Edgar to go on to accept C – which I'll unimaginatively call the *target included cases* – and the cases in which it is *not* intuitively rational for Edgar to go on to accept C – which I'll call the *target excluded cases*. A 'case' is just a situation in which a subject entertains some valid argument whose premises she accepts.

Using this terminology, the first horn of the dilemma is that not all cases are target excluded cases. At least some cases are target included cases. We can then think of the dilemma as arising separately for each of the target included cases. Either – on the first horn – our expressivist theory denies that it is really rational for Edgar to accept the conclusion in that case, or – on the second horn – our expressivist theory claims that it *is* rational for Edgar to accept the conclusion in that case, in which case Dorr argues, first, that the conclusion is adopted only because of a change in desire-like attitudes, and second, that it consequently counts as a case of wishful thinking.

It is helpful to think of the dilemma as arising separately for each case, because one way of responding to the problem is to make further assumptions about Edgar's case, and to try to use those assumptions in order to explain why Edgar's rationality in coming to accept C is not just a case of wishful thinking, because *in that case* Edgar has independent, ordinary descriptive, evidence for C, so that it is supported on the basis of Edgar's other, ordinary descriptive beliefs, and hence not only supported on the basis of P2, his desire-like attitude. In evaluating each of the proposals that this might be the case, the important thing for us to be keeping track of is not so much whether any such explanation *works*, as whether some such explanation works for *every* target included case. All that it takes for there to be a problem is that there are *some* target included cases for which no such explanation is possible.

On the other hand, a solution to the problem along these lines would not need to offer a one-size-fits-all solution that needs to apply to each and every case – it could be that different solutions go for different sorts of case, but each target included case is adequately covered by *some* such solution. So what we should be looking for, in evaluating these solutions, is whether they *jointly cover* the target included cases. The closer they come to jointly covering the target included cases, the less unintuitive residue will remain. But if any target included cases are left over, then the wishful thinking problem will not have been completely discharged.

Now, in principle several different responses to the wishful thinking problem are possible. The first is to embrace the first fork, biting the bullet and allowing that, even though a given case is *intuitively* one in which it is rational for Edgar to accept C, in fact this is really not so. A second response is to embrace the second fork, biting the bullet and agreeing that wishful thinking really is sometimes rational. A third response – which I'll say more about later on – is to agree that it is rational to accept C on the basis of no further evidence than P2 (together with P1), but to deny that this is really *wishful thinking*. But the main sort of response to the problem, offered in both published responses to date, is to try to find a way between the forks of the dilemma, by arguing that, in every target included case, Edgar is in possession of ordinary descriptive evidence for C, which can justify his concluding C without it being a case of wishful thinking.

This last strategy, of course, requires an account of where Edgar's descriptive evidence for C comes from. We can distinguish two possibilities for how this might happen. Since the only thing that changes when Edgar comes to accept P2 is that he comes to have a certain desire-like attitude, the first possibility is that the *fact that Edgar has this attitude* is itself ordinary descriptive evidence that Edgar comes by for C, by coming to accept P2. David Enoch (2003) has tried to exploit this possibility, by arguing that anyone who is *justified* in accepting P1 would also be justified in inferring C from the fact that he has the attitude expressed by P2.

A second possibility is that, since Edgar is *justified* in coming to accept P2 (otherwise this wouldn't be a target included case, because it's never justified to draw a conclusion on the basis only of unjustifiedly accepting a premise), he must have some evidence for it. So perhaps it is Edgar's evidence *for* P2 that is also evidence for C, and hence guarantees that Edgar's acceptance of C is, because it is supported by ordinary descriptive evidence, not merely wishful thinking. This second possibility is exploited by James Lenman (2003) in his response to Dorr. In Section 2 we'll look at how far these two possibilities can take us, starting with Enoch and the first, and moving on to Lenman and the second.

5. Enoch on accepting P2

The main idea of Enoch's proposed solution to the wishful thinking problem is that in every target included case, when Edgar comes to accept P2, he comes to have available an independent, purely descriptive, argument for C, which can justify him in accepting C without any wishful thinking. The new premise which Enoch holds becomes available to Edgar when he comes to accept P2 is P2*:

P2* I disapprove of lying.[3]

And so, to get a descriptive argument for C, Edgar must also have available the additional premise P1*:

P1* If I disapprove of lying, the souls of liars will be punished in the afterlife.

So, for Enoch's strategy to work, every target included case must be one in which Edgar is justified in accepting P1*.

His strategy for establishing this is piecemeal: noting that it can be rational for Edgar to conclude C on the basis of P1 and P2 only if he is justified in accepting P1, Enoch proposes to consider the different ways in which Edgar could be justified in accepting P1, and, for each, to argue that if that is how Edgar is justified in accepting P1 then he would also be justified in accepting P1*.[4] In this way, he proposes to cover all of the target included cases, dividing and conquering. One of the illustrative cases that Enoch considers is the case in which Edgar's justification for P1 comes from inductive evidence for its universal generalization, ∀P1:

∀P1 For any action A, if it is wrong to do A, then the souls of those who do A will be punished in the afterlife.

So let's walk through this case and evaluate whether someone with inductive evidence for ∀P1 would also have to have inductive evidence for ∀P1*, as Enoch claims.

∀P1* For any action A, if I disapprove of doing A, then the souls of those who do A will be punished in the afterlife.

The reason why Enoch thinks that anyone with inductive evidence for P1 would also have inductive evidence for ∀P1* is straightforward. It is that getting inductive evidence for ∀P1 involves having come across a significant series of cases of actions A, for which he thinks, 'doing A is wrong and the souls of those who do A will be punished in the afterlife,' without having come across any actions, B, for which he thinks, 'doing B is wrong and the souls of those who do B will *not* be punished in the afterlife.' But, Enoch reasons, every case in which Edgar thinks, 'doing A is wrong and the souls of those who do A will be punished in the afterlife' is one in which he is in a position to recognize that he disapproves of doing A, and hence in a position to think, 'I disapprove of doing A and the souls of those who do A will be punished in the afterlife', thereby collecting inductive evidence for ∀P1*.

This is clearly a very clever idea. But we should be suspicious of it. For one thing, the very same sort of reasoning would seem to predict that anyone is justified in accepting the following thesis:

hubris For any action A, doing A is wrong just in case I disapprove of doing A.

But surely expressivists should not accept a 'friendly suggestion' that leads to this hubristic prediction.[5]

In fact it turns out not to be hard to see that Enoch's reasoning is problematic in at least a couple of places. First, whenever Edgar thinks that doing A is wrong without thinking that he disapproves of doing A, he will collect inductive evidence for ∀P1 without collecting inductive evidence for ∀P1*. Second, it is possible – even rationally possible – for Edgar to be wrong about what he disapproves of. Suppose, for example, that Edgar does not disapprove of viewing pornography, but that consultation with his trusted psychotherapist has led him to believe that he does. And suppose, moreover, that Edgar further thinks that the souls of pornography-viewers are not, as it turns out, punished in the afterlife. In that case, Edgar will accept 'I disapprove of viewing pornography and the souls of pornography-viewers will not be punished in the afterlife' and hence be in possession of conclusive counter-evidence for ∀P1*, without being in possession of any counter-evidence for ∀P1. So he could be inductively justified in accepting ∀P1 without being inductively justified in accepting ∀P1*.

Enoch's reasoning also fails in a third way. Even if Edgar justifiedly thinks that he disapproves of something in precisely all and only the cases in which he does justifiedly disapprove of it, things can still go wrong. And that is because the appropriateness of inductive inferences depends on the suitability of the predicates that are being applied – on their *projectability*. Observation of a series of eagles to determine whether they fly will lead to a successful generalization to the effect that eagles fly. But observation of the same series of birds to see whether birds fly will not lead to a successful generalization. You might observe many birds that do fly, and generalize that all do, but the class of birds is heterogeneous with respect to locomotion in a way that the class of eagles is not. Enoch's reasoning requires the inductive evidence to work equally well when Edgar generalizes on what he thinks as when he generalizes on what is wrong. But there does not seem to be any *a priori* reason to think that this is so. In fact, Edgar may explicitly think that it is not.

So, in conclusion, it doesn't appear that Enoch's account could apply to *all* cases in which Edgar is inductively justified in accepting P1. Of course, it might, for all that, apply to *some* such cases. But it doesn't appear that it will succeed in covering the full range of target included cases, and the foregoing discussion makes it look like a poor candidate to cover even some of the most central and common sorts of cases.

6. The structure of Lenman's solution

On the face of it, it shouldn't be too surprising that Enoch's strategy ran into trouble. For it doesn't even make use of the full set of resources that ought to be available for explaining how Edgar is justified in accepting C. As Enoch points out, it is rational for Edgar to accept C on the basis of P1 and P2 only if he is *justified* in accepting P1 and P2. But Enoch's explanations only appeal to the assumption that Enoch is justified in accepting *P1* – no work is done by the assumption that Edgar is justified in accepting P2 – only by the assumption that Edgar *does* in fact accept P2. This both overgeneralizes the explanation of Edgar's justification for accepting C to cases in which intuitively Edgar should *not* be justified in accepting C (because he is not justified in accepting P2), and leaves a whole set of possible resources for solving the problem unutilized.

So a different strategy hopes to explain why Edgar always has ordinary descriptive evidence for C in target included cases, by trying to show that the evidence Edgar has for P1 and P2 must itself be descriptive evidence for C. I think this is the right way to understand the strategy taken by James Lenman (2003), in his reply to Dorr, and, when described in this way, it is easy to see why this is a more promising strategy than Enoch's, for the reasons just articulated.

Lenman actually adopts a very strong version of this strategy; he holds that whenever Edgar is justified in accepting both P1 and P2, it is on the basis of beliefs which, *independently of P1 and P2*, can be used to directly argue for C. The clearest example that he gives for how this might work is the following argument:

R1 Derek never contravenes the Decalogue.
R2 All and only contraventions of the Decalogue are wrong.

R3 Therefore: Derek never does anything wrong.
R4 Therefore: if looking at a woman with lustful intent is wrong, then Derek never looks at a woman with lustful intent.
R5 Looking at a woman with lustful intent contravenes the Decalogue.
R6 Therefore: Looking at a woman with lustful intent is wrong.
R7 Therefore: Derek never looks at a woman with lustful intent.[6]

In the example, R4 and R6 constitute a moral-descriptive *modus ponens* argument for R7 (just like Edgar's argument for C). But R4 is justified on the basis of R1 and R2, and R6 is justified on the basis of R2 and R5, and R1 and R5 (which are part of the justification of R4 and R6) constitute an independent, direct, descriptive argument for R7. So, given the way that R4 and R6 are justified, coming to accept R7 on the basis of R4 and R6 can't lead Edgar any more astray than his beliefs have already led him – because it is independently supported by R1 and R5.

7. How far does this solution go?

Lenman's case shows that there are at least *some* examples of target included cases that needn't involve wishful thinking in any objectionable way. So it solves the problem for at least some cases. But recall that there is still a problem, unless Lenman's solution covers *all* target included cases. This is exactly what Lenman claims his solution can do. He alleges that *all* target included cases are like this case, except perhaps simply a little bit more complicated. What Lenman says is that, if Edgar does *not* have background beliefs guaranteeing that he is in possession of an independent descriptive argument for C, then in *that* case the non-cognitivist may readily concede that Edgar, so characterized, is irrational. Such a concession is altogether harmless, as it is *independently* highly plausible – *whether we are non-cognitivists or not*. If Dorr insists on considering a case where this disconnection is total, we get irrationality by *anybody's* standards.[7]

What Lenman is saying here is that every case that doesn't meet the condition laid down in his account should be classified as being a target *excluded* case – one in which it is intuitively irrational for Edgar to come to accept the conclusion of the argument, anyway.

This is intuitively quite a surprising claim. There is no reason to suspect that, in *non-moral* arguments, someone is rational in accepting their conclusion only if they are in possession of some further, different, argument, which would independently justify its conclusion. In fact, that *can't* be the case, because it would lead to a vicious regress. *Some* arguments have to support their conclusions without the help of further arguments, or no arguments would support their conclusions at all. So, if Lenman's assumption is true of moral-descriptive *modus ponens* arguments, that would be quite a surprising and restrictive conclusion.

It is important, in order to see what is going on, to distinguish Lenman's thesis that the evidence for P1 and P2 must provide an *independent* justification for C from the weaker and more plausible thesis that the evidence for P1 and P2 must provide a justification for C. This latter thesis is compelling because, since C follows from P1 and P2, any evidence sufficient to justify both of them would also be sufficient, *derivatively*, to justify C *by way* of justifying P1 and P2. What Lenman's solution requires is the stronger thesis that there must be a *direct* argument from the evidence for P1 and P2 to C, as in his Decalogue case. This is what we've seen no reason to think is satisfied in the full range of target included cases.

8. What could Lenman be thinking?

What we've seen so far is that Lenman's claim that the assumptions required for his solution are independently plausible, 'whether we are non-cognitivists or not,' is clearly false. His argument requires the assumption that, every time someone is justified in accepting a moral thesis, it is justified partly on the basis of non-moral assumptions, which themselves suffice to justify any further non-moral conclusions that can be drawn from that moral thesis. Lenman claims that this is 'independently highly plausible – whether we are non-cognitivists or not,' but so far we've seen no reason why ordinary cognitivists must accept this assumption – indeed, it is easy to think of cognitivist views which are committed to denying it. For example, any intuitionist theory is committed to the view that at least some moral theses are directly justified – and hence not justified on the basis of any non-moral assumptions.

It is worth trying to sort out, however, what Lenman must have been thinking, and his Decalogue example is instructive here. In the Decalogue example, it is not the non-moral premises alone that justify the premises of the moral-descriptive *modus ponens* argument, but rather the non-moral premises *in combination with* the moral premise, R2, which says that all and only contraventions of the Decalogue are wrong. So there is at least one picture of the structure of moral epistemology which has the feature that, if we accept it, then we can adopt Lenman's solution. According to this picture of moral epistemology, anyone who is justified in accepting any moral thesis whatsoever is so justified on the basis of her acceptance of a completely general moral theory of the form 'all and only actions which are **** are wrong.'

If this is a correct thesis about moral epistemology, then, in any case in which a subject is justified in accepting the premises of a moral-descriptive *modus ponens* argument, it will have to be because she has derived them from this general moral theory, along with auxiliary non-moral assumptions – as in the Decalogue example. And hence these non-moral assumptions will be available to justify the conclusion of the moral-descriptive *modus ponens* argument. Perhaps Lenman accepts this overall picture of moral epistemology. Perhaps he even thinks that everyone should accept it. That may be what guides his thinking here. But this is an extraordinarily controversial thesis about moral epistemology – it is very implausible that most ordinary people even accept any perfectly general generalization of the form of R2, and even less plausible that their ordinary moral views are justified on that basis.

If I had to speculate, I would guess that Lenman may be being misled by considerations about supervenience. It *is* very plausible that the supervenience of the moral on the non-moral is an *a priori* constraint on competence with moral terms, and it is a familiar fact that strong supervenience entails the truth of some generalization of the form of R2 – provided that we are sufficiently liberal with what can be substituted for 'contraventions of the Decalogue.' But it is simply a mistake to think that this entails what Lenman needs; it is perfectly coherent to believe that the moral supervenes on the non-moral and even to think that things are wrong *because* of their non-moral features, without knowing just which non-moral features make something wrong. Indeed, the whole point of introducing talk of supervenience into philosophy in the first place was that we often find ourselves in this kind of situation: we know that there is a supervenience basis, but we don't know exactly what it is. So considerations about supervenience lend no support to the very strong assumptions about moral epistemology that Lenman needs in order for his solution to the wishful thinking problem to work.

What we've been observing about Lenman's solution is not that it is *wrong*, but that it relies on an extremely strong assumption about the structure of moral epistemology that – *contra* Lenman – is not at all obviously plausible independent of a commitment to non-cognitivism, or even independent of the wishful thinking problem, for that matter. What his solution shows is that non-cognitivists can solve the wishful thinking problem by taking on this kind of very strong picture about the structure of moral epistemology. And if you find it independently plausible, as Lenman does, that everyone accepts a comprehensive moral theory and bases his judgments about cases on that theory, then you might be happy with this solution. But, if this is the only way around the wishful thinking problem, then it is fair to say that the wishful thinking problem places very sharp constraints on moral epistemology – constraints that we might wonder whether non-cognitivists can do without.

9. What about the second fork?

So it seems that neither Enoch's nor Lenman's suggestions do quite what they are presented as doing. But it does seem to me that it is worth thinking about the merits of the second fork of the dilemma. A first observation is that 'wishful thinking' is something of a persuasive definition. True cases of wishful thinking are cases of wanting it to be the case that p, and coming to believe that p. That is clearly a bad way of proceeding, and deserves a special name. But it is not obvious that the connection between P2 and C looks like this, unless it turns out that 'lying is wrong' expresses the state of wanting the souls of liars to be punished in the afterlife. So it could be that some cases of getting to descriptive conclusions from, among other things, a desire-like attitude are not as bad as the paradigm cases of wishful thinking, and hence the name of the problem is itself efficacious in dissuading us from the second fork. If so, it would seem, we should be cautious.

A second observation is that, even though Dorr describes cases in which Edgar starts by accepting P1 and comes to accept P2, his acceptance of P1 is not, itself, irrelevant to the justification for C. But, though it is clear that accepting P2 is just having a desire-like attitude, it is not clear what sort of state is involved with accepting P1, until an adequate expressivist solution to the embedding problem and account of logical inconsistency and logical entailment is on the table. Whatever such a state turns out to be like, it will have to have the property that it can be involved in joint inconsistency with both beliefs and desire-like attitudes at the same time. It must turn out, for example, that it is inconsistent to be in the state expressed by P1, the desire-like attitude expressed by P2, and the belief expressed by the negation of C. It is very puzzling how there could be any state that could make this so, and that is an important part of why an especially hard part of the Frege–Geach Problem in the first place is to give an account that deals adequately with mixed moral-descriptive conditionals.[8]

So perhaps non-cognitivists should embrace the second fork of the dilemma, and argue that this is nevertheless sufficiently different from the ordinary cases of wishful thinking that it is not at all obvious that whatever is so bad about such ordinary cases carries over. Making good on this strategy would require making good on an explanation of precisely what is so objectionable about paradigm cases of wishful thinking, and an explanation of why those objectionable features don't arise in superficially similar cases like Edgar's. To make good on such explanations, we would need a much more complete understanding both of wishful thinking and of non-cognitivist theories of moral thought and inference.

10. Tools for progress

In this paper, we've been considering just one significant problem for non-cognitivism in epistemology – the wishful thinking problem. I have focused on it because it is relatively new and interesting, and because the responses to date on behalf of non-cognitivism have been intriguing but less than convincing, and it is not clear what satisfactory view could come out of it. But there are a variety of other significant problems for non-cognitivists in epistemology, and it is worth thinking about the wishful thinking problem in this broader context. For example, all along in the discussion in this paper, I have followed both Enoch and Lenman in assuming that, within a non-cognitivist framework, it will make sense to talk about 'evidence' for P1 and P2, and assumptions that 'justify' Edgar in accepting one or the other.

But it is very hard to see what account can be given of evidence for P2, in an expressivist view, or of what it is to be justified in one's moral views, as opposed to being justified in an ordinary descriptive belief. This is not to say that these concepts are beyond the reach of non-cognitivists, but they are certainly ones for which it is natural to expect that a better understanding of the non-cognitivist approach will lead us to further resources for getting our heads around the wishful thinking problem.

Consider the following comparison. Mathematicians worked for a long time with only an intuitive notion of continuity, because they didn't have the resources available to define it properly, which required the epsilon-delta definition of a limit. Discussing problems that turn on the notions of evidence and justification is like working with the intuitive notion of continuity – something like 'can you trace it without taking your finger off of the graph?' In the absence of the right tools for understanding how justification and evidence really work in a fully fledged non-cognitivist framework, it may in some cases be hard to tell whether we have a problem about justification, or a place in which our hand-wavy intuitive notion is breaking down.

The problem with this is that epistemological notions promise to be some of the hardest to get straight regarding what the right non-cognitivist account of them should be – not least because these epistemological notions are controversial in their own right. This is because, if someone knows something only if they truly believe it, then providing an expressivist account of knowledge will be at least as hard as providing an expressivist account of belief and providing an expressivist account of truth, put together – but non-cognitivist accounts of belief and of truth are themselves complicated topics, each in its own right. And that still leaves out whatever further condition is required to turn true belief into knowledge, which epistemologists have had enough trouble understanding, even on the assumption that non-cognitivism is false. So, all told, there are excellent reasons to expect the epistemological issues facing expressivism to be very difficult, as well as being particularly difficult to resolve without first resolving general issues about logic, truth, and belief.

Notes

1. Note that neither Dorr nor either of his commentators, Enoch (2003) or Lenman (2003), characterizes the problem as a dilemma; all assume that the second fork is obviously to be avoided.
2. See, for example, Schroeder (2009a; 2010, especially ch. 6).
3. Here I'm following the practice I've used elsewhere of using 'disapprove' as a generic term for that desire-like attitude toward lying, whatever it is, which is

what it is to think that lying is wrong, according to the non-cognitivist theory under discussion.

4. This gloss isn't completely accurate; things are slightly more complicated in the case in which Edgar is justified in accepting P1 only on the basis of testimony. In that case, the non-moral conditional which Enoch's account requires Edgar to be justified in accepting has the form, 'If Jack thinks that it is wrong to lie, then the souls of liars will be punished in the afterlife.' I believe that Enoch's treatment of this case is also flawed, but it isn't necessary to go into it for our purposes here.

5. See Schroeder (unpublished) for further discussion.

6. Lenman (2003, p. 272).

7. Lenman (2003, p. 269), italics in original.

8. See, for example, Hale (1993), Kölbel (2002), and Schroeder (2008), especially chapters 7–10.

7
Internal Reasons and the Motivating Intuition

Julia Markovits

Internalist theses, as they are usually stated, describe a necessary relation between an agent's having a reason and some other, usually motivational, fact about the agent. So, for example, internalists might claim that an agent can have a reason to perform some act only if he has a relevant desire, or only if he would be motivated to perform it in suitably idealized circumstances. Why should we accept internalism about reasons?

I'll begin by exploring the thought, appealed to by Bernard Williams and often cited in support of internalism, that reasons must be capable of *explaining* action: it must be possible for a fact that is a reason for an agent to act to be *the reason he acts – the reason that motivates him*. I'll call this the *Motivating Intuition*. As I will argue (in Section 1), it represents a key step in Williams' argument for internalism. And (as I will try to show in Section 2), the Motivating Intuition has much to be said for it. The problem is that versions of internalism that reflect the Motivating Intuition are vulnerable to numerous counter-examples, and that attempts to revise the internalist thesis to avoid these counter-examples introduce a divide between normative reasons and possible explanations of action. The result is that workable versions of internalist theses lose the support of the Motivating Intuition, and so begin to appear unmotivated. But the same counter-examples that forced the modification of internalist theses, and others, should also lead us to reconsider the Motivating Intuition itself. Indeed, I will argue (in Sections 3 and 4) that we should reject the Motivating Intuition, and that examples of reasons we have to act which cannot, or should not, be the reasons *why* we act are in fact quite common.

Where does this leave internalism? If the Motivating Intuition is misguided, should we reject the internalist thesis? Are there any other grounds for thinking there is a necessary connection between facts about our reasons and facts about our current motivational profile? I will close (in Section 5) by suggesting that there are.

1. Two arguments for internalism

According to Bernard Williams's version of *internalism about reasons*, which will serve as the hook on which I hang my own observations, for some agent A to have a reason to perform some action Φ, that action must be related to A's 'motivational set' in a particular way. Specifically, it must be the case that 'A could reach the conclusion that he should Φ...by a sound delibera- tive route from the motivations that he has in his actual motivational set – that is, the set of his desires, evaluations, attitudes, projects, and so on.'[1] Williams's formulation is somewhat misleading. One can have a reason to perform an action that is not a 'winning' reason – that is, a reason that is outweighed by other reasons not to perform the action. For something to be a reason for an agent to perform an action on the standard internalist picture, it must be the case that the agent would be *motivated to some extent* to perform the action if he deliberated rationally. But it need not be the case that he would be *moved* to perform the action, or that he would reach the conclusion that he should perform the action, *all things considered*.

Put in an oversimplified way, an internal interpretation of reasons is one that takes an agent to have a reason to perform an action only if she has some desire, the satisfaction of which will be served by her doing so.[2] The internalist account of reasons does not entail that any of our desires give us reasons, or that we will always be motivated by our reasons. False beliefs or bad deliberation may cause us to fail to recognize or be motivated by some of our reasons, and can give rise to desires we have no reason to fulfill. But the essential feature of an internalist account of reasons is that it ties the truth of a reasons claim to the presence of a suitable element in an agent's moti- vational set: according to internalism, what we have reason to do depends fundamentally on what ends, broadly understood, we already have.[3]

The first argument. Williams's argument for internalism about reasons in his seminal article 'Internal and External Reasons' seems to *begin* from the assumption that the concept of a reason *is* the concept of a considera- tion that could explain the actions of a rational agent. Williams thinks that, when we say someone has a reason to Φ, what we *mean* is that he would be motivated to Φ if he were rational. Though this claim is sometimes presented as the internalists' *conclusion*, it is in fact the *starting point* of Williams's argument. (For example, Williams claims that an *external* reasons statement (not just an internal reasons statement) 'implies that a rational agent would be motivated to act appropriately.'[4]) He then points out that it's easy enough to see what it would take for an *internal* reasons statement to be true of an agent. If A has an *internal* reason to Φ, this means that A would be moti- vated to Φ if he deliberated *in a procedurally rational way from his existing ends and motivations* (that's the internalist part), and it's easy enough to see why such procedurally rational deliberation might give rise to a new motivation, derived from one of the old ones. It's no mystery, Williams suggests, to see how an internal reason might serve to explain the actions of an agent who deliberates rationally.

It's much harder, Williams argues, to understand what it would take for an *external* reasons statement to be true of an agent. Because if claiming that an agent has a reason to Φ amounts to claiming that he would be motivated to Φ if he were rational, and if claiming the reason is *external* amounts to claiming that it does not apply to the agent in virtue of any of his existing motivations, then the external reasons theorist must explain *how* it could be true of the agent that a process of rational deliberation would motivate him to Φ, despite the fact that, by hypothesis, he need have no existing motivations from which the new motivation to Φ could be derived. And Williams finds it hard to imagine a process of rational deliberation that could give rise to a motivation to act, but not by taking any existing motivations as a starting point.

Williams considers the possibility that an external reason could explain the action of the agent whose reason it is, provided the agent is rational, by means of the agent's *coming to believe* he has the reason to act. Rational agents, after all, will form true beliefs about their reasons, and will be motivated to do as they believe they have reason to do, so, if an agent comes to believe an external reason to Φ applies to him, then if he is rational he will be motivated to Φ, regardless of his former motivations. And this, the thought goes, is enough to establish the truth of the external reasons claim.

An example might make this possibility clearer. The external reasons theorist will want to claim that Jim has a reason to give to charity, say, regardless of whether he has any desire, broadly understood, which might give rise, after procedurally rational deliberation, to a motivation to give to charity. That is to say, Jim has an external reason to give to charity. But if Williams is right about what all reasons claims (including external reasons claims) must mean, than this statement amounts to the claim that Jim would be motivated to give to charity if he were rational, regardless of his actual motivations. How could that be true? The suggestion under consideration is that the external reasons claim is true because, if Jim were rational, he would recognize that he has reason to give to charity, and (because he is rational) this recognition would motivate him to do so (regardless of his prior motivations).

But, Williams asks, what would Jim's 'recognition' amount to? If, again, Williams is right about our concept of a reason, it would have to amount to the recognition, on Jim's part, that he would be motivated to give to charity if he were rational (regardless of his existing motivations). It is a *true* belief in this proposition that is supposed to trigger in the rational Jim a motivation to give to charity. But now we do seem to have put the cart before the horse. After all, we were trying to determine how *that* proposition could be true. It doesn't seem to help to say that it can be true, because if it were true, and rational Jim therefore believed it and were motivated accordingly, then it would be true. So, Williams concludes, we can make sense of the idea of a normative reason, which, Williams says, just *is* the idea of a consideration that would motivate a rational agent, only if we accept the internalist thesis: that an agent can have a reason to perform some action only if he could be motivated to perform it by following a sound deliberative route from his existing ends and motivations.

The second argument. Some of the central claims of Williams's defense of internalism sow the seeds of another argument Williams himself does not make, but which is often attributed to internalists.[5] This argument begins from something like Williams's conceptual claim about reasons: 'It must be a mistake,' Williams writes, 'to simply separate explanatory and normative reasons. If it is true that A has a reason to Φ, then it must be possible that he should Φ for that reason; and if he does act for that reason, then that reason will be the explanation of his acting.' Similarly, the first premise of this second argument claims:

(1) It must be possible for me to be motivated by the reasons that apply to me. So a consideration can be a reason for me to Φ only if it can motivate me to Φ.

A second premise also looks familiar:

(2) A consideration can motivate me to Φ only if it is relevantly con-nected to my 'motivational set' – that is, only if it would motivate me to Φ if I were deliberating in a procedurally rational way from my existing ends and motivations.

The internalist conclusion follows from these premises:

(3) Therefore, a consideration can be a reason for me to Φ only if it would motivate me to Φ if I were deliberating in a procedurally rational way from my existing ends and motivations.

What should we make of this argument? One question it raises immediately is whether the notion of possibility at work in premise (1) is plausibly the same as the notion of possibility at work in premise (2), as it must be if the argument is to go through. The 'can' in premise (2) suggests psychological possibility: it identifies the conditions under which an agent who begins with a particular psychological profile might be motivated to perform some action. Is this also a plausible interpretation of the 'can' at work in premise (1)? Is it plausibly a conceptual constraint on when a consideration can count as a reason for an agent that there are circumstances in which that agent, burdened, at least at the outset, with his actual psychological profile, might be motivated by that consideration to act? If we take seriously Williams's claim that our concept of a reason is the concept of a conditional explanation of the actions of the agent for whom it is a reason, then this does strike me as a reasonable way of interpreting the argument's first premise. And the premise seems to gain some support from the *ought-implies-can* principle: it's very plausible that we *ought* to be motivated by the reasons that apply to us, so it's also plausible that it must be psychologically possible for us to be motivated by those reasons.

The second premise raises some additional worries. It looks like a version of what is sometimes called the Humean Theory of Motivation. Hume wrote:

> Where ... objects themselves do not effect us, their connexion [of effect to cause, which reason makes evident to us] can never give them any influence; and 'tis plain, that as reason is nothing but the discovery of this connexion, it cannot be by its means that the objects are able to affect us. ... [R]eason alone can never produce any action, or give rise to volition. ... Nothing can oppose or retard the influence of passion, but a contrary impulse. ... Reason is, and ought only to be the slave of the passions, and can never pretend to any other office than to serve and obey them.[6]

In its crudest form, the Humean Theory of Motivation claims that all motivation depends on a relevant antecedent desire. The argument I've outlined refines this thesis in one important respect: it expands the set of attitudes that can ground motivation to include more than just desires (narrowly understood). Williams makes clear that he means agents' 'motivational sets' to include, in addition to straightforward desires, 'such things as dispositions of evaluation, patterns of emotional reaction, personal loyalties, and various projects, as they may be abstractly called, embodying commitments of the agent.'[7]

Even so, the second premise of the argument is controversial at best. It looks to be making an empirical assertion about psychology – an assertion about what kinds of mental events can trigger the formation of new motivations – without backing it up with empirical research (never a promising strategy in philosophical argument). Why should we believe that the formation of a belief *never* triggers the formation of a new motivation?[8] After all, even a knock on the head could do that.

But we might again revise the premise to make it more plausible. Alfred Mele, for example, defends a view he calls the 'antecedent motivation theory' and attributes to Hume. He writes:

> in actual human beings, all motivation nonaccidentally produced by practical reasoning issuing in a belief favoring a course of action derives

at least partly from motivation-encompassing attitudes already present in the agent before he acquires the belief.[9]

Mele allows that beliefs might sometimes motivate, but claims that *reasoning* can motivate us *non-accidentally* only on the back of an antecedent motivation.[10]

It is not obvious how we are to understand the notion of non-accidental motivation, but it is possible that if we spell that notion out, and adjust our first premise accordingly, a version of the above argument for internalism may still go through. We might interpret the idea of practical reasoning non-accidentally producing motivation in terms of *rational motivation* – motivation that drives us when and because we are rational. If we amend the premises of the internalist argument accordingly, it reads:

(1*)   It must be possible for me to be *rationally* motivated by the reasons that apply to me. So a consideration can be a reason for me to Φ only if it can *rationally* motivate me to Φ: that is, motivate me to Φ *when and because I am rational.*

(2*)   A consideration can *rationally* motivate me to Φ only if it is relevantly connected to my 'motivational set' – that is, only if it would motivate me to Φ if I were deliberating in a procedurally rational way from my existing ends and motivations.

(3*)   Therefore, a consideration can be a reason for me to Φ only if it would motivate me to Φ if I were deliberating in a procedurally rational way from my existing ends and motivations.

Our new premise (1*) stays true to the intuition from which we began: that a reasons-statement – even a normative reasons statement – must still be able to serve as an explanation. After all, it was never the internalist's claim that any normative reason will serve as the actual explanation of the actions of the agent to whom it applies, since agents frequently fail to act as they have reason to act, whether because of ignorance or poor judgment or weakness of will. Rather, internalists appeal to the intuition that reasons should explain our actions when things go well – when we're not subject to such irrationalities. Reasons must be able to explain how we act when we are rational.

And consider the support the premise got from the *ought-implies-can* principle. I suggested earlier that premise (1) was plausible because it is entailed by *ought-implies-can* and another plausible claim: that we ought to be motivated by the reasons that apply to us. But it seems that we can plausibly claim more than this: it's better to be rationally responsive to our reasons than to be merely accidentally motivated by them. In other words, we ought to be not just motivated by our reasons, but *rationally* motivated by them.

Our new premise (2*) also improves upon the old premise (2). It no longer makes overreaching empirical claims about the conditions under which motivation *of any kind* is possible. And it sticks closer to its Humean origins in its focus on the role *Reason* can play in generating motivation. (3*) is identical to (3): our two new premises issue in the internalist conclusion as surely as the original ones did.

2. Motivating intuitions

Fleshing out the second argument for internalism along these lines brings out a striking similarity between this argument and the argument for internalism that Bernard Williams actually makes in 'Internal and External Reasons.' For it is now clear that the central premises driving both arguments are the same: both rely, first, on the claim that a consideration could be a reason for me to act only if it would motivate me to act if I was rational, and second on the claim that no process of rational deliberation could produce in me a new motivation to act except by taking my existing motivations as a starting point. Nonetheless, the arguments – at least their first central premises – are powered by different intuitions. Williams takes his first premise to be supported by intuitions about what our reasons statements *mean*. The second argument's first premise is supported by appeal to a conceptual connection between reasons (even normative reasons) and action-explanations, and also, I have suggested, by a plausible assumption about how we ought to be motivated, taken together with the *ought-implies-can* principle.

The argument's second central premise – the Humean one – has been the chief focus of the philosophical disagreement about the nature of reasons for action. Defenders of internalism about reasons have touted their theory's ability to reflect the myriad intuitions captured by the arguments' first premise: that practical reasons must be capable of motivating rational agents. Externalists have defended their view by attempting to block the implication from that first premise to the internalists' conclusion, largely by attacking the Humean Theory of Motivation in its various forms. But the first premise itself, and the intuitions underlying it, have received less scrutiny.

In what follows, I will describe in detail some of the varied intuitions that might be taken to support the claim that it must be possible for us to be motivated by the reasons that apply to us, at least if we are rational. Next, I will describe a series of counter-examples intended to undermine our confidence in that premise: reasons to act that cannot, or should not, motivate us to act are, I will argue, quite common. But, I will suggest, this should not lead us to abandon internalism. Some of the intuitions that were taken to support the internalists' first premise might nonetheless provide some direct support for a version of internalism that does not rely on that premise. And, because this version of internalism also does not rely on the Humean Theory of Motivation, it may be better placed to withstand the externalist attack.

So: why think that some consideration cannot be a reason for us to act unless it could motivate us to act, and would do so if we were rational? I touched on some of the reasons for thinking this in setting out the two arguments for internalism above. I'll begin with the intuition about the *meaning* of our reasons statements that, I have suggested, is the driving force behind the first argument for internalism – the one Williams actually makes explicitly. Why does Williams think that the conception of reasons – as facts that would motivate us if we were rational – is one that internalists and externalists *share*? Williams writes:

> There are of course many things that a speaker may say to one who is not disposed to Φ when the speaker thinks that he should be, as that he is inconsiderate, or cruel, or selfish, or imprudent; or that things, and he, would be a lot nicer if he were so motivated. Any of these can be sensible things to say. But one who makes a great deal out of putting the criticism in the form of an external reason statement seems concerned to say that what is particularly wrong with the agent is that he is *irrational*. It is this theorist who particularly needs to make this charge precise: in particular, because he wants any rational agent, as such, to acknowledge the requirement to do the thing in question.[11]

The whole point of ascribing a reason to someone, either internal or external, Williams thinks, is to make clear to them that, if they fail to act accordingly, they are failing by their own lights – they are failing to live up to a standard whose bindingness on them they must themselves, as rational agents, acknowledge: the standard of rationality. This is what makes such a charge different from saying merely that it would be better if they acted this way, or that we would wish them to do so, or would do so in their place. The shared etymology of *reason* and *rationality* is no accident. (Williams's claim is that, on this understanding of what reasons statements mean, only internal reasons statements can be *true*.) Reasons statements aim at objectivity, or at least intersubjectivity, and they add something to our arsenal only if we can use them, in this way, to appeal to the requirements of this shared standard.[12]

Williams's claim about what our reasons statements mean is backed up by an additional claim about the conceptual link between reasons and explanation. It is also no accident of etymology that we use the same word, 'reason,' to describe both the grounds on which we act – sometimes called motivating reasons – and the reasons *for us* to act – sometimes called normative reasons. In both cases, Williams suggests, reasons statements explain action: motivating reasons explain why we actually act the way we do, and normative reasons statements explain how we would act if all went well – if we did not succumb to weakness of will, or confusion, or ignorance, or poor judgment: if, in other words, we were rational.

So, Williams takes it to be a conceptual truth about reasons that they are the considerations that would move good practical reasoners. This certainly seems plausible, and it is reinforced by a claim that is often made about practical reasons: that they must be *action-guiding*. Reasons, the thought is, are not purposeless: they guide us in how to behave. But a reason that could not motivate us, even if we were perfect practical reasoners, could not play this action-guiding role. So all reasons must be capable of motivating us in so far as we are reasoning well.

Michael Smith has called the claim that 'what we have normative reason to do is what we would desire to do if we were fully rational' a 'platitude' about practical reasons. He argues that it follows naturally from considering what is involved in identifying our reasons: from how we should go about deciding what to do. When we deliberate about how to act, he says, we ask for *advice*. But we don't ask just anyone for advice; we look for advice from people who are better situated than we are to know what we should do – who are better informed, and more rational, and less subject to our weaknesses of will – but who know us, and what drives us, well. In other words, Smith suggests, suitably idealized, we are *ourselves* best placed to give ourselves advice. When we look for our reasons, what we want to know is how *we* would act if we were better placed than we actually are: if we were fully rational.[13]

Then there is the claim that I appealed to in support of the second argument for internalism, above. Surely, we *ought* to be motivated by any reason that applies to us – indeed, we ought to be so motivated when and because we are rational. Since *ought* implies *can*, it must follow that we *can* be motivated by any reason that applies to us, when we are rational. This thought becomes all the more forceful if we accept the very plausible claim that *virtue* is a matter of motivational responsiveness to practical reasons. For if we accept that thought, but deny that we ought always to be responsive to our reasons, then we are denying that we ought always to be virtuous.

The power of reasons to motivate rational agents might also help explain another fact that often comes up in the literature on internalism about reasons: that rational agents are reliably motivated to act as they judge they have reason to act. If considerations that provide reasons themselves have the power to motivate rational agents, this fact is neatly explained: rational agents are motivated to act by their judgment that they have reason to act because rational agents' judgments about their reasons are true, and are the discovery of facts that themselves have the power to motivate those agents when they are rational.

Finally, some philosophers have appealed to a somewhat more nebulous idea in support of the claim that our normative reasons must be capable of motivating us, at least when we are rational. They have suggested that a conception of reasons that allows that we might have reasons that could get no motivational grip on us, even when we're reasoning as we should, would unacceptably *alienate* us from our reasons. Peter Railton has made a point like this as part of a defense of an internalist account of an agent's *good*: 'it would be an intolerably alienated conception of someone's good,' he writes, 'to imagine that it may fail in any way to engage him.'[14] It's appealing to think something similar may be true of our reasons more generally. As Williams and others have argued, it may be a limiting condition on our moral obligations that they somehow reflect what *drives* us.[15] And there must be something about the reasons for me to act that makes them *mine*. Shouldn't it be a requirement on some consideration's providing *me* with a reason to Φ that *I* can appeal to it to justify myself when I do Φ? But I can appeal to such a consideration honestly only if it was one of the (motivating) reasons I *did* Φ. If a consideration can't motivate me to Φ, than how can I point to it to justify myself for having done so?

Taken together, these considerations provide compelling support for the claim that reasons must be capable of motivating the agents whose reasons they are, and will motivate them if they are rational. I will call this claim the *Motivating Intuition*. As I have argued, the Motivating Intuition plays an essential role in at least two important arguments for internalism about reasons. Unfortunately, as examples will show, the Motivating Intuition is false.

3. Counter-examples to the Motivating Intuition

The counter-examples to the Motivating Intuition that I will describe fall into three classes. The first, and most commonly discussed, class of counter-examples encompasses reasons we have *because* we are not perfectly rational. Some of these examples put pressure on the idea, which is reflected in part of the Motivating Intuition, that how we *should* act is determined by how we *would* act if we were more ideally rational than we are. Here are two such examples, both of which are, in some version, familiar from the literature on internalism:

> **The student of reasoning.** We surely have reason to take measures to improve our ability to reason: we have reason, for example, to take lessons in chess, or logic, and it is becoming increasingly common for universities to require students to take courses in 'reasoning and critical thinking.' But, if we were fully rational, we would not be motivated to take any such measures.

Even if our reasoning ability itself is unexceptionable, lack of self-control or weakness of will can also present us with obstacles that we ought to take into account:

> **The sore loser.** A squash player, who, after suffering an embarrassing defeat, rightly believes he will hit his opponent out of anger if he does not leave the court immediately surely has reason to leave, although if

he were fully rational, and so not weak-willed, he would be motivated instead to shake his opponent's hand.[16]

As these examples bring out, facts about how we would act if we were ideally rational can seem irrelevant to our actual, non-ideal circumstances, in which we face impediments that our perfectly rational counterparts do not. And we might wonder, more generally, why we should care about the motivations of people who are, after all, quite fundamentally different from us: what makes sense for Spock may make no sense for Captain Kirk.

What can we learn from these examples? They suggest that the Motivating Intuition, as I've stated it, is false; that (*contra* Smith) it is not, after all, a 'platitude' about practical reasons that what we have reason to do is what we would be motivated to do if fully practically rational; and certainly that Williams's claim about what our reasons-statements *mean* is mistaken: if we think someone has reason to improve his reasoning skills, despite acknowledging that he would not be motivated to do so if he were fully rational, we cannot plausibly *mean* by our reasons claim that he would be motivated to improve his reasoning skills if he were fully rational.

Where does this leave internalism? Examples such as these show that a simple version of the internalist formula, like the one that emerges as the conclusion of the two influential internalist arguments I set out above, is guilty of the 'conditional fallacy.' Our reasons can't be restricted to what we would be motivated to do if we were perfectly procedurally rational – rational relative to our existing ends and motivations. If we were fully rational relative to our existing ends and motivations, we would not be motivated to do things like taking chess or reasoning lessons, or abruptly walk off the squash court to avoid instigating a fight. So many internalists, Smith included, have replaced the simple internalist thesis with a more complicated thesis that avoids the conditional fallacy: they have suggested, for example, that we have reason to do what our fully procedurally rational *counterparts* would *desire or advise* us to do *in our actual situation*.[17]

Responses of this kind have some virtues. They allow internalism to retain the appeal to the shared standard of rationality that Williams considered so central to understanding reasons claims. And they also retain the tie between reasons and *advice* from a well-placed advisor that Smith appealed to in support of the supposed 'platitude' about practical reasons. But Robert Johnson has argued that revisions like this sacrifice the most appealing feature of internalism about reasons – its accommodation of the intuition that a reason for an agent to act must be capable of serving also as an explanation of how the agent acts, in the right circumstances:

Once one moves away from [simple internalism about reasons] in such ways in order to avoid the conditional fallacy, an explanatory gap opens up – in this case, between your better self desiring that you should do something and you yourself being motivated to do it. The gap opens because it may be impossible for the desire had by your rationally ideal self to play any role in the explanation of your actions.[18]

Johnson suggests that, if internalists are to retain their advantage over externalists, they must find a way of avoiding the conditional fallacy while continuing to satisfy the 'explanatory requirement' – the requirement that an agent's normative reasons be capable of explaining his actions, by serving as his motivating reasons for acting. The two examples I've discussed so far do nothing to undermine the force of that requirement: *we* can be motivated by the reasons we have not to harm people to walk away instead of instigating a fight, and *we* can be motivated by the reasons we have to improve our reasoning skills to take chess lessons or courses in critical thinking, even if our ideally rational counterparts cannot. But, as other counter-examples to the Motivating Intuition show, including the example on which Johnson himself focuses, the case for internalism about reasons would not be strengthened by its satisfying the explanatory requirement, because reasons need not be capable of motivating us, after all.

Let's start with Johnson's own example:

> **'James Bond.'** Let's say I become convinced I am James Bond. The fact that I am suffering from such a delusion may give me an excellent reason to see a psychiatrist for treatment. But it cannot motivate me to see the psychiatrist. For if this fact could motivate me to seek help, I would no longer be convinced I was James Bond. Someone who firmly believes he is James Bond cannot be motivated to seek a psychiatrist by the fact that his belief is a delusion.

Johnson is right that the versions of internalism about reasons that are revised to avoid the conditional fallacy must allow that 'James Bond' has such a reason, since it seems hard to deny that 'James's' perfectly rational counterpart would advise him to seek psychiatric help, or would wish that he'd seek help fortuitously, were he to suddenly find himself in 'James's' less-than-ideal position. And he is right that this shows that such revised versions of internalism do not satisfy the explanatory requirement. But the 'James Bond' example is as much a counter-example to the explanatory requirement itself as it is to simple, unrevised internalism. It suggests that internalists should perhaps not be trying to accommodate the explanatory requirement in the first place.

The story of 'James Bond' has the characteristic neatness and outlandishness of a philosopher's example. But I hope to demonstrate that cases of normative reasons that cannot motivate the agents for whom they are reasons are in fact quite common and familiar. I'll begin with an example from theoretical reasoning:

My Fallibility. I currently have some unjustified beliefs. Let's call this plausible proposition *my fallibility*. My current unjustified beliefs are reasons for me to believe that I have some unjustified beliefs. But they can't be the reasons *why* I believe in *my fallibility*. Because if I were convinced of *my fallibility* by the fact that I have those beliefs, then I would no longer count as having them. For example, imagine that I believe that Elvis is still alive, despite overwhelming good evidence to the contrary. Call the fact that Elvis lives *BEL*. I'm aware of *BEL*, and *BEL* provides good evidence of *my fallibility*. But I can't be convinced of *my fallibility* by *BEL*. If I were, I wouldn't really count as believing that Elvis lives, and so *BEL* would not obtain (and, of course, could no longer provide support for *my fallibility*).

Similarly (given that I believe Elvis lives), the fact that Elvis is dead and this has been well documented (call this fact *ED*) provides me with a good reason to believe in *my fallibility*. And I undoubtedly ought to believe in *my fallibility*. But I can't be justified in believing in it by *ED*, because if I believed *ED*, I couldn't really believe Elvis lives. In which case *ED* would no longer provide support for *my fallibility*.

We might respond to this case by questioning whether the fact that I believe that Elvis lives really gives *me* a reason to believe in *my fallibility*. But it clearly gives *you* a reason to believe in *my fallibility*, if you have access to exactly the same information as I have, both about Elvis and about my beliefs. And it would be strange if a fact that provided you with a reason didn't also provide me with a reason, when you and I have access to the same evidence. Similarly, I'm not tempted to conclude that, since I believe Elvis lives, *ED* isn't really evidence *I* have for *my fallibility*, and so isn't a reason for me to believe in *my fallibility*. It seems indisputable that I have reason to believe *ED*, and *ED* clearly establishes *my fallibility*.

The examples I've discussed so far all involve reasons we have because we are not perfectly rational. These reasons could not motivate us if we were fully rational, because they would not *apply* to us if we were fully rational. But there are other circumstances in which our reasons might not be capable of motivating us. One interesting class of counter-examples to the Motivating Intuition concerns things we have reason to do (and can do), but which we cannot *do for those reasons*, and so *could* not do if we were fully rational – and so fully responsive to our reasons – even if we wanted to. In a paper investigating some apparent paradoxes of deterrence, Gregory Kavka describes circumstances, which he calls 'Special Deterrent Situations' (or SDSs), in which agents would find themselves faced with reasons of this sort. An SDS arises when we have reason to *intend* to apply a very harmful sanction, affecting many innocent people, in retaliation for what would be a similarly extremely harmful and unjust offense, because *intending* to apply such a sanction is the likeliest means of deterring the offense. But, because the sanction is so harmful and its victims innocent, we have no reason to *actually apply* the sanction should the offense occur.[19] Such circumstances are likely not just the stuff of philosophy papers: a plausible real-life SDS (which Kavka discusses) is provided by:

Nuclear Deterrence. Perhaps the most likely way to deter a nuclear attack is to intend to retaliate against any attacking nation by responding in kind.[20] But, if an attack should occur, no good could come of actually retaliating. So, if I am responsible for the defense strategy of a nation threatened by nuclear attack, I have reason to *intend* to retaliate against any such attack with a nuclear attack targeting the aggressor. But I have no reason to actually retaliate. Because of this I cannot be motivated to form the intention to retaliate if I am fully rational: rational agents do not form intentions to act against their own (correct) assessment of the balance of reasons. And, what's more, they cannot intend to perform actions they know they will not perform when the time for performance comes: if the nuclear attack occurs, and I know I have conclusive reason not to retaliate, I won't retaliate. And since I know, now, that I won't retaliate were an attack to occur, I cannot intend to retaliate.

Kavka's familiar *Toxin Puzzle* provides a similar, if more fanciful, example:

Toxin Puzzle. If I am offered a million dollars today to simply *form the intention* tonight to drink a (non-lethal, but ill-making) toxin tomorrow, I cannot (certainly not if I am rational) be motivated to form the intention to drink the toxin by the reason (the million-dollar prize) I have to form it, since I know now that I will not need to drink the toxin to win the prize, and so have no reason to drink the toxin, and conclusive reason not to. When tomorrow rolls around, drinking the toxin can make me no richer, and will make me considerably sicker. So I would have to be very *irrational* to drink it. If I'm resourceful, I may succeed in finding another way to motivate myself to intend to drink the toxin (and to drink it) – for example, by betting a friend a substantial sum of money that I will drink it; but in this case I will not be motivated to form the intention by the original reason I had to form it – that is, by the million-dollar prize (though the prize will have motivated me to make the bet).[21]

The *Toxin Puzzle* and the problem of *Nuclear Deterrence* differ from the cases I've already discussed: they do not turn on reasons that I have *because* I am not fully rational. (If anything, the problems of motivation they bring to light afflict us because we are, in a sense, prisoners of our own rationality.) The reasons I have to intend to drink the toxin, or to intend to initiate a retaliatory attack, might not be capable of motivating me even when I'm not fully rational. This is simply not how the process of intention-formation works. The forming of intentions to act is driven by our motivations to perform the intended act. I cannot, through sheer force of will, form an intention to do something I believe I have no reason to do, and conclusive reason not to do, even if I believe I have reason to form the intention.

In being non-voluntary in this way, intention-formation resembles belief-formation. We cannot believe at will, simply because doing so would benefit us in some way, when our perception of the balance of epistemic reasons tips the other way. So here is a second counter-example to the Motivating Intuition from the realm of reasons for belief:

> **Pragmatic Belief.** I may have overwhelming pragmatic reasons to believe some proposition – perhaps that my disease is curable, if optimism would make me more likely to recover. But I cannot believe my disease is curable for that reason – I cannot be motivated to believe this by the fact that believing it will increase my chances of survival. Again, I may be able to bring myself to believe it by some other means; but I cannot believe it for the only genuine reason I have to believe it: my pragmatic reason.

Should we perhaps conclude that reasons such as these – reasons for believing that are not generated by the believed proposition's truth, or reasons for intending that are not generated by the intended action's value – are not genuine reasons after all? I don't believe so. After all, it may be possible for me to get myself to form the relevant intention or belief by other means: I might, in *Toxin Puzzle* (as I suggested), make a bet with a friend that gives me reason to actually drink the toxin, and so motivates me to form the intention to drink it; or I might, in *Nuclear Deterrence*, encourage in myself the kind of jingoistic fervor that I know will reduce my level of concern for the potential victims of a retaliatory attack to the point where I could intend to retaliate; or I might, in *Pragmatic Belief,* purposefully seek out medical opinions only from doctors with a reputation for optimism. If any of these methods of manipulating my own beliefs and intentions have a chance of success, I may have reason to undertake them. The very facts that could not motivate me to form the relevant beliefs and intentions give me reasons to try to bring it about that I form them in some other way. But it would be very strange if I had a reason to bring it about that I believe or intend something I have no reason to believe or intend. If I have no reason to believe or intend something, why trick myself into doing so? In order to explain why we might sometimes have reasons to manipulate ourselves in this way, we need to acknowledge that we can have reasons to believe or intend something that cannot motivate us to believe or intend it.

As Kavka notes, SDSs also bring out the somewhat surprising conclusion that we might sometimes have reason to corrupt ourselves – to bring about in ourselves dispositions to act against the balance of moral reasons, or to fail to be properly motivationally sensitive to some moral reasons. An agent faced with a genuine SDS, like *Nuclear Deterrence*, ought (if she can) to bring it about that she forms the deterrent intention – in this case, to retaliate – even though this means reducing her sensitivity to genuine moral reasons. This has important implications for our consideration of the Motivating Intuition. In particular, it seems to run counter to a thought which played an important role in our defense of the motivating intuition: that we *ought* always to be as virtuous as we can be, and therefore, since it's plausible that being virtuous is a matter of being appropriately motivationally sensitive to our moral reasons, that we ought always to be motivated by the reasons that apply to us. This thought, I argued, underlies the crucial first premise of the second argument for internalism I set out in Section 1. But, as Kavka's SDSs show, we sometimes have reasons to lessen our own sensitivity to reasons.

In *Nuclear Deterrence* and *Pragmatic Belief* we may have reason to corrupt ourselves because, unless we do, we will not be able to form intentions or beliefs we have good reason to form. In *Nuclear Deterrence*, the problem arises because of the partly involuntary nature of intention-formation: we cannot, at will, form the intention to do something we believe we have no reason to do. And cases where we have reason to intend to do something we have no reason to do may be quite rare. But the problem for the Motivating Intuition is in fact much broader than the example of SDSs suggests. It is, in fact, often true that we ought not to be motivated by reasons that apply to us.

Usually, when it is true that we ought not be motivated by our reasons, this is because we are more likely to succeed at doing what we have reason to do if we aren't motivated by those reasons.[22] A particularly grim version of this problem is faced by soldiers fighting in a justifiable war. The military historian Richard Holmes, who interviewed veterans of many wars, describes the problem faced by the soldier in this way:

> [a] soldier who constantly reflected upon the knee-smashing, widow-making characteristics of his weapon, or who always thought of the enemy as a man exactly like himself, doing much the same task and subjected to exactly the same stresses and strains, would find it difficult to operate effectively in battle. ... Without the creation of abstract images of the enemy, and without the depersonalization of the enemy during training, battle would become impossible to sustain. ... If ... men reflect too deeply upon their enemy's common humanity, then they risk being unable to proceed with a task whose aims may be eminently just and legitimate.[23]

This might be so even if the 'enemy's common humanity' underlies the justification for the war itself, and so provides a fundamental reason for fighting. That is:

> **Soldier in a Just War.** In a war fought on humanitarian grounds, soldiers may have reason to desensitize themselves to the common humanity of the inhabitants of an enemy state so that they can more effectively fight a war whose very justification is provided by that common humanity. If they have reason to fight in the war, and fight effectively then they ought not be motivated to fight by that reason.[24]

Pragmatic grounds not to be motivated by the reasons that apply to us are often generated when we are forced to act in emergency situations and against great odds, a fact that was strikingly demonstrated by post-crash interviews of Captain Chelsey Sullenberger, the US Airways pilot who miraculously succeeded in landing a commercial jetliner with no working engines on New York's Hudson River, improbably saving the lives of all 155 passengers and crew on board:

> **Emergency Landing.** On January 15th, 2009, Captain Sullenberger successfully emergency-landed an Airbus A320, which had lost all thrust in both engines due to a double bird strike, in the icy waters of the Hudson River, with no loss of life. Asked, in a *60 Minutes* interview by Katie Couric, whether he had been thinking about the passengers as his plane was descending rapidly towards the waters of the Hudson, Captain Sullenberger replied, 'Not specifically....I mean, I *knew* I had to solve this problem. I knew I had to find a way out of this box I found myself in....My focus at that point was so intensely on the landing...I thought of nothing else.'[25]

While the fact that many lives depended on his successfully landing the aircraft undoubtedly provided Captain Sullenberger with a reason to do so, it is also clear that it was a very good thing that the Captain was not in fact motivated by this reason as he guided the plane onto the water. Indeed, it seems likely that years of training in emergency preparedness coached the Captain, with good reason, not to think about the ultimate reasons for successfully handling a crisis situation when faced with the need to do so.

The lessons of *Soldier in a Just War* and *Emergency Landing* generalize. A specialist in a rarely curable disease may be able to cure more patients if she's in it for the social prestige than if she's in it chiefly to save lives, since her low success rate might otherwise drive her to quit. A surgeon may operate more successfully if she learns to suppress some normal sympathy for patients in unavoidable pain,[26] and she may be less likely to make nervous mistakes in delicate procedures if she is not thinking of the life that is at stake. In fact, many of us have found ourselves in situations in which we were fortunate that we were driven by ulterior motives, habit, instinct, or 'auto-pilot' rule-following to make decisions or react to threats which we would have likely reacted to less well if we had been responding motivationally to our reasons for doing so. If a child runs into the street right in front of my car, I hit the brakes automatically – I am not motivated by a concern for the well-being of the child. In a surprising number of cases, there is much to be said for *not* being motivated by our reasons.

4. What these counter-examples can teach us

What can we learn from these counter-examples? Has anything survived of the intuitions that supported the Motivating Intuition?

The examples of the *Student of Reasoning* and the *Sore Loser* show us that 'A has a reason to Φ' cannot *mean* 'A would be motivated to Φ if she were rational,' as Williams suggested, and that the Motivating Intuition does not state a 'platitude' about practical reason, as Smith suggested. We readily ascribe reasons to the *Student of Reasoning* and the *Sore Loser* despite the fact that we are perfectly aware that they would not be motivated to act on those reasons if they were perfectly rational (because they would not have those reasons).

While the *Student of Reasoning* and the *Sore Loser* would not be motivated by their reasons if they were perfectly rational (because the reasons would, in that case, no longer apply), their reasons could nonetheless serve as explanations of their actions in their *actual* circumstances – the circumstances in which they do apply. So does the conceptual link between normative reasons and possible *explanations* of actions, to which Williams also appeals, hold up? No: the examples of the deluded *'James Bond'* and of *My Fallibility* show that we can have reasons for both action and belief that could not possibly serve as explanations of our actions or beliefs, even in the circumstances in which they do apply to us.

Moreover, the problem is not just a result of our imperfect rationality, as the cases of the *Student of Reasoning*, the *Sore Loser*, *'James Bond'*, and *My Fallibility* might suggest. The predicaments presented by *Nuclear Deterrence*, the *Toxin Puzzle*, and the problem of *Pragmatic Belief* show that, even if we're fully rational, we might have reasons to act or believe that could not motivate us to act or believe accordingly. It won't always be possible for us to do as we have reason to do, *for* the reason we have to do it. In other words, it won't always be possible for us to act virtuously.

And finally, as the cases of the *Soldier in a Just War* and the *Emergency Landing* show, and as our own experience will confirm, even when we *can* be motivated to do something by the reason we have for doing it, it's not always true that we *ought* to be motivated by that reason. Sometimes, we are significantly more effective in doing what we have reason to do if we train ourselves to be motivated differently. If it's not always true that we *ought* to be (rationally) motivated by the reasons that apply to us, we cannot appeal to the *ought-implies-can* principle to derive the conclusion that we *can* always be (rationally) motivated by the reasons that apply to us.

Remember that the *First Argument* for internalism about reasons, the one explicitly made by Williams in 'Internal and External Reasons,' depended on the claim that the Motivating Intuition captures what our reasons-statements *mean*: that what we *mean* when we ascribe a reason to Φ to someone is that they would be motivated to Φ if they were rational. And remember my suggestion that the *Second Argument* for internalism about reasons, which also includes the Motivating Intuition as a premise, gained support from the *ought-implies-can* principle. As the counter-examples to the Motivating Intuition show, both of these influential arguments for internalism about reasons fail before we've even considered their controversial Humean premises. If, as Williams and Johnson have suggested and as the structure of the debate about internalism implies, internalism's ability to accommodate the Motivating Intuition were its chief virtue, then considering the counter-examples I've described should lead us to abandon internalism about reasons.

But I don't think we should abandon internalism. I believe internalism still receives some direct support from some of the considerations I appealed to in defense of the Motivating Intuition in Section 2. And I believe we have other good grounds for taking internalism about reasons seriously.

5. Why be an internalist about reasons?

I've argued that Williams was wrong to present the Motivating Intuition as an account of what our reasons-statements mean. But I think he was right to point out that, when we attribute a reason to someone, we intend to appeal to a shared standard of conduct that that person must, as a rational agent, recognize as authoritative. This is, indeed, what makes our ascription to someone of a reason to do something different from our merely claiming we would like him to do it, or would do it in his place: as I said before, reasons statements aim at objectivity. And internalist accounts of reasons may fit better with this idea that reasons-ascriptions appeal to a shared standard of rationality than externalist accounts.

I've also argued that Smith was wrong to suggest that the Motivating Intuition expressed a platitude about practical reasons. But, nonetheless, his suggestion that when we deliberate about our reasons we're interested in the advice of people who share our basic commitments but are better informed and more rational than we are may provide some *direct* support for the internalist view of reasons. This thought may spell out one way in which reasons may be action-guiding – not irrelevant to moral deliberation – even though, as I've argued, they cannot always motivate the agent whose reasons they are: an agent's reasons should at least guide *us*, when we advise her about how she should act.

And finally, even if we reject the Motivating Intuition, internalism about reasons may still help capture our instincts that what our reasons are should reflect what we care about – that an account of reasons that leaves it possible that we have reasons to act that do not reflect any of our value commitments unacceptably alienates us from our reasons.

In fact, I think internalism about reasons is supported by each of these more basic motivating intuitions – intuitions that *motivated* the Motivating Intuition. But the simple version of internalism with which I began – the version defended by Williams – must be false, since it entails the Motivating Intuition. A reason cannot be a consideration that *would motivate* me if I were deliberating in a procedurally rational way from my existing ends and motivations.

The essential feature of an internalist account of reasons is that it ties the truth of a reasons claim to the presence of a suitable element in an agent's motivational set: according to internalism, what we have reason to do depends fundamentally on what ends, broadly understood, we already have. Externalism, by contrast, holds that facts about our reasons do not fundamentally depend on facts about what we care about. The distinction is sometimes put differently: internalism embraces a *procedural* conception of practical rationality, according to which the rational requirement to hold certain ends is generated indirectly by the relation of those ends to other ends we already hold, as a result, in particular, of requirements of internal consistency and coherence. One might compare this to the case of theoretical reason, which may require us, by means of standards of internal consistency and coherence, to hold certain beliefs in virtue of their relationship to other beliefs that we hold. According to an externalist, *substantive* notion of rationality, reason may require us to hold some (moral and prudential) ends directly, and regardless of what else is true about us.

These ways of thinking about the disagreement between internalists and externalists make it clear that the internalists' claim about the necessary motivating or explanatory power of reasons is not an essential feature of the view. Our reasons depend on our antecedent ends not because those ends are the source of the (supposed) *motivating* force of normative reasons, but rather because those ends are the source of the *justifying* force of those reasons. As the example of a non-motivating theoretical reason provided by *My Fallibility* shows, a consideration (in that case, the fact that I have the unsupported belief that Elvis lives) can throw its justificatory weight behind my performing or believing an action or proposition (in that case, the proposition that I have some unjustified beliefs), even if it cannot *move* me to perform the action, or *convince* me of the proposition.

According to the version of internalism about reasons for action[27] that I am most interested in defending, a reason for an agent to Φ is a consideration that counts in favor of Φing – that throws its justificatory weight behind Φing – *in virtue of the relation it shows between Φing and the agent's existing ends* (for example, by showing that Φing is a means to one of those ends, or constitutive of it, or valuable in consequence of the value of that end). My account is internalist, because it takes what we have reason to do to depend fundamentally on what ends we already have. But, unlike many internalist accounts of reasons, my account does not rely on the claim that reasons must be capable of motivating rational agents, or necessarily motivate agents who recognize them: in my view, facts give us reasons when they are the source of a certain kind of *evidence* (given our other ends), not when they are the source of a possible *motivation* (given our other ends).

It may be helpful to think through how this version of internalism, unlike Williams's, can recognize the reasons for action and belief I've appealed to as counter-examples to the Motivating Intuition in the cases I've discussed. Take, for example, the case of Captain Sullenberger: although the Captain should not and perhaps *could* not have been motivated to take the necessary actions to land the plane safely by the fact that over 150 lives depended on his doing so, it is clear that the fact that his taking those actions would save those lives was evidence, relative to his antecedent value commitments, that taking the actions in question would be a valuable thing to do. The value of *that end*, in other words, was entailed by the value of his other ends and the consistency and coherence requirements of procedural rationality.

Similar arguments can be used to show that the soldier in my *Just War* example has an *internal reason* (as I understand it) to fight effectively (provided by the common humanity of the inhabitants of the enemy state); that the sick person in my example of *Pragmatic Belief* has a (practical) *internal reason* to believe her cancer is curable (provided by the survival benefits of believing this); that I have an *internal reason* to intend to drink the toxin when faced with the *Toxin Puzzle* (provided by the fact that so intending will win me the million-dollar prize); that the defense strategist in *Nuclear Deterrence* has an *internal reason* to intend to retaliate (provided by the deterrence benefits of the intention); that Johnson's *James-Bond*-delusional patient has an *internal reason* to see the psychiatrist (since, presumably, it is one of his important ends that he not be deluded); that the *Sore Loser* has an *internal reason* to leave the court without shaking hands (since this will prevent him from punching his opponent); and that the *Student of Reasoning* has an *internal reason* to take rationality-improving lessons. In each case the agents have value-commitments that, taken together with requirements of consistency and coherence and the reason-providing fact, entail the value of their taking such actions, despite the fact that they either should not, cannot, or could not if fully rational be motivated by those reason-providing facts to act.[28]

This version of internalism about practical reasons retains some of the features of Williams's internalism about reasons that made it an attractive view. It captures his thought that, when we attribute a reason to someone, we intend to appeal to a shared standard of conduct that the person must, as a rational agent, recognize as authoritative. Remember that the notion of rationality that plays a central role in the internalist account of reasons is *procedural*, not *substantive* (i.e., it concerns standards for proper relations *between* ends, but doesn't specify any end as rationally required, *per se*, regardless of its relation to things we already care about). The procedural standard of rationality, if not exactly uncontroversial, might nonetheless be agreed on by someone who disagrees with the internalist at the outset about what her *reasons* are. So it could serve as a kind of Archimedean point against which we might brace ourselves in disputes about reasons. Externalists, by contrast, if they want to appeal to a supposedly shared standard of rationality, must appeal to a substantive standard – one that simply incorporates, as a *rational requirement*, the need to respond to the very reason whose existence their interlocutor disputes. If she disputes the existence of the reason, she'll also dispute the existence of the corresponding rational requirement. The account of internalism I defend also avoids alienating us from our reasons: in the picture of reasons it presents, reasons are firmly rooted in facts about what matters to us.

Finally, the version of internalism I've defended here may still lay partial claim to a virtue that drew many philosophers to the Motivating Intuition, and thereby to Williams's internalism: its ability to explain the apparent motivating force of moral judgments. If, as the Motivating Intuition claims, considerations that provide reasons must be such as to motivate rational agents, we should expect rational agents to be reliably motivated to act as they have reason to act: rational agents' judgments about their reasons are true, and are the discovery of facts that themselves have the power to motivate those agents when they are rational. But counter-examples to the Motivating Intuition such as those presented by *Nuclear Deterrence, Just War*, and *Emergency Landing* show that, even if we are motivated to act as we judge we have reasons to act, it may not be *those reasons* doing the motivating. So the Motivating Intuition cannot explain the motivating force of such moral judgments. Nonetheless, the version of internalism I have sketched, which does not rely on the Motivating Intuition, should lead us to expect that the agents in these examples will be motivated to act as they judge they ought: after all, they have such reasons, on my account, because they each have ends that will be furthered by acting in this way, and (we've assumed) have the means to bring it about that they act as they ought – just for *other* reasons.

I have not undertaken a full defense of internalism about reasons here.[29] I have primarily been concerned with sketching a version of internalism that preserves the essential characteristics of the view without relying on or entailing the Motivating Intuition, and with arguing that this version retains some of the main attractions of traditional internalism about reasons. Even without the Motivating Intuition, there is, I believe, plenty to motivate internalism.

Notes

1. Williams (1995), p. 35.
2. Williams (1981b), p. 101. This way of stating the view oversimplifies the matter in at least two ways: firstly, as I have noted, Williams intends 'desires' to be understood broadly – they may include, in addition to ordinary present desires, evaluations, attitudes, projects, commitments, and so on – anything for the sake of which we act. Secondly, the notion of an action's 'serving' a desire suggests that reason plays a purely instrumental role. Williams, however, wants to allow for the possibility that we have reason to act in ways that serve our ends non-instrumentally – perhaps the action in question is constitutive of some end or commitment, or expresses that commitment (see p. 104).
3. This dependence does not necessarily rule out the possibility of universal reasons – reasons we all share. Some internalists defend the existence, for example, of universal internal *moral* reasons. See, for example, Michael Smith (1994a); I also defend a Kantian account of the existence of such reasons – see, for example, my (forthcoming). What makes such universal reasons *internal* is that they apply to us in virtue of the relation they stand in to our actual ends and desires, whatever those happen to be. But the possibility of such universal internal reasons will not occupy us here.
4. Williams (1981b), p. 109.
5. Thomas Nagel offers it on behalf of internalism (1970, p. 27), although he rejects one of the premises.
6. Hume (1739/1975), pp. 414–15.
7. Williams (1981b), p. 105.
8. That is, one not derived from our existing motivations.
9. Mele (2003), p. 89.
10. He contrasts this view with the 'cognitive engine theory,' which asserts: 'in actual human beings, some instances of practical evaluative reasoning, in or by issuing in a belief favoring a course of action, nonaccidentally produce motivation that does not derive at all from antecedent motivation.' (p. 89)
11. Williams (1981b), p. 110.
12. My own view is that thick moral concepts such as *cruel* or *selfish* also aim at objectivity – and so can be appropriately applied only when a reason-ascription is also appropriate. The charge of selfishness, for example, does not merely imply that the selfish person is more protective of her own interests than we would like her to be, say, or than is normal, but rather that she is more protective of her own interests than she has *reason* to be.
13. Smith (1994a), pp. 150–1.
14. Railton (1986), p. 9.
15. As Williams puts it, '[t]here can come a point at which it is quite unreasonable for a man to give up, in the name of the impartial good ordering of the world of moral agents, something which is a condition of his having any interest in being around in the world at all' (Williams, 1981a, p. 14).

16. The example is due to Michael Smith (1995, p. 111), who is elaborating on a character introduced by Gary Watson.
17. See, for example, Smith (1994a), p. 151.
18. Johnson (2003). See also Johnson (1999).
19. Kavka (1978).
20. Kavka (1978) notes that 'writers on strategic policy frequently assert that nuclear deterrence will be effective only if the defending nation really intends to retaliate' (p. 287).
21. Kavka (1983), pp. 33–34.
22. We can design science-fictiony cases to show that it might be possible for an agent to find herself in a situation where she cannot successfully do what she has reason to do if she is motivated by that reason. Phillip Stratton-Lake describes the following example:

    > Consider a world in which there is an omnipotent, evil demon whose aim is to stop good people from doing what they should in the light of the normative reasons why they should so act ... He achieves this by making it the case that if a good person ever acts from the normative reasons why she should so act, he will make it such that this action is wrong, and he tells them this. Every good person knows, therefore, that she cannot do the right thing from the normative reasons why this is right. For they know that if they are motivated to act in this way, then their actions will be morally wrong. (2000, p. 18)

    In Stratton-Lake's evil-demon world, we cannot do what we have reason to do *for that reason*, because the demon will ensure that the actions of well-motivated people bring about horrific consequences. But my focus in this paper is on real-world cases in which the motivating intuition fails.
23. Holmes (1985), p. 361. Soldiers in war also use the expression 'tango down' to indicate that a hostile human 'target' has been eliminated ('tango' represents the 't' in 'target'), whereas they use the expression 'man down' when one of their own fellow soldiers has been hit.
24. I don't want to suggest that such desensitization is easy to justify or usually justified. Indeed, the fact, described by Holmes, that soldiers often must be desensitized in this way to be effective soldiers is, I believe, one of the reasons why wars are hard to justify. Not only do wars require participants to 'corrupt' themselves to be effective soldiers (a cost with immediate and long-term effects that should not be underestimated), but the need for such self-corruption also creates a significant risk that soldiers will prosecute a potentially justifiable war in a manner that makes it unjustified; as Holmes says, 'if the abstract image [of the enemy, internalized by soldiers in training] is overdrawn or depersonalization is stretched into hatred, the restraints on human behavior in war are easily swept aside' (p. 361).
25. Katie Couric interviewed Captain Sullenberger on *60 Minutes*, airdate 8 February 2009, copyright CBS News. A summary of the interview that includes the quoted passages can be found at: http://www.cbsnews.com/stories/2009/02/08/60minutes/main4783580_page2.shtml?tag=contentMain;contentBody (accessed 17 September 2009).
26. As Kavka (1978) also suggests – see note 20, p. 287.
27. For reasons I won't go into here, but that I address elsewhere, I take the arguments for internalism about *practical reasons* – reasons for *action* – to be considerably stronger than parallel arguments one might make for internalism about *theoretical reasons* – reasons for *belief.* There are, I believe, much stronger candidates for

considerations that might count in favor of our adopting some belief regardless of the relation it stands in to our existing beliefs (e.g. basic sense-experiences). In fact, I think that thinking carefully about the ways in which practical and theoretical rationality come apart, and about what internalism and externalism about theoretical reasons might look like, gives us some reason to doubt that there could be external *practical* reasons. I make this argument in my (forthcoming).

28. I omit the case of *My Fallibility* because it concerns *epistemic* reasons for belief, and I am not concerned with the possibility of internal epistemic reasons here.
29. I undertake a more developed defense in my (forthcoming, *supra note 27*).

8
Beyond Wrong Reasons: The Buck-Passing Account of Value

Ulrike Heuer

The buck-passing account of value (BPA) is very fertile ground, which has given rise to a number of interpretations and controversies. It has originally been proposed by T.M. Scanlon as an analysis of value: according to it, being good 'is not a property that itself provides a reason to respond to a thing in certain ways. Rather, to be good or valuable is to have other properties that constitute such reasons.'[1] And also: 'being valuable is not a property that provides us with reasons. Rather, to call something valuable is to say that it has other properties that provide reasons for behaving in certain ways with regard to it.'[2]

As Pekka Väyrynen,[3] and subsequently Mark Schroeder[4] and Roger Crisp,[5] have pointed out, the account comprises two theses:

> **(BPA–)** The fact that something is good or of value is not itself a reason to respond to it favorably or to behave in certain ways with regard to it.

> **(BPA+)** The fact that something is good or of value consists in the fact that it has some other property P which is a reason to respond to it favorably or to behave in certain ways with regard to it.[6,7]

The two claims are, in principle, independent. As Crisp emphasizes, (BPA–) does not entail (BPA+). Perhaps goodness is not a reason, but it does not follow from this that goodness must consist in there being other properties that provide reasons.[8] The converse is also true: (BPA+) can be true, even if (BPA–) is false. Even if goodness consists in there being some other property P that provides a reason, goodness itself could also be a reason – in the way in which, if R is a reason, the fact that R obtains could also be a reason.[9]

Scanlon's original arguments attempt to show that (BPA+) is true because (BPA–) is. But these arguments are flawed.[10] I will not be concerned with them here. The most influential of these arguments – the one that Crisp[11] aptly dubbed 'the redundancy argument' – has been extensively discussed, and shown to be unsuccessful.[12]

Of course, the buck-passing account may be correct even if the arguments for it are not. But, since (BPA–) and (BPA+) are independent of one another, it may be asked why we should accept either of them. Some[13] have focused on (BPA–) as the claim the buck-passing account is ultimately concerned with. Viewed thus, (BPA+) may have been introduced only as an explanation of (BPA–), and an unsuccessful one at that. I am inclined, however, to think that (BPA+) is the more central of the two theses, and the theoretically more important one, as it suggests a metaphysical account of the relation of values and reasons. In this paper, I will therefore focus on (BPA+). I should add that, while I am going to discuss (BPA+) as suggesting a metaphysical account, there is also an interpretation of buck-passing as a conceptual analysis of 'good,' and of course the metaphysical and conceptual interpretations are compatible and could both be true.[14] Mainly for simplicity's sake, I will not run the two interpretations in tandem, but focus on the metaphysical one. (But I will draw your attention to the semantic alternative occasionally.)

In Section 1, I will show that BPA is not as obviously a successor of the fitting-attitude (for short: FA) analysis of value as some have thought. The much discussed wrong-kind-of-reasons (for short: WKR) problem afflicts buck-passing only in so far as it incorporates a version of FA analysis, or at any rate is expressed in terms of reasons for attitudes. There can be a buck-passing account of value that is not affected by the problem: one that limits the account to reasons for actions.[15] However, in so far as BPA does inherit elements of FA analysis, it also has a WKR problem. In Section 2, I will discuss this problem and its solution. I will show that it has been misidentified in the current literature, and that – once we understand the problem correctly – its solution is likely to be unavailable to the buck-passer. Hence we should reject any account of BPA that incorporates FA analysis. That leaves us with versions that do not: versions that formulate BPA+ in terms of reasons for actions only, rather than reasons for attitudes. Finally, in Section 3, I will discuss at least briefly why buck-passing seemed to be appealing to begin with, and whether a version of BPA that does not incorporate FA analysis is a viable alternative to a version of BPA that does, and hence whether such a version can enable us to move beyond the WKR problem.

1. Some background: buck-passing and FA analysis

Buck-passing stands in a complicated relation to the fitting-attitude analysis of normativity that reaches back to the work of Brentano and Ewing.[16] Proponents of FA analysis hold that, as a matter of conceptual analysis of goodness, something is good if it is fitting to have pro-attitudes of a certain kind towards it. The ambition of FA analysis is to explain all practical normativity in terms of the fittingness of attitudes, which – while being itself a normative concept – is the only normative concept that grounds all others.

Wlodek Rabinowicz and Toni Rønnow-Rasmussen[17] welcomed BPA as a contemporary version of FA analysis, and others have followed this suggestion.[18] But whether BPA should be regarded as a version of FA analysis is a moot point. First of all, the second disjunct in both formulations above – the phrase 'reasons...to behave in certain ways with regard to [something that is of value]' – has no obvious role in FA analysis. Let me begin, therefore, by dropping it for the moment and by focusing on the following shortened formulations of (BPA–) and (BPA+) (I will come back to the left-out disjunct later):

(BPA$_{FA}$ –) The fact that something is valuable is not itself a reason to respond to it favorably.

(BPA$_{FA}$ +) The fact that X is valuable consists in the fact that X has some other property P that is a reason to respond to it favorably.

The FA subscript indicates that in this form the formulations can be understood as part and parcel of FA analysis. Or can they? It depends on whether the fact that there is a reason to respond favorably to something is the same fact as the fact that it is fitting to have a favoring attitude to that thing. Thus the question is whether (BPA$_{FA}$+) is equivalent to:

(FA$_{BPA}$) The fact that X is valuable consists in the fact that X has some other property P that makes it fitting to have certain favoring attitudes towards X.[19]

There are at least two worries about this. First, not all reasons that we have by virtue of something being good are reasons to have favoring attitudes. Some of them are reasons to act. This is not a problem for BPA, because the second disjunct that I left out in the FA formulations of the view are precisely about reasons for actions: in Scanlon's formulation, there are reasons 'to behave in certain ways towards something that is good.' Adding this expressly, as in (BPA–) and (BPA+), shows that the account is not restricted to reasons for attitudes. It also shows that there is no assumption that reasons for actions can simply be derived from reasons for attitudes. But FA analysis would claim just that. If BPA+ were a version of FA analysis, reasons for actions would have to be derived from reasons for attitudes. That the original BPA formulations distinguish between reasons for attitudes and reasons for actions may be due to their author's skepticism about the FA project.[20] But, if so, BPA lacks the neatness, and perhaps also part of the motivation, that drives FA analysis.

Secondly, there is an obvious difference between 'there is a reason to have attitude A' and 'it is fitting to have attitude A.' Reasons are, *pro tanto*, requiring:[21] if there is a reason to have an attitude (and the reason is not defeated) I am at fault if I don't have it. Thus, if I have a reason to admire something (say), then, other things being equal, I am at fault if I fail to admire it. Fittingness is different: if I have an attitude, and it is fitting to have it, I am justified in having it, but it does not follow that I would have been at fault if I had not had the attitude at all. An example might help to show this. Take fear: it is fitting to feel fear only if there is danger – but a person who is not afraid, even though she is aware of danger, is not always (if ever) at fault. In other words: that it is fitting to have an attitude is not a reason to have it. Thus, it is not obvious that FA analysis could explain why a person may be required to have an attitude.[22] The normative force of 'there is a reason to have an attitude' and 'it is fitting to have an attitude' appears to be different. Perhaps 'fittingness' is a normative concept, but, if so, it is not clear how it translates into the language of reasons. It is not clear, therefore, that BPA is a version of FA analysis at all, even in its BPA$_{FA}$ formulations. None of this, of course, is any skin off the buck-passer's nose. There may be good reasons for departing from FA-analysis in the way she does. But those reasons have yet to be uncovered.

But, whether or not buck-passing is a version of or a development from FA analysis, it inherits one of its problems: the so-called wrong kind of reasons (WKR) problem.

2. The WKR problem

2.1. The problem

The so-called WKR problem is the problem that, intuitively, there seem to be reasons to have favoring attitudes towards objects that are devoid of value, as, for instance, when an evil demon orders you to admire him or else he'll torture you. You then have a reason to admire him, but he is not in any way good. Hence, the buck-passing account is false. The buck-passer's solution to the problem must be to narrow down the kinds of reasons of which BPA is true. Put schematically, the solution to the problem is to reformulate (BPA+) in a WKR-proof way, such as:

> The fact that X is valuable consists in the fact that X has some other property P which provides a reason *of the right kind* to respond to it favorably.

The difficulty is to describe the relevant kind of reasons in a non-circular way. Obviously, saying that only those reasons that obtain when the attitude's object is of value will not do. In the semantic interpretation, this would make BPA circular; in the metaphysical one, the account would become uninformative and uninteresting.[23]

There have been a number of attempts to solve this problem. Early on, Wlodek Rabinowicz and Toni Rønnow-Rasmussen suggested that a reason is of the right kind if it has the 'dual role' of both providing the content of the pro-attitude and justifying it: for instance, that a person is courageous is a reason for admiring her, and she is admired for her courage. The evil demon, on the other hand, is admired on account of his threat (the avoidance of the threatened punishment is the justifying reason for having the admiring attitude), but he is not admired *for* being threatening (in this case, it seems quite unclear what, if anything, he is being admired for). However, Rabinowicz and Rønnow-Rasmussen themselves are skeptical about the solution, because it meets with problems if the demon requires us to admire him for his own sake 'on account of his determination to punish us if we don't.' In this case, 'the demon's determination to punish us if we don't comply provides the reason for our admiration and at the same time appears in the intentional content of that attitude as the feature for which its object is being admired.'[24] The dual role solution has nonetheless received much attention, and a number of suggestions for developing it have been advanced in the recent literature.[25]

I am not going to discuss them in any detail here, though. One reason for not doing this is that I believe that the problem has not yet been identified clearly enough (I'll explain below). I want to approach the issue in a somewhat different way that will also allow us to place it within a broader context.

The WKR problem is a problem only for reasons for attitudes. There are no 'wrong reasons' for actions[26] – or so I will argue. Once we see why this is, the solution will take a different shape (I think).

2.2. Reasons for actions and reasons for attitudes

Only the reasons for attitudes disjunct of BPA gives rise to the WKR problem. Let me firstly explain why, and then, secondly, show how we can take a lead to solving the problem from this observation.

How do the evil demon examples work out if we focus on reasons for actions? Assume that the evil demon orders you to express your admiration for him (or for a saucer of mud) by bowing three times, or he will torture you. Clearly you now have a *pro tanto* reason to bow three times and do whatever else it takes to express admiration, and this reason is not of the wrong kind: it is a typical instrumental reason. If BPA+ were phrased in terms of reasons for action only, there would be no problem: the value of Φing (bowing, in our case) may consist in Φing's having other properties (e.g. being necessary to averting the demon's wrath) that give you a reason to Φ. The value in question is instrumental value. Thus, there is no problem with giving a buck-passing account of the value that relates to reasons for action – it is quite straightforward.[27]

But BPA has sometimes been suggested as an account of 'final value:' 'being valuable for one's own sake.' The account sets out to capture reasons to admire something for its own sake. Isn't it problematic, then, that the value of the action is instrumental value? But actions typically have instrumental (rather than final) value: their point is to achieve something, or bring something about. Yet there are exceptions: some actions may have final value (such as doing one's duty,[28] acting kindly or whistling a tune). How about those actions, then? If an evil demon orders you to do your duty (or else he'll torture you), you don't have a wrong reason – you just have an additional one. There may be a reason for doing your duty because of the final value of doing so, and there is now a further reason, because the demon orders you to do it, and you will be avoiding the punishment if you obey. This is no more problematic than, say, the reason to do your duty because if you don't you may lose your job. Perhaps the reason to do your duty because doing so has final value[29] is a sufficient reason, but there can nonetheless be additional reasons that are unrelated to the final value of so acting. As above, the evil-demon-reason is simply a typical instrumental reason. There is instrumental value in doing whatever it is that you are ordered to do, and there is no particular problem with giving a buck-passing account of this kind of value – I therefore don't see a reason for restricting the account to final value.

But what if the demon ordered you to do your duty for its own sake (or because of a sense of duty)? Again, there is no problem, since you have a reason to do that anyway. And finally, what if the demon ordered you to express your admiration of *his* final value, or to express that you admire him for his own sake? You may feel a bit pressed. But it is not because the reason is of the wrong kind, but because complying with it involves a kind of pretense or lying. You don't believe that the demon has 'final value' – but you could try to play-act. If the order is understood more stringently, as involving that you act out of the right attitude (and, being a demon, your torturer will know if you don't), the problem is with having the attitude, not with acting in a certain way.

I cannot at this point offer a general explanation for why reasons for actions do not give rise to the WKR problem, but I will be able to do so by the end of our journey (in Section 2.7). Bear with me.

Let us now look more closely at the WKR problem with reasons for attitudes. If the demon orders you to admire him, or else he'll torture you, the reason is of the wrong kind, because, while you now have a reason to admire the demon, this is not because admiring him is a fitting response to his value – *ex hypothesi*, being evil, the demon has no value.[30]

This description brings back the circularity worry: we know independently that the demon is 'evil,' and therefore the reason to admire him must be of the wrong kind: it is of the wrong kind because it does not relate to his value. This explanation is suspicious if offered by the buck-passer. If our only way of ascertaining that certain reasons are 'the wrong reasons' were that our independent understanding of value allowed us to characterize them as 'wrong' from the perspective of the analysis, one might begin to wonder why the analysis seemed tempting to begin with. It seems that we already understand value, independently of the analysis, and, furthermore, this understanding is presupposed by the analysis.

But, since this worry is couched in epistemic terms, the buck-passer can shrug it off: buck-passing is not offered as an account of our knowledge of values.[31]

The proponent of BPA may reply that the lesson that the 'evil demon' recipe for generating counter-examples teaches us is a different one: the disvalue of the evil demon is stipulated, and thus does not show that we have epistemic access to value that is independent of our knowledge of reasons. The examples, rather, show that there could be reasons for admiring *anything* – because there are no limits to what the evil demon can order you to admire. But we know that it is not true that just anything is of value. Hence some of the reasons must be of the wrong kind. While the examples make this clear by stipulating the evilness of the demon, the general point is independent of this.

Yet, there is a more important worry lurking behind the epistemic one. Take a neutral example: some person, P, orders you to admire something, X, or else P will punish you. Neither P nor X are described in evaluative terms, and you don't know whether P is a good person, or X is an admirable thing. Is your reason for admiring X of the wrong kind? It seems to me that it is. We can say that much without knowing whether X has value or not: even if it does, its value does not consist in the reason that is provided by being ordered to admire it. But why is the reason of the wrong kind? Not because you know independently that X has no value – we assumed that you don't know this. X may be the most admirable thing. This, I believe, is a start towards showing what is wrong with the way the WKR problem has been set up: the reason is of the wrong kind, but not because the thing in question has no value. Or, to put it differently, whether or not a reason for admiring is of the wrong kind does not depend on the value of what is to be admired.

To see this more clearly, let's take out the uncertainty (and the epistemic taint of the previous example). Imagine that your benign and caring benefactor wants you to love a beautiful painting that she is going to bequeath to you. You have one reason for loving the painting anyway, namely that it is beautiful, and you have a further reason, because your benefactor wishes it. Your reason is not the avoidance of a torture threat in this case, but perhaps a reason of gratitude or a reason not to disappoint your benefactor. This reason you would have even if your benefactor, not being the best judge in matters aesthetic, were mistaken on this occasion, and the painting were but a poor, inept attempt at artwork. And, furthermore, this second reason for loving the painting is of the wrong kind in the very same way as the reason to admire the evil demon. In this example it is not because we stipulated that your benefactor is evil and has no value – on the contrary: we stipulated that she is good. Of course, the object of the attitude is not your benefactor but the painting. But, even if we assume that the painting is indeed beautiful and deserves to be admired, the reason of gratitude towards your benefactor for loving it is of the wrong kind. It is just not true that the goodness of a beautiful painting consists in its having other properties, such as being commended by a kindly person to whom you owe a debt of gratitude. If anything, its value consists in its aesthetic qualities – this we know *a priori*.

Thus, perhaps, the problem has not been identified clearly enough. It is not the problem that there can be reasons for pro-attitudes towards things that are devoid of value. Some reasons for admiring things are of the wrong kind, whether or not those things are of value or admirable.

2.3. Placing the problem

Let me, therefore, make a fresh start. Quite intuitively speaking, there are different kinds of reasons for having attitudes. If I am being promised £100 if I believe that it's sunny outside, I have a reason to believe it, even in the face of pouring rain, the reason being that it will earn me the money. But that seems to be a peculiar reason. The example has nothing to do with the buck-passing account of value and the WKR problem, since BPA is not concerned with reasons for belief. However, the reason is peculiar, in perhaps the same way as wrong reasons are.

Joseph Raz has recently suggested that the mark of reasons of this kind is that they cannot be followed directly.[32] That is, I cannot form a belief that it is sunny directly in response to the reason that it will earn me £100. I can comply with the reason, however. Perhaps I mistakenly happen to believe that it is sunny anyway; or I can undergo hypnosis, and end up with the relevant belief, thereby earning the money. In either case I would comply with the reason for having the belief. But I cannot form the belief directly, *for that reason*. We can respond directly to reasons for belief only if they are truth-related.

This is not meant to be a remark about psychology. The idea is not that we are psychologically unable to form beliefs in certain ways directly (even though that may by and large be true); it is, rather, a claim about the normative structure of belief: if someone were to form a belief about the weather directly in response to finding that this would earn her £100, then she must be conceptually confused (not understanding what 'it is sunny' means) or irrational.

Raz proposes to distinguish the two kinds of reasons as 'standard' and 'non-standard' reasons. As Raz sees it,

> [s]tandard reasons are those which we can follow directly, that is have the attitude…for that reason. Non-standard reasons for…an attitude are such that one can conform to them, but not follow them directly.[33]

Standard reasons for belief are truth-related reasons. But there are other reasons for having beliefs – perhaps again reasons of the evil demon variety, but also more mundane ones: believing that Iraq has biological or chemical weapons might help a politician to get along with allies and colleagues. Hence, she has a reason for having the belief, but she can't directly follow that reason. As before, she can do so indirectly: by having the false belief anyway, by visiting a hypnotist, by being self-deceived, and so on. And, again, the 'can' and 'cannot' should not be understood as being supported by empirical findings about our psychology, but as claims about the nature of belief. If a person were to follow that reason directly, it wouldn't show that it was, after all, a standard reason, but, rather, that she was conceptually confused or self-deceived.

Reasons for affects and emotions are similar: take reasons for admiration or fear. Perhaps it would be good to be afraid in a certain situation because it would make you more alert to changes in your enviroment, or perhaps it would be good if you admired your boss, because that would make it more likely that you would get promoted. Therefore you have reasons to be afraid, or to admire, which are independent of danger and admirability. But you cannot be afraid or admire someone for those reasons (even though they are perfectly good reasons for having those attitudes).

The so-called 'wrong reasons' that haunt BPA are non-standard reasons for attitudes. They, too, are reasons that cannot be followed directly. But they can be conformed with. A person can take steps towards acquiring the attitude that the evil demon command requires, even if she cannot form it directly. Or she can just happen to have it (for no reasons, or bad reasons). The non-standard reason itself provides a perfectly 'good' reason for having the attitude, albeit one that cannot be followed. An example of John Skorupski's illustrates this nicely:[34] a demon orders someone to admire a lousy violin performance. She can conform with this reason in various ways, one being that, having bad taste in music, she believes that it is an excellent performance and therefore admires it. While her false belief that the performance is excellent is no reason to admire it, the demon's order (as ever, backed by threat) is.

Raz identifies non-standard reasons with practical reasons – reasons to bring about or take steps towards having the relevant attitude. But the example shows that this is a bit rash: complying with a non-standard reason may require taking action of some kind, but it need not. Non-standard reasons can on occasion give rise to practical reasons – but they are not themselves practical reasons. The reason to admire the bad concert is not itself a practical reason, since it can be complied with in the absence of taking any action (simply by being a bad judge), but it is nonetheless true that the reason cannot be followed directly. Even the bad judge cannot respond directly with admiration to the demon's threat.

2.4. Explaining non-standard reasons

But why is it, then, that there are these two kinds of reasons for the attitude? Because attitudes, it seems – at least those attitudes we have been considering so far – have an inherent standard. As Raz sees it,

> [r]easons are adaptive [i.e. 'standard reasons'] if they mark the appropriateness of an attitude in the agent independently of the value of having that attitude, its appropriateness to the way things are. (p. 46)

Truth is the standard in the case of belief; admirability (or perhaps excellence in its various forms) in the case of admiration; danger in the case of fear. All those attitudes can be formed directly only in response to reasons that relate to the respective standards.

In the case of belief, it is not difficult to explain why some reasons are standard reasons whereas others are not: the non-standard ones are unrelated to the truth of the belief. Admiration is similar: the standard reasons for admiring are those that speak to the admirability of that which is admired; the non-standard reasons are unrelated to admirability. They are, however, related to value: there is a non-standard reason to admire something if and because it would be good to have the attitude, or because the having of the attitude is of value.[35]

2.5. Parfit's distinction of state- and object-given reasons

Derek Parfit discusses, but rejects, a somewhat similar distinction between state- and object-given reasons for attitudes (such as beliefs or desires).[36] Parfit does not introduce the distinction in the context of buck-passing. While he endorses a version of BPA, he does not address the WKR problem. This is not, I think, an oversight on his part; it is because his brand of buck-passing doesn't have a WKR problem. Parfit's buck-passing account is only concerned with reasons for actions[37] and, as explained above, there is no WKR problem with reasons for actions. But let's investigate the suggestion, since it may be of use to the buck-passer who wishes to include reasons for attitudes and has a problem with non-standard reasons.

Parfit rejects the idea that there could be both state- and object-given reasons for attitudes. A state-given reason for an attitude would be a reason to have that attitude because it would be good to have – it is 'grounded' in properties of the attitude.[38] An object-given reason is provided by properties of the 'object' towards which the attitude is held. That is to say, there is reason to believe that 2 + 2 = 4, because it does. The object of the belief is '2 + 2 = 4', and it is true. Parfit considers whether there could be a state-given reason to believe that 2 + 2 = 1, if – the move is familiar now – an evil demon will torture you unless you do. Parfit thinks we should reject this idea.[39] His worry is that, if there were both state- and object-given reasons for forming beliefs about the sum, those reasons could compete or conflict. It would then be a sensible question to ask: 'Do I, all things considered, have most reason to believe that 2 + 2 = 4, or that 2 + 2 =1?' Parfit wishes to reject this question, because he imagines that, in some circumstances, the reason to avoid the demon's threat could be conclusive: you would then have most reason to believe that 2 + 2 = 1. Since your reason to believe that 2 + 2 = 1 is stronger than your reason to believe the alternative, we would have to conclude that, in this situation, it is rational to believe that 2 + 2 = 1. But it plainly isn't. It would be good if you did, but it would not be rational. To avoid this problem, Parfit suggests that we should distinguish between reasons for having beliefs (and other attitudes), which are all object-given, and reasons for *causing ourselves to have such attitudes* (which may be state-given). A reason for causing ourselves to have an attitude is not a reason for the attitude, and therefore there are not both state- and object-given reasons for attitudes. If we make this distinction, it becomes clear that the reasons respond to different questions. State-given reasons are practical reasons, and object-given reasons are epistemic reasons (at least in the case of belief). Hence, state-given reasons in this sense do not speak to the rationality of belief. They are relevant with regard to the rationality of taking certain actions.

The problem with accepting the possibility of state-given reasons for attitudes that Parfit points out is real enough. It gets us as close as we will come (in this paper) to understanding what is wrong with 'wrong reasons.' However, I think that we should reject Parfit's distinction for a number of reasons.

First, the idea of an object-given reason is confusing. Take epistemic reasons: that it's overcast is an epistemic reason to believe that it will rain – hence, according to Parfit, an object-given reason. But the reason is not a property of the belief, or of the content of the belief, that it's going to rain. 'That it is overcast' is not a property of 'it's going to rain.' It is an epistemic reason because it is truth-related, not because it is a property of the object of the belief. Something similar holds for the math example above: that $2 + 2 = 4$ is *not* itself a reason for believing that $2 + 2 = 4$.[40] Any reason for believing this will not be a property of the 'object' of the belief.

Raz's distinction of standard and non-standard reasons is more helpful. The distinctive characteristic of standard reasons is not that the reason is provided by a property of the object of the attitude, but that the reason relates to the standard that determines the appropriateness of the kind of attitude it is.

The second reason for rejecting Parfit's approach is that it rests on too frail a distinction: the distinction between a 'reason to have an attitude' and a 'reason to cause oneself to have an attitude.' The reason to cause oneself to have an attitude could quite naturally be regarded as a reason for having that attitude. To keep the distinction in place we would have to regiment language, and make it terminological.

But, even if we did, we would come up against a third problem: state-given reasons are reasons to cause oneself to have an attitude only if one doesn't have it anyway (due to mistaken beliefs, bad taste, etc). Since state-given reasons can be complied with without 'causing oneself...', they are not properly captured by that phrase. (They are not, as such, practical reasons.) They are, in the first place, reasons to *have* the attitude, just like object-given reasons – the 'causing' comes in only as one way of acquiring it, because the attitude cannot be acquired by following the reason directly.[41]

Luckily, Parfit's distinction between causing and having an attitude is not necessary for avoiding the problem. As we have seen in the context of Raz's discussion, standard and non-standard have very different explanations. Only standard reasons for beliefs are epistemic reasons, because only they relate to the epistemic standard. Hence they are the only reasons that determine the epistemic rationality of believing. That there are non-standard reasons for believing (independently of epistemic reasons) does not undermine this. 'You have most reason to believe that 2 + 2 = 1' is a statement that could mislead someone into thinking that having this belief is, in some circumstances, epistemically rational. But it would not be difficult to explain why this is not the case: the reasons for having the belief aren't epistemic reasons – hence, they cannot establish the epistemic rationality of the belief. Similarly in all other cases: 'there is most reason for admiring the evil demon' could mislead someone to conclude that the evil demon is admirable. But the explanation of the reason would make it clear that it is unrelated to admirability. That is simply what 'non-standard reason' means.

2.6. Buck-passing and the standard /non-standard reasons distinction

We have now found a way of distinguishing between different kinds of reasons for attitudes, which maps onto the buck-passer's distinction between right and wrong reasons. Does it then help the buck-passer? Is the story we told available to her?

If the suggestion I have been exploring is correct, then the wrong reasons are non-standard reasons in the sense that they cannot be followed directly. The explanation for why some reasons are standard reasons that can be followed directly, and others aren't, is that some reasons relate to the inherent standard that governs the forming of the attitude, whereas others are provided by the value of having the attitude. The problem for the buck-passer is to explain the distinction in a non-circular way: to avoid explaining reasons for those attitudes that BPA is concerned with in terms of value. Does the standard / non-standard reasons distinction escape the circularity worry?

You may think that it does, because the standard that governs the attitude needn't be evaluative at all: truth-relatedness is not (I think) an evaluative standard. It doesn't govern beliefs because it is good to have true beliefs. Even if, by and large, the point of forming true beliefs is that it is good for us to have them, there'll be some beliefs that are not good to have (for some person, in some circumstances), and yet they are appropriate and conform to the relevant standard.

However, the standards of evaluative attitudes, such as 'admirability', are evaluative standards. But it doesn't follow that having the attitude is in any way good. There may be no point at all in my admiring some admirable things (e.g. if I will never have a chance to engage with them; they aren't accessible to me; they are beyond the reach of my sensitivities, etc.). Yet it would be appropriate. Forming attitudes in accordance with their inherent standard, then, needn't be of any value. At the very least we should regard it as an open question whether there is value in having true beliefs (let alone believing all that is true), or in being afraid when there is danger (let alone fearing everything that is dangerous). Having a standard reason for having an attitude is independent of the value of having that attitude.

There is value, however, in complying with non-standard reasons. There is a non-standard reason for having an attitude if and because it is good to have the attitude. While non-standard reasons are provided by the value of having the attitude, and thus relate to value in a very direct way, standard reasons only relate to whatever standard governs the appropriateness of the attitude, and, even if this is an evaluative standard, it doesn't follow that having the appropriate attitude is *ipso facto* of value.

The buck-passer is not concerned with just any attitudes but only with *pro-attitudes*, like desiring, respecting, loving. Of the ones I have discussed above, only 'admiring' comes within her purview. Furthermore, her claim is not that having the attitude is of value, but that some object's, X's, being of value is the same property as there being a reason for having an attitude of a certain kind towards X, which is provided by some property of X, P, and P ≠ 'being good.' According to our suggestion, a standard reason for admiring X is that X has some property, P, that makes X admirable.

Is this just a simplified version of BPA? It isn't. First, there is no suggestion that X's admirability is the same property as there being a standard reason for admiring it. There is no property identity claim involved. (I'll get back to this point in Section 3 below.) Secondly, there is no reason to assume that P (the standard reason for admiring) couldn't be that X is (in a certain respect) good. Therefore, none of the distinctive features of BPA finds its way into the standard / non-standard reasons distinction.

Furthermore, the suggestion differs from BPA not only in detail, but also in spirit: it explains reasons for admiring in relation to an evaluative standard, admirability. It therefore abandons the buck-passer's ambition to explain value in terms of reasons and instead explains reasons (for evaluative attitudes) by their relation to value. Therefore, as a response to the WKR problem, the distinction of standard / non-standard reasons is circular in the way that the buck-passer needs to avoid. We said that the wrong reasons are reasons for admiring that cannot be followed directly because they are unrelated to the admirability of the thing in question. The buck-passer needs a distinction between right reasons that are independent of admirability (or of value) and wrong reasons. The standard / non-standard reasons distinction does not help her. It explains both the standard and the non-standard reasons for pro-attitudes in terms of value: the relation to the evaluative standard and to the value of having the attitude, respectively.

If the explanation thus far has been convincing, then, as far as I can see, there is no way of spelling out the distinction that salvages the buck-passing account. Starting from the distinction between wrong and right reasons that the buck-passer brought to our attention led us to a distinction between reasons for attitudes that can be followed directly and those that can't, which has applications beyond evaluative attitudes – in the case of reasons for belief, for instance. Thinking about the significance of the WKR problem – which is a circularity worry that arises for the FA analysis of value and for BPA, in so far as it purports to explain value in terms of reasons for attitudes – leads me to the view that we should not try to solve the problem, but should abandon BPA. If we eschew BPA, there is a distinction between different kinds of reasons for attitudes – as described above – but none of them is the 'wrong kind,' and there is no problem with them being of different kinds.[42]

2.7. Reasons for actions and wrong reasons

I started the section by arguing that there are no wrong reasons for actions. Alternatively, we could (and perhaps should) reject the distinction as applied to reasons for actions. We explained standard reasons ('right reasons') as reasons that we can follow directly in forming an attitude. If the only way of forming an attitude in response to a reason would be by taking some action that results in having the attitude, the reason for doing so would be a non-standard reason. (But remember that I rejected Raz's and Parfit's claims that non-standard reasons *are* practical reasons.) Viewed from this angle, it seems that either practical reasons do not fit into the standard / non-standard reasons distinction, or they are all non-standard reasons. I think we should accept the former claim, because the latter is just needlessly confusing. The standard / non-standard reasons distinction is really concerned only with reasons for attitudes.

The main reason why the distinction sits badly with reasons for action is that there is no equivalent to reasons that can be followed directly with regard to actions. After all, following a reason by taking actions is a typical instance of complying with a reason that cannot be followed directly.

What should we say, then, about a buck-passing account that is couched in terms of reasons for action only? The following thesis would perhaps describe it:

(BPA$_{PR}$ +) 'X is good' consists in X's having some other property, P,[43] that provides a reason for action.[44]

There could be a circularity worry here as well: it might turn out that we can explain reasons for action only in relation to value. But this worry is not a variant of the WKR problem. The problem is not that a certain intuitive difference between kinds of reasons needs to be explained, while avoiding circularity. There are no such different kinds of reasons when it comes to reasons for action. The problem is simply to come up with a substantive account of reasons for action that does not explain them by their relation to value (or as deriving from reasons for attitudes, lest the WKR problem return). Thus, even if the WKR problem cannot be solved, this version of buck-passing could still be viable.

Two qualifications: it does encounter the old WKR problem in all those cases where a reason for action requires that the action is done with a certain attitude – if acting out of gratitude requires that you actually feel gratitude, for instance, the problem is back, for there could be an evil demon ...

Secondly, this is neither a version nor a development of FA analysis. Whatever can be said in its favor will be independent of FA analysis. What can be said in its favor?

3. Why buck-passing?

The buck-passing account of value brought back a theme that had retreated somewhat into the background of philosophical discussions:[45] the explanation of the relation of values and reasons. BPA explains this relation by putting forward two theses: BPA+ and BPA–.

As before, I will focus on the positive claim and on its metaphysical rather than the semantic interpretation, and I will now be only concerned with $BPA_{PR}+$, assuming that $BPA_{FA}+$ falters because of the WKR problem. In its metaphysical interpretation BPA+ is a claim about property identity.

Why does the buck-passer suggest property identity of the particular kind that BPA+ describes? BPA+'s characteristic emphasis is on the claim that being of value consists in there being properties *other than being of value* which are reasons. It is not altogether clear why the buck-passer takes this view. One reason that has been offered is that being good itself is not a reason; that is, BPA– is offered as a reason for accepting BPA+. As shown in the beginning, BPA– does not entail BPA+; and, as shown elsewhere, BPA– is false. I will therefore disregard this consideration.

Could an argument for BPA+ be grounded in some view about the relation of being good and the other properties that are alleged to provide reasons? It cannot, for two reasons: even if there is a necessary relation between goodness and the reason providing properties, such as pleasantness (as there would be, if the relation is one of supervenience, say), there wouldn't be property identity. A supervening property is not identical with any of the properties it supervenes upon. More importantly, we would be looking for property identity at the wrong level. According to the buck-passer, goodness is a second-order property. It is not identical with any first-order property (or properties). The claim is that goodness is the same property as the property of there being a reason to act or to have a pro-attitude of some kind.

But there does not seem to be any (valid) argument in favor of this view, and furthermore, as has been pointed out by a number of philosophers, it begs the question against some deontological views of normative ethics.[46] Some deontologists claim that, while there is a reason to keep one's promises (say), or not to kill an innocent person, it doesn't follow that it would be good to act in these ways. It also begs the question against some accounts of reasons, such as Williams's internalism, which rests on the assumption that an account of practical reasons has to explain the difference in meaning and truth conditions between the propositions 'there is a reason to Φ' and 'it would be good to Φ.'[47] The same goes for value-based views of practical reasons, which explain reasons through values, claiming that there is a reason *because* acting in some way is good. The identity claim does not allow for the explanatory distance of the 'because.' It seems that the buck-passer (of the metaphysical variety) will have to claim that the deontologist, the reasons internalist, and the reasons externalist who offers a value-based explanation of reasons are all mistaken; the semantic buck-passer would add that they are also conceptually confused. Both are strong claims – and, as far as I can see, the buck-passer has provided no reason to accept them.

I take it that the virtue of BPA is that it raises interesting questions, in particular the question of how to explain the close (perhaps necessary) relation of values and reasons. Yet, we are not quite sure how closely related the two are – various normative theories and theories of reasons allow for different kinds of distances. Assuming that none of their proponents is simply conceptually confused, can we settle the issue by going for metaphysical buck-passing? This seems to be closing off certain possibilities by fiat and without argument.

Therefore, while the question is important, I don't see any reason to accept the buck-passer's answer.[48]

Notes

1. Scanlon (1998), p. 97.
2. Ibid., p. 96.
3. Väyrynen (2006).
4. Schroeder (2009b).
5. Crisp (2008).
6. Perhaps the thesis should allow that goodness consists in a plurality or combination of other properties and thus BPA+ should read: 'The fact that something is good or of value consists in the fact that it has some other properties P1, P2, ... Pn which are reasons to respond to it favorably or to behave in certain ways with regard to it.'
7. The formulations are mine, but I take it that they are in keeping with Väyrynen's, Crisp's and Schroeder's views. Väyrynen, in his formulation of BPA+, emphasizes that goodness is supposed to be the higher-order property of other properties that provide reasons. I will discuss the property identity claim that this formulation brings out in Section 3.
8. Crisp wishes to argue that, while BPA– is a plausible claim, we should not commit ourselves to BPA+. I disagree with him on this point in more than one way: I don't find BPA– plausible at all, but I also don't believe that there is much interest in it independently of its connection with BPA+.
9. For a more detailed argument, showing how this could be so, see my 'Wrongness and Reasons,' as well as Schroeder (2009b).
10. I have argued for this point in detail in Heuer (2006) and Heuer (2010), and so have Crisp (2005), Väyrynen (2006) and Schroeder (2009b).

11. Crisp (2005).
12. In Heuer (2006) I called the argument 'the argument from explanation,' but I think that Crisp's label is better, and more to the point, and I will therefore adopt it here.
13. As for instance Crisp (2008), also Parfit, if not quite as explicitly.
14. For instance, Rabinowicz and Rønnow-Rasmussen, as well as Daniellson and Olson, take this view. Scanlon seems to vacillate between the two interpretations.
15. I take it that Parfit's version of BPA is an example of this.
16. Brentano (1934), Ewing (1947). For a recent discussion see Bykvist (2009).
17. Rabinowicz and Rønnow-Rasmussen (2004).
18. See for instance, Daniellson and Olson (2007).
19. I use the subscript 'BPA' for the version of FA, because it emphasizes that it is properties *other than being valuable* that make the attitude fitting.
20. In his first book (1998), Scanlon claims that all reasons are reasons for attitudes – beliefs and intentions, respectively. But he does not seem to pursue this approach anymore. Scanlon (2008) claims that intentions are based on reasons for action, rather than the other way around.
21. Unless there are, as Jonathan Dancy (2004b) has it, 'enticing reasons' – reasons that do not require compliance (other things being equal). However, if Dancy is right and there are enticing reasons in this sense, they wouldn't be relevant in our context, because BPA is concerned with all reasons for pro-attitudes, whereas 'enticing reasons' would be a subclass of those, distinguished by their content.
22. Joseph Raz suggested to me that a proponent of FA analysis may claim that an attitude is required if it is fitting to have it and unfitting not to have it. This requires that 'unfitting' is different from the negation of fitting (different from 'non-fitting'). Or rather: if it is fitting to have an attitude, it is not *eo ipso* unfitting not to have it – as the example of fear above has shown. It may be fitting to be afraid, but it is not unfitting not to be afraid. In those cases, where to have the attitude is fitting and it is also the case that it would be unfitting not to have it, the agent may have a reason to have the attitude. If the proponent of FA analysis can make sense of these concepts and their logical relations, she may have a way of analysing 'required' – but, as this shows, the explanation is not straightforward.
23. I take it that the problem is roughly the same on both interpretations: a circular analysis fails, because it presupposes an understanding of the concept that it sets out to explain, and similarly a metaphysical account that is uninformative fails because it does not provide the kind of explanation that it is supposed to establish: in our case, showing that reasons for attitudes are explanatorily prior to value.
24. Ibid., p. 419.
25. Olson (2004); Rabinowicz and Rønnow-Rasmussen (2006); Lang (2008).
26. *Pace* Schroeder (forthcoming) who recently argued that there are.
27. Parfit (2001) agrees that BPA is particularly well suited to account for instrumental value of this kind.
28. At least, according some deontological accounts thereof.
29. I assume that it does for the sake of argument.
30. And the demon does not even have instrumental value – it is only acting in a certain way that has.
31. Interestingly, Wallace (forthcoming) argues that the buck-passing view ought to be defended as a view about the epistemology, rather than the metaphysics, of values. He observes that we are sometimes unsure whether a certain feature or property is evaluative or normative. He suggests that if we wonder whether (for example) the pleasantness of a resort is a normative property, the question to pose and answer is whether it provides reasons. Thus our knowledge of reasons may be prior to our knowledge of values. However, in the current context this

approach would probably fail. If, in doubt whether being the order of an evil demon is an evaluative property, you ask 'does it provide reasons?', the answer is 'yes'. Why, then, presume that the reason in question is a 'wrong reason', if you don't have independent knowledge of value? By the way, I do not doubt Wallace's observation, or his suggestion that we 'test' the normativity of alleged evaluative properties by trying to figure out whether they provide reasons. All this seems entirely accurate to me. But I am doubtful that it should be seen as underwriting a buck-passing account of values.

32. Raz (2009).
33. Raz (2009), p. 40.
34. Skorupski (2007).
35. This relation of non-standard reasons to value seems to be Raz's reason for claiming that non-standard reasons are 'practical reasons'. As remarked above, this doesn't seem quite right, as it is not necessary to take any action in order to comply with a non-standard reason.
36. Parfit (2010), Appendix B.
37. To my knowledge, while Parfit (2001 and 2010) endorses buck-passing, he does not spell out anywhere the proposition that describes his version of the account. But, judging from the context, his claim is probably something like: 'x is good' consists in x's having other properties that provide *reasons for acting* in certain ways. Furthermore, he explicitly discusses buck-passing for instrumental value (which is important in the context of reasons for action, as I have explained in Section 2.2 above).
38. Following Olson (2004, p. 297), we should perhaps say more precisely that it is the properties (or properties of consequences) of having of the attitude that provide the reason.
39. Both Rabinowicz and Rønnow-Rasmussen (2004) and Olson (2004) reject the distinction for a different reason: properties of the attitude can be recast as properties of the object of the attitude. Hence there is no real distinction here. (For a discussion of the many responses and counter-responses, and further suggestion along these lines, see Lang, 2008.) I will not concern myself with this worry, because I believe that the introduction of Raz's distinction helps to put it to rest. The distinctive characteristic of standard reasons is not that the reason is provided by a property of the object of the attitude, but that the reason relates to the standard that determines the appropriateness of the kind of attitude that it is.
40. Alternatively, we could allow that the fact that it rains (for example) is *a* reason for believing that it rains. I think that this is a mistake, but I don't have space to argue this point. But, even if we were to accept that the fact that p is a reason to believe that p, it would at best be *a* reason for the belief – most reasons will be different. Normally, the reason for believing that p will be the fact that q, and q ≠ p. Therefore, normally the reason for believing that p will *not* be 'object-given' (on the understanding of the term that I explored above).
41. For a related comment see Rabinowicz and Rønnow-Rasmussen (2004), p. 411f.
42. The WKR problem simply is the circularity worry for BPA – there is no other problem. In a recent response to Olson, Rabinowicz and Rønnow-Rasmussen (2006) seem to embrace the circularity. It is not clear to me what is left of the buck-passing view if it allows that reasons can be explained in terms of values.
43. Or other properties, P1 ... Pn
44. The 'PR' subscript stands for 'practical reason'.
45. Having been in the foreground, especially in early twentieth-century ethics, as a question about the relation of the right and the good.

46. See, for instance, Dancy (2000b), Crisp (2008). Olson (2007) suggests a reply to this objection, on behalf of the buck-passer.
47. It is one of the express aims of Williams's internalism to uncouple values and reasons. Take the following example from Williams (1995): 'I shall presumably say, whatever else I say, that it would be better if [a cruel husband] were nicer to [his wife]. There is one specific thing the external reasons theorist wants me to say, that the man has a reason to be nicer. [...] The question is: what is the difference between saying that the agent has a reason to act more considerately, and saying...that it would be better if they acted otherwise' (p. 39f). Williams assumes that there *is* a difference.
48. I am grateful to Joseph Raz and Michael Brady for very helpful comments.

9
A Wrong Turn to Reasons?

Pekka Väyrynen

1. Introduction

Much of recent metaethics, and meta-normative inquiry more generally, displays a turn to reasons. In the air wafts a confidence, even if not a definite program easily attributable to particular people, that appealing to reasons – in the normative sense in which reasons are good grounds for acting, thinking, or feeling in certain ways – will better enable us to account for various normative and evaluative phenomena than appealing to value or any other notion. This paper argues that it is hard to reconcile taking reasons as fundamental in explaining various evaluative and normative phenomena with certain explanatory demands regarding reasons themselves. Its aim is to sound a skeptical note against the confidence that turning to reasons will offer special advantages in dealing with real theoretical problems when it comes to explaining various normative and evaluative phenomena.

Section 2 sets the stage: it describes why evaluative and normative phenomena typically call for explanation and what constraints apply to such explanations under a turn to reasons. Section 3 quickly delineates some different forms that such explanations might take. Sections 4–7 then argue that various explanations of each form either fail to favor turning to reasons in particular or else are inadequate with respect to the constraints that apply to them, unless perhaps a kind of reductionism about reasons, which is typically rejected by those who favor turning to reasons, is true. Their way of turning to reasons thus enjoys no special advantages over other ways of meeting comparable explanatory demands regarding normative and evaluative phenomena. Turning to reasons offers no short cut.

2. Normative explanation and reasons

It is widely agreed that nothing is brutely right or wrong, good or bad, admirable or terrifying, just or unjust. Things bear normative and evaluative properties in virtue of some other properties. The distribution of normative and evaluative properties over these other properties seems neither accidental nor groundless; there should be some explanation of their distribution. If this piercing feeling in my neck is bad, that is no brute fact; or so I want to say. Suppose I say that the feeling is bad in virtue of being painful. This looks like an explanation: it specifies something *because of* which the feeling is bad, something that is at least part of *why* it is bad.[1]

But now I have another evaluative fact to explain. For the explanation that I gave presumes that the painfulness of the feeling makes it bad to some degree or in some way. The truth of this kind of evaluative claim isn't a brute fact either; or so I want to say.[2] When such claims are true, in virtue of what are they true?

Normative facts concerning reasons for actions or for attitudes are, on the face of it, no different: they aren't groundless and they typically call for explanation. Here I mean 'normative' reasons: units or considerations that make systematic contributions to, and thereby explain, the overall normative statuses (such as 'required,' 'permitted,' 'appropriate,' etc.) of the actions or attitudes for which they are reasons. Normative reasons can be stated by saying that some considerations are a reason, weaker or stronger, for some person in certain circumstances to do something.[3] Such statements refer to a relation that holds between a proposition or a fact P, a set of conditions C, and an activity of Φing (such as taking a course of action or adopting an attitude like belief, intention, approval, etc.), when P is a reason (of degree of strength D, at time T) for someone in C to Φ.[4] When I talk about reasons, I have in mind this type of relation. When I talk about properties or features that 'provide' reasons, I mean properties ascribed to things by the facts or propositions that slot in for 'P' in reason relations. I'll simplify by omitting degree and time references and by taking 'conditions' or 'circumstances' to include the properties of agents. (This doesn't sacrifice theoretical neutrality; normative reasons may still be held to depend on whether they bear some suitable relation to some motivational fact about the agent.[5]) Reason relations can then be expressed by a relational predicate R(P, C, Φ). Reason claims of this form entail that, when there is a reason to Φ, there must be something that is the reason, something that speaks in favor of Φing or makes Φing sensible in C. This fact or proposition P will often, if not always, be some ordinary fact or proposition about the world. It will be a further normative fact about P that P is a reason to Φ in C.[6]

Now consider some specific examples. If the only way I can save my life is to jump out of the window, the fact that jumping will save my life is a reason to jump. If I promised my mother that I would call her, the fact that calling her will fulfill a promise is a reason to call her (but, one hopes, not the only reason). The fact that there is loud music and chatter coming from across the street is, in many circumstances, a reason to believe that the neighbors are having a party. Many people would allow that the fact that parachuting is thrilling is, in many circumstances, a reason for those who desire a thrill to go parachuting. What I want to say is that the truth of claims about what is a reason for what isn't a brute fact. So, again, we should be able to ask in virtue of what these normative claims, when true, are true.

Suppose I say that the fact that jumping will save my life is a reason to jump because prudence requires me to save my life, and that the fact that calling will fulfill a promise is a reason to call because morality requires me to fulfill my promises. These explanations presume that requirements of prudence and morality distribute in a certain way over other facts.[7] But what I want to say is that their distribution isn't a brute fact. Various facts about reasons call for explanation as much as any other normative and evaluative facts. Just as one wants not merely a list of valuable things but also an explanation of why value distributes in that way, so one wants not merely a distribution of reason relations over facts, circumstances, and actions or attitudes, but also an explanation of why that distribution is the one that holds.

It feels difficult to find a satisfactory explanation of many of these sorts of normative and evaluative facts. So I take it that there is a real problem concerning their explanation.[8] Would turning to reasons advance this enterprise? Such hope is in the air. For instance, some people find it hard to assess whether something is of intrinsic value (roughly in the sense of Moore, 1922) until they begin to consider how they have reason to act or feel towards it.[9] Such a response suggests that reasons can be invoked to analyze or explain what it is to be intrinsically valuable.[10] But, although the idea is in the air, little has been done to state it clearly. I'll articulate my target by describing different forms a turn to reasons might take.

It is common to claim that the normativity of all that is normative consists in its relation to reasons. But claims to this effect can be more or less inclusive with respect to the category of the normative.[11] If 'normative' means 'deontic,' as contrasted with 'evaluative,' such claims entail only that reasons are fundamental with respect to other deontic notions, such as *right*, *wrong*, and *ought*. This is compatible with thinking that reasons are grounded in considerations of value or explained thereby, or that neither deontic nor evaluative notions are explained by the other.[12] If 'normative' includes also the evaluative (for instance, if value is, *inter alia*, such as to generate reasons), then taking reasons as fundamental in the normative domain entails that they are fundamental with respect to other deontic and evaluative notions.[13] My interest concerns this more inclusive turn to reasons.

Irrespective of its scope, a turn to reasons can take at least three forms, depending on whether reasons are supposed to be conceptually, metaphysically, or explanatorily fundamental. A conceptual turn holds that the concept of a reason is the fundamental normative concept, in the sense that this concept is the sole normative element in any normative concept. Most of those who endorse this claim also take the concept of a reason to be primitive: it can be at most paraphrased, but not analyzed, in other terms, normative or otherwise. A common paraphrase is that a reason to Φ is a consideration that 'counts in favor' of Φing.[14] So reasons are conceptually fundamental in the domain of normativity.

A metaphysical turn to reasons holds that the nature of normative properties of various sorts – moral rightness and wrongness, various forms of value, or whatever the normative includes – has to do with the relation to reasons for actions or for attitudes. One local instance of a metaphysical turn is the claim that moral rightness (wrongness) consists in having properties that provide reasons of certain kind and strength for (against) action. If the normative includes the evaluative, then other local instances include the kind of 'buck-passing' account of value according to which to be good or valuable is to have some other properties that provide reasons of an appropriate kind to favor their bearers,[15] and the view that such evaluative facts as that something is terrifying or that something is amusing consist in there being reasons of an appropriate kind to be terrified by it or amused by it. So reasons are metaphysically fundamental in the domain of normativity in the sense that the nature of normative properties, or at least their normativity, consists in their relations to reasons.

An explanatory turn to reasons holds that normative notions are to be accounted for in terms of reasons. One local instance of this kind of turn to reasons is the kind of 'buck-passing' view of value according to which the fact that something is valuable is explained by its having other properties that provide reasons of an appropriate kind to favor it. In general, in so far as evaluative and normative facts generally call for explanation in the way discussed above, they can be understood or explained in terms of reasons that there are, in certain circumstances, for actions or for attitudes such as beliefs, intentions, or feelings. So reasons are explanatorily fundamental in the domain of normativity.

Explanation of normative facts might not be a concern to all of these versions of the turn to reasons. A conceptual turn to reasons, for instance, might not be troubled by a demand for such explanations. It allows that when some fact is, in some circumstances, a reason to Φ, there is an explanation why, but it appears to carry no particular commitment as to what explains this. It is perfectly possible that the concept of a reason has no analysis in other terms, normative or otherwise, and yet picks out a relation that consists in some complex of independently characterizable factors, such as the promotion of value or of desire satisfaction, or the instantiation of which can be explained in some such terms.

The explanatory turn to reasons, however, is subject to the explanatory demand. It grants that various normative and evaluative facts call for explanation. Since the grounds for thinking that they do so seem to apply equally well to facts about reasons, then reasons also call for explanation. Much the same holds for the metaphysical turn to reasons in so far as it grants that normative facts to the effect that some fact P is a reason to Φ in C aren't brute or groundless. My interest in what follows lies in an explanatory turn to reasons, understood to include this sort of a metaphysical turn. The idea of such a turn is in the air, even if no writer has fully articulated it or explicitly endorsed it in full generality.[16] How far an appeal to reasons in understanding various normative and evaluative phenomena can be pushed is also of significant interest independently of whatever actual currency the idea happens to enjoy.

One might still wonder whether it really is reasonable to hold an explanatory turn to reasons to the demand that there must typically be an explanation of why some fact P is a reason to Φ in some circumstances C (or, for short, why a reason to Φ is a reason to Φ).[17] One sort of thought is that reasons will need no explanation in so far as reason relations hold necessarily, when they hold at all, and that at least the fundamental reason relations do hold necessarily. (The particular facts that provide reasons often hold contingently, when at all, but contingent facts can stand in necessary relations.)

Many necessary truths, however, call for explanation and don't seem brute. One example is the widely accepted, if not uncontroversial, supervenience of the normative on the non-normative. Supervenience relations hold necessarily, when they hold at all, but most philosophers agree that if there can be no normative difference (and hence no difference in reasons) without a non-normative difference, this requires explanation.[18] But surely it isn't the mere number of metaphysical impossibilities in how reasons and non-normative facts may be recombined that makes supervenience require explanation. Just the same demand for explanation applies to such specific claims as that it is metaphysically impossible that the entire universe could be exactly like it actually is in all non-evaluative, non-normative respects but the fact that my mother is my mother is a reason for me to torture her (Schroeder 2007, p. 71). But now notice that we are at least very close to thinking that reason relations also typically require explanation even if they hold necessarily. Why should they be special in requiring no explanation?

Another sort of thought is that some reasons need no explanation because it strikes us as obvious that they are reasons. Suppose that the fact that a person's child has died is a reason for her to feel sad. Or suppose that, for a person in control of a car, the fact that if the steering wheel isn't turned the car will injure or perhaps kill a pedestrian, but if the wheel is turned the car will hit no one, is a reason to turn the steering wheel.[19] If these claims strike us as obviously true, then explanations of the reasons they report might be superfluous with respect to many epistemic functions which explanations typically serve.

This doesn't, however, mean that a theoretical demand for an explanation of reasons is out of place. For a fact may be obvious and yet not brute or inexplicable. Nor does it follow that there is nothing more to say about why, or in virtue of what, a fact cited as a reason to Φ is a reason to Φ. To illustrate, suppose that value is normative in the sense that something is good (bad) only if there are reasons to favor (or disfavor) it. So far as this goes, it could be that it is the goodness of something that explains the reasons to favor it or that some third factor explains both its goodness and the reasons, rather than that the reasons to favor it explain its goodness. So there had better be something to say in explanation of these reasons which shows why explanations that don't involve turning to reasons are closed off.

These considerations suggest a constraint on explanations of reasons under an explanatory turn to reasons. If reason relations typically require explanation but they are explanatorily fundamental relative to other normative and evaluative notions, then explanations of reasons must typically satisfy a 'normative fundamentality' constraint:

NF constraint: When a fact P is under conditions C a reason to Φ, explanations of this normative fact may not appeal to any evaluative or normative factors which don't themselves concern reasons.

The NF constraint is by no means trivial. It would be a substantive claim to say that every explanation of why P is a reason to Φ in C is itself a reason, even if by other name. (Clear cases of this kind, as when a derivative reason is explained by the reason whence it derives, don't exhaust explanations of reasons.[20]) But, in so far as explanations of reasons failed the NF constraint, reasons wouldn't be metaphysically or explanatorily fundamental in the normative domain. If reasons to Φ could be explained, for instance, in terms of the prospective value of Φing, then it wouldn't seem to be very plausible that what it is for Φing to be of value is for it to have other properties that provide reasons of an appropriate kind to Φ. Or, if what it is for something to be a reason to Φ were for it to play a role in explaining why one ought to Φ, then it wouldn't seem to be very plausible that reasons are explanatorily fundamental with respect to what one ought to do, since their normativity would derive from that of *ought*.

An explanatory turn to reasons can take different forms depending on what counts as an appropriate explanation of reasons. We saw that, even if some evaluative and normative facts don't call for explanation relative to some epistemic functions of explanation, a demand for some other type of explanation can still be legitimate. One type of explanations which figure in understanding a wide variety of phenomena are 'constitutive' or 'grounding' explanations. These explain phenomena by laying out the conditions in which those phenomena consist or in virtue of which they obtain. The fact that I am older than my sister consists in my age, her age, and a certain ordering between them. And something is a member of the singleton {Pinky} by being Pinky, not Pinky in virtue of being a member of {Pinky}; the fact that something is a member of {Pinky} consists in the fact that it is Pinky.[21] If reason relations aren't explanatorily brute or groundless, a demand for a constitutive explanation of why P is a reason to Φ in circumstances C would often seem to be legitimate. Surely at least sometimes, when such a reason relation holds, there will be conditions in which the fact that P is a reason to Φ in C is grounded or consists, or in virtue of which the reason relation holds.[22]

One might doubt that a demand for a constitutive explanation of reasons is typically legitimate. Contextually variable reasons clearly call for explanation. If some facts are a reason to Φ in some circumstances but not others, then there should be some explanation as to why those facts are a reason to Φ, when they are, and why they aren't a reason to Φ, when not. But explanations in these cases might work by contrasting some cases in which those facts are a reason with other cases in which they aren't and by relating the case at hand to that contrast, or they might work by laying out the circumstances in a certain kind of way or order. Such explanations might, in other words, rest on coherence or narrative relations among various non-normative features of situations, instead of appealing to factors in virtue of whose presence or absence the facts in question are or aren't a reason to Φ.

Even here, however, it seems to be legitimate to ask why some particular contrasts or differences between circumstances, but not others, make for a difference in what certain facts are a reason to do or what it is about the particular contextual constellation of features that makes it the case that those facts are a reason to do one thing and not a reason to do something else. How else is laying out the circumstances of the context or contrasting them with others supposed to explain why some facts are a reason to Φ, if not by indicating *why* some contextual features or differences are relevant to whether those facts provide reasons? One might have thought the normative bedrock to run deeper than that.

What I take away from all this is that it remains reasonable to demand that an explanatory turn to reasons provide constitutive explanations of why a reason to Φ is a reason to Φ which satisfy the NF constraint. One way to explain reasons consistently with the NF constraint would be to show that reason relations reduce to some non-evaluative, non-normative properties or relations. (An example would be the view that the reason relation reduces to some non-evaluatively specifiable utility property, such as happiness, plus the maximizing relation.) Such a reduction base wouldn't consist in evaluative or normative factors which don't themselves concern reasons. And yet, if As are reducible to Bs, then we can use the B-phenomena in the reduction base to explain the reducible A-phenomena (Horgan, 1993). Note here that, if reasons were so reducible, other evaluative and normative notions might be reducible in a parallel way. A substantial question would remain whether those notions could also be systematically explained in terms of reasons, leaving reasons explanatorily fundamental within the normative domain.

In fact, however, most of those who are sympathetic towards turning to reasons reject reductionism about reasons. They would therefore have to try to satisfy the NF constraint through explanations of reasons which take some different form. Much of the discussion to follow works through various possible solutions to this problem.

My focus will be specific: can an explanatory turn to reasons explain facts about reasons consistently with the NF constraint but without being pushed in the direction of reductionism? But the problem is a general one when it comes to explaining evaluative and normative facts under fundamentality constraints such as the NF constraint. Analogous constraints are thus likely to apply to other putative explanatorily fundamental factors in the normative domain. Much of the discussion to follow may thus generalize fairly directly to proposals to turn to other evaluative or normative notions. This wouldn't, however, affect the main upshot of this paper, which is that turning to reasons offers no distinctive advantage in solving hard and deep problems concerning the explanation of normative facts.

Some readers may be inclined to draw a further moral that some suitably sophisticated reductionist account of normative and evaluative properties is beginning to look like an attractive explanatory hypothesis. So long as our notion of reduction isn't Neanderthal, a reductionist account needn't involve implausible semantic claims, or eliminate the reduced property, or otherwise make it any less real. Reductionism about reasons may or may not be true, but it isn't the bogey man of normativity that it is sometimes taken to be.

3. Reasons and explanation: some distinctions

Putative explanations of reasons can be classified along at least two dimensions. One concerns what kind of facts can be reasons. That is, what kind of facts may slot in for 'P' in R(P, C, Φ)? The other concerns what kind of factors explain the (further, distinct) normative fact that some fact P is a reason to Φ in C. Distinctions under these headings can be used to generate templates for explanations of reasons.[23] One distinction under the first heading is that the facts that are reasons will be either non-evaluative, non-normative aspects of the world or else at least partly evaluative or normative in character. One distinction under the second heading is that either the factors that explain why certain facts provide the reasons they do are distinct from those facts or they aren't. Irrespective of whether these explanatory factors are distinct from reasons, they will likewise be either non-evaluative, non-normative aspects of the world or else at least partly evaluative or normative in character.

4. Intrinsicality

One tradition in moral philosophy regards acts as duties simply because of the types of acts that they are.[24] One way of trying to explain why certain facts are reasons would be to generalize this idea and say that some facts are reasons *intrinsically* and other reasons are explained in terms of their relation to these. Something is intrinsically F if it has intrinsic properties in virtue of which it is F. For instance, the property *being square* is an intrinsic property and the property *being square or married* is an extrinsic property; but the latter is a property that all squares have intrinsically, in virtue of being squares.[25] Similarly, G.E. Moore denies that being valuable is an intrinsic property but thinks that some things are intrinsically valuable: their value is intrinsic in the sense that they have it solely in virtue of their intrinsic properties (Moore, 1922, p. 260). Since we can think of the claim that something is F in virtue of some intrinsic properties as entailing that its possession of those properties at least partly explains why it is F, this strategy might be thought to fit with an explanatory turn to reasons. If some facts were reasons intrinsically, these reasons could be explanatorily fundamental without requiring a deeper explanation in terms of some distinct further factors.

If some things are reasons intrinsically, then the intrinsic features in virtue of which they are reasons will be either non-evaluative and non-normative, or else at least partly evaluative or normative, in character. Some evaluative and normative facts would seem to be good candidates to be intrinsically reason-giving facts, in virtue of their particular evaluative or normative character. If you have a right to physical integrity, this might be a reason not to hit you, and if treating you in a certain way would be bad for you, this might be a reason not to treat you in that way. But, unless these descriptions of the facts are mere shorthand for claims about reasons, the explanations of reasons they provide violate the NF constraint. And, if they are shorthand for claims about reasons, the reasons to which they refer will require explanation. Thus an explanatory turn to reasons cannot allow reasons to be explained in terms of any evaluative or normative character that they might have intrinsically.

So might any non-evaluative, non-normative features be reasons intrinsically? If any were, pain would seem to be a good candidate. After all, nearly everyone agrees that, if something is painful, that is (at least defeasibly) a reason to avoid it or make it stop. But would it be plausible to claim that it is intrinsic to, or otherwise part of, what pain *is* that the fact that something is painful is (at least defeasibly) a reason to avoid it or make it stop?[26]

I have three distinct worries here. The first is that theories of pain tend not to support this kind of normative claim. For instance, most functionalist and other physicalist theories of pain provide no resources for defending it. The second worry concerns errors and disagreement about reasons. If someone denies that the fact that something is painful is a reason to avoid it or make it stop, it seems neither that their mistake is mere ignorance about what pain is, nor that our disagreement concerns merely the nature of pain. The third worry is that, if the fact that something is painful were intrinsically a reason to avoid it or make it stop, then painfulness would be a normative property. This would be a surprising metaethical commitment for an explanatory turn to reasons to carry. Furthermore, appealing to the nature of pain in explaining reasons would in this case seem to violate the NF constraint after all.[27]

The general point I am making doesn't require that all of these worries be effective with respect to pain in particular, but only that they generalize well enough to make it doubtful that there would be enough intrinsically reason-giving non-normative facts to explain the rest of the reasons there are. The worries raised above make this much doubtful.

5. Evaluative facts and reasons

Next I'll discuss the role of evaluative and normative facts in explanations of reasons. Such facts might figure in such explanations in two ways. First, some evaluative and normative facts might count as reasons in virtue of their particular evaluative or normative character.[28] For instance, one reason to go shopping today might be that there are lots of good things on sale today. An explanation of this normative fact would presumably rely on the positively valuable aspects of the things on sale, other than just their low price. (Otherwise reasons would turn us to the likes of Poundland and Dollar Store much more than they actually do.) And pointing out what is valuable about friendship might be a good way to explain why the fact that someone is my friend gives me reasons to act in certain ways. Second, the factors that explain why some non-evaluative, non-normative facts provide the reasons they do might be evaluative or normative in character. For instance, it might be that what explains why the non-evaluative fact that a holiday resort is pleasant is a reason to visit it and recommend it to friends is that, if a resort is pleasant, this makes it good in certain ways or respects.

So-called 'value-based' accounts of reasons presumably take one or the other of these forms.[29] Unsurprisingly, then, each is inconsistent with an explanatory turn to reasons, unless the claims about goodness in the reason statements or explanations of reasons which they offer are mere shorthand for claims about reasons.[30] But this is unclear, to say the least.

Suppose that the following may in some contexts be an adequate explanation of what is bad or inappropriate about taking pleasure in making others suffer:

> In taking pleasure in the suffering of others one is displaying insensitivity to their suffering, and a lack of concern for it, which is particularly reprehensible if one is oneself the cause of the suffering, and could have prevented it. (Raz, 2001, p. 52)

This explanation could be taken to specify in what the badness of taking pleasure in making others suffer consists, at least proximately if not ultimately. It appeals to factors that have evaluative flavor, so it may be subject to further explanatory demands. As I have indicated, the explanatory issues at stake are general, not specific to reasons. What isn't easy to see, however, is what further illumination would be provided by saying that the fact that taking pleasure in the suffering of others would display insensitivity to their suffering, and lack of concern for it, is a reason against doing so, and an especially strong reason if one is oneself the cause of the suffering.

What emerges here is that, if reasons are to be explanatorily fundamental in the normative domain, then neither things that are reasons nor factors which explain their status as reasons should involve evaluative or (non-reasons-based) normative aspects of our circumstances. This commitment of an explanatory turn to reasons is further confirmation that it is subject to the NF constraint. The extent of (explanations of) reasons which are most plausibly treated as evaluative in character – and with it the plausibility of a turn to reasons – depends on many controversial issues.

One way to illustrate the potentially wide sweep of this commitment is to consider how so-called 'thick' concepts and properties, such as *generous*, *courageous*, *brutal*, and *cruel*, matter to explanations of reasons. A maximally non-committal characterization of thick concepts is that they have some substantive non-evaluative content and their use is connected, in some close-knit way, with evaluation. According to a popular family of views, they are evaluative concepts whose applicability typically implies or signals the presence of reasons for action.[31] What would an explanatory turn to reasons say about such reasons?

It is a matter of dispute whether thick concepts and the properties they can be used to ascribe are evaluative in the same way as thin concepts, such as *good*, *right*, and *ought*, or evaluative at all. But suppose such facts as that something is cruel or that it is generous at least sometimes provide reasons even if they aren't evaluative facts. Those reasons would presumably require explanation. Thus, on the one hand, if thick concepts aren't evaluative but the properties they ascribe provide reasons, these reasons are among those which an explanatory turn to reasons is committed to explaining either in non-evaluative, non-normative terms or else in normative terms which only concern reasons. For otherwise it will fail the NF constraint. If, on the other hand, thick concepts and the properties they ascribe are in themselves evaluative, then their bearing on an explanatory turn to reasons depends on whether or not their evaluative and non-evaluative aspects can be divided into distinct components. For instance, if generosity can be understood as the property of being disposed to act in certain ways $F_1, \ldots, F_n$ (specifiable in wholly non-evaluative terms) towards others, and being good in a certain way for being so disposed, then it will be coherent to understand this latter, evaluative component in terms of reasons provided by the fact that something has or would manifest such a disposition. But, if thick concepts cannot be understood in this way, then it would seem that the reasons provided by the properties they ascribe will have to be explained in evaluative terms.[32] So, if thick concepts are evaluative, they can be used to explain reasons consistently with the NF constraint only if their evaluative and non-evaluative aspects are separable. This would be a controversial substantive commitment.

A further worry about reasons associated with the applicability of thick concepts concerns their explanation under the NF constraint. Suppose generosity is a complex property divisible into two components: a disposition to act in certain ways towards others plus there being reasons to respond to people in certain favorable ways in virtue of their having or manifesting this disposition.[33] This might seem to be able to explain why the fact that someone is generous implies reasons to respond to it in certain favorable ways. For such a fact is now understood in terms of the existence of reasons to respond favorably plus a specification of what provides those reasons. But what explains why having or manifesting the disposition provides the reasons that it does? The normative element of generosity itself merely states that it does. The NF constraint requires either that the explanation be non-evaluative and non-normative or else that it appeal to some other factors concerning reasons.

In short, an explanatory turn to reasons faces exactly the same questions that arise for any account of thick concepts, and comes with controversial commitments regarding thick concepts in so far as these come with reasons. But, for all that, it seems to provide no distinctive advantage in answering these questions or explaining these reasons.

6. Non-normative explanations of reasons

We have seen that explaining reasons consistently with the NF constraint requires that the facts that are reasons be non-evaluative, non-normative facts. Thus, reasons to go to a concert will be such things as that doing so would be stimulating or fun, reasons to add a certain spice to what one is cooking will be such things as that adding it would bring out, balance, or complement such-and-such flavors of such-and-such other ingredients, and so on. And we have seen that the NF constraint doesn't allow explaining the status of such facts as reasons in non-evaluative or normative terms. I'll now discuss whether their status as reasons can be explained in non-evaluative, non-normative terms or else in normative terms concerning reasons.

The most straightforward version of the former, non-normative option is the claim that the fact that P is a reason to Φ in C consists in P, C, and Φ. No doubt reason relations are in some sense grounded in their relata. But surely merely listing their relata fails to explain them, unless something about the relata explains why they are so related. The clearest such cases are factors that have evaluative or normative content, in so far as these might be reasons intrinsically. But on the present view the reason relata are to be described in non-evaluative, non-normative terms. So this option is unpromising for an explanatory turn to reasons.

A better way to assess the prospects for non-evaluative constitutive explanations of why P is a reason to Φ in C is to consider the properties of such explanations. Even if we don't understand exactly what it is for something to consist in some conditions or obtain in virtue of them, or how explanations that appeal to such a relation work, we know some things about what the relation isn't like. One example (an unsurprising one, given that supervenience relations often require explanation themselves) is that the supervenience of reasons on the non-normative as such isn't enough to furnish it. Even if there can be no difference in reasons without a non-normative difference, this alone determines no particular distribution of reason relations. It entails the existence of some reason relations to begin with only if reasons nihilism is false.[34] For, if there were no reasons, it would follow trivially that, if two cases differ with respect to reasons, they must also differ in some non-normative respect.

Even if we conjoin supervenience with substantive normative assumptions to the effect that some particular non-normative way things are is co-instantiated with a particular reason relation, reasons won't be explained by their supervenient character. For supervenience provides only a non-symmetric and purely modal sort of determination, whereas explanatory relations are asymmetric and not purely modal.[35] Facts can be determined, in that sense, by conditions which don't constitute or explain them. For example, given a coarse tripartite division of the space of temperature conditions, *being neither hot nor cold* determines *being warm* (Oddie, 2005, p. 153). But clearly the latter doesn't consist in the former. Thus factors $F_1, \ldots, F_n$ can well fail to explain why P is a reason to Φ in C even if this reason relation cannot fail to hold when $F_1, \ldots, F_n$ obtain. This means also that truth-makers of reason claims may not provide constitutive explanations of them. The literature on truth-making nearly uniformly assumes that, if an entity α makes a proposition P true, then α couldn't exist without P being true. Such necessitation isn't enough for explanation. But what more there might metaphysically be to the truth-making relation is rarely discussed.

Supervenience can be used to illustrate one further constraint on constitutive explanations. The supervenience base for any property can be taken as a disjunction of every possible minimally sufficient set of conditions for the instantiation of that property. But it would be a significant theoretical cost if the distribution of reason relations over non-evaluative, non-normative features of the world had only a fundamentally disjunctive explanation. For that would mean that the reasons in this distribution would have nothing distinctively in common. Moreover, the supervenience relation itself allows each disjunct to include an extremely broad set of non-evaluative features, or even, at the limit, all of the non-evaluative features of the entire possible world in question. But being forced to allow that P's being a reason to Φ in

C may consist in the entire world being a certain non-evaluative way $F_1, ...,$ F_n would seem to be a significant theoretical cost. For that would be to allow that constitutive explanations may fail to differentiate those aspects of the world in virtue of which P is a reason to Φ in C, those in virtue of which Q is a reason to ψ in D, and so on.

The conditions which constitutive explanations select as those in which P's being a reason to Φ in C consists must also support the modal properties of reasons. Recall from Section 2 the idea that it is metaphysically impossible that the entire universe could be like it is actually in all non-normative respects, but the fact that my mother is my mother is a reason for me to torture her (Schroeder, 2007, p. 71). Whatever reasons the fact that my mother is my mother gives me, the conditions in which these reason relations consist should support metaphysical impossibilities of this kind where they hold. And if some reason relations hold necessarily, the conditions in which their holding consists should support their necessity.

In sum, then, if reason relations have constitutive explanations in non-evaluative, non-normative terms, there are strong reasons to think that the conditions in which the various reason relations consist aren't fundamentally disjunctive and that this constitutive relationship isn't purely modal but can support or ground the sorts of modal features that reason relations may have. These constraints can be met if reason relations are reducible to non-evaluative and non-normative properties or relations, since there will be no other way for P to be a reason to Φ in C than for P, C, and Φ to have these properties or stand in these relations, and nothing else will be required for them to do so.[36] But it is hard to imagine a plausible account of constitutive explanations of reasons in non-evaluative, non-normative terms which doesn't push towards a reductionist account of reasons. Other explanatory domains don't readily suggest a model for such explanations.

An independent consideration against the plausibility of constitutive explanations of reason relations in non-evaluative, non-normative terms concerns their fit with the 'autonomy of ethics', the thesis that there is no reasonable inference, deductive or non-deductive, from purely non-evaluative, non-normative premises to evaluative or normative conclusions. Ordinary normative discourse obeys this constraint. For instance, if we see someone realize that jumping out of the window is the only way they can save their lives and infer that this fact is a good reason for them to jump, we tend not to think that they have drawn a terrible inference. We tend instead to interpret the inference charitably as implicitly relying on further evaluative or normative premises, such as that their life is worth continuing and that one has a reason to take the necessary means to worthwhile courses of action.[37]

Explanatory relations may not themselves be inferential relations. But one would still expect that, if A explained B, this would say something about what would be reasonable or good about an inference of B from A. If P's being a reason to Φ in C consists in conditions $F_1, ..., F_n$, one would expect there typically to be a reasonable, even if non-monotonic, inference from $F_1, ..., F_n$ to $R(P, C, \Phi)$, even if such an inference were unavailable in our pragmatic situation.[38] If so, and if reason relations had constitutive explanations in non-evaluative, non-normative terms, then the possibility of reasonable inferences from such premises to evaluative or normative conclusions would seem to follow.

These considerations push naturally towards reductionism about reasons. For, if reason relations were reducible to some non-normative, non-evaluative properties and relations, then the connections that underwrite the reduction could perhaps be used to indicate, consistently with the autonomy of ethics, what would be reasonable or good about the relevant inferences. Otherwise it isn't easy to see what features of those inferences would make them so.

I conclude that I can see no plausible account of explanations of reasons in non-evaluative, non-normative terms which satisfies the NF constraint on explanations of reasons without naturally pushing in the direction of a reductionist account of reasons.

7. Explaining reasons in terms concerning reasons

My argument so far pushes an explanatory turn to reasons to the claim that the facts that are reasons are non-evaluative, non-normative facts, and their status as reasons can be explained by appeal to normative factors concerning reasons. I'll now discuss three strategies for trying to construct plausible explanations of this kind which might also satisfy the NF constraint.[39]

One sort of normative factor concerning reasons which could be used to explain reasons is the set of conditions under which something is a reason to do something. To satisfy the NF constraint, such conditions cannot be stated in some further normative terms. For instance, it would be ineligible to say that, when P is a reason to Φ in C, this is because P plays a role in explaining why one *ought* to Φ. Such conditions must also be stated in informative terms, not in terms which do little more than paraphrase reason talk. For instance, it would be either insufficiently informative or in violation of the NF constraint to say that, when P is a reason to Φ in C, this is *because* those who consider P would be motivated to Φ if they were fully informed and rational. This explanation isn't informative if talk of informed rational motivation merely paraphrases talk of reasons. But, if the notion of informed rational motivation is sufficiently independent of the notion of a reason to explain the status of some facts as reasons, then such explanations violate the NF constraint. For the fundamental explanatory work in such accounts isn't done by normative reasons. Rather, reasons will be a function of the desires of fully informed agents whose overall mental economy satisfies various rational requirements of coherence and the like.[40] It seems doubtful that there will turn out to be further normative reasons to be rational in this sense.

Another sort of normative factor concerning reasons which could perhaps be used to explain reasons is a certain sort of substantive claims about reasons. One idea along these lines is that it is part of the notion of a reason that certain non-evaluative, non-normative facts stand in reason relations. For instance, perhaps reason relations are by their nature such that the fact that something is painful is a reason to avoid it or make it stop. But this seems too strong. One widespread feature of normative discourse is that, when a pair of speakers find out that they favor very different sorts of things, they tend not to think that they have different enough normative concepts to be talking past each other. Rather, each tends to think that the other has mistaken, or at least idiosyncratic, normative views.[41] This, I take it, is how someone who denies that something's being painful is a reason to avoid it or make it stop would usually be classified. I also don't find it convincing that such people, although they share a concept of a reason with us, would have to be classified as mistaken about what reasons are, rather than as mistaken simply about what considerations are reasons for what.

A different way of appealing to substantive claims about reasons would be to explain why particular facts are reasons by subsuming them under general principles to the effect that certain facts are a reason to Φ in C. But, even apart from the question of whether a particular normative fact can sensibly be said to consist in, or hold in virtue of, a general normative principle plus suitable particular non-normative facts, this strategy would commit an explanatory turn to reasons to a surprising range of controversial implications. It would require some sort of 'covering law' theory of explanation. It would imply that particularist accounts of reasons are false. And it would carry a commitment to some particular set of substantive principles about reasons. Most importantly, however, this strategy would only push the explanatory problem a level up. General principles that specify what is a reason for what, necessary or not, seem no more brute or groundless than particular facts about what is a reason for what. So this strategy won't help.

A third sort of factor concerning reasons which could perhaps be used to explain reasons is some metaethical account which takes reasons to be a certain kind of function of a certain kind of collection of *judgments about* reasons. This general idea can be developed in different ways. One is constructivism. On this view, the normative fact that P is a reason to Φ in C is constituted by the fact that taking P to be a reason to Φ in C would withstand scrutiny from the standpoint of all the other normative judgments endorsed by the agent.[42] Another is expressivism. On this view, to judge that P is a reason to Φ in C is to express a certain kind of psychological attitude, and such a judgment counts as correct if it belongs to a set of such attitudes that cannot be, in a certain sense, improved upon.[43]

The only point I can make here about these views is dialectical. Constructivism and expressivism apply equally to reasons and other evaluative and normative notions, and nothing in discussions of constructivism and expressivism which touch on the relevant explanatory issues seems to point to any rationale for putting reasons in particular at the center stage. So, even if these metaethical accounts succeed in explaining reasons in terms of judgments about reasons, neither supports an explanatory turn to reasons in particular.

I conclude that there seems to be no account of explanations of reasons in terms concerning reasons which would support an explanatory turn to reasons. But this conclusion requires a caveat. It can be introduced by considering (theoretical) reasons for belief.

It is plausible that theoretical and practical reasons involve normative reason relations of the same type. But it seems that the demand to explain why some fact (e.g., that there is loud music and chatter coming from across the street) is a reason for some belief (e.g., that the neighbors are having a party) might be easily met by something like the following explanatory schema: given the fact in question (plus some body of background information or facts), the proposition that is the content of the belief is likely to be true. Where such explanations are best located in this paper's framework for explanations of reasons deserves a fuller discussion than I can give here. But I suspect that truth and probability, and concepts of epistemic utility constructed out of them, aren't themselves normative notions. (They are, of course, co-opted into normative standards in epistemology.) Thus it would seem that either explanations of reasons for belief in terms of truth and probability are explanations in terms of non-normative factors or that probability-raising considerations count as reasons for belief only if, and because, false belief is in some sense bad and true belief good (at least when the truths are non-trivial and sufficiently important or interesting).

The caveat to my conclusion above is that this second option might not have to violate the NF constraint. Some philosophers think that something like the explanatory schema above follows from the very nature of belief as an attitude that has a 'constitutive aim' of truth.[44] If fact F makes proposition P likely to be true (or is otherwise indicative of the truth of P), then F is a reason to believe P, given what belief is. The status of a fact as a reason for belief could thus be explicable in terms of some norms of reason which somehow derive from the aim of truth and by which belief is constitutively regulated. True belief might then be held to be good in the sense of according with such norms of reason. This might come close enough to counting as an explanation of reasons for belief in terms concerning reasons.

Whether a general explanatory turn to reasons is a significant option here depends on the prospects for similar explanations of why certain facts are reasons for action, intention, and desire, for the various reactive and affective attitudes, and, on the theoretical side, for attitudes such as supposing and guessing. The bet would be that actions (and so on) also have some or other 'constitutive aim'[45] and, moreover, that reasons for action (and so on) can be explained in terms of that aim. It is highly controversial that acting and a variety of attitudes for which there can be reasons each have a constitutive aim to begin with, and that, if they do, that aim is of the right sort, and sufficiently rich, to ground and explain a sufficiently wide range of reasons for action.[46] I suspect that making all this plausible will prove too tall an order. But here I can only note the caveat that this is an option for an explanatory turn to reasons which my arguments don't rule out. Its assessment must be left for future work.

8. Conclusion

For all that this paper shows, there may be constitutive explanations of reasons that satisfy the NF constraint without pushing towards reductionism about reasons. I may simply have failed to find them. But it is far from clear where to look for such explanations, save perhaps for controversial ideas about constitutive aims of action, belief, and all the other attitudes for which there are reasons. Thus it seems fair to cast my discussion as a challenge to those who find themselves sympathetic to an explanatory turn to reasons to construct such explanations. My aim has been to force such philosophers into a choice that many of them wouldn't like: either endorse reductionism about reasons or abort the turn to reasons in particular.

The concerns over explanation of evaluative and normative facts which fuel this challenge are, as I have noted, quite general. It is therefore possible that the considerations I have given can be recruited to generate parallel challenges against proposals to take some other factors than reasons as explanatorily fundamental in the normative domain. I don't particularly worry that this means that my discussion shows too much for my purposes. If everyone faces a certain problem over explaining evaluative and normative facts, that doesn't mean that no one has a problem. And, in fact, nothing I say here challenges reductionism as a general explanatory hypothesis regarding evaluative and normative facts. Whether and to what extent reductive explanations of various evaluative and normative facts or notions are plausible depends on such further issues as how well those explanations can capture the evaluative or normative character of these facts or notions.

Some people might be inclined to conclude instead that the constraints on explaining evaluative and normative facts must be weaker than the NF constraint and its analogues. That would affect the main thrust of this chapter. Although Section 2 defends the idea that evaluative and normative facts typically call for explanation, the strength and scope of such a constraint clearly deserves further discussion. For what it is worth, my own inclination is to think that the rational intelligibility of normative and evaluative distinctions and facts significantly constrains what can be regarded as brute in the normative domain and where no further explanation is possible. And, again for what it is worth, I suspect that, if there are evaluative or normative facts that have no further explanation, they will be more concerned with whether certain aspects of our situation in the world have some or other sort of normative significance than whether the particular form that their significance takes is constitution of value, provision of reasons, or something else. Thus, the current fashion of putting reasons at center stage in moral philosophy fails to strike me as a significant innovation in the important enterprise of explaining evaluative and normative phenomena.[47]

Notes

1. So by 'explanation' I mean the content of an answer to a why-question, not the activity of giving such an answer. We may need to add that something counts as an explanation only if it also satisfies certain epistemic conditions. For example, it may be that the content of an answer to a why-question counts as an explanation only if it is (or represents) a body of information that is structured in such a way that grasping that body of information would constitute a certain kind of epistemic gain regarding what is being explained.
2. Those who agree include, for example, Raz (2001, p. 50). Parfit (2006, p. 331) thinks the bedrock lies nearer the surface.
3. This isn't the only kind of reason predicate we deploy, even when talking just about normative reasons, in contrast to 'motivational' and 'explanatory' reasons. We can also talk of 'overall' reasons to Φ, based on taking into account everything that counts for or against Φing (although how to understand such talk is controversial), as well as of 'sufficient' reasons to Φ (see, e.g., Skorupski, 2006).
4. There is controversy over which ontological category includes the considerations that provide reasons, but there is a broad consensus that they are facts or propositions. I keep the assumption disjunctive because, although reason statements often specify facts that are the case, we can also talk about whether something would be a reason if it were the case, and so statements of the form R(P, C, Φ) aren't uniformly factive with respect to P.
5. Thus these simplifications don't prejudge debates between internalist and externalist theories or Humean and anti-Humean theories of reasons. A huge literature is devoted to these debates, but see, for example, Williams (1981b), Smith (1994a), Dancy (2000a), Schroeder (2007), and, for a useful survey, Finlay and Schroeder (2008).
6. The distinction between facts that are reasons and the normative facts that they are reasons is most explicitly drawn by McNaughton and Rawling (2003). For a relevant critical discussion of some work on reasons which plays fast and loose with the distinction, see Olson (2009). We should probably make the distinction tripartite by adding another dimension: the source or ground of the normative fact that P is a reason to Φ in C.
7. They also presume that the fact that prudence requires me to do something is a reason to do it, and so is the fact that morality requires me to do something. Whether these might be brute facts is unclear.
8. The problem may be a generalization of the problem mentioned for the moral case in Pritchard (1912).

9. Note also that skepticism about intrinsic value isn't uncommon, but in the case of reasons one more commonly finds claims such as the following: 'Genuine skepticism about...whether anything ever counts in favor of anything else in the sense typical of reasons...would be a very difficult position to hold' (Scanlon, 1998, p. 19). Such claims often rely on the thought that any argument for skepticism about reasons for belief would be self-defeating. But it seems not at all clear that an argument for the truth of the claim that there are no reasons for belief must be committed to the existence of reasons for believing its conclusion (cf. Olson, 2009, p. 177).

10. It is common to group proposals to explain value in terms of the 'fittingness' or 'appropriateness' of a certain sort of response with a turn to reasons. I won't do this here, because fittingness or appropriateness needn't be understood as a function of reasons or vice versa. Thus the claim that a certain response to something is fitting and the claim that there is a reason to respond to it in that way may not be equivalent.

11. Claims to this effect, but of varying determinacy regarding the scope of the normative, can be found in Hampton (1998, p. 115), Scanlon (1998, p. 17), Raz (1999, p. 67), Dancy (2004a, ch. 1), and Schroeder (2007, p. 81).

12. For the first view, see, for example, Raz (1999, p. 1). The second is mentioned as an option in Dancy (2000a, pp. 29–30). It is perhaps endorsed by Crisp (2006, p. 62), but this isn't clear.

13. Or fundamental in so far as the normativity of these other notions is concerned. Some of these other notions might have non-normative elements which aren't exhausted by their relation to reasons.

14. See, for example, Scanlon (1998, p. 17) and Dancy (2004a, ch. 1), among many others.

15. See, for example, Scanlon (1998, pp. 95–100), Stratton-Lake and Hooker (2006), and Väyrynen (2006).

16. The idea comes up in conversations. Skorupski (2006, p. 26) mentions it with approval. I take the general tenor of the early chapters of Scanlon (1998) strongly to suggest it. See also Parfit (forthcoming, ch. 1).

17. Note that this kind of explanatory demand is compatible with a wide range of views about reasons. It can be reasonable not merely if the concept of a reason is primitive, but also if reasons are best explicated in terms of their role in explaining what one ought to do (Broome, 2004) or in terms of their bearing on practical questions (Hieronymi, 2005). If some fact forms part of an explanation of why one ought to Φ, or part of an answer to the question of whether to Φ, then it is presumably not a brute or arbitrary fact that it does so.

18. See, for example, the literature on the 'supervenience argument' against moral realism originated by Blackburn (1971). Many writers on necessity deny that there are unexplained necessities (see, e.g., Cameron, 2010).

19. I owe these examples to T.M. Scanlon (The John Locke Lectures, University of Oxford, 2009).

20. To a first approximation, P is a non-derivative reason to Φ if P is a reason to Φ but not (only) because some fact Q distinct from P is a reason to Φ. Instrumentalist theories of practical reasons will typically count some instrumental reasons as non-derivative in this sense, which seems to be the right result.

21. See Fine (1995, p. 271). Väyrynen (2009a) discusses several different kinds of relations which the term 'in virtue of' may be used to express.

22. No uniform terminology exists here. Such relations as *A consists in nothing more than B* and *A is nothing over and above B* are called 'grounding' (Fine, 2001, pp. 15–16)

and 'constitution' (Shafer-Landau, 2003, p. 77), among other things. These locutions are usually meant to allow that A and B may be numerically distinct.

23. It is one thing to say that something is a reason to Φ, another to say that it is part
of what explains why something is a reason to Φ. It might not be the case that all
explanations of reasons to Φ must themselves be reasons to Φ. But, if so, then it
is possible for something to play the latter role without playing the former.

24. One example would be the notion of a basic *prima facie* duty, in the sense of Ross
(1930, ch. 2).

25. For this example and a useful survey of intrinsicness and intrinsicality, see
Weatherson (2008).

26. See Quinn (1993), Lance and Little (2006), and Heuer (2006) for remarks that
seem sympathetic to this claim.

27. Unless, surprisingly indeed, to be painful is to have other properties that provide
certain kinds of reasons.

28. See Raz (2001, pp. 165–6), Wallace (2002, p. 448), Scanlon (2002, p. 513), and
Dancy (2004a, ch. 2).

29. Different forms of value-based accounts of reasons can be found, for example, in
Moore (1903), Quinn (1993), Lawrence (1995), Raz (1999; 2001), Audi (2006), and
Heuer (2006).

30. For instance, being a good-making feature would have to be nothing over and
above providing certain kinds of reasons for actions or attitudes.

31. See Williams (1985, pp. 128–9, 140–1) and much of the literature following his
discussion. Against this, Väyrynen (2009b) argues that the evaluations which
may be conveyed by using predicates expressing thick concepts aren't located in
their sense or semantic content.

32. This claim is developed and endorsed by Stratton-Lake and Hooker (2006,
p. 152).

33. This is to understand the fact that something is generous as an existential fact
that there are reasons, given by certain properties, to respond to it in certain
favorable ways. According to the buck-passing account of value, the fact that
something is good is a similar existential fact. Such existential facts about reasons can be derivative reasons.

34. This can be seen by considering the antecedent in the standard formulation of
weak and strong property supervenience of the normative on the non-normative.
Strong supervenience holds that: $\Box[(\exists x) (B^*x \And Ax) \supset \Box(\forall y)(B^*y \supset Ay)]$, where A
is a normative property and 'B^*' is the 'total' non-normative base property. Weak
supervenience drops the second necessity operator ('$\Box$'). The antecedents of
these supervenience claims hold only if something has the normative property
A; normative nihilism denies this. Varying the modal strengths of the necessity
operators generates different versions of these supervenience claims.

35. These claims aren't in dispute in the supervenience literature. See, for example,
McLaughlin and Bennett (2008).

36. For a sustained defense of reductionism about reasons along these lines, see
Schroeder (2007, ch. 4).

37. See Sturgeon (2002). As Sturgeon notes, similar inference barriers seem to appear
in many other domains. For an extended discussion of inferring 'ought' from 'is'
without such auxiliary premises, see Zimmerman (2010, ch. 5). (I am here ignor-
ing the well-known 'cheap' counter-examples to the autonomy of ethics.)

38. At least in so far as such explanations are abductive or non-monotonic, there
is no reason to suppose that they would always have to predict or retrodict the
holding of particular reason relations. A perhaps related point is that explanation

of reasons is one thing (theoretical), deliberation about what to do is another (practical).

39. Another strategy, which I cannot discuss properly here, is to argue that what explains why P is occurrently a reason to Φ is that P has a *disposition* to be a reason to Φ in C and the circumstances C obtain. (For a discussion of such 'normative dispositions,' see Robinson, 2006.) But I suspect that the arguments I have given so far can be applied also against taking such normative dispositions as the fundamental units of explanations of reasons. If properties are the sorts of things that can have dispositions to begin with, it might be plausible that some evaluative and normative properties are disposed to give reasons to Φ in C in virtue of their particular evaluative or normative character; but this would violate the NF constraint. It seems much harder to motivate the idea that non-evaluative, non-normative properties are disposed to give reasons to Φ in C. That certain such properties bear such a normative disposition isn't a brute fact, in my opinion. But what in such properties would explain why they are so disposed? This question might have a satisfactory answer if normative dispositions were reducible to a non-evaluative, non-normative basis that explains why the disposition is manifested when it is. But I don't see how an appeal to normative dispositions that doesn't involve reductionism can help explain reasons consistently with the NF constraint. Still, it may well be that these doubts are too hasty and deserve further discussion.

40. For an analysis of normative reasons in such terms, see, for example, Smith (1994a, ch. 5).

41. For one recent discussion of this point and some of its implications, see Merli (2009).

42. See especially Street (2008) and the works cited therein. Constructivists of this sort don't usually think that the attitude of taking something to be a reason can be characterized in non-normative terms, but only in certain sorts of primitive normative terms (see Street, 2008, 239–42). Note also that this view wouldn't seem to furnish a transcendental argument to the effect that, if there are to be any reasons at all, there must be reasons for thinking along the lines of some procedure for determining what reasons there are for particular agents to do what.

43. See, for example, Blackburn (1988) and Gibbard (2003, pp. 188–91). Although expressivists think that what reasons one has can only be assessed against a standpoint constituted by other judgments about reasons, they also think that the attitude expressed by such judgments – the attitude of counting P as favoring Φing in C – can be described without using the concept of a reason. But this prong of expressivist accounts of reasons doesn't seem to be intended to furnish the sorts of explanations of normative reasons that are the focus of this paper.

44. The literature on the 'aim of belief' is extensive, but see, for example, Velleman (2000, ch. 11) and Wedgwood (2002).

45. The literature on the 'constitutive aim of action' is again extensive, but see, for example, Velleman (2000, ch. 6–8 and 'Introduction'), Korsgaard (2009), and, for one representative critical discussion, Enoch (2006).

46. Various specifications of such constitutive aims would be of the wrong sort to suit an explanatory turn to reasons. If the constitutive aim of action were *the good*, then explanations of reasons for action in terms of this aim would violate the NF constraint. And would it be informative and non-circular for an explana-

tory turn to reasons to exploit a constitutive aim of action if that aim were *acting in accordance with reasons?*

47. Thanks to audiences at Universities of Birmingham, Leeds, and Oxford, and especially to Hanne Appelqvist, Michael Brady, Daniel Elstein, Geoffrey Ferrari, Joseph Raz, Jussi Suikkanen, and anonymous referees, for helpful discussions and comments regarding this paper. Support is acknowledged from the European Community's Seventh Framework Programme (FP7/2007–2013) under grant agreement n° 231016.

10
Shmagency Revisited
David Enoch

1. The Shmagency challenge to constitutivism

In metaethics – and indeed, meta-normativity – constitutivism is a family of views that hope to ground normativity in norms, or standards, or motives, or aims that are constitutive of action and agency. And, mostly because of the influential work of Christine Korsgaard and David Velleman (and, some would say, because of the also influential work of Kant and Aristotle), constitutivism seems to be gaining ground in the current literature.

The promises of constitutivism are significant. Perhaps chief among them are the hope of providing some kind of answer to the skeptic about morality or, perhaps, practical reason, and the hope of securing for practical reason a kind of objectivity that is consistent with its practical, motivationally engaged nature. The former philosophical motivation for constitutivism – most clearly present in much of Korsgaard's relevant work[1] – relies on the fact that constitutive norms seem to be less mysterious than not-clearly-constitutive norms. There is arguably nothing mysterious about, say, the norms of certain reasonably well-defined activities, such as building a house, or playing chess. And challenges by the relevant skeptic – the one asking 'Why should I make sure the house I'm building can shelter people from the weather?' or 'Why should I avoid being checkmated?' – seem very rare, barely intelligible, and in any case remarkably easy to cope with. We should explain to the misguided skeptic that, if he doesn't even try to build something that can protect people from the weather, he's not in the business of building a house at all; that, if she doesn't even try to play by the rules of chess, she's not in the business of playing chess at all; and so on. It would be nice, the constitutivist hope seems to go, if we had something equally powerful by way of a response to the skeptic asking 'Why be moral?' (and related skeptics).

The other main motivation for constitutivism – most clearly present in David Velleman's relevant work[2] – starts from a commitment to some rather strong kind of existence-internalism about reasons: an agent has a reason to Φ, according to such views (commonly associated with Williams's influential 'Internal and External Reasons', 1981), only if she can come to Φ, or at least to be motivated to Φ, by sound deliberation starting from her actual motivational set. What reasons we have, on such a view, is a function of what motivations we have. And, of course, different people have different motivations. So objectivity is threatened. But if some motivations are necessarily shared by all possible agents – if, in other words, some motives are constitutive of agency – then objectivity can be restored, consistently with internalism. The reasons grounded in the motives constitutive of agency – if such exist – necessarily apply to all agents.

If it can be defended, then, constitutivism promises to yield significant payoffs.[3] But constitutivism seems to be subject to a powerful objection. For agents need not care about their qualifications as agents, or whether some of their bodily movements count as actions. They can, it seems, be perfectly happy being shmagents – non-agent things that lack the thing purportedly constitutive of agency, but that are as similar to agents as is otherwise possible – or perhaps being something else altogether. If so, constitutivism cannot make good on its promises: for, when Korsgaard replies to the agent who asks, say, 'Why should I care about the hypothetical and categorical imperatives?' with 'Well, otherwise you wouldn't even count as an agent, you wouldn't even be in the game of performing actions,' the skeptic can discard this reply with a simple 'So what?' What is it to her, as it were, whether she qualifies as an agent or not? She would be analogous not to the chess-player who asks why she should play according to the rules, but to someone who enjoys the aesthetic qualities of (what we call) the chess board and pieces. If we tell this person that he must not move his king to a certain position because it's against the rules, and if he breaks them he won't count as playing chess, he can perfectly rationally shrug us off with a simple 'So what?' He doesn't care whether his manipulation of the chess pieces qualifies as chess-playing. And at this point the objectivity Velleman hopes for also collapses, because the practical reasons whose objectivity Velleman wants to secure will not reach the person who is happy being a shmagent-rather-than-an-agent, or perhaps something else entirely. The general point here is that the status of being constitutive of agency does not suffice for a normatively non-arbitrary status. Of course, if there were some independent reason to be an agent (for instance, rather than a shmagent), or to perform actions, this objection would go away. But the price would be too high, for such an independent reason – one not accounted for by the constitutivist story, but rather presupposed by it – would make it impossible for constitutivism to be the whole, or the most foundational, account of normativity, or to deliver on its promised payoffs.

Or so, at least, I have argued in my 'Agency, Shmagency: Why Normativity Will Not Come from What Is Constitutive of Action' (2006).[4] Several people have responded to that paper, defending constitutivism against the shmagency challenge.[5] I think that engaging these responses justifies a further discussion of the shmagency challenge. This is so, first, because of the prominence of constitutivism in the current literature (since the publication of 'Agency, Shmagency,' for instance, both Velleman (2009) and Korsgaard (2008) have published already influential constitutivist books). If there is no successful answer to the shmagency challenge, this is of some significance to the current meta-normative debate. Furthermore, a detailed examination of the possible lines of response available to constitutivists may – even if they do not end up refuting such views – improve our understanding of constitutivist views and of the motivations underlying them, and this too should count for philosophical progress. Indeed, from Velleman's response to the shmagency challenge (and related difficulties) we can already learn much more about at least his version of constitutivism than we could from his previous writing on the topic, as I hope will become clear later on. Finally, some of the topics to be discussed below are, in fact, of much wider philosophical interest. Or so, at least, I hope.

Before proceeding, though, I need to make two preliminary points. First, in order to isolate the discussion of the shmagency challenge as much as possible from other possible challenges to constitutivism (or to specific constitutivist theories) I will grant for the sake of argument – as I did in 'Agency, Shmagency' – much of what the constitutivist wants. In particular, I will grant that action and agency do have a constitutive aim (or aims, or standards, or motives, etc.), and I will not quibble over what it is (though, of course, different constitutivists may differ among themselves here). Also, I will have nothing at all to say specifically about morality here: perhaps constitutivists have some further challenges they need to address when it comes to morality.[6]

Second, I will be using Velleman's discussion of the shmagency challenge and related issues as my focal point here. But I will not start this discussion with a clear, orderly presentation of his reply. My reason is that his reply (and to an extent, also Ferrero's) is not easily put in a clear, orderly way. Rather, his response seems to be comprised of several related lines of thought, which together disarm the challenge and show constitutivism to emerge victorious. So it is more convenient to discuss these lines of thought in turn, and then return – in the concluding section – to the bigger picture, in order to do some score-keeping. And, indeed, this is how I will proceed.

2. Does playing chess suffice for having a reason to checkmate?

One of the points I emphasized in 'Agency, Shmagency' (p. 185) was that, even if you find yourself engaging in a kind of activity, and, indeed, even if you find yourself *inescapably* engaging in it (inescapability will shortly take center stage), and even if that activity is constitutively governed by some norm or is constitutively directed at some aim, this does not suffice for you to have a reason to obey that norm or set your sights on that aim. Rather, what is also needed is that you *have a reason* to engage in that activity. The example I use here – following Velleman – is that of games. Even if you somehow find yourself playing chess, and even if checkmating your opponent is a constitutive aim of playing chess, still you may not have a reason to (try to) checkmate your opponent. You may lack such a reason if you lack a reason to play chess. The analogy is clear enough: even if you find yourself playing the agency game, and even if agency has a constitutive aim, still you may not have a reason to be an agent (for instance, rather than a shmagent).

But one may want to reject this initial claim, even with regard to chess. For it may be suggested that playing chess *does*, after all, suffice for having a reason – *some* reason, at least, perhaps a weak one, perhaps one that is outweighed by others – for checkmating your opponent. Perhaps there is no need after all for another reason, namely, a reason to be playing chess (or perhaps to play this specific game of chess)?[7] If so, we may proceed to conclude that our merely playing the agency game suffices for us having a reason to direct ourselves towards its constitutive aims.

As a general thesis, though, this cannot be true. We can define many cooked-up variations of chess, with slightly different rules, or perhaps slightly different ways of winning (say, you only win if you checkmate your opponent in an even number of moves; or when she still has her queen; or when she looks away; or if you move your castle diagonally three times when your opponent looks away; etc.). Whenever you find yourself playing chess, you also find yourself (in sufficiently early stages of the game) playing these cooked-up games chess*, chess**, chess***, and so on. But it doesn't seem that you have reasons to win at chess*, or at chess**, or at chess***. This is so, presumably, because you don't have a reason to play chess*, or chess**, or chess***. So this little example suffices to show that it's not generally true that engaging in some activity – satisfying some relevant descriptive criteria – suffices for having reason to direct oneself at its constitutive aim.[8]

So, if you think that the game of agency is different – if you think, in other words, that playing it suffices for having a reason to play it well, or to achieve its constitutive aims, or some such – then you must be able to come up with an answer to the question: What's so special about agency? Why is this true of agency, even though it's not true in general? I can't think of an answer to this question (except perhaps in terms of inescapability, to which we will return shortly).

But, it may now be argued, I have mischaracterized the analogy. The right analogy is not to the person who finds herself satisfying the descriptive criteria that apply to those playing chess. Rather, the right analogy is to those *already* caring about playing chess (rather than playing chess*, or doing something else entirely). And, when it comes to *those*, their playing chess and caring about whatever aim is constitutive of playing chess does suffice for their having a reason to achieve it. This, I think, is a different line of thought, and it is the topic of the next section.

3. But you do care!

The thought, then, may be this. What is arguably constitutive of action is not just its being subject – in some yet-to-be-specified objective sense – to certain norms, or its being directed – in some yet-to-be-specified objective sense – at some aim. Rather, what is constitutive of action is *caring* about the relevant constitutive aim. Velleman, for instance, believes that the constitutive aim of action is some special kind of intelligibility, making sense of oneself by acting in a way that makes sense *to* oneself. And what is necessary, on his account, for a behavior to qualify as an action is that the agent performing it be motivated to (thereby) achieve self-understanding. It is, on this view, constitutive of agency that agents have this motive geared at achieving self-understanding. It's not just that an action can only count as successful if (and to the extent that) it achieves self-understanding. Rather, it can only count as an action if the one performing it is partly motivated to achieve (by performing it) self-understanding. On this suggestion, then, we should be careful with the game analogy. The analogous claim to the one sketched here is not that an episode of chess-playing cannot count as (fully) successful unless it achieves the constitutive aim of chess (checkmating your opponent). Rather, it is that you don't even count as playing chess unless you are committed to achieving that aim, unless you care about checkmating your opponent, unless you (to an extent, at least) want to checkmate your opponent.[9] If *this* is the constitutivist claim about chess-playing, then it becomes *much* more plausible that merely playing chess (and so also caring about checkmating your opponent) suffices for your having a reason to checkmate your opponent (regardless of whether or not you have a reason to play chess). And, similarly, if the constitutivist claim about agency is that *caring about self-understanding*, or *being motivated to achieve self-understanding*, is constitutive of action, then it becomes much more plausible that merely being an agent, merely being in the business of performing actions (and so caring about self-understanding) gives you a reason to aim at self-understanding.

What is of importance here, then, is the distinction between two ways in which the game analogy can be used – one in which games are an example of an activity that is constitutively governed by certain norms (so that the relevant success criteria are given by those norms), and another in which it is (arguably) necessary, in order to count as taking part in a certain activity, that one already care about (what is arguably) its constitutive aim. In 'Agency, Shmagency' I wasn't clear enough about this distinction, and so I wasn't explicit enough about rejecting this second way of using the game analogy. In my defense, I do not think it was completely clear in constitutivist texts that this was what they were after.[10] And, at least with regard to Korsgaard, I do not think this *is* a plausible reading of her constitutivism (a point to which I return in the next section). But it is very clear that this is what Velleman (2009) has in mind, and it is important to address this line of thought directly.

To see more clearly how it is relevant, it helps to think of things in dialogical terms. The one putting forward the shmagency challenge asks something like: 'Why should I care about self-understanding? Even if you are right about its constitutive status, why should I care about *that*?' The constitutivist we are now considering answers: 'But you *do* care! You are, after all, an agent, as is evidenced even by your mere asking of these very questions. And it's a necessary condition for being an agent to care about self-understanding. So you do already care about self-understanding!' Notice that this answer – problematic though it may be, as I am about to argue – is different from the kind of answer I explicitly discuss in 'Agency, Shmagency' (p. 179), in terms of the imagined dialogue between Korsgaard and the skeptic, where she threatens him that if he doesn't care about morality (or some such) his bodily movements will not merit being called 'actions.' (I return to this skeptic – and to Korsgaard – in the next section.)

Well, how good is this reply? Remember, we are granting here for the sake of argument that self-understanding is constitutive of action in the second way outlined above, and so that the one putting forward the challenge already cares about self-understanding. When someone of whom all this is true asks 'But *why* should I care about self-understanding?' how good is the retort 'But you *do* care!'?

I want to argue that it is not good at all, for two reasons. The first is that this reply is highly implausible. The second reason – the more important one in our dialectical context – is that it is beside the point; it fails to engage the question. I will discuss implausibility first, irrelevance later.

3.1. Implausibility

With regard to implausibility, then, let me start with the following rather obvious structural constitutivist tension: the more you pack into whatever it is you claim is constitutive of agency, the less plausible is the claim that it *is* so constitutive. On the other hand, the less you pack into whatever it is you claim is constitutive of agency, the less by way of norms of practical reason you can extract from it.[11] The challenge for constitutivists, then, is to come up with a constitutivist account that packs enough into whatever it is that is claimed to be constitutive of action for the account to be interesting, but packs sufficiently little into it to be even remotely plausible. And the restriction relevant here is this latter one: it is one thing to say that the rules of chess, or perhaps the relevant success standards, are somehow constitutive of the game of chess. Myself, I am not even sure that *this* claim is true. But what I want to emphasize now is that it is *much* weaker, and so also much more plausible, than the claim that *caring* about checkmating your opponent is constitutive of chess-playing. Suppose I am playing chess (or, well, sort-of playing chess) with my daughter; I obey the rules quite strictly, but I do not care who wins. Perhaps I even intentionally let her win. On the (chess-analogue of the) suggested constitutivist account, I am not really playing chess.[12] And this seems like a huge stretch. Certainly, in common parlance we would be happy to describe the situation as one in which I am playing chess with my daughter.[13]

Getting back, then, to action and agency: it is one thing to say that some criteria of success are constitutive of agency. It is quite another to claim that *caring* about them is constitutive of agency. All that is needed as a counter-example to *this* claim is a possible creature who – though perhaps causally governed in some way by the 'aim' of (for example) self-understanding – doesn't care about it, and whom we are still happy to classify as an agent, as performing actions, and so forth. By relying on the but-you-do-care response to the why-should-I-care question, then, the constitutivist makes his constitutivist claim (even) less plausible. But, because I am for the most part granting for the sake of argument the constitutivist claim (that so-and-so is constitutive of agency), I will not dwell on this point further.

Before proceeding to discuss the irrelevance of the but-you-do-care response, though, let me quickly make two further points. First, the current version of the chess analogy (from two paragraphs back) shows not only how implausible the constitutivist claim must be, but also that there's something silly about this whole discussion. After all, the question of whether someone who seemingly plays chess but doesn't care about winning should *really* count as playing chess seems terribly uninteresting, and one on which the answer to nothing at all deep can hang.[14] Who cares whether this counts as chess-playing? Most clearly, nothing of any normative significance can depend on it. So, if this is the right version of the chess analogy, the analogous worry about the constitutivist claim seems imminent: I'm not sure whether someone who doesn't care about self-understanding (or whatever is supposed to be constitutive of agency) should *really* count an agent. But, whether she should or not, this seems like a somewhat silly question,[15] on the answer to which nothing of any importance can hang. This too, I think, should give the constitutivist pause.[16]

Second, I often hear the claim that I have failed to make it reasonably clear what it is to be a shmagent. When characterizing shmagents, I said (p. 179) that they are non-agent creatures who lack whatever it is that is constitutive of agency, but are otherwise as similar to agents as is possible.[17] But it may be thought that – lacking the constitutive aim of agency – shmagents can be nothing at all like agents.[18] However, we already know that this claim cannot possibly be right. Perhaps when I seemingly play chess with my daughter, not caring about who wins, I do not *really* play chess. But the claim that I don't even do anything *similar* to playing chess is too much to swallow. Similarly, I would say, for agency. Indeed, it follows from things Velleman says in this context (e.g. p. 128) that, even if agents cannot act, they can certainly *behave*. And, while action may be a very interesting and special particular instance of behavior, the claim that non-action behavior is nothing like action is just too much to swallow. After all, if they were so dissimilar, we would not need the careful work of good philosophers of action to help us see the distinction, at least in outline.

3.2. Irrelevance

So much, then, for the implausibility of the but-you-do-care response to the why-should-I-care-about-(e.g.)-self-understanding challenge. What I want to argue now is that, even if we ignore this implausibility, still this response cannot possibly work, because it does not even qualify as a response – it fails to address the challenge. The thought here is very simple: noting that I do Φ is never a good answer to the question of whether I should Φ. This is true for actions, and it is just as true for carings. Perhaps I do care about something; but how does noticing this fact count as an answer to the normative question of whether I *should* care about it, or indeed as a reason for caring about it?

The point is not merely an 'is-ought gap' kind of point. True, some of us have somehow become very good at convincing ourselves that sometimes an ought can, after all, be derived from an is, or that some normative facts or properties just are some natural facts or properties, or some such. But what we are up against here is an *especially* problematic instance of such a move – it is the move immediately from someone caring about something to it being the case that she *should* care about it, or at least that she has a reason to care. I take it that even those of us with the strongest stomach for naturalistic fallacies should not be happy with such a move. When someone asks 'Why should I care about self-understanding?' (or whatever else is constitutive of agency), and the response comes 'But you *do* care!', all that is needed by way of counter-response is 'So what? I asked whether I *should* care, not whether I *do*. You haven't answered my question.' The but-you-do-care response is thus no response at all. It is utterly irrelevant.

Constitutivists like to emphasize that the agency game is not just one we *do* play, but also one we cannot avoid playing; agency is – in certain senses – inescapable for creatures like us. Constitutivists then sometimes suggest that the inescapability of agency somehow helps with the shmagency challenge (and related challenges).[19] Thus, Velleman (2009, pp. 136–7) distinguishes two senses of inescapability, suggesting that their combined strength helps in answering the why-should-I-care-about-self-understanding challenge. His two senses may be labeled *natural* and *dialectical*.[20] Let me postpone discussion of dialectical inescapability to sections 5 through 7. The natural inescapability of agency seems to come down to the fact that we cannot opt out of the game of agency; such opting out is just not something we can do. We can, of course, choose to end our lives, but, as I also noted in 'Agency, Shmagency' (p. 188), far from opting out of the game of agency, this would be a major move *within* the game. And we can temporarily opt out of the game, say by going to sleep. But still, acting and choosing is, as Korsgaard likes to put things, 'our plight.'[21]

I want to concede that agency is indeed naturally inescapable for us. But I also want to note (as I did, to an extent, in 'Agency, Shmagency' (p. 188 and on)) that such inescapability does not matter in our context, and in particular does not render the but-you-do-care response any better. For the move from 'You inescapably Φ' to 'You should Φ' is no better – not even the tiniest little bit – than the move from 'You actually Φ' to 'You should Φ.'

Perhaps Velleman appreciates this point. Perhaps this is why he suggests (2009, p. 137) that the inescapability of agency (and so, in his theory, of caring about self-understanding) does not so much show that one should care about self-understanding, as it renders moot the question of whether one should care.[22] And, of course, there is something to this point: it would, for instance, seem unwise to devote many resources to an attempt to answer the question of whether I should Φ, when I cannot avoid Φing. But we are not here in the business of allocating research grants. Rather, we are in the business of finding the best theory of normativity – after all, it is the constitutivist ambition to give us such a theory; and it was my point in 'Agency, Shmagency' that constitutivism cannot live up to this ambition. And, because this is the nature of our project, the mootness of the why-should-I-care question is simply beside the point. Its very intelligibility – and the fact that so far we do not have an adequate constitutivist reply to it, even if it is in some practical sense moot – suffices to cause serious trouble for constitutivism.[23]

Perhaps an example can help here. I am a latent and grudging patriot.[24] I reject patriotism and nationalism as morally unjustified. I am willing to defend this position in a philosophical or political argument. And yet I find myself moved by the sorts of thing patriots are moved by (say, a flag, the national anthem, the success of a local sports team). In a sense, then, I care about such things. I can ask, and often have asked 'Why should I care about such things?', and I'm rather confident that the answer is that I should not. If someone then tells me: 'But you *do* care!' what she says will be true. Perhaps it's even true that (in some sense) patriotism of this kind is inescapable for me, that I cannot avoid it (for what it's worth – I've tried). But this does not even begin to answer the question of whether I should especially care about, say, how well my country's tennis team does in the Davis Cup, and, if so, why. That the question whether to care is in a sense moot for me – I cannot stop caring – is neither here nor there.

There may be a complication here. Constitutivists are typically existence-internalists about reasons; they believe in a very strong connection between the reasons an agent has and her subjective motivational set. After all, and as stated at the outset, a major motivation for constitutivism is precisely the attempt to account for some kind of objectivity consistently with such internalism. And it may be thought that, *assuming internalism*, the objection above fails. Assuming internalism, showing that you do care about something, *can*, so this thought goes, show that you have a reason to care, because internalism is precisely the claim that what you have reason to do and care about is very closely related to (roughly) what you care about.

But this line of thought is mistaken. Internalism does indeed assert a close connection between your reasons and what you care about, but it does not take caring about something as *sufficient* to having a reason to care about it. An internalism that would commit itself to such a claim would be extremely implausible (as the grudging patriot example shows), and no internalist I know of takes this line. So, even if we are willing to assume – for the sake of argument – some constitutivist-friendly version of existence internalism about reasons, still this cannot bridge the gap between the why-should-I-care question and the but-you-do-care answer. Even on internalism, more is needed for having a reason to care, and so the constitutivist still has not adequately addressed this question.

As I've already hinted several times, Velleman seems to notice these points. Though he says that the inescapability of agency renders the question 'Why should I care about self-understanding?' moot, he also continues to further discuss it, suggesting – even saying explicitly (2009, p. 138) – that it still calls for an answer, that 'But you do care!' does not suffice as an answer. We will return to what he has to say here in Section 5.

4. Which constitutivism?

Before doing that, though, let me briefly comment on the scope of constitutivist views to which the but-you-do-care line of thought applies. And let me start here with the following point: the but-you-do-care reply does not show that the relevant skeptic is *wrong*. Rather, it shows that he is *impossible*, that none of us is, or indeed can be, such a skeptic, someone who just doesn't care about whatever it is that is constitutive of action.

Of course, this is a possible line to take (and one that I anticipate in a footnote in 'Agency, Shmagency' (p. 199, footnote 44)). But it is a rather surprising one. And it is especially disappointing if your motivation for going constitutivist in the first place was the hope of answering the skeptic.[25] This is clearest in Korsgaard – she hopes not to show that no one is a skeptic, but rather to show that the skeptic is wrong, or confused, or some such. And this means that she cannot utilize the but-you-do-care reply, at least not without some further story.

True, if you claim not to care (*de re*) about whatever it is that is constitutive of action or agency, and we can then show that – being an agent – you do care about it, we've shown that you are in some less-than-fully-precise sense inconsistent, and so (presumably) in a sense also irrational. This would amount to showing that you are wrong in some of your commitments. But it would not show that it is your commitment *to skepticism* that is wrong. Perhaps, after all, it is your caring about the constitutive aim of action that is wrong, and perhaps this is the commitment that should be discarded in order to regain consistency.[26]

Or think again about the two ways I distinguished above of understanding the game analogy. Korsgaard's way of talking strongly suggests that she utilizes such analogies (as in the house-building case) in the first of the two ways, as examples of activities with constitutive objective standards of success (rather than as ones where what is constitutive of the activity is the *caring* about the relevant success conditions).[27] If this is a fair characterization of her views – and, because of the unclarity with which Korsgaard's views are presented, I cannot be confident that this is so – then Korsgaard cannot rely on the but-you-do-care response, even if Velleman and others can.

I don't know of any attempt to defend a Korsgaard-style constitutivism from the shmagency challenge – Korsgaard and her followers, it often seems, are just not that much into responding to objections. And so it's important to note here that, even if Velleman's way of dealing with this challenge – or related ways – succeeds, it may only vindicate a Velleman-style constitutivism. In 'Agency, Shmagency' I was putting forward the challenge as one that refutes all constitutivist theories with just one blow. If Velleman's reply succeeds, this is not so. But the challenge still stands – even if everything else I say in this paper fails – against Korsgaard's theory.[28]

5. The mistake of the adversarial stance

As you recall, Velleman argues that agency, for us, is inescapable in two ways. The first way – the one I called natural inescapability – comes down to our inability to opt out of the game of agency (with few and irrelevant exceptions). The second – the one I'll call *dialectical* inescapability – is nicely illustrated by the following quote:

> To ask 'why should I have the aim of making sense?' is to reveal that you already have it. If you don't seek to do what makes sense, then you are not in the business of practical reasoning, and so you cannot demand reasons for acting or aiming. (Velleman, 2009, p. 137)

The point seems to be that no one can consistently occupy the position of the relevant skeptic: by the very raising of the challenge to the agency-religion, you show yourself to be a devoted follower. And – so the thought seems to go – this goes some way towards vindicating agency, and with it presumably constitutivism. A similar line of thought is especially clear in Ferrero's reply to the shmagency challenge. Thus, he writes:

> The inescapability of agency, however, shows that there is no standpoint external to agency that the shmagent could occupy and from which he could launch his challenge. (Ferrero, 2009, p. 311)

This way of putting things seems to dramatize the challenge, in something like the following way: there is this character, a real flesh-and-blood person and agent (or perhaps shmagent); call her 'the skeptic.' And this character challenges us – non-skeptics that we are – to a kind of adversarial duel. She has her position to defend, and we have ours. If this is the dramatized scene, then it is only natural to think that, if the skeptic's position (or argumentation) is somehow unstable, then we win. After all, in an adversarial setting, showing your adversary to be wrong amounts to vindicating your own position.

Thus, the situation here is similar to one often occurring in discussions of epistemological skepticism, where it is sometimes argued that skeptics defeat themselves. The interesting skeptic puts forward an argument, say, relying on premises, using rules of inference; but, if his skeptical conclusion is right, no one is epistemically justified in believing any premises, using any rules of inference, and so on. So his skeptical challenge fails even by his own lights. And this, we are sometimes told, shows that at least some kinds of skeptical challenges are not to be taken seriously, because they defeat themselves; there is, therefore, no ground a skeptic of this kind can safely occupy, from which he can launch his skeptical attack. The skeptic, we are told, is guaranteed to lose, and so we have won.

But this line of thought (which I anticipate in 'Agency, Shmagency', pp. 183–4) cannot succeed, either in our context or in the epistemological one. The error here is already present in the very first step, the specific dramatization of the dialogue. The skeptic is not – certainly she need not be – an actual character, with a position to defend. The skeptic, rather, is the embodiment of a problem *we* face, because of *our* commitments. I put the point in 'Agency, Shmagency' by noting (p. 184) that skeptical challenges are best seen as *ad hominem* arguments, with all of us non-skeptics as the relevant *homini*.[29]

Perhaps an example can help here. Assume a philosopher – call her the paper-skeptic – who believes that there's something intellectually corrupting about the papers analytic philosophers are so fond of reading and writing. Philosophical progress, she thinks, can only be achieved by writing books. The paper-frenzy is just a race to philosophical superficiality, and an incentive to substitute technical skills for deep philosophical insights. Being a conscientious professional, she writes this all down, presenting her analysis and arguments, culminating in the conclusion that philosophers should not write papers. But – in order for the example to be interesting – she writes all this down in the format of a paper, and proceeds to submit it to her friendly neighborhood philosophy journal (by which it is rejected, without comments, eleven months later).

Now, we paper-writing philosophers are eager to defeat the paper-skeptic's challenge. To do that, is it sufficient to show that she has no stable ground to stand on while she's launching her attack, that in a sense she defeats herself because she expressed her paper-skepticism in the form of a paper? Perhaps – though I doubt it – this shows that our paper-skeptic is in some sense in trouble. But it certainly does not show that *we* are *out of* trouble. If her arguments still work, then we – committed as we are to writing papers – are in trouble. We need a substantive answer to the challenge she puts in a sort-of self-defeating way. The challenge is real enough. It is real enough even if expressing her paper-skepticism in the format of a paper is for some reason inescapable for her. Indeed, the challenge is real enough even if a paper-skeptic does not, or even cannot, exist. And so it is better to tell the story without anthropomorphizing the arguments at all. There are arguments attempting to show that we shouldn't be so seriously into writing papers. We need to deal with these arguments. It just doesn't matter whether there is a character – the paper-skeptic – who can help us make this debate more dramatic. And, even if there is such a character, we should not mistake finding fault with her for vindicating our paper-writing practices. We should not, in a term I borrow from Crispin Wright (1991, p. 89), commit the mistake of the adversarial stance.

The analogy, I hope, is clear. Showing that the practical-reason-skeptic (the one asking 'Why should I care about (e.g.) self-understanding?') has no safe grounds from which to launch his attack is neither here nor there. It does not even begin to vindicate practical reason. Thinking otherwise is like settling – in the discussion with the paper-skeptic – for noting that she's written a paper, without tackling her arguments against paper-writing head on. And so here too – as in the paper-skepticism case – we are better off avoiding the dramatic effects and anthropomorphizing the challenge. The challenge is a challenge for *us*, non-skeptic as we are.[30] It is *we* who have to come up with a theory of normativity that will be adequate (at least) by our own lights. It is we who must be convinced that agency is not normatively arbitrary (for us), that we do have, even upon reflection, reason to care about whatever it is that's constitutive of action and agency,[31] even if, regardless of having or failing to have such a story, we inescapably do care about it. And, so, it is we who are vulnerable to the shmagency challenge. Whether or not there is an agent (or a shmagent) who can stably embody this challenge is just beside the point.

6. The distinction between internal and external questions

As I have already mentioned several times, Velleman (p. 137) concedes that merely noting the inescapability of agency (even of both the natural and the dialectical kinds) does not suffice here, because we can still ask for a jus-tification, for some reason to pursue the aim that is constitutive of action. Here he seems to concede (though not explicitly) a major part of my origi-nal shmagency challenge: merely noting that this aim (whatever exactly it is) is constitutive of action in no way settles the normative question of why (and even whether) we have any reason to pursue it. But, with regard to the request for such justification, Velleman (p. 138 and on) seems to be presenting the following dilemma (which I present here in my own words): either this request or question is understood *internally*, as asked from the point of view of an agent already committed to self-understanding, or it is understood *externally*,[32] as asked by someone with no such commitment;[33] if the former, then we are entitled – in answering it – to rely on the already-present commitment to the aim of self-understanding; and then all that is needed in order to show that we have a reason to pursue self-understanding is to show that pursuing self-understanding is something that promotes (in the appropriate way) our self-understanding; and it does – after all, it makes sense to make sense, or to try to.[34] Understood internally, then, the chal-lenge is a legitimate one, and it can be coped with as a normative challenge, utilizing all the normative apparatus available to us – including, of course, that of the constitutive aim of agency. If – and this is the other horn of the dilemma – the challenge is supposed to be external, to be raised from out-side any committed point of view (like that of the agent), then it is nonsen-sical; it is not even a legitimate challenge to begin with. Either way, then, constitutivism wins – the challenge can be understood internally, and met on its own terms; or it can be thought of externally, and then be shown to be incoherent.

The claim that the challenge – thought of as an external one – is nonsensi-cal is an important one, and I discuss it in the next section. As to the claim that, understood internally, the challenge can be met: for the most part, I want to grant this claim for the sake of argument. Let me just quickly note here that Velleman's relevant discussion is *very* quick (p. 138), and pretty much comes down to *asserting* that it makes sense to make sense. Given the centrality of this claim to Velleman's defense of constitutivism, more could have been hoped for.[35] Velleman does emphasize (pp. 141–2)[36] – and I agree with him on this – that there need be no flaw in the kind of circularity that is involved when some most basic criterion or norm is justified in terms of its living up to its own standards. Indeed, though Velleman (p. 141) thinks that there is a disanalogy here with the case of theoretical reason, I have argued elsewhere (Enoch and Schechter, 2008) for a very similar point in the most general epistemological context.[37] Of course, some further condi-tions need to hold. As Velleman rightly notes (p. 142), at the very least we need a further story that distinguishes between benign and vicious circular justifications. And in Enoch and Schechter (2008) we go to great lengths trying to give such a story. All that Velleman does here (p. 142) is to point again to the fact that the aim (for pursuing which he's giving a circular justification) is constitutive of action. But, in conceding earlier that this does not settle any justificatory question, Velleman seems to have undermined this move too.

But, again, this is not the main point I want to take issue with here. What I want to do in the rest of this section, rather, is to raise some questions about the very distinction between the internal and external understandings of the why-should-I-care-about-(e.g.)-self-understanding question. For it is anything but clear how this distinction is to be understood,[38] and Velleman does nothing to explain or even explicitly state his understanding of it. I doubt that such a distinction can be taken as primitive.

Before quickly going through some possible ways of understanding the distinction, let me just note the adequacy constraints on such understandings. If it is to help in the defense of constitutivism (against the shmagency challenge, or more generally), the internal–external distinction must be understood in a way that supports its role in Velleman's argumentation; that is, it must be understood in a way that renders both horns of Velleman's dilemma plausible; that is, the distinction must be understood in a way that makes it plausible to say that the internal question can be adequately (though somewhat circularly) addressed, and that the external question is incoherent or nonsensical. With this in mind, then, how are we to understand the internal–external distinction?

One possibility is to understand the distinction between internal and external questions in terms of the commitments of the person asking them.[39] Thus, if the person accepts (in some sense) the aim of self-understanding, her question is internal, and if she does not the question is external. But this suggestion is hugely problematic. First, we are still owed a story of this acceptance or commitment – is it a belief? A motivational disposition? Some other thing? At the very least, then, more details are needed. And there are challenges facing the attempt to complete these details. For instance, if this acceptance is a belief – certainly an explicit belief – then the suggestion that the external question is incoherent becomes quite unbelievable. Doesn't the question – asked by a person who is motivationally committed to the self-understanding aim, but who lacks the belief that this aim is worth pursuing – make perfectly good sense? If the relevant acceptance has to do with some motivational disposition, then it becomes utterly unclear how, understood internally, the question is guaranteed to be answerable. For the relevant motivation may be misdirected in any of a number of ways. And it's not clear what other options are available here. Second, this way of understanding the internal–external distinction – in terms of the mental states of that infamous character, the skeptic – commits, of course, the mistake of the adversarial stance. There is no such character, and we don't need to know anything about him (whom?) in order to understand the challenge.

How else can the internal–external distinction be understood? It may be thought that the distinction should be understood in more dialectical terms. The question is understood internally in a dialectical setting in which it's legitimate to rely on the premise that the aim of self-understanding is worth pursuing; it is external otherwise. But, thus understood, the suggestion that the internal question can be satisfactorily answered fails. For now the circularity becomes paradigmatically vicious: *of course* in a dialectical setting in which we can rely on the premise that the self-understanding aim is worth pursuing we can prove that, well, the self-understanding aim is worth pursuing (and note that this is so regardless of whether it makes sense to make sense, as Velleman argues). It is hard to take this as a justificatory victory.

Perhaps, though, the distinction should be understood differently. Let us again utilize the game-analogy. Suppose I ask whether I have a reason to (try to) checkmate my opponent. Here it does make sense, I guess, to say that from within the framework of a game of chess, or from a point of view of a chess-player, the answer is 'yes.' And perhaps it is also true to say that it is not at all clear how this question can be understood externally, not from within the chess-game framework. Should the distinction between an internal and an external reading of the why-care-about-self-understanding question be understood analogously?

The problem, though, is that it is not at all clear how to understand talk of points of view (or the like) in the chess case either.[40] So, while the game analogy is not without value – it shows that, at least sometimes, something naturally put in terms of the internal–external metaphor does seem to make sense – still it cannot solve Velleman's problem here. Furthermore, perhaps the right account of the distinction in the chess case cannot be applied in the agency case. At the very least, then, more needs to be said here.

Let me not overstate my case here. I do not claim that the internal–external distinction does not make sense. What I do claim, however, is that Velleman has said far too little about it to be able to rely on it in defending his constitutivism; that some natural ways of understanding this distinction fail; that it's not clear how exactly to understand it; and that it's therefore unclear whether an appropriate understanding of it can support Velleman's dilemma. (In the next section I will offer yet another possible understanding of the internal–external distinction.)

7. Which questions make sense?

When the why-care-about-self-understanding question is understood externally, Velleman – rather than answering it – suggests that there's something wrong with the question. The suggestion is that such practical why-questions – requests for practical reasons – only make sense within some constitutive framework or another. Asked with the ambition of being understood outside any such framework (agency, or even shmagency, or some other one), the question is supposed to be semantically defective. At times, Velleman writes as if the question, understood externally, committed some category mistake, 'like asking whether a telephone is correct rather than a tree' (p. 145).[41] But this does not seem to be the right thing to say here. I think that what Velleman has in mind is that a request for practical reasons that is not made from within a framework in which there is some constitutive aim or other is just *not well-formed*, because crucially *incomplete*; it uses an n-place predicate with only n–1 arguments. Until you say whether you want an answer given the aim constitutive of agency, or of shmagency, or whatever, 'You aren't owed an answer, because you haven't yet asked a question' (p. 144); 'Until you specify what you want guidance for, you haven't posed a determinate question' (p. 143).

Perhaps the following example – which Velleman does not use in this precise context – will help to make this clear. The question 'How can I play well?' is, as it stands, semantically defective. Until you specify which game you're talking about, you are not owed an answer, because you haven't asked a determinate question. Indeed, you haven't asked *any* question, because your attempt at a question is not well formed. You are missing one argument for your central predicate. I take it that Velleman thinks the question 'Why care about self-understanding' – like any other request for practical reasons – suffers from a similar flaw, unless it is clear what 'game' is being played. Of course, here as in the game case, it is not required for the value of the further argument to be given explicitly, as in 'How can I play chess well?' It can also be completed implicitly, by the context. If, for instance, we're now playing chess, or have been discussing chess for a while, or some such, then the question 'How can I play well?' may be understood to be about playing *chess* well, and thus be unproblematic. But that the question can be completed implicitly should not blind us to the fact that it does most certainly need completing. Similarly for 'Why care about self-understanding?': in many contexts (perhaps in all of them, except those that involve a skeptical challenge in a philosophical discussion of normativity; or perhaps even more widely, in all contexts except that of coping with the shmagency challenge), it is clear that the question is asked within the framework of the agency-game. But that the question can often be completed implicitly need not blind us to the fact that it does most certainly need completing. And this is the nature of the mistake of the person attempting to ask the why-care-about-self-understanding question externally: he (well, I) fails to see that, thus understood, the question is not well formed, and is thus not a question at all.

This way of understanding Velleman on the defectiveness of the external question[42] also has the following two virtues: first, it helps in understanding Velleman's surprising claim that the question of whether to care about self-understanding can be asked not just from the point of view of an agent, but also that of a shmagent, and presumably also that of many other kinds of creature – although, from the mouth of a shmagent, it will not be a request for reasons for action, but rather for some other thing (say, shmeasons for shmactions).[43] The ill-formed how-to-play-well question can be made whole, after all, by mentioning chess, or checkers, or football, or any number of games. What would make the why-care-about-self-understanding question semantically defective in the way described is not asking it outside the agency framework, but asking (or attempting to ask) it outside *any* such framework.[44]

The second advantage of this way of understanding the flaw Velleman finds in the external question is that it helps with the difficulties discussed in the previous section. As you recall, the problem there was that it was very hard even to make sense of the internal–external distinction. But we are now in a position to suggest another way of understanding it. The question is internal if it specifies – explicitly or implicitly – the nature of the 'game' regarding which we are asking how to play it well. It is external otherwise. And there is nothing mysterious about the distinction thus understood – it just comes down to a distinction between different numbers of arguments. Furthermore, it renders plausible Velleman's claim that the question understood internally is not too problematic. It all comes down, then, to the claim that an external question – roughly thus understood – is semantically defective in the way described.

But *is* it semantically defective in this way? We must not be blinded by powerful analogies. The how-to-play-well question is (unless implicitly referring to a determinate game) defective in this way. But what reason have we been given to believe that the why-care-about-self-understanding question, or indeed the what-do-I-have-reason-to-do question, is (unless implicitly referring to some constitutive framework) equally defective? Think about it this way: when we are presented with linguistic creatures like 'How can I play well?' or 'The Empire State Building is Taller,' we immediately sense the incompleteness, and indeed that's why we feel the pressure to assume an implicit reference to the value of the missing argument. But when I ask 'What do I have reason to do?' or 'Why should I care about self-understanding?', these questions certainly do not *feel* semantically defective in anything like the same way. I do not want to overstate the point – sometimes, I'm sure, semantic defectiveness doesn't have a 'feel,' and we may be mistaken about such things, just as we may be mistaken about anything else. But still, that a question seems to make sense is at least some evidence – rather strong evidence, I would say – that it does.[45] By insisting on not understanding an (external) question that certainly seems to make sense, Velleman is thus in danger of satisfying David Lewis's (1986, p. 203, footnote 5) characterization of a competent philosopher:

[A]ny competent philosopher who does not understand something will take care not to understand anything else whereby it might be explained.

Of course, just noting the dangers of pronouncing a seemingly legitimate question defective does not amount to an argument establishing that the question *is* indeed legitimate. How, then, are we to make progress? If, as I suggested, apparently making sense is strong *pro tanto* evidence of making sense, the dialectical situation is not symmetrical. The burden is on Velleman to show some countervailing reason, some reason to believe that appearances here are misleading, and that the external question that appears to make sense in fact does not.

And here it is I who need to make a partial concession. In 'Agency, Shmagency,' I was hoping to put forward a challenge to constitutivist theories that was largely independent of the details – and explanatory successes and failures – of specific constitutivist theories. But, even if this was possible for the presentation of the initial challenge, it is no longer possible in thinking about Velleman's response to the challenge. For one way of making progress in shouldering the burden above – giving us reasons to believe that the external question that seems to makes sense in fact doesn't – is to present a theory with considerable explanatory advantages, which entails that the external question is semantically defective. If this can be done, then the explanatory advantages of the theory count as reasons for believing that the question is indeed defective. I take it this is a part of Velleman's *point* (e.g. p. 144): in numerous works over many years now, he has developed his constitutivist theory, attempting to show its explanatory payoffs in numerous contexts. And it follows from his theory that the what-do-I-have-reason-to-do question is in the relevant respects like the how-can-I-play-well question. His theory, then, should be evaluated holistically, and if it is still the best theory overall then we should take the discrepancy between it and the appearances (regarding the legitimacy of the external questions) as reason to reject these appearances, not Velleman's theory.

Let me concede the methodological point. And let me also concede – this time, only for the sake of argument – that Velleman's theory is indeed in other respects explanatorily very powerful. Still, this does not suffice to save Velleman's constitutivism (by dooming the external question to semantic defectiveness), for the following two reasons: first, for the other explanatory advantages of the theory to justify accepting that a seemingly legitimate question is semantically defective, it is not sufficient that *there are* such advantages. Rather, it is also necessary that these advantages are *sufficiently significant*, weighty enough to justify rejecting the appearance of coherence of the external questions. Of course, it is always hard to quantify the significance of different explanatory (and other) advantages of a theory, and any conclusion here is bound to be controversial. So let me settle for pointing out that there is here some unfinished business for Velleman: he has to show that the explanatory advantages of his theory are weightier than the reason we have to believe that the external questions make sense (namely, that they seem to make sense).

Second, and more importantly, explanatory advantages are always *comparative*. And, even if Velleman's theory scores significant explanatory points against *some* other theories, it does not do as well against *all*. Consider a theory that affirms a reason to care about the aim constitutive of agency, where this reason is robustly realistically understood,[46] that is, it is not understood along constitutivist lines. Such a theory is inconsistent with constitutivism, of course, as it incorporates at least one reason that is not constitutivistically friendly.[47] But it can explain whatever Velleman's constitutivism can explain, and just as well: it just starts with this robust reason, and then plugs in Velleman's own explanations. And notice that, on this theory, the external why-should-I-care-about-self-understanding question makes perfect sense, even if – depending on the other details of the theory – its answer may not be extremely informative. The only possible remaining explanatory advantage of Velleman's theory over *this* alternative is that this alternative is committed to a robust not-constitutivistically-accounted-for reason to care about self-understanding (or some such), whereas Velleman's constitutivism is not so committed. But first, to my ears this does not sound like a significant explanatory advantage, and second, and more importantly, invoking this explanatory advantage as a reason to doom the external questions to semantic defectiveness is especially suspicious: after all, we can always avoid the need to assume an answer to a question by declaring it semantically defective. Now, perhaps there are normative reasons to doubt – even assuming a robust realism of sorts – that there is a reason to care about whatever it is that is constitutive of action and agency. If so, the sketched alternative theory fails. But if so, so does Velleman's theory, for whatever reasons doom this alternative theory.

Though I agree, then, that other explanatory advantages of a theory may justify ruling a seemingly legitimate question semantically defective, for the above reasons I do not think that the explanatory advantages (assumed here for the sake of argument) of Velleman's theory suffice to do that. If so, Velleman has not given us sufficient reason to believe that the external questions are semantically defective. And because they certainly *seem* semantically legitimate – because they do not sound like how-to-play-well questions, for instance – I conclude, then, that they are.[48]

8. Score-keeping

So where does all of this leave us? It seems to me that what is *really* at stake between Velleman and myself are the questions discussed in the previous section. Given Velleman's concession that the justificatory question remains open even given the but-you-do-care reply, even when this reply is strengthened by some inescapability point, his major line of response to the shmagency challenge consists simply of denying that the challenge – understood externally, as I meant to present it – even makes sense. The other points in (the relevant parts of) his text, and indeed in this paper, are relevant only derivatively. Thus, the precise account of the internal–external distinction is relevant for a better understanding of the claim that external questions are semantically defective; and the whole discussion of inescapability – natural and dialectical alike – is only relevant, as far as I can see, either as a part of the straightforward, supposedly benignly circular answer to the internal question, or as helping to make the semantic-defectiveness claim (with regard to the external questions) plausible.

But, if the arguments above are sound, none of this can succeed. Starting from the conclusion: the external challenge seems to make sense, and – because no convincing reasons have been given for why we should reject this appearance – we are justified in taking it at face value, as semantically legitimate. My argument for this conclusion was independent of the other flaws I found in Velleman's reasoning. Furthermore, it is very hard to see how the natural inescapability of agency can be seen as anything but normatively arbitrary, and so it is equally hard to see how it could help here. The discussion of dialectical inescapability misunderstands the nature of skeptical challenges (by committing the mistake of the adversarial stance). And that we already do care about whatever it is that is constitutive of action – if indeed we do – is just neither here nor there.

How much of this discussion was ad-Velleman? Can it be generalized to apply to constitutivists more generally? As I argued above (in Section 4), Korsgaard's constitutivism seems to be in even more serious trouble than Velleman's in responding to the shmagency challenge. And, while I conducted much of the discussion in Vellemanesque terms, nothing of significance, I think, hinged on my doing so. Nothing in my discussion, for instance, depended on the constitutive aim of action being that of self-understanding. Velleman's argumentative moves are, I think, in a sense precisely the moves any constitutivist should employ in response to the shmagency challenge. True, the claim that everything here boils down to the controversy over the semantic status of external questions may be somewhat ad-Velleman – other constitutivists need not share his concession regarding the openness of the justificatory issue even after the but-you-do-(inescapably)-care card has been played. Nevertheless, something feels right about the debate boiling down to the question of whether the external challenge and questions make sense. Indeed, the fact that this is what the debate boils down to may partly explain the they-just-don't-get-it feeling, common on both sides of this and related debates.

Let me note another possible line of a constitutivist reply, one that – to the best of my knowledge – has not been developed by any constitutivist, but that it may be interesting to hint at here. The shmagency challenge is closely related to more common open-question-argument-like challenges, challenges that demand some explanation for the normative status of the relevant target – here, agency, or the aim constitutive of it, or some such. And I have hinted above – as well as in 'Agency, Shmagency' – that the most natural way of defending the normative non-arbitrariness of such things is by invoking a general, constitutivism-independent reason to be an agent. It's just that this line is not available to constitutivism. But there is reason to believe that not all explanations of normative status take this form. Rather, as Schroeder (2005) convincingly argues, some normative explanations must take a more constitutive form. Applied to the case of constitutivism, such an explanation would state that (say) we have a reason to pursue self-understanding because *that's just what it is to have a reason*; it's to be related in the relevant way to the pursuit of self-understanding. Such a claim would be analogous to a claim made by the divine command theorist that we have a moral duty to obey God's commands, not because there is some God-independent moral duty to do as He says, but rather because that's just what it is to have a moral duty to do something; it's to be commanded by God to do it.

This is not the reply Velleman gives, and perhaps it is not a reply Velleman wants to give: after all, on such an account, the external questions make sense, but get answered (positively) rather quickly. Furthermore, on this reply, it is not clear how it could be possible to raise the question from within alternative, competing frameworks (think about the divine command theorist again). And, regardless of what Velleman says or wants to say, it is not clear how plausibly it may be argued that this is indeed just what it is to have a reason. But nor is it clear to me that this line of thought can-*not* succeed, and, because I haven't anticipated it in 'Agency, Shmagency,' I quickly note it here.

But until this line of thought is adequately developed and defended, or until some other reply can be made to work, I conclude that the shmagency challenge stands. Korsgaard has not responded to the skeptic. Velleman has not shown how something like objectivity can be accommodated consistently with his existence-internalism about reasons. And there remains a strong reason to suspect that constitutivism cannot be the foundational story of normativity it aspires to be.[49]

Notes

1. See discussion and references in my 'Agency, Shmagency' (2006), pp. 171–2.
2. See discussion and references in my 'Agency, Shmagency' (2006), pp. 172–4. For the clearest, most recent statements of such hope, including one referring to it as 'the purpose' of Velleman's Kantian strategy, see Velleman (2009, pp. 120, 139).
3. In my 'Agency, Shmagency' (2006) I call the second position in the text above 'quasi-externalism.' I also mention another advantage – that of assisting the naturalist in dealing with the best version of the Open Question Argument. And there may also be other advantages to constitutivism, perhaps when it is considered as a corollary of constructivism. For some discussion here, see my 'Can There Be a Global, Interesting, Coherent Constructivism about Practical Reason?' (2009).
4. That paper was original, I hope, in much of its argumentative details. But the general thrust of this objection to constitutivism has been, I think, 'in the air'

for a while. See, for instance, Railton (1997); FitzPatrick (2005). In that paper, I use three examples of constitutivism – Korsgaard, Velleman, and (to an extent) Connie Rosati. In conversation, though, Rosati has explained to me that I have misunderstood some of her central claims in Rosati (2003), so – although I still think that the reading of that paper in my 'Agency, Shmagency' is a plausible one – I no longer use Rosati as a constitutivist example here.

5. Ferrero (2009); Velleman (2009, pp. 135–146, though the explicit discussion of 'Agency, Shmagency' starts on p. 142); references to Ferrero and Velleman below are to these texts. I have also seen relevant drafts by Matty Silverstein and by Scott Forschler.

6. Korsgaard seems rather confident that this can be done. Velleman is *much* more pessimistic. For his partly concessive 'Kinda Kantian' strategy of defending morality, see Velleman (2009, p. 149 and on).

7. Velleman does not, I think, take this line. But I have heard it elsewhere (for instance, from Matty Silverstein), and, because this is not something I discussed in detail in 'Agency, Shmagency,' I think it is important to briefly address it here. Also, this discussion will naturally lead us to the more central one in the next section.

8. As Michael Brady rightly pointed out, you may want to understand 'engaging in some activity' in a thicker way, so that in my example you don't count as engaging in the game of chess* even though you do satisfy the descriptive criteria of engaging in that activity. But, if this is something the constitutivist wants to rely on in this context, then it seems to me he is shifting to the but-you-do-care response to the shmagency challenge, the one I proceed to discuss in the next section.

9. I am here sliding over possibly important differences between wanting and caring on one side, and being committed on the other. I try to show that employing some richer notion of commitment won't save the constitutivist below, in Section 6.

10. In 'Agency, Shmagency' I was explicit about not distinguishing between claims about what is constitutive of action and what is constitutive of agency (p. 170, footnote 1). But can it perhaps be argued that it is time to draw – and rely on – this distinction? For it may be argued that, while *caring* about (for example) self-understanding is constitutive of being an agent, being directed at self-understanding in some more objective sense is constitutive of actions. I don't think this interesting suggestion can work here, though, for two reasons. First, textually (and so somewhat boringly), I do not know of any suggestion along these lines made by any constitutivist. Second, and much more importantly: if one thing is constitutive of agency, and another of action, it can no longer be taken for granted that all and only agents can perform actions.

11. Setiya (2003) argues that there is not enough content to whatever norms may be plausibly considered constitutive of action.

12. Perhaps we need a distinction between *caring* about winning and *being motivated* to win, in the thinner sense in which I make (what I believe to be) the right moves, and so on. And it is, I concede, more plausible to say that being motivated to checkmate is constitutive of playing chess than to say that caring about checkmating your opponent is. But this won't save the constitutivist: what is needed for the 'But you *do* care' reply is actually caring, not just this thinner kind of being motivated. To settle for this being-motivated rather than caring is to render the irrelevance problem (which I am about to move on to in the text) even more serious than it already is.

13. I hint at such considerations in 'Agency, Shmagency' (p. 189, footnote 44), and I return to this point later in the text.
14. See, in this context, Ferrero's (pp. 312–13) characterization of such a character – in two adjacent sentences – once as playing chess half-heartedly, and once as only pretending to play chess. His official position, though, is that such a person is not really playing chess (p. 313).
15. The whole 'shmagency' way of talking (of which Velleman (p. 143) is no big fan) was partly meant, of course, to convey the feeling that something silly is going on.
16. There is perhaps something a touch unfair in this way of putting things. What is at stake, someone like Velleman can argue, are all of the explanatory payoffs of the relevant theory of action and agency. I return to this line of thought – in a more concessive mood – later in the text.
17. Actually, this is not the precise wording I used there. I concede that I should have.
18. See Ferrero (pp. 311–12). I've heard this claim made also by Matty Silverstein. And there's a hint of it also in Velleman (p. 144).
19. As even the title of his paper makes clear, this is a major theme in Ferrero (2009).
20. Ferrero (p. 308) also distinguishes two senses of inescapability (which together constitute agency's inescapability in the sense that is supposed to help with the shmagency challenge). One of them, which he characterizes using the term 'closure,' is not completely clear to me, at times sounding like Velleman's natural inescapability, at times like his dialectical inescapability, at times like an intermediate position of sorts. The other – characterized in terms of 'an enterprise with largest jurisdiction' – is unclear to me. If the point is supposed to be about the *aspiration* of agency, as it were, then shmagency is also with largest jurisdiction. If, on the other hand, the point is about agency's *success* in establishing largest jurisdiction (success which is not shared by the enterprise of shmagency), then assuming this from the start amounts in our context to begging the question against the shmagency challenge. Later on, Ferrero (p. 322) introduces another sense in which agency is arguably inescapable – the *concept* of agency is one we cannot do without. I have no idea whether this is true, and how – if it is – this helps the constitutivist in dealing with the shmagency objection. And there are also hints of dialectical inescapability in Ferrero, as when he says (p. 326): 'This status is…presupposed in raising the practical question.'
21. See 'Agency, Shmagency' (pp. 188–9, footnote 42), and the references there.
22. I've heard similar suggestions – sometimes put in terms of 'practical irrelevance' – from Matty Silverstein and from Scott Forschler. And, later on, Velleman (p. 138) seems to concede that something from the why-should-I-care question remains unanswered even after the but-you-do-care reply. I return to what Velleman has to say on that in Sections 6–7 below.
23. Again, the discussion that follows the mootness declaration seems to show that Velleman himself acknowledges this point.
24. Ferrero (pp. 312–15) discusses (following comments I make in 'Agency, Shmagency' (p. 188)) what he calls 'alienated participation' in the enterprise of agency. In reply to such examples he argues that such alienated participation is – in the case of agency – impossible. I find this suggestion both implausible and irrelevant, for reasons similar to those given in the text about inescapability in general. Note that the example of the grudging patriot shows not only that such

cases are possible (in the case of agency as well, I would say), but also how much more complicated the relevant motivational structure can be.

25. Ferrero (p. 316, and in conversation) concedes this point, at least with regard to the most ambitious way of defeating the skeptic.

26. Also, this attempt at a response commits the mistake of the adversarial stance. See the next section.

27. This is also sometimes true of Ferrero's formulations (see, for instance, p. 305), but in conversation he assures me that his is a version of the but-you-do-care response.

28. It is not clear to me whether Velleman's other argumentative moves – those discussed in sections 6–7 below – can be utilized by Korsgaard too, without the support of the but-you-do-care reply.

29. Ferrero (p. 317, footnote 27) says he agrees with me on this point. But still, throughout his paper he commits (as the quote above shows) the mistake of the adversarial stance. Note that the suggestion in the text is not (as Ferrero (p. 317) mistakenly understands it to be) that *constitutivism* is found to be inconsistent; rather, it's that constitutivism is found to be inconsistent *with some other of our pretheoretical commitments*, including (as I proceed to explain in the text) about which questions make sense.

30. When describing my main argument in 'Agency, Shmagency', Ferrero (p. 305) says that I ask the reader to imagine the shmagent, putting forward his objection. But this is not how I present the challenge. The challenge is not put forward by a shmagent – and starting with imagining a shmagent is a clear instance of the mistake of the adversarial stance. The important point is not *who* is putting forward the challenge, but its content – namely, what reason do we have to be agents (rather than, for instance, shmagents). So Ferrero's comparison of a 'conversation' with a shmagent and a 'conversation' with a parrot is beside the point – the content of a philosophical objection can be quite devastating even coming from the mouth of a parrot.

31. Precisely for this reason, there is a grain of truth in Velleman's insistence on understanding the question (why care about self-understanding?) internally, from the point of view of someone who already does care. I return to this point in the next section.

32. Ferrero (p. 306) also uses the terms 'internal' and 'external' in a similar context.

33. Actually, Velleman (p. 143) discusses a third option – the question may be asked from within a framework, but not of agency – perhaps, for instance, of shmagency. I return to this complication below.

34. See also Ferrero (p. 326).

35. Ferrero (Section 7, starting on p. 322) rightly emphasizes that there is nothing obvious about agency being self-vindicating in this way.

36. For a similar point, see Ferrero (p. 323).

37. Like Velleman (and explicitly drawing on him), Ferrero (p. 324) both tries to vindicate some kind of circularity here and suggests that nothing of the sort can be done in the theoretical context.

38. Though Velleman does not put things in terms of the internal–external distinction, he does come very close, for instance, when he writes (p. 143): '[The Kantian strategy] merely insists that questions must be asked and answered *within* the framework of some constitution' (emphasis added). Putting things in terms of the distinction between internal and external questions may remind the reader of Carnap's (1956) similar distinction. I think Carnap's distinction raises the exact same problems as Velleman's.

39. At least at one point, this is how Ferrero (p. 323) seems to understand it.
40. In the jurisprudential context, Hart (1961) has famously distinguished between the internal and external points of view, and Raz (1979) has famously classified a class of judgments as judgments-from-a-point-of-view. I'm afraid that these (perhaps related) sources do not help (me) in clarifying the internal–external distinction Velleman uses, both because I'm not at all confident I understand *them*, and because it's not guaranteed that Velleman's understanding of this distinction is identical to either of these two.
41. See also the reference there to Street's example – asking whether the Empire State Building is taller, without specifying taller than what; though this seems to be an example of another flaw, the one I proceed to discuss next in the text.
42. Ferrero (p. 329) also suggests that some question in the vicinity here is defective, though not semantically. It is not clear to me what exactly the nature of the defect is supposed to be.
43. He reconciles this observation with the attempt to accommodate (some kind of) objectivity by relying again – if I understand him correctly – on the inescapability of agency (pp. 144–5).
44. In this way, then, Velleman here partly takes back the dialectical inescapability point, for he concedes that the question can be asked by someone who is not committed to the aim constitutive of action – by a shmagent, for instance. This is only a partial concession, though, because the very same words uttered by a shmagent presumably express a somewhat different question than when expressed by an agent.
45. "[T]he fact that a notion appears to make sense is strong *prima facie* evidence that it does make sense" (Fine, 2001, p. 13). And for a similar point see Zangwill (1992, p. 160).
46. Like the Robust Realism I sketch in my (2007), and in more detail in my *Taking Morality Seriously* (forthcoming). Note that I do not there commit myself specifically to a reason to be an agent, or to care about whatever aim (if any) is constitutive of agency.
47. In 'Agency, Shmagency' I mention (p. 187) the possibility of postulating a robust reason to be an agent (or some such), noting that doing so is inconsistent with constitutivism and with its underlying philosophical motivations.
48. There's a rather delicate dialectical issue here, regarding who begs which question against whom. Velleman seems to suggest (p. 141) that the very raising of the why-care-about-self-understanding question, when it is understood externally, begs the question against him (by assuming that this question makes sense). I, on the other hand, believe that Velleman comes very close to begging the question against me when he says (p. 139) things like 'But in relation to what criterion of correctness do you suspect intelligibility-seeking agency of error?', because he suggests that such a criterion must be specified if the question is to make sense at all. But the situation is not symmetrical here, because of the *pro tanto* evidential force of the external questions seeming to be semantically legitimate.

 I'm not sure what exactly is going on in the footnote in which Velleman hastily proclaims robust realism to be nonsensical (p. 145, footnote 32). But, to the extent that I understand it, Velleman here too begs the question about the semantic defectiveness of certain external questions.
49. For helpful comments on previous versions, I thank Michael Brady and Luca Ferrero.

11
The Authority of Social Norms

Nicholas Southwood

An important recent development in metaethics has been a broadening of its scope. Traditional metaethics was concerned mainly with trying to understand the normative character of *moral* norms. Contemporary metaethicists are now also turning their attention to a range of other normative – or putatively normative – phenomena and trying to understand the normativity of, for instance, norms of rationality (Broome, 2005; Kolodny, 2005; Schroeder, 2009c; Southwood, 2008), norms of prudence (Brink, 2003; Bykvist, 2006; Laden, 2009), epistemic norms (Chrisman, 2007; Chuard and Southwood, 2009; Jenkins, 2007), and so on.

I want to focus here on a phenomenon that has not received a great deal of attention from metaethicists to date: *social norms*.[1] Social norms are interesting, in part, because they seem to have two aspects that pull in rather different directions. On the one hand, they seem to have an important *customary* aspect. They seem to be constitutively tied to what is normal, conventional, habitual. It seems profoundly relevant to the existence of a social norm that there is an assumed practice of behaving in a certain way – passing the port to the left, wearing black to funerals, holding one's fork in one's left hand – that behaving in that way 'is the way things are done.'

On the other hand, social norms also seem to have an important *normative aspect*. For one, they *require* things of people: to wear black at funerals, to refrain from uttering certain kinds of expletives in certain kinds of company, to bring a small gift for one's host when invited for dinner, and so on. Moreover, they seem to be normative in ways that go beyond mere constitutive rules, such as the rules of cricket and chess. When one's chess partner moves a rook as if it were a bishop, she is simply not playing chess. But when someone arrives at a funeral in a pink tutu, or gets a little too close to one in the subway, or turns up empty-handed at a dinner party, she seems to have gone wrong in some deeper way. This can be seen by the fact that we are typically inclined to deploy a much richer set of reactive attitudes in response to those who violate social norms (Brennan and Pettit, 2004).

My aim in this article is to sketch a theory of social norms that can explain these two aspects. My thesis, roughly, is that at least core paradigmatic cases of social norms are constellations of genuine rather than merely apparent normative judgments, which are nonetheless distinct from other normative judgments such as judgments of morality, prudence and so on. What makes them distinctive, I shall suggest, has to do with the particular role that what I shall call social practices are playing in grounding the judgments.

I shall begin by considering two alternative ways of understanding social norms: as social practices, on the one hand (Section 1); and as constellations of moral judgments, on the other (Section 2). I shall conclude that the first can explain the customary aspect of social norms but not the normative aspect, and that the second can explain the normative aspect but not the customary aspect. I shall then propose the positive account of social norms as constellations of practice-dependent normative judgments (Section 3). Finally, I shall conclude by arguing that we should understand social norms as serving the function of creating a particular kind of social authority.

1. Social norms as social practices

It is widely accepted that there is some kind of important relation between social norms and social practices, such as conventions, customs and tradition. Where there is a social norm this will typically be accompanied by a corresponding social practice of this kind. One view of social norms goes further and holds that they just are – or at least entail – corresponding social practices.[2]

Such a view has the virtue of offering a straightforward explanation of the customary aspect of social norms. Social practices are special kinds of behavioral regularities. More precisely, they are behavioral regularities among the members of a group that are explained by the presence within the group of pro-attitudes (or beliefs about the presence of pro-attitudes) that are a matter of common knowledge. So, the view that social norms are or entail social practices holds that for there to be a social norm among Oxford dons requiring one to pass the port to the left is (at least in part) for there to be a regularity of behavior among the dons (the dons will generally pass the port to the left), which is explained, at least in part, by the fact that the dons generally have certain pro-attitudes towards passing the port to the left (or at least they generally believe that others generally have such pro-attitudes) and the fact that this is common knowledge among the dons. The customary aspect of social norms is thereby rendered unmysterious.

The view faces two serious problems, however. The first is that it makes it impossible for there to be widespread failure to conform with a social norm (Southwood and Eriksson, MS). Social practices, such as conventions, customs and tradition, are (albeit special kinds of) behavioral regularities. If social norms are or entail corresponding social practices, it therefore follows that social norms also entail corresponding behavioral regularities. So, where there is a social norm among a group requiring individuals to behave in a certain way, it follows that individuals generally do behave in the required way. It does not follow that *all* individuals *always* behave in that way. But it does follow that where failure to behave in the required way becomes sufficiently widespread, such that it is no longer true that most individuals generally behave in the required way, the social norm must necessarily cease to exist.

This seems to be an unfortunate implication of the view. Surely there is nothing in the concept of a social norm to rule out the possibility of widespread non-compliance. Suppose, for example, that it is a social norm in Moldova that one must not urinate in public swimming pools. Moldovans accept that one mustn't urinate in swimming pools. They disapprove of others if they become aware of their having done so. Urinating in swimming pools is, as far as most Moldovans are concerned, 'just not the done thing in Moldova.' Despite this, suppose that, in fact, unbeknownst to the Moldovan public, urinating in swimming pools is in fact widespread. Just about everyone does it. To be sure, no one fesses up to the fact. Indeed, they do everything they can to hide it. When they do it themselves, they feel rather guilty (though perhaps also a certain frisson of guilty pleasure). They have no idea, and would be appalled to discover, that others are behaving in exactly the same way. This scenario involves massive hypocrisy on the part of the Moldovans. But it does not seem to be incoherent.

There is another reason for which one might be suspicious of any theory that rules out the possibility of social norms that fail to attract general conformity. This is that it seems to violate an important platitude about normativity. It is sometimes said that norms entail the possibility of failure.[3] It has to be possible to fail to comply with them (as well as possible to succeed in complying with them). The intuitive idea is that norms involve demands on one; and demands are the kinds of things that one can fail to live up to. Perhaps 'ought' implies 'can', but it doesn't imply 'does.' That would be to milk the norm of its normative oomph. The idea is usually understood as applying to particular individuals. But there is some temptation to think that it may also have application to groups of individuals. There is something excessively normatively fragile about the idea of a demand that is guaranteed to go out of existence simply on account of individuals generally failing to act in accordance with it. That would not be a demand worthy of the name. Yet that is in effect what we would have to conclude about social norms if they were – or entailed – social practices.

This brings us to the second problem with understanding social norms in terms of social practices, namely, that such a view appears unable to explain the normative aspect of social norms. Even leaving aside worries about the possibility of failure, we are confronted with a more prosaic concern. Social norms are, as we noted above, constituted by requirements. Where there is a social norm – say, a social norm involving not getting too close to others in public places – the members of the group in which it is a social norm must generally accept a *requirement* not to get too close to one another in public. They must generally judge that one *must not* get too close to one another and be disposed to *disapprove* of those who flout the requirement. But the existence of a social practice seems quite the wrong kind of thing to appeal to in order to explain the tendency of individuals to make such normative judgments. It need not be the case that social practices involve any such tendency on the part of their members.

This is perhaps clearest in the case of conventions, understood in something like David Lewis's sense as solutions to coordination problems (Lewis, 1969). It is not obvious that pure conventions of this kind need involve any evaluative judgments whatsoever (Southwood and Eriksson, MS). What they involve is conditional desires to act in a certain way. So, for example, where there is a convention among the males in a certain office of wearing a brightly colored tie to work on Fridays, this entails that the individuals party to the convention generally have a desire to wear a brightly colored tie to work on Fridays conditional on others (generally) doing likewise. It is not obvious that they need also judge that wearing a brightly colored tie to work on Fridays is good or worthwhile or important. It might be simply something that they, as it were, whimsically desire to do.

Suppose, however, that the tie-wearers *do* regard wearing a brightly colored tie to work on Fridays as in some way valuable. Perhaps the tie-wearing practice is more than a mere Lewisian convention. Perhaps it has acquired the character of a full-blooded custom or tradition. Even where this is so, clearly it need not be the case that the tie-wearers accept a *requirement* to wear such a tie, that they judge that one *must* do so, or that they are disposed to *disapprove* of those who opt for boringly conventional hues. That might be to impute a kind of mandatory significance to the enterprise that it simply lacks. Indeed, it might even be true that the tie-wearing practice is predicated on an explicit understanding among those party to it that there is no requirement to wear a brightly colored tie; ongoing participation in the practice is taken to be wholly optional on all sides. It might even be a precondition for continued enjoyment from participation in the practice, and perhaps even its very continued existence, that participants do not regard it as in any way mandatory. Were it to come to be seen as mandatory, the practice might dissolve. Perhaps it is, as we might say, an essentially non-normative social practice. The possibility of non-normative practices suffices to show that social practices are simply the wrong kinds of things to appeal to in order to explain the normative aspect of social norms. What social practices involve is mere pro-attitudes. But social norms involve full-blooded normative attitudes. To explain the normativity of social norms, we shall have to look elsewhere.

2. Social norms as moral judgments

This brings us to a second possible view of social norms, namely, as some-how dependent on and deriving whatever normativity they possess from *moral judgments*. As we have seen, social norms involve constellations of normative attitudes. Where there is a social norm, individuals accept a requirement of some kind; they judge that one must (or must not) X and be disposed to disapprove of those who do otherwise. Moral judgments are, of course, the paradigmatic instances of such genuine normative judgments. It might seem, therefore, that social norms should be understood as con-stellations of shared moral judgments. For there to be a social norm in a particular group to the effect that one must X just is – or entails – the pres-ence among the members of the group of some kind of moral judgment that entails, given other generally held beliefs, that one must X.

A view along these lines has great appeal. Not only does it appear to offer a compelling account of the normative aspect of social norms, it also allows us to make sense of the fact that social norms often have some kind of important moral content. The social norm that one must bring a bottle of wine for one's host when invited for dinner appears to enshrine significant moral values such as generosity and reciprocity. The social norm that one must refrain from nudity in public places may be seen as a specific appli-cation of more general moral ideas such as modesty and consideration for others.

The challenge facing such a view is, of course, to explain the customary aspect of social norms. Moral judgments as such need not have any sig-nificant customary aspect. Members of a group or community – the Danes, say – may generally judge that one must not murder, and this may be com-mon knowledge among the Danes. The claim that one must not murder entails the claim that one must not murder one's children. So the Danes accept a requirement not to murder one's children. Customary considera-tions don't seem to be playing any role here whatsoever. Indeed, to adduce them seems positively inappropriate. We would think there was something very strange going on if a Dane were to cite, as a relevant consideration, a social practice of not murdering one's children. Something would be truly rotten in the state of Denmark.

However, one might feel that the view could be refined so as to meet this challenge. One possible refinement would be to hold that social norms may be explained specifically by reference to moral judgments with the explicit content that one must obey the social practices of one's group. Just as some philosophers believe that we have a moral obligation to obey the law of the state in which we are citizens, so too it might be argued that we have, and generally take ourselves to have, a moral obligation to honor the social practices of the group or community of which we are members. What this means is that where there is a presumed social practice within a particular group – a social practice of Xing – individuals within that group will generally hold the moral judgment that one must X. Social norms just are or entail moral judgments of this kind.

This is not a plausible view. For one, it is substantively implausible. No one thinks that we are morally required to honor *all* social practices. We do not think that we are morally required to hold our knife in our right hand, even if there is a social practice within one's group or community of holding one's knife in one's right hand. Yet we do think that we are required to do so in some sense. For another, it has some odd implications. It is commonly accepted that, where we violate a moral obligation, other individuals in general (and not just the members of our community) have some kind of legitimate complaint against us; it is generally appropriate for them to blame us or regard us in a negative light. Appealing to the presence of a general moral obligation to honor the social practices of one's group therefore seems to imply that those who are not members of our group have a legitimate complaint against us in so far as we violate social norms. That may be plausible in some cases, but it doesn't seem plausible in all. Suppose that a bitter Oxford don passes the port to the right. At most, this seems to be the business of other dons.

A more promising way of refining the view would be to hold that social norms are to be explained in terms of moral judgments that entail conclusions about what we must do *in concert with relevant social practices*. Consider the following example. Singaporeans accept a requirement to drive on the left. It is tempting to suppose that this is due to Singaporeans generally subscribing to a prior moral judgment, something along the lines of 'One mustn't knowingly endanger others' lives.' In and of itself, this does not entail that one must drive on the left in Singapore. It only does so in so far as there is a presumed convention in Singapore of driving on the left. Given the existence of this convention, to do otherwise than drive on the left would be to knowingly endanger others' lives. On this view, the customary aspect of social norms consists in the fact that social practices activate the conditions under which prior moral judgments apply.

Such a view faces certain difficulties, however. One difficulty is that it is not obvious that it has sufficient generality. It seems most plausible in the case of social norms that involve actions that are linked to core interests of the kind that play an important role in morality – interests such as the interest in survival and the interest in not being harmed. But there are many social norms that involve actions in which such interests are playing at most a peripheral role. Consider, for example, the multifarious norms associated with communal dining. Some of these doubtless reflect and exemplify important moral considerations such as health and hygiene, equality, respect, and so on. But many others seem to resist being accounted for in terms of antecedent moral ideas. Consider the hackneyed example of norms concerning the respective hands in which one must hold one's knife and fork, or norms concerning the direction in which the port must be passed, or norms concerning the order in which dishes are served and eaten. It seems deeply implausible to try to give these judgments a moral interpretation. There do not seem to be any plausible candidates for moral judgments that are in the background of the judgments. Moral considerations just seem beside the point.

More generally, it appears to mistake the nature of the role that social practices are playing in the normative judgments that are constitutive of social norms. To repeat, it holds that their role consists exclusively in activating the conditions under which moral judgments apply. But, in fact, social practices seem to be more intimately connected with social normative judgments. Where there are social norms, it seems that individuals' judgments that one must act in this way or that reflect some sense of identification with the practices of the groups of which they are members.

One way to bring this out is to consider the difference between those who are and those who are not participants in the relevant social practices. Suppose that there is a social norm among Finns that one must touch tongues when one makes a toast. Let us suppose that such tongue-touching constitutes a successful way of ensuring that others feel that they are all on an equal footing, an important moral value. Now suppose that you are a visitor to Finland and present at an event where toasts are being proposed. Both you and the Finns agree in your moral evaluation that one is required to make people feel that they are all on an equal footing. And you are made aware that going through the tongue-touching ritual is something that has a certain significance for Finns such that it will help to ensure that others feel that they are on an equal footing. So you may well come to the conclusion that you must touch tongues with your fellow toasters. Still, there seems to be an important difference between you and the Finns. There is a kind of normative significance that tongue-touching has for the Finns that you, as an outsider, are unable to enjoy. In judging that you must touch tongues, you are occupying an external perspective with respect to the Finns' social practice. By contrast, when the Finns judge that one must touch tongues, they are in some sense affirming the social practices in which they are participants and expressing their membership in the group. The problem with understanding social norms as moral judgments is that it fails to appreciate the way in which, in the case of social norms, the normative and customary aspects are effectively intertwined.

3. Social norms as constellations of practice-dependent normative attitudes

We have seen that social norms must involve more than social practices if we are to be able to do justice to their normative aspect. Social norms are constellations of genuine normative attitudes. One thing this might mean is that they are constellations of moral judgments. But we have seen that the most promising ways of developing this idea fail to offer a compelling explanation of the customary aspect of social norms. I shall now argue that we should understand them instead as constellations of *distinctive kinds* of normative judgments – ones in which social practices play a pivotal role.

To get a rough sense of what this involves, it is useful to imagine a certain kind of challenge to a normative judgment that one holds. Suppose, then, that one judges that one must wear black at funerals. Now imagine that one were to be challenged as to why one must wear black at funerals. If one's judgment is the kind of judgment constitutive of a social norm, it seems that at least part of the answer will involve adducing a presumed social practice. At least part of the answer must be something along the lines of 'Wearing black at funerals is just the way things are done around here. Wearing black at funerals is just what we do.' Again, suppose that a Finn judges that one must touch tongues when one makes a toast. And again imagine that the Finn is subjected to the following normative challenge: 'Why do you think one must touch tongues when one makes a toast?' In so far as this is the kind of judgment constitutive of a social norm among Finns requiring one to touch tongues, the answer has to involve a corresponding social practice. It has to be, at least in part, 'Touching tongues when we make a toast is just what we Finns do.'

It is important to be clear about the role that social practices are playing. It is not the case that the subject is simply judging that there *is* a social practice of a certain kind – a practice of wearing black at funerals or a practice of touching tongues when making a toast. Nor need it be the case that the social practice is *explaining* why the subject *holds* or *continues to hold* the judgments. Rather, a presumed practice is part of what is *grounding* the judgments. That is to say that a social practice that the subject takes to exist constitutes part of what *justifies*, in his or her mind, the normative principle to which the social practice corresponds. So, in the mind of our Finn, the social practice in Finland of touching tongues when toasting (which he takes to exist) is part of what justifies the requirement to touch tongues when toasting. This, I suggest, is what is essential to the kinds of judgments that are constitutive of social norms.

I have said that the practice must constitute part of what justifies the principle *in one's mind*. It is natural to suppose that this means simply that one *believes* that the social practice is part of what justifies the normative principle. But this might be thought to be too strong. Perhaps it is enough that the social practice *appears* to one to be related to the principle in a certain way, that one somehow *sees* the practice as legitimating the normative principle to which it corresponds, or *feels* that it renders certain conduct obligatory and licenses us to regard those who violate the principle in a certain negative light. Whatever it involves precisely, the point is that it needn't be the case that the practice *in fact* does anything to justify the principle. The practice may not even exist, as in the case of our hypocritical Moldovans. Even if it exists, the practice and the principle to which it corresponds may be completely *un*justified, as when the male members of sexist and misogynistic societies judge that women must bow and scrape in their presence, because 'that's just how things are done.' The point is that the social practice of female genuflection is part of what justifies the requirement to bow and scrape *in their mind*.

Note, moreover, that I have said that the practice must constitute *part* of what justifies the principle in one's mind. Clearly it need not be the whole story. The grounds of our normative judgments will obviously be various. Among the considerations that ground our judgments, it will typically be the case that practice-independent considerations also figure. Thus, where we judge that one mustn't go naked on the beach, the grounds of the judgment will typically include a mishmash of miscellaneous considerations, such as thoughts about the importance of modesty, decorum, social stability, and so on. The point is just that a presumed social practice must be in the mix. Granted that the justification in our minds for the requirement not to go naked on the beach will derive in part from the fact that licensing people to go naked on the beach would conflict with God's commandments, or thwart female emancipation, or whatever, the thought that there is a social practice – that going completely naked on the beach 'is just not what we do' – must also play a role. In particular, a presumed social practice must be playing a *non-derivative* (that is, a not wholly derivative) role in justifying the requirement. Sometimes, as we saw, social practices may simply activate the conditions under which principles that we accept apply, as in the case of the Singaporean's judgment that one must drive on the left. In a sense, it is true that the presumed existence of the drive-on-the-left convention is part of what justifies the requirement to drive on the left in the mind of the Singaporean. But it is playing a wholly derivative role. From the perspective of the Singaporean, what justifies the requirement has to do with the importance of not endangering the lives of others. The role of the convention consists simply in changing what behaviors fall under the description. Contrast this with the case of the Finn who judges that one must touch tongues when toasting. Like the Singaporean, the Finn believes that there are valuable practice-independent considerations that tongue-touching realizes; it makes people feel that they are equals. But this isn't the whole story. Also important in the Finn's mind is the mere fact that there is a social practice in which he is a participant, a social practice that in some sense defines what it is to be Finnish, which is an aspect of an identity that, at least to some extent, he sees himself as having. In short, the social practice has a kind of justificatory significance in his mind that cannot be recast in wholly practice-independent terms. It has an importance in and of itself.

This might strike us as singularly odd. How can the mere fact that there is a social practice of acting in a certain way – the fact that acting in that way is 'what we do' – have this kind of normative significance? The very idea might seem preposterous. It might seem to involve an obnoxious presumption in favor of the status quo, a kind of culturally blinkered vision, and indeed a disturbing sort of bootstrapping. Part of the answer to this challenge might involve evoking other kinds of agent-relative considerations. Take the fact that a particular bad-tempered and rather smelly individual happens to be 'one's best friend;' or the fact that a particular tarnished, coffee-stained, unstable piece of furniture happens to be 'one's desk;' or the fact that collecting broken pieces of Georgian tea-pots happens to be 'one's project' – that it is just 'what one does.' These are generally taken to have a kind of importance for us that may not be reducible to the intrinsic properties of the individual, desk or project. The idea that social practices may confer justification in and of themselves may not be any more odd than these various other familiar forms of agent-relative justification.

Still, we might wonder how. The answer, I believe, must have something to do with a sense of identification with the social practices of one's group. Social practices may represent for one an aspect of what it is to be a member of a group of which one sees oneself as a part and to which one sees oneself as in some way accountable. For the American, wearing black at funerals represents an aspect of what it is to be an American. For the don, passing the port to the left represents an aspect of what it is to be a don. For the Finn, touching tongues represents an aspect of what it is to be a Finn. Social practices say something about the kind of people we are and take ourselves to be. When we make normative judgments that are responsive to social practices, we are in effect affirming these identities and our membership in the group.

It is important to reiterate, however, that what I am saying is that the normative judgments constitutive of social norms are ones in which presumed social practices have this kind of normative significance *in our minds*. I am not saying that social practices *in fact* have any normative significance whatsoever. Perhaps presumed social practices are not normatively on a par with personal relationships, objects and projects. Perhaps they are all equally nonsensical. Either way, perhaps we have mistakenly imbued social practices with an importance they lack, such that anyone whose normative judgments are grounded in presumed social practices is guilty of committing a kind of mistake. If so, then social norms will be constituted by mistaken normative judgments. But they are no less normative for being mistaken.

I have suggested that what is distinctive about the normative judgments that constitute social norms is that they are grounded, in part, in presumed social practices. In this sense the judgments are essentially *practice-dependent*. Social norms just are constellations of such practice-dependent normative judgments.

This view is quite different from the two views we considered above. It is quite different, first, from the view that social norms are or entail social practices. For one thing, practice-dependent judgments are genuine normative judgments. For another, unlike social practices, practice-dependent normative judgments only entail *presumed* social practices, that is, that individuals generally *take* there to be corresponding social practices. The individuals may perfectly well be mistaken, as the Moldovans are about the presence of a social practice of not urinating in swimming pools. To be sure, cases like this are presumably not especially common. Most social norms involve requirements of which the fulfillment or non-fulfillment will be readily discernible by others. Even in the more familiar cases, however, there may be a measure of denial on the part of individuals, who, in the face of mounting evidence of non-compliance, continue to think of their society as one in which certain social practices exist. (Think of an elderly person who continues to believe that there is a social practice of young people ceding their seats to the elderly in buses.)

The view that social norms are constellations of practice-dependent judgments is also quite different from the view that they are constellations of moral judgments. Suppose that Kofi judges that one must not commit genocide. And suppose that, when challenged as to why he thinks that one mustn't commit genocide, he responds, 'Committing genocide is just not done around here. Genocide is just not what we do.' Assuming that he is speaking truly – a presumed social practice of not committing genocide is indeed part of what is grounding his judgment that one mustn't commit genocide – it seems clear that we should conclude that Kofi isn't really making a moral judgment, properly speaking, at all. Moral judgments do not permit social practices as part of their grounds. In this sense, they are essentially practice-independent. The judgments that are constitutive of social norms, in contrast, are inexorably linked, and beholden, to presumed social practices.

4. The authority of social norms

I have presented a theory of what social norms are. They are constellations of practice-dependent normative judgments. I have suggested we should accept this theory on account of its explaining two core aspects of social norms. In conclusion I want to say something very briefly about what it implies for the purpose or *function* social norms serve, what they're *for*.

Consider the following two familiar functions that different sorts of social facts might be thought to serve. First, they might primarily serve a coordination function. That is to say that they facilitate our reaching mutually beneficial outcomes where our interests are moderately well aligned. This seems a pretty good description of what many conventions, such as the convention of driving on the right or the left, are doing. Second, social facts might serve the function of being, as it were, morality's handmaiden. That is to say that they help us to comply as much as possible with the dictates of morality – say, by presenting us with a series of practicable moral rules of thumb or by changing the payoffs associated with moral compliance and deviance. This is effectively the function of what H.L.A. Hart (1961) calls principles of 'positive morality.' On one view, it is also the primary function of criminal law.

Clearly, particular social norms *can* serve these functions. But understanding the core function of social norms primarily in these terms seems mistaken. Take the coordination function. Neither of the two core aspects of social norms makes sense on the assumption that they are supposed to be facilitating coordination (Southwood and Eriksson, MS). The normative aspect of social norms seems epiphenomenal. Social practices are not necessarily normative; and this in no way undermines their ability to facilitate coordination. The customary aspect of social norms seems to fall short of what is required. Effective coordination requires that individuals generally *behave* in ways that others expect them to behave. But, as we saw, social norms do not require that individuals generally behave in accordance with them.

Here is another way of bringing out the inadequacy of thinking about social norms primarily as instruments for facilitating coordination. Suppose that coordination is either impossible or unimportant. Under these circumstances, it seems obvious that there might still remain an important role for social norms. Indeed, many of the most important social norms fall into this category. Think of social norms requiring us to perform actions especially costly to the individual. Or think of social norms compliance with which signals our sense of identification with the group. Or think of social norms with which we express our shared values. If we are thinking of social norms as a coordinating device, these kinds of norms must strike us as somehow eccentric or deficient.

What about the morality-buttressing function? It's clear that social norms can and do help in this regard. They can provide us with additional motivational resources, ones that are tied to our sense of membership in a group. However, there are also limitations to understanding social norms in these terms. One is that, as we have already noted, many social norms don't seem to have anything much to do with morality at all. It seems a mistake to regard these as idiosyncratic outliers. Moreover, the customary aspect of social norms makes for a very uneasy alliance with morality. For one, the judgments constitutive of social norms take as their normative anchor the social practices of particular contingent associations of individuals. This represents a significant curtailment of the moral point of view, which aspires to a kind of transcendence with regard to such practices and associations. For another, it is often thought to be a peculiarity of morality that it matters not just what one does but why. Even where the dictates of morality and social practices line up, and they often won't, there is a worry that social norms involve a mode of thinking that crowds out moral motivation.

If social norms don't primarily serve either of these functions, what function do they serve? I suggest that what they do is give us a certain sort of
shared *authority* over one another. Part of what this means is that that social
norms give us a recognized shared right to demand and expect things of
one another (see Coleman, 1990). Possessing authority is therefore quite
different from the sort of reliable information about how other individuals
will act that is required for effective coordination. To enjoy authority over
one another implies a normatively significant modification in our relations
with them. We are in a position to hold one another to account.

But this cannot be the whole story. Moral norms also plausibly involve
authority in this sense. Stephen Darwall has influentially argued that moral
norms depend 'on presupposed authority and accountability relations
between persons' (Darwall, 2006, p. 8). What is distinctive about the kind
of authority that social norms bring about, I want to suggest, is its peculiarly
social nature. Social norms involve a distinctively *social* kind of authority –
a kind of authority that is tied to the group. To understand its nature we
must understand the peculiar role it plays in constituting and reconstitut-
ing the group. This is so in at least three ways.

First, the kind of authority that is at issue is limited in scope. We only
recognize as having authority those with whom we share a common membership in a social group. Contrast this with the kind of authority at play in
moral norms. In the case of moral norms, there is no such restriction. The
familiar Kantian idea is that we are accountable to each and every moral
agent, that every such agent has the right to demand us to take her into
account in deciding what to do. Moral norms, in other words, purport to
create a kind of authority that is unlimited in its scope.

Second, when we exercise the authority, it seems that we somehow do
so *in the name of the group*. Our authority to make moral demands of one
another seems to reside with intrinsic properties that we possess as individual agents. An affirmation of our authority to make moral demands is an
affirmation of our valuable status as individuals. But, in the case of social
norms, affirming one's authority amounts to standing behind and affirming the values of the group – in effect, to affirming the status of the group
of which one is a member. Whereas in the case of moral demands individual
agents appear to be the ultimate arbiters, in the case of social norms it is the
group's values that are, in some sense, the highest court of appeal.

Third, this last idea suggests an even more intimate connection with the
group. It seems, indeed, that the kind of authority at play in social norms
is partly *constitutive* of the group. Clearly it is part of what constitutes the
group into the particular group it is – a group with these values rather than
those. But it seems that it may be playing an even more central role. Any
association of individuals in which the members acknowledge one another's right to demand and expect things of one another seems to be of an
importantly different kind from an association in which the members make

no such acknowledgement, even if they act in ways that are responsive to one another's interests. Consider the contrast between friends and mere acquaintances. These are different, in part, due to the fact that we recognize the right of our friends to demand and expect things of us that we wouldn't dream of recognizing in the case of mere acquaintances: to spend time with them; to listen to them when they have a personal problem; to indulge them (within limits). Similarly, it seems that, by virtue of recognizing others' authority over us, our relation with those others is relevantly transformed. Some kind of tighter bond seems to be in existence. An association of individuals has become something more, a group in the full-blooded sense.

Though social norms and moral norms both involve authority, then, my contention is that the kind of authority they involve is crucially different. Social norms, in particular, create a distinctly *social* kind of authority – one in which the status of the group is paramount. It is social in at least three ways. First, it is social inasmuch as its scope is limited to members of particular groups. Second, it is social inasmuch as the group is the ultimate source of authority; and claiming authority amounts to acknowledging the status of the group in our lives. Third, it is social in the sense that it is partly constitutive of the groups in which it resides.

It shouldn't be too hard to see why social norms are the perfect tools to create authority of this kind. Consider the normative aspect of social norms. Norms are constellations of *normative* attitudes. For there to be a social norm, it is not enough that people judge, 'I shall do this.' Rather, they must judge, 'I must do this.' Social norms entail that the members of the group accept normative requirements. When we accept a normative requirement, we accept the right of others to expect us to comply with the requirement. In doing so, we regard ourselves as accountable to others so far as complying with the requirement is concerned.

In this context, it is also worth mentioning the fact that social norms allow for not being generally complied with. This is also readily explicable according to the hypothesis that social norms serve an authority-creating function. Consider a teacher whose commands are recognized by the students as legitimate, but only because the teacher always commands the students to do only what he knows the students will do anyway. This would not be a teacher with genuine authority. To make authority dependent on one's authoritative demands being generally complied with would be to give up on authority altogether.

What of the customary aspect of social norms? This seems important to their capacity to create the distinctively *social* kind of authority. We only accept a justificatory burden in the case of those who are participants in the shared social practices that are part of what justifies particular requirements in our mind. Moreover, as we have seen, the social practices of one's group can be thought of as instantiating shared values of the group. So affirming one's authority in this context amounts to standing behind and affirming these values and the status of the group of which one is a member – and perhaps even to constituting it in the light of these values.

If social norms are well suited to creating social authority, social practices and constellations of moral judgments aren't. Social practices lack the right kind of normativity and are behavioral regularities, which we saw was antithetical to genuine authority. Moral judgments are practice-independent in ways that disqualify them as phenomena that can do justice to the social character of social authority.

Social norms, then, serve the function of creating authority. This is not meant to be a defense of social norms. Like any tool, they can be abused. Knives serve the function of cutting. Unfortunately, this means that they can be used to murder as well as to cut tomatoes. Conventions serve the function of facilitating coordination. Unfortunately, this means that they can be used to facilitate the endeavors of villains as well as saints. Social norms are no different. Creating patterns of mutually recognized rights to demand and expect things of each other is simply *what norms do*.

It is time to conclude. My aim in this article has been to present a theory of social norms. I have argued that we should think of them as constellations of practice-dependent attitudes that serve the function of creating a distinctively social kind of authority. Doing so, I have suggested, offers the best hope of vindicating their customary and normative aspects.

Notes

1. To be sure, they have received plenty of attention within the philosophy of social sciences. See for a sample Bicchieri (2006), Brennan and Pettit (2004), Elster (1994), Gilbert (1989), and Ullmann-Margalit (1977). But the task of clarifying their distinctive normativity has tended not to be central to the ambitions of these theorists.
2. Adherents of this view include David Lewis (1969, pp. 97–100), H. Peyton Young (1998, pp. 144–5), Cristina Bicchieri (2006, ch. 1), Eric A. Posner (1998; 2000), Thomas Voss (2001, pp. 108–9), and Bruno Verbeek (2002).
3. For critical discussion see Lavin (2004).

12
Moral Epistemology

Alison Hills

1. Introduction

I will begin with a puzzle about moral epistemology. At first sight, the puzzle is primarily a problem for moral realism, since it highlights some ways in which moral epistemology differs from the epistemology of non-moral matters of fact. But I will argue that the problem is much broader, that it affects not just moral realism but other major metaethical theories.

I will set out four features of moral epistemology. Three are related to one another, but the fourth presents a significant problem in that it seems to be inconsistent with the other three. In the next sections I will discuss how moral realism and non-cognitivism might try to account for these four features of moral epistemology. I will show that none of these theories can comfortably accommodate all of them. In the final sections of the paper, I explain how I think that the problem should be solved.[1]

2. Four features of moral epistemology

The first interesting feature of moral epistemology is the treatment of testimony. Trusting the testimony of other people about non-moral factual matters – what time it is, where the train station is, when the next train is leaving – is acceptable. Indeed, it is a vital way of finding out about the world, one which we could not do without. Of course, you should not trust the word of everyone all of the time. But at least when you have reason to think that the speaker is trustworthy (perhaps even when you have no reason to believe her untrustworthy) you can and should trust her.

Many people think that forming your beliefs about moral matters on the basis of the word of someone else is, by contrast, in many circumstances unacceptable. Of course you may find out factual information from another person and, under special circumstances, trusting their word on a specifically moral matter may be acceptable. But, in normal circumstances, trusting testimony about a moral question is problematic in a way that trusting testimony about other non-moral matters of fact is not. Suppose that you are not sure what is the right thing to do, or you are not sure how powerful are the moral reasons you have to act. For example, you are wondering whether you should join your union and support your colleagues by going on strike, even though doing so would harm those you usually help and might produce no benefits. You ask a colleague who says: 'yes you should.' It would be odd simply to take her word for it and do what you were told, even if you thought that she was usually right about such things.

In fact, the status of moral testimony is more complicated. Learning about morality from your parents or peers when you are a child is both normal and perfectly acceptable. It is only when one becomes older and more mature that it seems important not simply to take someone else's word on what you ought to do.[2]

Secondly, deferring to the opinions of experts about non-moral matters of fact is wise. For example, when you buy a house, it is sensible to ask a surveyor whether it is structurally sound and a lawyer to look at your contract, and to defer to their opinions. But deferring to the beliefs or judgments of others about purely moral matters is problematic. There are no moral experts to whom it is rational to defer, as there are experts about other matters of fact.

Thirdly, we tend not to give weight to others' opinions about moral questions as we would about other matters of fact. Many moral issues are extremely controversial, with many sensible people taking opposing views about the morality of euthanasia, abortion and capital punishment, whether it is ever right to lie to someone for her own benefit, to what extent you could be morally be required to sacrifice your own interests for the sake of complete strangers, whether animals have similar rights to humans, and so on. A wide variety of different people disagree about these questions, including some whom it is reasonable for you to regard as similar to you in judging these questions, or even better (that is, as likely as you or more likely to get the answer right). If you took the opinions of others into account, it is likely that you would have to suspend judgment on any controversial moral issue.[3] Most of us do not do this, nor do we think that we should.

These three features of moral epistemology are plainly related. Taking people's words or beliefs or judgments into account on moral matters seems to be problematic, though doing so is perfectly acceptable, even required, with regard to non-moral matters of fact.

The fourth feature of moral epistemology is that taking advice from other people is acceptable and often a very good idea. For example, suppose again that you are considering whether to join the union. Asking your colleagues what they do, asking your friends and family what they think you should do and why, can be an invaluable guide to your own thinking. There is no need for you to try to work out what to do all by yourself and no benefit in doing so – but using what they say as a guide to your own reflections is very different from simply putting your trust in the answer they give you. Taking advice is not the same as trusting testimony.

At first sight, the first three features of moral epistemology seem to be a problem for moral realism, for they are important differences between the epistemology of morality and that of non-moral facts. In the next section, I discuss how moral realists might respond.

3. Moral realism

According to moral realism (as I will understand it here), there are objective facts about morality that do not depend on our beliefs or attitudes about them. Killing the innocent is wrong, for example, no matter whether or not we believe that it is, disapprove of it and so on. There are many challenges that can and have been made to moral realism. But the issues that I have raised in the last section have not been much discussed. Moral realists think that moral questions are similar in important respects to non-moral matters of fact, so they need to explain why the epistemology of the two is so different.

One feature of moral epistemology that I picked out in the last section is easy for moral realists to explain. Taking advice about moral questions is a good idea, if moral realism is true, because others may be better placed than you to recognize the moral facts, and their advice may help you form true beliefs.

But if others can help you form moral beliefs with their advice, why not with their testimony? Why should you not trust their word and take their opinions into account, deferring to them if they are experts? There are some obvious and uncontroversial reasons why we might not defer to moral experts.[4] There are no widely acknowledged moral experts as there are experts in other fields. If you need to find an expert surveyor to assess your house, you can check that she has the appropriate professional qualifications. Not only is there no widely recognized qualification for a moral expert, but it is hard to imagine that one could possibly be devised. There is so much disagreement about who has good judgment about moral matters and what qualities someone needs to have good judgment that no test for moral expertise will ever be widely (let alone universally) accepted.

But, if you cannot identify an appropriate expert, there is no reason for you to defer to anyone else's judgment; you might even think that there was reason not to do so. It might be better to make up your own mind than to rely on someone else whose judgment may be badly flawed.[5]

But, even though it may be difficult to find a moral expert, this is not a strong reason never to accept moral testimony and never to defer to the judgments of others. It is not that difficult to discover someone who has better judgment or more experience than you in some particular area or about some single issue. And there would be no reason not to take their word on at least that moral question.[6] Moral realists tend to be quite optimistic about the possibility of moral knowledge. But, if some people have moral knowledge, why can't they transmit it to others through testimony, or by those others deferring to them?

Moreover, suppose that it was indeed difficult to find anyone whose moral judgment you should trust. What would be the point of asking for their advice? Either their judgment is no good, in which case there would seem to be no benefit in taking their advice (it might even make things worse). Or if their advice was useful, what could be the problem with trusting their testimony or deferring to their judgment? It is hard for a moral realist to explain why it is not reasonable to trust moral testimony, without claiming that it is hard to find anyone whose judgment you should trust, and therefore without also suggesting that there is no point in taking moral advice.

4. Non-cognitivism

Moral realism has difficulties in explaining why it is a mistake to trust moral testimony or to defer to moral experts. One possible reason for this is its commitment to *cognitivism*, that is, the claim that moral judgments are expressions of belief and that they can be evaluated as true or false.[7] Non-cognitivist accounts of moral judgment, according to which in making a moral judgment you are not representing the world, but are expressing your attitudes towards it, may seem to be well placed to explain why trusting moral testimony and deferring to moral judgments of others is not a good idea. In this section I discuss whether simple or sophisticated versions of non-cognitivism can explain all four features of moral epistemology.

4.1. Simple non-cognitivism

According to simple non-cognitivism, moral judgments are expressions of approval or disapproval or combinations of these and other non-cognitive attitudes. Here is Ayer's classic statement of simple non-cognitivism:

> The presence of an ethical symbol in a proposition adds nothing to its factual content. Thus if I say to someone 'You acted wrongly in stealing that money' I am not stating anything more than if I had simply said, 'You stole that money.' .. If now I generalize my previous statement and say, 'Stealing money is wrong', I produce a sentence which has no factual meaning – that is, expresses no proposition which can be either true of false... Another man may disagree with me about the wrongness of stealing, in the sense that he may not have the same feelings about stealing as I have, and he may quarrel with me on account of my moral sentiments. But he cannot, strictly speaking, contradict me. For in saying that a certain type of action is right or wrong, I am not making any factual

statement, not even a statement about my own state of mind. I am merely expressing certain moral sentiments. (Ayer, 1936, p. 107)

If moral judgments are all expressions of our attitudes, there is no such thing as moral truth and no such thing as moral knowledge. And if (as is plausible) trusting testimony about matters of fact is reasonable because it can be a source of knowledge, and there is no such thing as moral knowledge, there could be no reason to trust moral testimony.

Since moral judgments are simply expressions of attitudes, according to simple non-cognitivism, and no one's attitudes can be regarded as better in any respect than those of anyone else, we are all equally well placed to make moral judgments. Of course, some of us may have more factual information and could count as experts in that sense. But there would be nothing distinctively moral about our expertise. Indeed, it is hard to see how anyone could distinguish herself as a moral expert, according to simple non-cognitivism. Since there are no moral experts, there is no one to whom it is rational for us to defer.

Similarly, since all you are doing when you make a moral judgment is expressing your attitude, there seems to be no reason why you should suspend judgment when you discover a 'disagreement', that is, someone else expressing a different attitude. You are not, as Ayer says, strictly speaking contradicting one another (two propositions can contradict one another, strictly speaking, only if they each can have a truth-value, but of course moral judgments cannot be true or false, according to this view). So there is a good sense in which you are not disagreeing at all. In any case, moral 'disagreements' are clearly quite different from ordinary factual disagreements, and it is not surprising that different responses are required in each case.

Simple non-cognitivism gives an account of moral judgments according to which it is easy to see why trusting moral testimony is usually unacceptable, why there are no moral experts to whom one should defer and why you are not required to suspend judgment in response to moral disagreements. It might appear, then, that it gives a better account of moral epistemology than does moral realism. But this is not really so.

In the first place, it cannot give an adequate account of how we make moral judgments. We can and do subject moral claims to scrutiny, we think carefully about them, try to work out which factors are morally relevant and how much they matter and so on, and it certainly seems that our moral beliefs are better justified if we carry these out well. Simple non-cognitivists insist that there are no benefits to thinking carefully about moral matters. But a complete denial that careful deliberation about moral matters has any point is not a very attractive view. It is not very plausible that thinking about moral questions is a complete waste of time.

In the second place, simple non-cognitivism is not able to explain all the features of moral epistemology. For, after all, we do take moral advice, and it is hard to see why we would do so if making a moral judgment were merely expressing an attitude. Why should you regard their expression of an attitude as relevant in any way to your expressing your attitude?

There are reasons why you might be interested in someone else's attitudes. You might simply be curious. You might want to be like that person (and share her attitudes) or unlike her (and develop different attitudes). Discussing moral questions with others may help you to refine your own attitudes, to change them or to endorse them. But this is not a particularly good account of moral advice. In asking for and taking moral advice, you seem to be asking what you should think about moral questions and what you should do. It is not clear that simple non-cognitivism can capture this feature of moral advice.

Moreover, while in many circumstances we do not trust moral testimony, in some situations we do, and we think that doing so is right. Some people – notably children – should listen to moral testimony. The kind of non-cognitivism that insists that there are no better or worse moral opinions, that deliberation and consideration can play no role in ethics, apparently cannot explain why it is ever a good idea to trust moral testimony.

4.2. Sophisticated non-cognitivism

Any plausible non-cognitivist theory will be more sophisticated than this very simple non-cognitivism. I will discuss one well-known sophisticated version of non-cognitivism, Simon Blackburn's quasi-realism (Blackburn, 1998).

Blackburn claims that ethical evaluations are typically practical issues on which we want to coordinate or have to coordinate. Initially, therefore, we must understand moral judgments as expressions of non-cognitive attitudes, rather than as attempts to represent the world in any particular way. But moral judgments take on a new form, the moral proposition: a 'propositional reflection' of these non-cognitive attitudes.[8]

The moral proposition acquires many features that appear realist. For example, Blackburn also adopts minimalism about truth, the view that to assert 'p is true' is to do no more than to assert 'p.' Since it is proper for us to assert moral propositions such as 'murder is wrong,' we are also entitled to assert propositions such as 'it is true that murder is wrong,' which appear to commit us to moral truths. Similarly, there is no problem in talking about moral knowledge. According to Blackburn, we talk of knowledge that p when we are convinced that no improvement has any chance of reversing our commitment to p; we might even find ourselves saying that we know moral propositions to be true.[9] In addition, we can have genuine disagreements, for we are disagreeing about how to coordinate together: obviously, if I want to coordinate with you in a way that is incompatible with the way that you want to coordinate with me, we are disagreeing with one another.[10]

A sophisticated version of non-cognitivism, such as Blackburn's view briefly sketched here, is a much better account than simple non-cognitivism.

It allows that thinking through moral questions does have a point, and that some of us have more time, opportunity, relevant experience and perhaps ability, so that we will do so better than others. It can explain why we sometimes listen to moral testimony and why we take moral advice, because we want to coordinate with other people and the coordination for which we make moral judgments is particularly important.

But, unfortunately, sophisticated non-cognitivism cannot explain all the features of moral epistemology either. Suppose that you are more careful in forming your moral judgments than I am. If there are benefits to careful deliberation in forming your moral beliefs, why can't you share those benefits with me by telling me the results of your deliberation? And why shouldn't people like you, who have spent longer thinking more carefully and more accurately about moral questions, count as moral experts? If there are moral experts, should we not defer to them?

The problem, of course, is that the closer that sophisticated non-cognitivism comes to moral realism, the greater the difficulties it has in retaining the appealing parts of the moral epistemology of simple non-cognitivism.

Neither moral realism nor the versions of non-cognitivism considered here could solve the puzzle about moral epistemology. Indeed, we might be inclined to think that it is not so much a puzzle as an actual inconsistency in moral epistemology. It is simply impossible to reconcile all four features, for any argument in favor of taking moral advice must apply also to trusting moral testimony and deferring to experts; and any argument against trust and deference in ethics also suggests that we should not take moral advice or ever listen to moral testimony. But in the following section I will argue that we can give a coherent account of moral epistemology that accommodates all four features of moral epistemology, one that is compatible with both moral realism and the kind of sophisticated non-cognitivism mentioned above.

5. Moral understanding

When discussing moral realism, I suggested that, if we could gain moral knowledge through testimony, we would have reasons to trust moral testimony. But that assumes that we want, or have reason to try to gain, moral knowledge. Perhaps we prefer or have stronger reasons to try to gain something else: moral understanding.[11]

If you ask someone else what it is morally permissible or morally right for you to do, and they tell you, you may know what to do and you may as a result do the right action. But you could not give an explanation of the reasons why the action is right – you may have absolutely no idea why it is right. You could not work out what to do in a similar situation in the future. In short, you do not *understand why* your action is right.

Moral understanding, as I conceive of it, is *factive* and it is *not transparent*. You cannot understand why killing the innocent is always morally acceptable, even if you think that you do, because killing the innocent is not always acceptable. In these two important regards it is similar to knowledge. But understanding why p is true is quite different from knowing that p is true. Moral understanding requires a grasp of the reasons why some action is right, or why some policy or practice is morally wrong. This grasp involves a set of abilities, including the ability to give explanations and to make judgments about similar cases. These abilities go beyond what is required to know that some action is right, and even what is needed to know why it is right. If you understand why p (and q is why p), then in the right sort of circumstances you can successfully:

  (i) follow an explanation of why p given by someone else
 (ii) explain why p in your own words
(iii) draw the conclusion that p (or that probably p) from the information that q
(iv) draw the conclusion that p' (or that probably p') from the information that q' (where p' and q' are similar to but not identical to p and q)
 (v) given the information that p, give the right explanation, q;
(vi) given the information that p', give the right explanation, q'

To understand why p, you have to have the abilities (i)–(vi) to at least some extent.[12] For example, to understand why killing the innocent is wrong, you might to be able to explain that people's lives are valuable, that it is wrong to end their lives prematurely, particularly when they have not given their consent. It follows that you cannot really understand why some isolated fact is true; you need to have a grasp of moral considerations that will have implications for other moral questions (for instance, in this case, the question of whether it is ever morally acceptable to kill someone whose life is no longer worth living and who wishes to die might be relevant).

Since it essentially involves a set of abilities, moral understanding is closer to know-how than to ordinary propositional knowledge.[13] And, like know-how, it is usually not successfully transmissible by testimony. In order to acquire moral understanding, it is important that you develop the abilities to draw conclusions about what is morally right from the reasons why it is morally right. Being told the correct conclusion, or finding out what some expert believes, will usually not help: you need to practice. Of course, you cannot begin to develop moral understanding before you have any moral beliefs at all, because it requires to some extent a systematic grasp of moral considerations. So it is not surprising that we expect children to learn most of their moral beliefs from testimony. It is only when they have acquired sufficient moral beliefs in this way, and have to some extent the ability to give explanations of moral truths and to draw conclusions on the basis of the reasons why certain moral claims are true, that they can develop moral understanding. And, as we would predict, it is at this point that we expect children no longer to trust testimony or defer to moral experts, but to make up their own minds.

I suggest that not only is it important that we acquire the abilities characteristic of moral understanding, but it is also important that we *use* our moral understanding to draw conclusions and to offer explanations (I will be arguing that to do so is an essential part of morally worthy action). If this is right, then not only is it a mistake to fail to acquire moral understanding, but it is also wrong to trust testimony or defer to moral experts when you could have used your own judgment instead.

Now we can also distinguish between taking advice and trusting testimony. When you trust testimony or defer to experts, you base your belief solely on the authority of the other person. You make no attempt to assess whether their reasons for their opinion are any good. It does not, of course, follow that you trust the testimony of anyone or that you treat everyone as an expert. You may take into account how expert and trustworthy the speaker is. You may rate her as a source of moral testimony or of moral expertise. But you are essentially judging the person, not what she says or thinks about this particular issue. So you cannot be responding to the reasons why p is true – you might have no idea of the reasons why it is true, but even if you do (the other person may have offered an explanation) you do not base your belief on that, but on the fact that she said or thought that p.

By contrast, you may take their views as *moral advice*, which you subject to critical scrutiny and then decide whether or not to accept *on its own merits*. Here you take into account what others have said to you as a guide to your own reflections. If you come to the same conclusion (that p), you do so on the basis of the reasons why p – reasons that they may have helped you to become aware of or to appreciate properly – rather than basing your belief on them. Since, when you take moral advice, you develop and use your moral understanding, whereas trusting testimony and deferring to experts is a rival way of forming beliefs, if moral understanding is important in the way I have suggested it is clear why taking moral advice is acceptable when trusting testimony and deferring to others is not. The only exception, I think, is if for some reason you have no moral understanding and could gain none (perhaps you do not have the relevant experience, or you have poor moral judgment), in which case it might be better to trust moral testimony or to defer to someone who was better placed than you.[14]

If I am right that using moral understanding is important, then it also makes sense not to suspend judgment when in moral disagreements, no matter how intractable, and, in general, you have good reason not to give any weight to the opinions of others on moral questions, whatever their level of expertise. For, if you do have moral understanding and they do not, you could have used it to come to the right answer, and paying attention to others would make things worse. On the other hand, if you had got the answer wrong and had no understanding, you would not gain understanding by putting some weight on the fact that others believed that not-p (independently of the weight that you give to their reasons for that belief). For the fact that some people believe that not-p is not usually a reason why not-p is true. So giving weight to that fact is not a way for you to grasp the connection between the reasons why not-p is true and not-p, and to form your belief that not-p on that basis. Treating the opinions of others as having any weight is a different way of forming moral beliefs than using your moral understanding, and, if I am right about the importance of moral understanding, it is a mistake to do so. Since you should not give weight to the moral beliefs of others (independently of their reasons for those beliefs), you should not suspend judgment in response to moral disagreements.[15] If moral understanding is important in the ways that I have suggested, we can explain all four features of moral epistemology.

6. Moral worth

Why does it matter whether or not you have and use your moral understanding? In the first place, moral understanding may be valuable for its own sake. It may simply be worthwhile to grasp the connections between the reasons why p and p (where p is some moral truth), and to form moral beliefs on that basis.

Secondly, moral understanding plays an important role in certain kinds of moral action. If you know what to do, you can do the right action. But what will be your reason for action? That you are doing what you are told? You might do the right action, but you will not be acting for the right reasons. Your action will not be *morally worthy*.

Morally worthy action is right action for the right reasons, that is, for the reasons that make the action right. If you have moral understanding, if you grasp why your action is right, and you act on that basis, you will act for the right reasons.

The most familiar examples illustrating the difference between right action and morally worthy action involve different types of motivation. Recall Kant's well-known two grocers. One treats his customers honestly in order to have a good reputation. He is not really acting well: he is doing what is morally right, but only because it is in his interests to do so, whereas the grocer who gives the right change precisely because doing so is fair is acting well and his action has *moral worth*.[16] But I suggest that, as well as your desires and goals, your beliefs and the ground of those beliefs are also crucial to morally worthy action.

Suppose that you give your customers the right change, not because you realize that doing so is fair and that you should treat your customers with respect, but because you were told by someone whom you trust that doing so is right. Suppose that you reflect on why this might be, and, realizing that all your customers are local, you think that it must be because it is wrong to cheat local people. Unlike the honest shopkeeper who recognizes that all his customers deserve to be treated fairly (no matter where they are from), you do not understand why giving your customers the right change is morally right. You may have good motivations (unlike the selfish shopkeeper) but you did not choose your action on the basis of the reasons that make it right, so you did not act for the right reasons.

I have argued that moral understanding differs from moral knowledge, and that, if you want to acquire and use moral understanding, it does not usually make sense to trust moral testimony, to defer to moral experts, or to suspend judgment on controversial moral issues, but that taking moral advice is worthwhile. I have suggested that having and using moral understanding may be valuable for its own sake, but it is also needed in morally worthy action (of a certain kind). In the next section, I will consider two objections to my argument: first, that you can perform morally worthy actions on the basis of moral knowledge rather than moral understanding, and, secondly, that not all moral claims are closely linked to action.

7. Objections to the argument

(i) Is moral understanding necessary for morally worthy action?

Moral understanding is not essential for morally worthy action, because you need not act on the basis of explicitly moral beliefs in order to act for the right reasons. But, if you do, then moral understanding is essential.

Why isn't moral knowledge sufficient? Obviously knowledge that some action is right is not sufficient, because you could have that without any idea of why the action is right, and so you would not be able to act for the reasons why it is right. But what about, for example, acting on the basis of testimony that X is right *and* the reasons why it is right?

I do not think that knowing that X is right and knowing why is sufficient for morally worthy action, if you do not have moral understanding. That is because, even if you act on the basis of that knowledge, you are not really responding to moral reasons yourself; you are responding to the testimony or the judgments of others who may be themselves responding to those reasons.

To act for the reason that p, your belief that p must be among the causes of your action. The causal connection is necessary to distinguish the reasons for which you act – your reasons – from all of those for which you might have acted (some or all of which you may be aware of). For example, there might be many reasons to go for a walk: to get some fresh air, to get some exercise, to buy something useful from a shop. But, even if you are aware of these reasons and you go for a walk, they will not be your reasons for going for a walk unless you act because of them. For example, if your belief that going for a walk will give you some exercise is among the causes of your action, that may be among your reasons for action. This causal connection between your belief and your action may not be sufficient, for well-known reasons (the causal connection may be of the 'wrong' kind), but I think it is certainly necessary.[17] So, if there is no causal connection between your belief that p and your action, you do not act for p.

Suppose that you have been told that giving the right change to your customers is the right action because doing so treats them with respect. The speaker was someone whose judgment you trust, so you believe them, and as a result you know what it is right to do, and you know why. But, before they had told you what to do, you saw nothing wrong with cheating your customers, provided that you could get away with it and as long as they were not local people. You still have no moral understanding, so you could not draw the conclusion that giving the correct change is right from reasons why it is right on your own, and you certainly could not do so in similar cases (for example, about whether it is acceptable to lie to your non-local customers about the best before dates of your produce). If you give the right change, the explanation of that will be that you believed that doing so is right because you trusted your interlocutor. The explanation will not include: you thought that doing so was right because you would be treating your customers with respect. Of course you now do believe that doing so is right because you would be treating your customers with respect (for you were told so). But that belief is not the cause of your belief that the action is right. Instead, the testimony is a *common cause*: both of your action and of your belief that that the action is right because it treats your customers with respect.

Right action for the right reasons, when it involves explicitly moral belief, also requires moral understanding. You must use your ability to derive a conclusion (of what to do) from the reasons why it is morally right, in order to act for the right reasons. Testimony is a rival way of finding out what to do, but a morally problematic rival, because if you base your moral belief on testimony rather than moral understanding (you trust the testimony, rather than treating it critically as moral advice) you cannot be acting for the right reasons.

(ii) Why aim for moral understanding if your moral beliefs
are not going to be used in action?

Sometimes our moral beliefs are very closely connected to action. The kinds of example I have been discussing here include beliefs about whether actions are right or wrong, and whether or not we have moral reasons to perform them.

But sometimes moral beliefs are unlikely to be put in to action: for example, beliefs about the character of long-dead people, beliefs about whether particular actions in distant lands, perhaps in the past, were right or wrong. We can call these *remote moral judgements*. Circumstances in which remote moral judgments would be put into action are hard to imagine. Of course it is not impossible that action on these beliefs might be appropriate; they may have consequences which reach right the way to the present. So you could not rule out the possibility that you might act on any of your moral beliefs. But there is a more important reason why moral understanding may be important here.

Moral evaluations of a person or an action have implications for moral evaluations in other circumstances. That a person is just or cowardly or cruel for acting in some particular way has implications if you or those around you act similarly. And, if actions in the past or in distant lands are morally right or wrong because of some set of features, actions with those features in the present will also be morally wrong. So, while a particular moral judgment may be unlikely to lead to action, it will have implications for moral judgments that will lead to action. So if you did not understand why the remote moral judgment was true but merely knew that it was true (or even knew why it was true), and derived from that knowledge a moral judgment that you put into action, unless you somehow acquired moral understanding in the meantime, your action would not be based on moral understanding and would not be morally worthy. So there are good reasons why we should try to gain moral understanding with regard to any moral belief, though the reasons are strongest when we are deciding what we morally ought to do.

8. Conclusion

I introduced a puzzle about moral epistemology, which at first sight seemed like a problem for moral realism: how to explain four features of moral epistemology. But I suggested that the problem was much broader, affecting anti-realist theories like non-cognitivism, and that the difficulty in reconciling the four features was serious. But it can be done, provided that we distinguish between moral knowledge and moral understanding and recognize that it is understanding, not knowledge, that we typically seek, and that we have good reasons to do so.

Notes

1. Some of these features and my solution to them are discussed in Hills (2009) and Hills (2010).
2. In fact, the status of moral testimony is controversial. While acknowledging that it is widely believed that trusting moral testimony is wrong, several philosophers have recently defended trusting moral testimony, including Jones (1999), Driver (2006), and Hopkins (2007). All three argue that trusting moral testimony is legitimate as a way of gaining moral knowledge.
3. The rational response to disagreements about ordinary factual matters is itself a matter of considerable disagreement. For example, Elga (2007; forthcoming) argues that it is always rational to suspend judgment when you disagree with an 'epistemic peer' (that is, anyone whom, laying aside your current dispute, you

judge to be as likely as you to get the answer right). Kelly (2005; forthcoming) defends a different view, according to which suspending judgment is not always rationally required in response to disagreement. Nevertheless, I think that, even if Kelly is right, moral disagreements are of a kind for which suspending judgment is normally appropriate. So in either case, if moral disputes were like ordinary factual disputes, it would be rational to suspend judgment about any controversial moral issue.

4. These reasons are elaborated in Driver (2006).

5. When your decision is particularly important, you may well prefer to trust your own judgment rather than defer to someone who may or may not be an expert. However, this cannot explain why in general we defer to non-moral experts but not moral experts, as Hopkins points out, for some moral truths are trivial, and some non-moral matters (will the house I am going to buy remain upright for the next few years?) are extremely important (see Hopkins, 2007, pp. 621–3).

6. Hopkins makes this argument for gaining moral knowledge by testimony (Hopkins, 2007, pp. 623–6).

7. Some versions of cognitivism can make sense of our treatment of testimony, deference and disagreement in morality, however. Consider a simple form of cognitivist relativist theory, according to which a judgment that X is morally wrong means 'I disapprove of X.' If you are wondering about whether some possible action is morally wrong, according to this view, what you need to establish is whether you disapprove of that action. Since you are typically much better placed to discern your attitudes than others are, there is no point in trusting the testimony of others, nor is there any point in deferring to the judgment of others. In fact, no only is there no point, since you are more expert than others on your own attitudes of approval and disapproval, but their testimony and their judgments are actually misleading. For when someone else says that X is morally wrong, she is not telling you that you disapprove of X, but saying that she disapproves of X. So the testimony and judgments of others about what is morally right and wrong are wholly irrelevant. Similarly, there would be no point in suspending judgment in response to moral disagreements with others, no matter what epistemic virtues they had, for their judgment would be irrelevant to whether you disapproved of X, and hence whether X was morally wrong (in fact, of course, there would be a good sense in which you were not really disagreeing at all). However, if the testimony and judgments of others about what is morally wrong are irrelevant to your own judgement, what could possibly be the point of asking moral advice? Doing so would be a puzzling waste of time, for others would not be talking about what is relevant to your judgment – your attitudes – they would be describing their own attitudes.

8. Blackburn (1998), p. 77.

9. Blackburn (1998), p. 79.

10. In fact, Blackburn claims that, even if we don't have to coordinate together, we cannot tolerate sufficiently serious differences in attitude (Blackburn, 1998, p. 69).

11. The term 'understanding' can be used in a variety of ways, including the locutions 'understand that p', 'understand p' (where p is a proposition) and 'understand X' (where X is a subject matter). I have nothing to say about these uses of the term. My account of moral understanding is restricted to understanding why p (where p is a moral proposition). As will become clear, my account of moral understanding is quite different from most accounts of understanding in the literature (there are no accounts specifically of moral understanding of which I am aware). In particular, unlike Zagzebski (2001), I think that understanding is

factive, and, unlike Kitcher (2002), Woodward (2003, p. 179), Lipton (2004, p. 30) and Grimm (2006), I do not think understanding why p is the same as knowing why p. The accounts of understanding most similar to mine are by Pritchard (forthcoming) and Kvanvig (2003), though I am not sure that either would agree with all the details of my conception of moral understanding.

12. You can have these abilities to a greater or lesser degree, which may make it tempting to say that moral understanding comes in degrees. You have minimal moral understanding if you correctly believe that q is why p and you can follow an explanation of why p. You have greater understanding if you have (i)–(vi) to some extent and you have full understanding if you have (i)–(vi) to the greatest extent. Alternatively, there might be a cut-off point before which you do not count as having understanding, and after which you do. This cut-off point might be contextually determined.

13. It is, of course, controversial whether know-how is a species of propositional knowledge or not. I think that there are two reasons for thinking that moral understanding is not a type of propositional knowledge. First, unlike propositional knowledge, it requires the abilities mentioned above. Secondly, I think that it is compatible with certain kinds of luck, which knowledge is not. For example, if you learn that q from a source that is usually unreliable but is now telling the truth, and from that you draw the conclusion that p, you can understand why p, though you do not know that p (or know why p).

14. Jones (1999) argues that testimony can be a useful source of moral knowledge, albeit 'second-hand,' and her main example (of Peter, who is not very good at picking out examples of sexism or racism) is of this type. Peter has good reason to think that he has not got the right sort of experience or judgment for these sorts of moral issues, and it would be better for him to trust the testimony (or to defer to the judgment) of those who do.

15. In fact, this is a significant oversimplification. For suppose that you cannot gain moral understanding: your moral judgement is too poor, or you have too little information. Then it would make sense to trust testimony and to give weight to the opinions of others (it might even make sense to defer to them, if they are moral experts). So, when you decide how to respond to a moral disagreement, you have to weigh up the possibility that you do have moral understanding, and would make things worse by suspending judgment, and the possibility that you cannot gain moral understanding by using your own judgment and you would do better to take into account the opinions of others. I think that it is likely still to be rare that suspending judgment in response to moral disagreements, even widespread and apparently intractable moral disagreements, is required.

16. What is it to act for the right reasons? One possibility is that, to do the morally right act for the right reasons, you must choose it under an explicitly moral description, such as 'the morally right action.' But the use of an explicitly moral concept is not essential to morally worthy action. What matters is that you respond to moral reasons, not that you do so under an explicitly moral description.

17. Davidson (1980, pp. 3–19) defends the 'standard' view that a reason for action is a belief and a pro-attitude that cause action, and raises the problem of 'deviant' causal chains. Problems for the standard model have been raised by Velleman (2000) and Setiya (2007), but I think their objections are more convincing against the model as a sufficient account of acting for reasons than as a necessary condition. In other words, I think that any plausible account of what it is for an agent to act for the reason that p will include the condition that his belief that p is among the causes of his action.

13
Aesthetics and Particularism

Sean McKeever and Michael Ridge

1. Starting points

We begin with a pair of scenarios:

> On Tuesday, Edgar is hosting an opening at his gallery, Art Maison, for his friend, the up and coming painter Andrew. Knowing that this is an important opportunity for Andrew, Edgar has assured him that he will do his best to bring off the event successfully. Edgar also knows that proper lighting is critical for art to look its best, and several bulbs at the gallery have recently gone dead and need to be replaced. But a trip to the store is inconvenient, and, for no better reason than that, he neglects to replace them. As a consequence, at the opening Andrew's paintings are less impressive than they otherwise would be.

Now consider another dimension and perspective:

> Andrew is having an opening at the gallery of his friend Edgar on Tuesday night. The event is important to him and he wants his paintings to be as good as they can be. In preparation for the show, he is working on a small abstract entitled Mood. The work is pleasing and competent, but hardly stands out. It lacks excitement and cannot hold viewing interest. After looking at the work in progress for some time, Andrew decides to divide the canvas horizontally with a thickly painted dark red line. Once applied, Mood comes together in a way it hadn't before. It is dynamic and holds the eye.

The facts reported in the first vignette may prompt the following judgments:

> Edgar was wrong not to replace the bulbs.
>
> The facts that proper lighting was important for a successful opening and that Edgar had assured Andrew he would try to make the event a success are moral reasons for Edgar to replace the bulbs.

The facts reported in the second vignette may prompt similar judgments, such as:

Mood is beautiful (or aesthetically good).[1]

The horizontal red line makes Mood beautiful.

Without proposing to analyze these judgments, our discussion takes the following as starting points.

First, each of these judgments is justified. They merit the credence we place in them and do not fall short of ordinary standards of justification, while still subject to revision and refinement. Most obviously, the coming to light of further, so far unspecified, facts might force one to abandon entirely any of these judgments. Less obviously, additional thought or facts might lead one, justifiably, to refine these judgments, especially the second in each pair. The judgments do not purport to offer fully precise or complete explanations of, in the first instance, Edgar's wrongdoing or, in the second instance, Mood's beauty. Just as someone who claims that faulty wiring was the reason for the fire might refine their explanation without withdrawing it, so too someone might refine without withdrawing a judgment about what made an omission wrong or a painting beautiful.

Second, both the moral and the aesthetic case are arguably characterized by holism of the sort explored by Jonathan Dancy (2004a). For present purposes, holism can be characterized as the possibility that a feature that makes something good or bad (whether morally or aesthetically) in one context might not have the same moral or aesthetic import in another case. It might have the reverse import or none at all. Mood is made beautiful, we suppose, by the horizontal red line. Transpose such a line to another work, and it may fail to do its beauty-making work. It may even disrupt a work that otherwise would have been beautiful and leave it ugly. In the ethical case, the fact that Edgar had assured Andrew is a wrong-making feature. But in other circumstances, such assurances may be ethically inert. According to the holist, then, moral and aesthetic relevance comes in several flavors. Features may be morally or aesthetically relevant because they are good-making features. Other features may be relevant as defeaters or enablers (or, countenancing negative facts, absences of these), which make it the case that some other feature is (or is not) a good-making feature itself.

Whether holism is true – whether it describes a genuine possibility – must depend upon the true story about what the good-making features actually are. Since we have already conceded that our characterization of the good-making features is subject to refinement, it is possible that the ultimately proper refinement of good-making features will reveal features that are context invariant. If the proper way to refine our conception of good-making features is to consider all manner of possible cases, we might even find features whose evaluative import is context invariable. Even so, our ordinary and unrefined judgments about what is good-making presuppose holism, and as yet we see no good grounds for thinking that the process of refinement *must* excise holism from the scene. So, for present purposes, we assume the reverse. We assume that the holism we find reflected in our intuitive judgments is indicative of how the evaluative functions quite generally and is not an illusion generated by our relative ignorance.

One point on which we shall insist, however, is that holism does not lend credence, much less establish, that there are no true and exceptionless principles governing either morality or aesthetics. Such principles would convey sound explanatory information about why, for example, some acts are wrong or some objects beautiful. The crux of the argument, which we have given in more detail on prior occasions, is this (McKeever and Ridge, 2005). A principle can itself make reference to how defeaters and enablers function in relation to a potential good-making feature. The fact that we must (if holism is true) take account of enablers and defeaters is perfectly compatible with the thesis that these contextual features behave in quite predictable ways that sound principles might capture. In fact, we have argued that, in the moral case, our knowledge of particular cases presupposes the availability of moral principles, even on the assumption that holism is true.

It is at this point that trouble begins. Whether one's philosophical proclivities run to particularism or generalism, a good question to ask oneself is how far one is prepared to press either thesis before embarrassment kicks in. For generalists such as ourselves, the problem is this. If one accepts that our knowledge of Edgar's wrongdoing presupposes that generalism is true in ethics, are we forced to agree that our knowledge of Mood's beauty presupposes generalism in aesthetics? Both cases, we are prepared to admit, are characterized by holism and susceptible to knowledge. Does our defense of generalism, as a particularist might charge, turn out to prove too much? In effect, this paper aims to address this particularist challenge to our defense of moral generalism.

The simplest route for us would be to leave the parallel undisturbed and defend generalism in aesthetics. But for two reasons we find this unsatisfactory. First, like many philosophers, we find ourselves much more sympathetic to particularism in aesthetics than in ethics. It seems possible to us that what makes Mood beautiful is the horizontal red line. But it is quaintly ridiculous to suppose that there is some default principle governing horizontal red lines. Even if true, such a principle seems uninformative and uninteresting. What is gained by way of understanding beauty once we know that horizontal red lines always make objects beautiful unless there is some specific defeating condition that prevents their doing so?

Those sympathetic to generalism in aesthetics would do better to deny that what makes Mood beautiful is its horizontal red line, and instead to insist that what makes Mood beautiful is some feature of more plausible general relevance. Perhaps the line gives Mood a balanced composition, and it is the balance that makes Mood beautiful. It is not our aim to argue against this possibility, but neither do we wish to be committed to it. In short, we would like to be able to argue for generalism in ethics while leaving generalism in aesthetics an open question.

The second reason we find the clean route unsatisfactory by itself is that it leaves unexplored whether there are good grounds for the *apparent* asymmetry. Even if generalism is true in aesthetics, as we agree it may be, we are surely not alone in finding particularism more attractive in the aesthetic case than in the ethical case. One of the best ways to motivate particularism in ethics is by analogy to particularism in aesthetics. This raises the question: are there salient differences between the aesthetic and the ethical case that explain why particularism appears more attractive in aesthetics (even if this appearance is misleading)? To find such an explanation, one must be prepared to disturb the parallel between the case of Edgar's wrongdoing and Mood's beauty.

Another route of escape denies that we have knowledge in the aesthetic case. We do not wish here to take on the burden of arguing for aesthetic knowledge, but neither do we wish to deny such knowledge. One reason is dialectical. An advantage we claim for our argument for generalism in ethics is that it does not require any particular metaethical analysis of moral judgments or moral knowledge. Our argument, as we put it, runs 'downstream' from the possibility of moral knowledge in particular cases and to moral principles. In this dialectical context, however, the assumption that we have moral knowledge of particular cases functions as a piece of common sense that we share with particularists. But common sense also includes claims to knowledge in the aesthetic case. Another and more important reason to shun this route is substantive. Even if our common sense claims to aesthetic knowledge in particular cases are unsound, this would not show that our common sense claims to aesthetic knowledge do not presuppose generalism. It would simply be the case that generalism is false because we actually lack aesthetic knowledge. But this threatens to leave in place the conditional claim that we could have aesthetic knowledge only if there were aesthetic principles.

A better solution, so we think, is to distinguish the cases. We begin, in the next section, by briefly reviewing the main outlines of our argument for generalism in the moral case. In Sections 2 and 3, we turn our attention to aesthetic judgment and argue that many of the assumptions critical to our argument for moral generalism lack ready analogues in the aesthetic case.

2. Revisiting generalism as a regulative ideal

In *Principled Ethics* (McKeever and Ridge, 2006), we argued, sequentially, for four theses. First, there are true and non-vacuous hedged moral principles. Such principles convey genuine explanatory information about what makes something have the moral qualities it has, but they are hedged by a certain kind of *ceteris paribus* clause. Second, it is in principle possible to 'trim the hedges' and replace the *ceteris paribus* clause with a concrete specification of what could make things not otherwise equal. Third, we have good moral reason to engage in the kinds of reflection that yield principles, both hedged and un-hedged. Fourth, such principles can have a valuable role to play in guiding the virtuous agent. For present purposes we will focus on the first two theses and our arguments for them.

Default principles, we claim, can be drawn from our knowledge of particular cases. Assuming holism for the sake of argument, this simply reflects the fact that, whenever a feature has one moral valence in one context but a different moral valence in another context, there will be some explanation for this. Again, particularists agree, for they accept supervenience, and argue that when a feature loses its moral relevance this is due to the presence of a 'defeater.' The particularist just argues that these defeaters cannot be codified in humanly manageable terms, and anyway that moral practice gets along just fine without doing so. We argue that, even if the particularist is right about the multiplicity of possible defeaters, we can still derive a very modest 'hedged' principle from our moral knowledge in the case at hand. For we can formulate a principle which simply *quantifies over* all possible defeaters (and other relevant contextual features). So we might have a principle of the form:

> *If an action would produce pleasure then that is a reason in favor of the action unless some other feature of the situation explains why it is not.*

An important and familiar objection to '*ceteris paribus*' laws, whether in morality or in the philosophy of science, is that they are trivially true. If hedged principles come to little or nothing more than 'F is a reason except in those cases where it is not', they will be of little interest. In the moral case, our reply to this objection turns on the claim that not any feature can be a moral reason. Many features can never be reasons. For example, the fact that an action is done in a leap year is never a moral reason to perform the action. If that is right, then the following is not, on our account, a sound hedged principle.

> *(LY) For all actions (x): If (a) x would be done in a leap year and (b) no other feature of the situation explains why the fact that x would be done in a leap year is not a moral reason not to x, and (c) the reasons in favor of x do not explain why x is not wrong in virtue of the fact that x would be done in a leap year, then x is wrong in virtue of the fact that x would be done in a leap year.*

The principle is unsound because the failure of the leap year fact to be a reason is not explained by any contingent 'feature of the situation.' Being done in a leap year can never be a moral reason, and so no contingent fact explains this. Whether there is an explanation at all turns on whether necessary truths admit of explanation. The proper answer to this question does not directly bear on our argument. In either case, no feature of the situation is needed to do the explaining.

This is important for two reasons. First, it confirms that our argument really does depend upon moral knowledge of particular cases. It is this knowledge that guarantees that we have identified a feature that at least can be a moral reason. Second, it shows that default principles can be informative. They discriminate between the features that can be moral reasons from the many that cannot be.

One might accept that default principles can be sound and informative while nevertheless thinking that defeating and enabling conditions are themselves so multifarious and complex that particularism lives on in the hedges. In the second stage of our case for generalism as a regulative ideal, we argue that, in the moral case, we can 'trim the hedges.' In particular, we argue for the availability of moral principles whose defeating and enabling conditions have been fully and finitely spelled out in descriptive terms. We argue for the availability of such principles on three grounds.

Our first argument for trimming the hedges turns on an ideal of practical wisdom (in the moral case) that we take to be widely shared. We claim that this ideal is best explained by the availability of unhedged principles. To motivate the argument, we rely on a thought experiment involving an interstellar journalist named Wanda, who is by hypothesis a person of practical wisdom. Recently assigned to cover some recent events in an alien culture, Wanda wants to write a story which not only presents the facts, but also offers a moral opinion. She has a source who is entirely honest and forthcoming but will provide only the empirical facts and not moralize one way or the other. Our argument was that in this case, in virtue of her practical wisdom, Wanda would know what questions to ask to find out the relevant facts, and that, on the basis of the answers to these questions, she would be in a position to tell her readers the whole story. We then argued that her ability to know which questions to ask, and when she could reasonably stop and draw a conclusion, showed that the number of potential moral reasons, relevant defeaters and meta-defeaters, and so on was both finite and not beyond the ken of the person of practical wisdom. From this we argued that we could 'trim the hedges' – that is, that unhedged moral principles were available to us in so far as we approximate practical wisdom. Whether this argument can be transposed will depend upon identifying a corresponding ideal of aesthetic wisdom, something we will argue against in Section 4.

Our second argument for trimming the hedges was that the availability of such principles helps sort the *a priori* from the *a posteriori* in the ethical case. There are good reasons, in the moral case, for supposing that our knowledge in a particular case can be divided sharply into *a priori* and *a posteriori* components. Moral principles are known *a priori* and cooperate with contingent facts known *a posteriori* to yield particular moral conclusions. Whether this argument can plausibly be transposed to the aesthetic case will depend upon whether a sharp distinction between *a priori* and *a posteriori* knowledge remains sound in the aesthetic case. We return to this issue in Section 4.

Our last argument for trimming the hedges in the moral case was intuitive. We pointed out not only that this view has had many philosophical defenders throughout much of the history of Western thought, but that ordinary philosophy students do not find the idea strange or obviously hopeless or confused. When presented with W.D. Ross's short list of '*prima facie* duties' most students wonder whether the list is long enough or too long, but do not tend to object to the very idea of listing all the reasons in this way, for example. As we have already acknowledged, however, when it comes to aesthetics, particularism is, if anything, more pre-theoretically plausible than generalism. Why this is so, we shall now try to explain.

3. Aesthetic default principles?

Our purpose in the remainder of this paper is to see whether what we take to be the best arguments for moral generalism can be transposed plausibly into arguments for aesthetic generalism. Recall that we argued that a principled account of morality is available and worth articulating. In this section and the following one, we focus just on the arguments that a principled account is available, turning first to the possibility of default principles and then to the possibility of trimming the hedges. Our conclusion is that these arguments do not carry over plausibly to the aesthetic context.

First, it is worth pausing to consider what would follow if the argument did transpose. It might seem to follow immediately that aesthetic 'default principles' are in fact available. This, however, would misconstrue the force of our argument in the moral case. In the moral case, we did not argue for the possibility of substantive moral knowledge. Instead, we took this as common ground between ourselves and the moral particularists. Strictly speaking, our argument in the moral case therefore establishes only a conditional conclusion: if we have moral knowledge in particular cases, then from that knowledge we can derive non-trivial default principles. Instead of denying that aesthetic knowledge is possible (or insisting that it is in any event rare), we shall focus on what aesthetic knowledge would be like, if there is any. To be clear, we shall not attempt here to offer a full theory of aesthetic judgment. Our more modest aim is to draw out some important contrasts between our pre-theoretical conceptions of aesthetic and moral knowledge and to show how these bear on arguments for generalism.

It is tempting to hold that one can have aesthetic knowledge only of those things one has directly observed. However, this temptation should be resisted. For a start, we can have aesthetic knowledge based on the testimony of reliable judges. If ten critics whose judgment I rightly respect all say a new film is rubbish, then I will be well justified in inferring that the film has very little aesthetic value. If this assessment is correct then my belief looks like a good candidate for knowledge.[2] Furthermore, there is the possibility of aesthetic knowledge based on induction. If I know from experience that every single film by Ed Wood to date has been horrible, then I might well be justified in inferring that his latest release will also not be very good. If I also happen to know that he threw the film together at the last minute and that the script got lost midway through shooting, then my justification might be strong enough that (assuming my belief is true) again I might have knowledge.

These objections from testimony and induction suggest a friendly amendment. Instead of holding that a person's aesthetic knowledge is limited to what he has directly observed, perhaps we should hold that such knowledge is always *parasitic* on direct observation by someone of either the object of evaluation itself or of some class of objects of evaluation reasonably taken to be similar in salient ways to the object of evaluation. After all, if none of the critics on whom I relied had actually seen the film (but simply had read the script, say), then it is not clear that I would have aesthetic knowledge. Similarly, if my judgment about Ed Wood's latest in the induction case was based not on having seen his previous films, or at least the testimony of someone who had seen his previous films, then it is not at all obvious that my judgment can constitute knowledge. The friendly amendment seeks to maintain what is distinctive about the original proposal – the necessity of direct observation – while allowing for the transmission and extension of aesthetic knowledge via testimony and analogical reasoning.

Even this amended version of the 'direct observation' thesis is untenable, though. The view requires revision not at the periphery but at the core. The basic worry is that the direct observation view remains unacceptably restrictive. Without further specification direct observation suggests a straightforwardly perceptual encounter that ill fits many important candidates for aesthetic knowledge. We shall mention several, but our argument does not depend upon the proper interpretation of any one case. Though one might resist one or more of the cases on their own, collectively they are enough to motivate an alternative to the direct observation view.

Mathematical proofs and other abstract objects: We often characterize abstract objects, such as mathematical proofs or chess combinations, as beautiful. Clearly, such beauty is not found via ordinary sensory perception, however.[3]

Artworks not yet created: A composer may know that a line of melody is beautiful without ever literally hearing it. Though one might try to accommodate such cases by counting quasi-perceptual simulations as observations, it is not clear that even quasi-perceptual simulation is necessary. Perhaps simply seeing the notes on the page would be enough. In any case, quasi-perceptual simulation seems to us to be insufficient to capture the full range of cases. Such as...

Conceptual art: Though conceptual art typically has perceptual features, its beauty is often thought to lie in the ideas it conveys.

Narrative art: Though engaging with narrative arts typically involves ordinary perception, this may not be central to the aesthetic experience. One would be surprised, for example, if those who read Huckleberry Finn by sight were better able to appreciate its success as a novel than those who read it by Braille.

Though much more deserves to be said about each of these cases considered in its own right, collectively they suggest how we might build on the direct observation view. Though we should abandon the view that aesthetic knowledge requires direct perception, we should continue to think that aesthetic knowledge must always be parasitic on some sort of direct engagement with the object of evaluation. We suggest that the notion of direct engagement should include the direct apprehension of the soundness and simplicity of a mathematical proof, or of the simple and forcing nature of an unexpected chess combination, or other such abstract objects.

It is hard to precisely characterize this broader notion of 'direct engagement.' Without claiming to give a full account of direct engagement, we hope to spell out some of its central features. To start, here is a suggestive passage from John Barker, who argues (against Nick Zangwill) that talk of beauty can be literally true even in regard to abstract objects:

> ...we do not literally *see* proofs, nor do we perceive mathematical objects and results through the senses. However, non-inferential and even non-conceptual knowledge play a strikingly similar role in the understanding and appreciation of mathematical proofs. First, simply *understanding* a proof requires more non-conceptual knowledge than many people realize. As any aspiring mathematician soon realizes, there is a difference between understanding a proof as a whole, and understanding each individual inference in the proof. Grasping a proof, understanding its gist, seeing why it works, is an important further step, and an essential step if one is to become a competent mathematician. However, simply by following each move in a proof, one has learned everything that is explicitly stated in the proof. Therefore, in really understanding a proof, one must be learning something that is not explicitly stated in it.
>
> Moreover, I think it is pretty clear that this extra something constitutes non-conceptual knowledge. That is, it constitutes something that cannot be stated in language, or at least, that can be grasped independently of one's ability to state it in language. If this were not the case, then the

extra knowledge could simply be written down as a further line of the proof, or as a remark following the proof, saving the reader much trouble and effort.

Likewise, in judging a proof to be elegant, we rely on insight, not inference. We simply see the proof as elegant. I actually suspect that the parallel to perception here is strong, though how strong is a psychological question outside the scope of this paper. In either case, we detect higher-order features, either of a scene or a proof, in a non-inferential process of analysis and integration. (Barker, forthcoming, pp. 11–12)

There are several ideas at work in this rich passage. First, there is the idea that even understanding a mathematical proof requires a sort of engagement with the object of evaluation which is (a) non-inferential, (b) non-conceptual, and (c) global. This last point is less explicit but meant to capture the crucial difference 'between understanding a proof as a whole, and understanding each individual inference in the proof.' Moreover, on Barker's account, in the case of aesthetic appreciation, we must detect the 'higher-order features' of the object of evaluation. A global engagement brings into view how the various parts of the object relate to one another.[4]

We want to build on Barker's basic approach without committing to all of its details. In particular, we remain agnostic about whether the relevant understanding is non-conceptual. However, the idea that the relevant sort of engagement with the object of evaluation must be non-inferential and global seems very plausible indeed to us. Moreover, this seems equally plausible in the case of non-abstract objects of evaluation, like paintings and landscapes. In those cases, a proper appreciation of the object of evaluation's beauty requires non-inferential and global engagement of some kind (here literally sensory engagement) with the object of evaluation.

So we propose that aesthetic knowledge is always parasitic on direct engagement of this sort (non-inferential and global) with the object of evaluation. Again, we say 'parasitic on' to allow for indirect forms of knowledge such as knowledge via testimony or knowledge via induction. These forms of knowledge, however, must somehow 'bottom out' in knowledge via direct engagement.

One might wonder just why aesthetic knowledge must always be parasitic on direct engagement in this way. Unfortunately, a full answer to this question would require a comprehensive theory of aesthetic judgment. Providing such a theory would go far beyond the scope of this paper, and anyway we do not have such a theory 'up our sleeves.' We will, however, pause to speculate on what the basic contours of such an explanation might look like.

Aesthetic judgement, at least in its paradigmatic form, is often thought to involve taking pleasure of some kind (perhaps a suitably 'disinterested pleasure') in the object of evaluation. Perhaps the notion of pleasure is too narrow, as some works of art impress us as aesthetically good but do so by being depressing or frightening in the right way. We shall not try to resolve the debate over the range of relevant subjective responses, but the idea that aesthetic judgment is somehow essentially tied to subjective responses of some kind to objects of evaluation seems right to us. A species of creatures entirely incapable of any of the range of subjective responses we associate with aesthetic judgment would in our view be incapable of full-blooded aesthetic judgment. They might, like the color-blind, be able to make second-hand aesthetic judgments in a derivative sense by tracking the classifications of those who are capable of the relevant sorts of subjective responses, but, just as in the case of the color–blind, this falls well short of making the relevant judgments in a full-blooded way.

We think that perhaps this element of subjective response holds the key to explaining the special role of direct engagement in aesthetic judgment. For the relevant sort of subjective responses are precisely responses we have in light of our engagement with the object of evaluation taken as a whole. One does not properly judge the beauty of a painting or statue by focusing on the various components of the painting, working out their individual value, and then doing the sums. Instead, one takes in the painting as a whole, reflects on it as a whole and sees what one makes of it.

Our claim here is meant to be compatible with the familiar fact that in aesthetic experience our attention is often directed to some features more than others, and it can seem that our aesthetic responses are to these, especially salient, features. When I judge a song to be great, this may be cued to the 'groove' of its rhythm, not the lilt of its melody. Moreover, our claim should not really hinge on whether our responses are responses *to* the whole or *to* the parts. On this point, intuitions will differ and one would need to go beyond our pre-theoretical conception of aesthetic judgment to settle the point. What is crucial from our point of view is that our responses must be made in light of our engagement with the parts as they are situated relative to one another and in the larger whole. If we judge a song good, this may be on account of the groove of its rhythm, but if our judgment is really of the song then we must be engaging with the rhythm in the larger context of the song. The rhythm may 'stand out' but we must be engaged with the background against which it stands out. Moreover, in order to produce the right sort of subjective response to the object as a whole, this engagement will need to be non-inferential (and *perhaps* non-conceptual). A critic who only understands via inference that the painting has properties A, B, and C will not thereby appropriately appreciate the painting as a whole.

The special role of direct engagement may explain the ubiquity in the aesthetic realm of what G.E. Moore called 'organic unities,' in which the value of the whole is not equivalent to the sum of the value of the parts.[5] Generalizing on Moore, we might extend the idea of an organic unity to hold that the value of the whole is not even equivalent to any mathematical function of the value of the parts, where that function remains constant across all contexts of evaluation. It is striking that clear examples of Moorean organic unities are much easier to generate in the aesthetic realm than in the moral realm. Indeed, in aesthetics, they seem to be the norm rather than the exception. Perhaps this reflects the centrality of direct engagement with the object of evaluation taken as a whole in combination with the fact that such holistic engagement can create a sort of perceptual (or pseudo-perceptual, in the case of abstract objects of evaluation) gestalt, such that our subjective reaction to that gestalt is in no way a sum of the subjective reactions we would have to the parts of the object of evaluation. Actually, independently of the fancy idea of a gestalt, the simple fact that our subjective reaction to a higher-order pattern may not systematically be a function of our reactions to its parts would seem to explain this phenomenon.

In any event, suppose that aesthetic knowledge is always dependent on direct engagement with the object of evaluation. Does this mark a difference from moral knowledge, and, if so, is the difference relevant to the debate over particularism and generalism? Here we need to disentangle the two aspects of direct engagement in our sense – being non-inferential and being global. Whether moral knowledge is always parasitic on non-inferential engagement with the object of evaluation is a matter of controversy. On a broadly intuitionist approach to moral epistemology, of the sort defended by Ross and others, perhaps this is true.

For example, on an intuitionist view, knowing that pain is bad may require non-inferential knowledge of what pain is like, *and* non-inferential knowledge that anything that feels 'like that' is bad. In fact, such putative knowledge is now less secure than Rossians might once have supposed. For apparently certain analgesics lead patients to report that the pain 'feels just the same' but that they 'no longer mind it.' If these phenomenological reports are accurate, then we do not really learn that pain is bad simply by learning what it feels like; this is an unexpected overgeneralization. We would not remark on this specific instance were it not for the fact that the badness of pain is often taken to be one of the most obvious normative facts there are, in which case knowledge of the badness of pain might be seen as one of the best cases for an epistemology that makes use of ideas such as 'immediate self-evidence' and the like, as intuitionists often do.

In any event, intuitionism is but one view. On other models of moral epistemology, our moral knowledge is not non-inferential in this way. A Kantian constructivist, for example, will presumably offer a very different account, and one that may involve considerable inference and 'construction' (in some sense) of the relevant moral facts. Whether constructivism can in some sense go 'all the way down' or requires some basic normative facts which might be known more immediately is hotly debated.[6]

However, we shall not try to settle this difficult dispute in moral epistemology here. Already, though, it is worth noting that there are interesting approaches to moral epistemology that would eschew giving pride of place to non-inferential knowledge when accounting for our fundamental moral knowledge. We do not want our arguments to rest on such a controversial and potentially question-begging assumption, though. After all, those sympathetic to moral particularism are typically also sympathetic to some kind of intuitionist epistemology, broadly construed. Moreover, our arguments (in *Principled Ethics*) were explicitly and self-consciously neutral on this issue. So let us suppose that fundamental moral knowledge is, as the intuitionist suggests, paradigmatically non-inferential.

This is not yet enough for an exact parallel with the aesthetic case, though. For, in the aesthetic case, the relevant sort of direct engagement was not only non-inferential, but also global. For simplicity, we here focus on one paradigmatic object of evaluation: action. The contrast we draw, however, if sound at all, should generalize from the evaluation of action to moral evaluation more generally, for example to the evaluation of character traits or states of affairs.

Is the moral evaluation of an action parasitic on direct engagement with the action itself? Assuming for the sake of argument that such knowledge requires non-inferential engagement of some kind, the crucial question becomes whether the relevant sort of non-inferential engagement must be global, in the intuitive sense that our judgment must somehow involve 'taking it all in' in some immediate way. In our view, moral judgment is not global in this way, though we have allowed elsewhere that it may well be holistic in the sense that the particularist emphasizes. That is, we allow that moral judgment may require sensitivity to certain features of the context and not just to the facts that are the reasons for action. However, we have argued that those features are themselves finite and limited, so being sensitive to those features is not the same as being sensitive to *all* of the features of the action. Moreover, being sensitive to features, in the sense that one's judgment is counterfactually cued to them in the right ways, is not the same as actually attending to them in the way that one seems to need to attend to the object of evaluation as a whole in the aesthetic case. So we think that denying globalism is consistent with accepting holism in the sense that holds that reasons for action can be context-sensitive.

Of course, the fact that denying globalism in the moral realm is consistent with endorsing holism in the moral realm is hardly an argument for holding this combination of views. Why, then, do we deny globalism in the moral case? Simply by reflecting on how we actually reach moral judgments, and contrasting this with the way in which we reach aesthetic judgments, the intuitive differences seem clear to us.

Consider someone trying to decide whether a given action would be morally wrong. The person deliberates for some time, and then reaches a verdict. We ask the person on what grounds he reached his verdict, and he might cite what he took to be the relevant reasons and how he weighed them one against the other in context. If he is more thorough in his answer, and thinks reasons can be context-sensitive, then he might tell us what features of the situation 'enabled' the facts that were reasons to be reasons. Suppose he tells us something like the following:

> Well, the fact that volunteering for this departmental job would be unpleasant is a reason not to do it. It would also take me away from my family a bit more, which is a reason not to do it too. On the other hand, I have not done as much as the other members of the department in the way of doing onerous jobs that are not assigned to someone *ex ante*. This fact provides a reason of fairness or perhaps of equity in favor of my doing it. The background context is one in which there is very good reason for *someone* to do this job – otherwise the students will be unhappy, they will learn less, and the department's reputation will suffer, all of which are reasons to do it. I judge that fairness trumps the unpleasantness of the job and the distraction from family in this case, and so I conclude that I ought to do it.

This sounds like a reasonable rationale for the view taken, though of course someone might disagree with the weight assigned to the reasons. We allow, of course, that someone might intelligibly suggest that the agent has left something out. Perhaps, say, the fact that he is not very good at the job in question is a reason for him not to be the one to do it. We do not pretend that moral decisions are easy or that the reasons in play are typically few or easy to weight. We do, however, think that it is implausible and even bizarre to complain simply on the grounds that the agent had not directly engaged with the action as a whole. In case some remain tempted by globalism in the moral case, however, we offer two further and related considerations.

First of all, there seems to be an important asymmetry in the moral assessment of possible actions and the aesthetic evaluation of possible bearers of beauty. In the moral case, the ability to make reliable judgments of non-actual cases is essential. Without it, we could hardly hold people responsible for their deliberations, in so far as deliberation requires assessing merely possible courses of action. In the aesthetic case, by contrast, it *may* be possible to make reliable judgments of non-actual cases, but it is far from clear that it is routine, much less essential. Even if one thinks that those who reliably create good art do so by engaging with their works as a whole prior to creation, this does not show that this is a general ability possessed by competent aesthetic judges. By contrast, a moral agent unable to make judgments of non-actual cases would fall short of even minimal competence.

This is connected to a second point. Merely possible actions are determinable types with many determinate instances. The action of doing this onerous job is multiply realizable. The action can be performed at different times, in a different frame of mind, with differing levels of dedication and concentration, in different clothes, while listening to music or not, and so on indefinitely. It would be weird and mistaken to think that I must some-how imagine and directly engage (in my imagination) with the action as specified in all of these indefinitely many different ways before reaching a conclusion about whether the action as such is morally obligatory. Similarly, when judging actual actions it is enough to identify the action as belonging to a relevant type. The resulting judgment will, on our view, typically be defeasible, but that is because additional features (which themselves are of a finite and manageable number) could lead us to reclassify the act as belong-ing to another type.

By contrast, paradigmatic objects of aesthetic evaluation are typically determinate tokens (the *Mona Lisa* or a given token performance of a given opera), or fully determinate types, anyway, as with a mathematical proof considered as an abstract object or an opera or novel understood as another sort of abstract type. We acknowledge that the relationship between token objects of aesthetic evaluation, for example a particular musical perform-ance, and corresponding types is a contested one.[7] For now, our point is this. The aesthetic assessment of tokens is *sui generis* because the aesthetic judgment depends upon taking in the token – with all of its determinate features – as a whole. One need not see the token as a token of some aesthetic type that is (generally) good or bad. One can recognize a bad performance of *Hamlet* while seeing its failure as due simply to the failure of its concrete elements to work well together. Contrast this with the moral case. Here, too, we recognize bad tokens of good types. For example, one may think an apology was obligatory in some specific case while also thinking that the particular apology given fell short of the mark. In this case, though, we sup-pose one classifies the apology as belonging to more than one salient type. It might be an apology (and so obligatory) but also insincere, or overdue, or self-serving (and so not fully virtuous).

A third difference, and one that is critical from our point of view, turns on what can ever be a moral or aesthetic reason (or good-making feature). As we have already noted, there are some features, such as being done in a leap year, that can never be moral reasons. In fact, however, when moral evaluation is at stake, many of the possible features of action are features that could never be moral reasons for action (or enablers, or disablers, or intensifiers, etc.). If this does not seem obvious, we suspect that this is due to neglect of a necessary distinction between direct and indirect relevance. Features may be relevant indirectly. For example, if I promise to return your lawn tools on Thursday, then the fact that it is Thursday is morally relevant, but its relevance – and the underlying force of my moral reasons – is due to my promise. In the moral case, particularists sometimes say things like, 'In the right context, any old feature could be morally relevant – even shoelace color or sea level.' Perhaps anything can be indirectly morally relevant, as the example of promising might suggest. Furthermore, it seems likely that anything could be a reason *to believe* that you have a reason to act in some way, since perhaps anything could reliably indicate the presence of a reason to act. But a reason to believe there is a moral reason to act is not itself a moral reason to act. Our claim, for which we have argued on previous occasions, is that many features can never be directly morally relevant; some things can never be reasons to act. Claims about the moral relevance of sea level are amenable to innocent reinterpretation, but, if offered as claims about what can be directly morally relevant, they are, we claim, false. If this is right, then it promises some explanation of why direct engagement is unnecessary in the moral case; there is no need to engage with features that will never, in any case, be relevant.

In aesthetics, however, any old feature of an object of aesthetic evaluation *could* be directly relevant to the aesthetic value of the whole. At least, we cannot be sure that this is false. The relevant 'could' here is epistemic. One might take this epistemic possibility as evidence of a further metaphysical possibility. Starting from the claim that, *for all we know*, a dab of red paint can make something beautiful, one might infer that, in the right context, a dab of red paint *can* make all the difference to the aesthetic value of a painting.[8] But should we draw this inference? To be sure, there are cases that should give one pause. It is difficult to imagine, for example, that the day of the week on which a poem was composed could be directly relevant to its beauty. At the same time, it is difficult to define limits on what is potentially relevant. For example, we should not be sure that objects are made good only by their phenomenal properties, or only by their intrinsic properties. For example, conceptual art or mathematical proofs are not beautiful in virtue of their phenomenal properties. And a piece of art is often beautiful for the ways in which it represents or otherwise references the world beyond it. A painting might be made beautiful not by the fact that it includes a brushstroke that is red (assuming for the sake of argument that this is an intrinsic property of the painting), but because it includes a brushstroke that is the color of blood. We remain uncertain whether anything can be an aesthetic good-making feature, but our present purposes do not require such a claim. As we shall now argue, our inability to define limits on what might be directly aesthetically relevant means that we are not forced to accept aesthetic generalism. Because our argument turns on this weaker claim, we are also not forced to accept aesthetic particularism. For us the issue remains an open question.

Recall that a critical challenge to our argument for default principles was that they would be trivial or vacuous. Our response to this objection turned on the claim that not any feature can be a moral reason. To be sound, a default principle must specify some fact as being a reason unless some feature of the circumstances defeats it. When it comes to features that can never be reasons, then, this condition is not met precisely because the failure of such facts to be reasons (if it is amenable to explanation at all) is not explained by the particular circumstances of the case. This response is not available in the aesthetic case, however, for the simple reason that we have no firm sense of the limits of what might be aesthetically relevant.

Strictly speaking, aesthetic principles may not be vacuously true – true simply in virtue of their logical form. If one were willing to say, for example, that the day of the week on which a poem was written can never be directly aesthetically relevant, then an aesthetic default principle along these lines would be unsound, just as the fanciful leap year principle is in the moral case. But our response to the vacuity objection in the moral case was intended to do more than to answer a narrow logical point. For principles to have a meaningful role in moral practice it is important that they help us to distinguish, in a helpful way, what can be morally relevant. They do this, we think, by identifying a comparatively few features that can ever be moral reasons against a vast background of features that never are. This is not to deny that there are deep disagreements about what can be morally relevant. The point is that even those who deeply disagree – for example a strict Kantian and a hedonistic consequentialist – will typically have quite a bit in common when it comes to the irrelevance of much of the background. Even if aesthetic default principles are not strictly vacuous, they look extremely uninteresting. We won't learn anything from the default principles that we could not learn by directly engaging with the objects of our aesthetic evaluations; indeed, we learn much less than we learn by experience. This is quite different from the moral case, in which we might learn of a very small list of possible facts (a Rossian might vote for five here, given Ross's considered list of *'prima facie* duties') that they can function as moral reasons, and that no other such facts can.

One might object at this point that the preceding argument assumes without argument that the beauty-making features of an object of evaluation are its descriptive properties. Perhaps richly normative properties such as 'having a balanced composition' are better candidates for the good-making features in aesthetics. We have two replies. First, though we shall not put much weight on this, locutions such as 'having a balanced composition' are arguably evocative metaphors rather than literal truths anyway. In that case they are not well suited to being good-making features; we assume that a good-making feature must be a feature which the object of evaluation literally instantiates. Second, given the supervenience of the aesthetic on the descriptive (which we take to be very plausible) as well as our practice of citing certain descriptive features when explaining something's beauty to someone who just doesn't get it, we think it is more plausible to take the good-making features to be purely descriptive. We need not insist on this point, though. For suppose the good-making features are these rich and 'thick' evaluative features, and that they do not in turn 'bottom out' in descriptive features. That would be a further reason that the argument from *Principled Ethics* for default principles does not carry over. For our aim there was precisely to defend default principles that were informative to those with no antecedent moral view. To that end, it was crucial that the antecedents of those principles not use any moral concepts. In so far as aesthetic default principles depart from this model, this is a significant respect in which our argument does not carry over.

Let us take stock. In this section we have argued for an asymmetry between aesthetic and moral evaluation. The asymmetry is that, in the aesthetic case, knowledge involves a kind of direct engagement with the object of evaluation that is not essential in the moral case. This direct engagement is global, and this reflects our inability to define limits on what might be aesthetically relevant. We must attend to the whole thing to be sure we do not miss the contribution of some feature.[9] This difference, in turn, explains why our argument that default principles are not vacuous or trivial does not carry over.

4. Trimming the hedges?

In *Principled Ethics*, having argued for the availability of non-trivial and manageably few default principles, we went on to argue for the codifiability of morality in a much more ambitious sense. In particular, we argued that morality can and should be codified in a way that captures all of the moral truths and which is made up entirely of principles that have purely descriptive antecedents and moral conclusions. We are, admittedly, a long way from having any such theory which demands wide assent or which is obviously true, but that is no objection to the thesis that such a theory is available to us in principle and that we ought to seek it. By way of analogy, certain theorems in mathematics or laws of nature may currently be unknown to us but still may be both available to us in principle and worth discovering and articulating. Recall that here we argued that the most plausible account of ideal practical wisdom for creatures like us entailed the availability of such principles. The question we shall explore in this section is whether an analogue of this argument carries over to the aesthetic case.

The argument of the preceding section counsels skepticism. If we cannot secure default principles, then it seems even less likely that we could establish much stronger unhedged principles. This is too hasty, however. For, even if our case for generating default moral principles fails for the aesthetic case, this only counts against one argument for aesthetic generalism, not against aesthetic generalism itself. Furthermore, our argument from practical wisdom is actually somewhat free-standing, and might hold up even if the argument for default principles breaks down for the reasons given in the previous section. As we shall now argue, however, there are good reasons to think that aesthetic and moral wisdom are quite different, even if both are in some sense practical.

The main premise of our original argument was that the best explanation of the possibility of ideal practical wisdom for creatures like us was a principled one – that is, one that attributed a suitable stock of moral principles to the person of ideal (humanly attainable) practical wisdom. We argued for this premise on three different grounds: (1) that the best account of the ability of the person of practical wisdom to have knowledge about fictional cases through description is one which invokes such principles, (2) that a principled explanation sorts the *a priori* from the *a posteriori* in a more plausible way than the alternatives, and (3) that the availability of such principles has some intuitive support independently. This last argument can safely be set aside, since robust aesthetic principles are, if anything, counter-intuitive. So our question now is whether analogues of either of our first two arguments can be carried over plausibly to the aesthetic realm.

How about the argument from knowledge in fictional cases? The analogue here presumably would be aesthetic knowledge of merely possible objects of aesthetic evaluation, where this knowledge can be gained simply by an adequate description of the object of evaluation. Here again the role of direct engagement seems relevant. We do not paradigmatically appreciate the beauty of the *Mona Lisa*, say, by reading a description of it. Indeed, even reading an incredibly detailed description of the painting does not seem sufficient for a proper appreciation of its aesthetic value. We do not deny that one can have aesthetic knowledge of non-actual objects. In fact, an eagerness to allow for this possibility motivated us to move from talk of the role of observation to the role of engagement. But, when one has aesthetic knowledge in these cases, a description is not enough. That alone is enough to spoil the analogue of our argument in the moral case, which was meant to invoke an ideal which is possible for creatures like us. However, it is worth pausing to see whether a version of the argument invoking a conception of aesthetic wisdom that is not specifically a conception meant to be appropriate for creatures like us might fare better. Although such an argument would be less practically relevant, given its utopianism, it might still be of interest.

One immediate worry is that the notion of aesthetic wisdom seems unlikely to be a notion we can understand while simultaneously abstracting from the sorts of creatures in question. This again reflects the intuitive idea that aesthetics is somehow more subjective than morality. Even if aesthetic value is not relative to individuals, it might at least be relative to *species*. The problem would then be that there will be many ways to idealize beyond the limitations of the human condition, and what counts as aesthetic wisdom may vary depending on how these idealizations are understood. On this sort of view, the *Mona Lisa* may be beautiful for us, aesthetically worthless for the Vulcans, and mediocre for the Martians.

A distinct, but related, worry is whether an ideal aesthetic wisdom for creatures like us, understood as a single unified phenomenon, is a coherent one. It may be that aesthetics is pluralistic in a deeper way than morality or practical reason more generally. In particular, it may be that certain forms of aesthetic value can be properly appreciated only by someone with a sensibility that would make it impossible for the person to appreciate other sorts of aesthetic value. For example, perhaps someone ideally suited to appreciating the aesthetic value of depressing arthouse films would thereby not be well suited to appreciating the aesthetic value of a slapstick comedy or a Hollywood action blockbuster.

Let us waive this worry as well. How might a species of creatures be able to go from an adequate description of an object of evaluation to a proper appreciation of the object and then to aesthetic knowledge? Given the need for direct engagement, the key idealization here would be an unlimited ability to go from any fully determinate description of the features of an object of evaluation to an accurate, though merely imagined, direct engagement with it – as a notional object of imaginative experience, that is. Human beings cannot go from (for example) a fully determinate pixel-by-pixel characterization of an arbitrarily fine-grained digitization of the *Mona Lisa* to a vivid and fully accurate act of direct acquaintance with it in imagination, but the species of creatures we are imagining by hypothesis can. Is the best account of the aesthetic wisdom of such a species of creatures plausibly taken to be a principled one?

Given the apparently open-ended nature of aesthetic value, and the way in which any feature can be good-making in the right context, we cannot give an affirmative answer. There is no reason in advance to believe that such creatures would not extract as many principles as there are possible objects of aesthetic evaluation. To us, this seems actually to be the most plausible hypothesis; in so far as we have a coherent ideal of aesthetic wisdom, we suspect it is *not* principled. Our purposes here, however, do not require us to insist on this last point. Our aim is not to establish the truth of particularism in aesthetics, but instead to explain why it is and should be more attractive than moral particularism.

What about the argument from sorting the *a priori* and the *a posteriori* in the right way – does that argument at least have a plausible analogue in the aesthetic case? Here we find it useful to draw a distinction between a proposition being *a priori* in principle and its being *a priori* for us. There may be certain mathematical propositions that are true, but are simply too complex for creatures like us ever even to comprehend, much less know. If so, such propositions are not *a priori* for us, though they might well be *a priori* for God. Lest the relativity of the *a priori* seem strange, recall that the *a priori* is usually defined modally – in terms of whether the proposition *can* be known in a certain way. We are simply pointing out that, if we understand 'can' in a way that takes contingent limitations of the judge into account, then there will be a useful distinction of this sort to be drawn.

Now return to our imagined creatures who can go from fully determinate descriptions to a vivid and fully accurate imaginative acquaintance with a representation of the object of evaluation. Perhaps there is a sense in which a principle going from the relevant features of the painting (those in virtue of which they find it beautiful, say) to the conclusion that it has a certain aesthetic value is *a priori* for them. For perhaps they can know such a principle simply by reflecting on what such an object of evaluation would be like, and this may count as *a priori*. Does this represent an advantage for such a principled account of aesthetic wisdom, putting to one side the worries already raised about such an account?

Again, this does not seem to us to be any kind of advantage for the view on offer. It is not as if we had some strong pre-theoretical intuition that aesthetic knowledge might in this way be *a priori* in principle even though it is not typically *a priori* for us (though it may sometimes be – again, knowledge of the elegance of a mathematical proof comes to mind). We can let the chips fall where they may on this count, but it hardly seems like an advantage for the account of aesthetic wisdom on offer that it can divide the *a priori* from the *a posteriori* in this unusual way.

5. Conclusion

Let us again take stock. In *Principled Ethics*, we argued that the best account of ideal practical wisdom for creatures like us is a principled account. Here we have argued that there is no plausible analogue of this argument in the aesthetic case. In many ways, our two main grounds for this are (a) that aesthetic wisdom is different from practical wisdom for creatures like us in that the former but not the latter requires direct engagement; this makes the ideal of aesthetic wisdom needed to support the argument rely on imaginative capacities that far exceed anything that human beings will ever even approximate, and (b) even for more idealized creatures without such imaginative limitations, there would likely be as many principles on offer as there are possible objects of evaluation. We also argued that the argument from the ability to sort the *a priori* from the *a posteriori* did not carry over, in that here there is no pre-theoretical basis for assuming some such distinction is needed anyway.

So the arguments given in *Principled Ethics* do not transpose smoothly into the context of aesthetics. Furthermore, the differences in virtue of which the arguments do not transpose smoothly provide some indication of why some form of particularism might pre-theoretically seem more attractive in the context of aesthetics than in the context of ethics. In particular, the essential role of direct global engagement makes particularism considerably more plausible in the case of aesthetics than in ethics, where such engagement does not seem essential. To be clear, we do not say that generalism is false in the case of aesthetics, but instead only that our arguments do not support it and that we can explain why particularism might seem intuitively more plausible in the case of aesthetics.

Notes

1. In the discussion that follows we will use beautiful simply to mean aesthetically good.
2. We here put to one side distracting complications arising out of the possibility of 'Gettier' cases – cases in which a justified true belief falls short of knowledge in certain characteristic ways. Although such cases clearly are as possible here as anywhere else, we think that their very ubiquity means that they will cut right across the moral/aesthetic divide and not help explain any relevant asymmetries. See Gettier (1963) for the classic statement of the sorts of cases we have in mind.
3. Some have argued that these uses of 'beautiful' and cognate terms are all metaphorical, and that all literal beauty and aesthetic value supervenes on features amenable to sensory perception. See Zangwill (1998). For a reply, see Barker (forthcoming).
4. An alternative term is 'holistic.' But since this term is already used to mark a number of quite different distinctions in the particularism/generalism debate we eschew it here.
5. See Moore (1903, chapter 6).
6. See Street (2008) for discussion.
7. We wish here to remain agnostic about how best to account for aesthetic judgment of types. One possibility is that we directly engage with types and so can have direct knowledge of their aesthetic properties. Another possibility is that our judgments about types must be reached via induction from judgments about tokens.
8. In the text we rely on a distinction between direct and indirect relevance; we discuss this more in *Principled Ethics* in the moral case when we discuss the distinction between direct and indirect reasons for action. There is an analogous distinction between direct and indirect evaluative relevance. There are, for example, good-making properties, and properties that simply explain why the thing has the good-making properties, and these will be distinct.

   Here we think that, in so far as the day of the week could matter to an aesthetic evaluation, this will be parasitic on some more broadly relevant aesthetic feature, like its resonance with a theme of the work. If, for example, a painting is about the importance of resting on the Sabbath, then the fact that the painting was finished on the evening before the Sabbath might be relevant. Its relevance, though, will in our view be explained by this broader and more generic fact about thematic resonance. We admit, though, that in the aesthetic case this distinction may be more problematic. If it is, and if even the day of the week can, in the right context, be aesthetically relevant, then that is just grist for our mill. For that simply bolsters the contrast we are after even more.
9. One complication we shall not explore here is the sort of modality involved in talk of what we 'can' directly engage with. In one sense, we can directly engage with the microtextual features of the *Mona Lisa*, but we don't think that these sorts of features are or even could be aesthetically relevant. We think that what counts as available for direct engagement in the relevant sense is somewhat slippery and context-sensitive. However this difficulty is worked out, though, the idea is clearly broad enough to make the analogue of default principles come out as very trivial and uninteresting, which is our main point here.

Bibliography

Alston, W.P. (2000) *Illocutionary Acts and Sentence Meaning* (Ithaca, NY: Cornell University Press).

Audi, R. (2006) 'Intrinsic Value and Reasons for Action', in T. Horgan and M. Timmons (eds) *Metaethics after Moore* (Oxford: Clarendon Press), 79–106.

Ayer, A.J. (1936/1946) *Language, Truth and Logic* (London: Victor Gollancz).

Barker, J. (forthcoming) 'Mathematical Beauty', *Art and Philosophy*.

Bedke, M. (2010) 'Might all Normativity be Queer?' *Australasian Journal of Philosophy* 88, 41–58.

Bicchieri, C. (2006) The Grammar of Society: The Nature and Dynamics of Social Norms (New York: Cambridge University Press).

Blackburn, S. (1971) 'Moral Realism', reprinted in his *Essays in Quasi-Realism*, 111–29.

Blackburn, S. (1984) *Spreading the Word* (Oxford: Clarendon Press).

Blackburn, S. (1988) 'How to Be an Ethical Anti-Realist', reprinted in *Essays in Quasi-Realism*, 166–81.

Blackburn, S. (1992) 'Morality and Thick Concepts', *Proceedings of the Aristotelian Society*, Suppl. Vol. 66, 285–99.

Blackburn, S. (1993) *Essays in Quasi-Realism* (Oxford: Oxford University Press).

Blackburn, S. (1998) *Ruling Passions* (Oxford: Oxford University Press).

Blackburn, S. (2002) 'Replies', *Philosophy and Phenomenological Research* 65, 164–76.

Blackburn, S. (2006) 'The Semantics of Non-Factualism', in M. Devitt and R. Hanley (eds) *The Blackwell Guide to the Philosophy of Language* (Oxford: Blackwells).

Blackburn, S. (2009) 'The Absolute Conception: Putnam vs Williams', in D. Callcut (ed.) *Reading Bernard Williams* (New York: Routledge).

Block, N. (1987) 'Functional Role and Truth Conditions', *Proceedings of the Aristotelian Society* 61, 157–81.

Block, N. (1993) 'Holism, Hyper-Analyticity and Hyper-Compositionality', *Philosophical Issues* 3, 37–72.

Blome-Tillman, M. (2009) 'Non-Cognitivism and the Grammar of Morality', *Proceedings of the Aristotelian Society* 103, 279–309.

Boyd, R. (1988) 'How to Be a Moral Realist', in G. Sayre-McCord (ed.) *Essays on Moral Realism* (Ithaca: Cornell University Press), 181–228.

Brandom, R. (1984) 'Reference Explained Away', *The Journal of Philosophy* 81, 469–92.

Brandom, R. (1994) *Making It Explicit* (Cambridge, MA: Harvard University Press).

Brandom, R. (2000) *Articulating Reasons* (Cambridge, MA: Harvard University Press).

Brandom, R. (2008) *Between Saying and Doing* (Oxford: Oxford University Press).

Brennan, G. and Pettit, P. (2004) *The Economy of Esteem* (Oxford; New York: Oxford University Press).

Brentano, F. (1934) *Vom Ursprung sittlicher Erkenntnis* (Leipzig: Felix Meiner).

Brink, D.O. (1984) 'Moral Disagreement and the Argument from Queerness', *Australasian Journal of Philosophy* 62, 112–25.

Brink, D.O. (1986) 'Externalist Moral Realism', *Southern Journal of Philosophy* 24: 23–40.

Brink, D.O. (1989) *Moral Realism and the Foundations of Ethics* (Cambridge: Cambridge University Press).

Brink, D.O. (2003) 'Prudence and Authenticity', *Philosophical Review* 112, 215–45.

Brink, D.O. (2007) Review of A. Gibbard's *Thinking How to Live*, in *Philosophical Review* 116, 267–72.

Broome, J. (2004) 'Reasons', in R. J. Wallace, M. Smith, S. Scheffler and P. Pettit (eds) *Reason and Value* (Oxford: Clarendon Press), 28–55.

Broome, J. (2005) 'Does Rationality Give us Reasons?', *Philosophical Issues* 15, 321–37.

Budolfson, M. (unpublished) 'Non-Cognitivism and Rational Inference.'

Byrne, A. and Hilbert, D. (2003) 'Color Realism and Color Science', *Behavioral and Brain Sciences* 26, 3–21.

Bykvist, K. (2006) 'Prudence for Changing Selves', *Utilitas* 18, 264–83.

Bykvist, K. (2009) 'No Good Fit: Why the Fitting Attitude Analysis of Value Fails', *Mind* 118, 1–30.

Bykvist, K. and J. Olson (2009) 'Expressivism and Moral Certitude', *Philosophical Quarterly* 59, 202–15.

Cameron, R.P. (2010) 'Necessity and Triviality', *Australasian Journal of Philosophy* 88, 401–15.

Carnap, R. (1935) *Philosophy and Logical Syntax* (Bristol, UK: Thoemmes Press).

Carnap, R. (1956/1983) 'Empiricism, Semantics, and Ontology', in *Meaning and Necessity* (2nd ed.) (Chicago: The University of Chicago Press), 205–21; reprinted in P. Benacerraf and H. Putnam (eds) *Philosophy of Mathematics: Selected Readings* (2nd ed.) (Cambridge: Cambridge University Press), 241–57.

Chrisman, M. (2007) 'From Epistemic Contextualism to Epistemic Expressivism', *Philosophical Studies* 135, 225–54.

Chuard, P. and N. Southwood (2009) 'Epistemic Norms without Voluntary Control', *Noûs* 43, 599–632.

Coleman, J. (1990) *The Foundations of Social Theory* (Cambridge, Mass.: Harvard University Press).

Copp, D. (1995) *Morality, Normativity and Society* (Oxford: Oxford University Press).

Copp, D. (2007) 'Realist Expressivism: A Neglected Option for Moral Realism', in D. Copp (ed.) *Morality in a Natural World* (Cambridge: Cambridge University Press), 153–202.

Copp, D. (2010) 'Normativity, Deliberation, and Queerness', in R. Joyce and S. Kirchin (eds) *A World Without Values* (Dordrecht: Springer).

Crisp, R. (2005) 'Value, Reasons, and the Structure of Justification: How to Avoid Passing the Buck', *Analysis* 65, 80–5.

Crisp, R. (2006) *Reasons and the Good* (Oxford: Clarendon Press).

Crisp, R. (2008) 'Goodness and Reasons: Accentuating the Negative', *Mind* 117, 257–65.

Cuneo, T. (2006) 'Saying What We Mean: An Argument against Expressivism', in R. Shafer-Landau (ed.) *Oxford Studies in Metaethics*, Volume 1 (Oxford: Oxford University Press).

Cuneo, T. (2007) *The Normative Web* (Oxford: Oxford University Press).

Dancy, J. (1993) *Moral Reasons* (Oxford: Blackwell, 1993).

Dancy, J. (2000a) *Practical Reality* (Oxford: Clarendon Press).

Dancy, J. (2000b) 'Should We Pass the Buck?', in A. O'Hear (ed.) *Philosophy, the Good, the True and the Beautiful* (Cambridge: Cambridge University Press), 159–74.

Dancy, J. (2004a) *Ethics without Principles* (Oxford: Clarendon Press).

Dancy, J. (2004b) 'Enticing Reasons', in R.J. Wallace, P. Pettit, S. Scheffler and M. Smith (eds) *Reason and Value* (Oxford: Clarendon Press).

Dancy, J. (2004c) 'On the Importance of Making Things Right,' *Ratio* 17, 229–37.

Dancy, J. (2006a) 'Nonnaturalism', in D. Copp (ed.) *The Oxford Handbook of Ethical Theory* (Oxford: Oxford University Press), 122–45.

Dancy, J. (2006b) 'What Do Reasons Do?', in T. Horgan & M. Timmons (eds) *Metaethics After Moore* (Oxford: Oxford University Press), 39–59.

Danielsson, S. and J. Olson (2007) 'Brentano and the Buck-Passers', *Mind* 116, 511–22.

Darwall, S. (2006) The Second-Person Standpoint: Respect, Morality, and Accountability (Cambridge, Mass.: Harvard University Press).

Davidson, D. (1980) 'Actions, Reasons and Causes', in his *Essays on Actions and Events* (Oxford: Oxford University Press).

Davis, W. (2003) *Meaning, Expression, and Thought* (Cambridge: Cambridge University Press).

Dorr, C. (2002) 'Non-cognitivism and Wishful Thinking', *Noûs* 36, 97–103.

Dreier, J. (1990) 'Internalism and speaker relativism', *Ethics* 101: 6–26.

Dreier, J. (2004) 'Meta-Ethics And The Problem Of Creeping Minimalism', *Philosophical Perspectives* 18, 23–44.

Dreier, J. (2006) 'Negation for Expressivists: A Collection of Problems with a Suggestion for their Solution', in R. Shafer-Landau (ed.) *Oxford Studies in Metaethics*, Volume 1 (Oxford: Oxford University Press), 217–33.

Dreier, J. (2010) 'Mackie's Realism: Queer Pigs and the Web of Belief', in R. Joyce and S. Kirchin (eds) *A World Without Values* (Dordrecht: Springer).

Driver, J. (2006) 'Autonomy and the Asymmetry Problem for Moral Expertise', *Philosophical Studies* 128, 619–44.

Dummett, M. (1978) *Truth and Other Enigmas* (London: Duckworth).

Dworkin, R. (1996) 'Objectivity and Truth: You'd Better Believe It', *Philosophy & Public Affairs* 25, 87–139.

Elga, A. (2007) 'Reflection and Disagreement', *Noûs* 41, 478–502.

Elga, A. (forthcoming) 'How to disagree about how to disagree', in R. Feldman and T. Warfield (eds) *Disagreement* (Oxford: Oxford University Press).

Elster, J. (1994) 'Rationality, Emotions and Social Norms', *Synthese* 98, 21–49.

Enoch, D. (2003) 'How Noncognitivists Can Avoid Wishful Thinking', *Southern Journal of Philosophy* 41, 527–45.

Enoch, D. (2006) 'Agency, Shmagency: Why Normativity Won't Come From What Is Constitutive of Action', *Philosophical Review* 115, 169–98.

Enoch, D. (2007) 'An Outline of an Argument for Robust Metanormative Realism', in R. Shafer-Landau (ed.) *Oxford Studies in Metaethics*, Volume 2 (Oxford: Oxford University Press), 21–50.

Enoch, D. (2009) 'Can There Be a Global, Interesting, Coherent Constructivism about Practical Reason?', *Philosophical Explorations* 12, 319–39.

Enoch, D. (2010) 'How Objectivity Matters', in R. Shafer-Landau (ed.) *Oxford Studies in Metaethics*, Volume 5 (Oxford: Oxford University Press), 111–52.

Enoch, D. (forthcoming) *Taking Morality Seriously: A Defense of Robust Realism*.

Enoch, D. and Schechter, J. (2008) 'How Are Basic Belief-Forming Methods Justified?', *Philosophy and Phenomenological Research* 76, 547–79.

Ewing, A.C. (1947) *The Definition of Good* (London: Routledge & Kegan Paul).

Ferrero, L. (2009) 'Constitutivism and the Inescapability of Agency', in R. Shafer-Landau (ed.) *Oxford Studies in Metaethics*, Volume 4 (Oxford: Oxford University Press), 303–33.

Fine, K. (1995) 'Ontological Dependence', *Proceedings of the Aristotelian Society* 95, 269–90.

Fine, K. (2001) 'The Question of Realism', *Philosophers' Imprint* 1, 1–30. http://www.philosophersimprint.org/001001/

Finlay, S. (2006) 'The Reasons that Matter', *Australasian Journal of Philosophy* 84, 1–20.

Finlay, S. (2008) 'The Error in the Error Theory', *Australasian Journal of Philosophy* 86, 347–69.

Finlay, S. (2009) 'Oughts and Ends', *Philosophical Studies* 143, 315–40.

Finlay, S. and M. Schroeder (2008) 'Reasons for Action: Internal vs. External', in E. Zalta (ed.) *The Stanford Encyclopedia of Philosophy*, Fall 2008 Edition. http://plato.stanford.edu/archives/fall2008/entries/reasons-internal-external/

FitzPatrick, W.J. (2004) 'Reasons, Value and Particular Agents: Normative Relevance Without Motivational Internalism', *Mind* 113, 285–318.

FitzPatrick, W.J. (2005) 'The Practical Turn in Ethical Theory: Korsgaard's Constructivism, Realism, and the Nature of Normativity', *Ethics* 115, 651–91.

FitzPatrick, W.J. (2008a) 'Robust Ethical Realism, Non-naturalism, and Normativity', in R. Shafer-Landau (ed.) *Oxford Studies in Metaethics*, Volume 3 (Oxford: Oxford University Press), 159–205.

FitzPatrick, W.J. (2008b) 'Morality and Evolutionary Biology', in E. Zalta (ed.) *The Stanford Encyclopedia of Philosophy*. http://plato.stanford.edu/entries/morality-biology/

'Flight 1549: A Routine Takeoff Turns Ugly.' CBS News, 5 July 2009 (first published 8 February 2009; updated 4 July 2009), accessed on 6 March 2010. http://www.cbsnews.com/stories/2009/02/08/60minutes/main4783580.shtml?tag=content Main;contentBody

Fodor, J. and Lepore, E. (1991) 'Why Meaning (Probably) Isn't Conceptual Role', *Mind and Language* 6, 329–43.

Foot, P. (1972) 'Morality as a System of Hypothetical Imperatives', *Philosophical Review* 81, 305–16.

Foot, P. (1978) 'Moral Beliefs', in *Virtues and Vices* (Berkeley: University of California Press), 110–31.

Garner, R.T. (1990) 'On the Genuine Queerness of Moral Properties and Facts', *Australasian Journal of Philosophy* 68, 137–46.

Geach, P.T. (1965) 'Assertion', *Philosophical Review* 74, 449–65.

Gert, J. (2002) 'Expressivism and Language Learning', *Ethics* 112, 292–314.

Gert, J. (2004) *Brute Rationality: Normativity and Human Action* (Cambridge: Cambridge University Press).

Gert, J. (2007a) 'Normative Strength and the Balance of Reasons', *Philosophical Review* 116, 533–62.

Gert, J. (2007b) 'Cognitivism, Expressivism, and Agreement in Response', in R. Shafer-Landau (ed.) *Oxford Studies in Metaethics*, Volume 2 (Oxford: Oxford University Press), 77–110.

Gert, J. (2008) 'Michael Smith and the Rationality of Immoral Action', *The Journal of Ethics* 12, 1–23.

Gert, J. (2009) 'Response-Dependence and Normative Bedrock', *Philosophy and Phenomenological Research* 79, 718–42.

Gettier, E. (1963) 'Is Justified True Belief Knowledge?', *Analysis* 23, 121–23.

Gibbard, A. (1990) *Wise Choices, Apt Feelings* (Cambridge, Mass.: Harvard University Press).

Gibbard, A. (2003) *Thinking How to Live* (Cambridge, MA: Harvard University Press).

Gibbard, A. (2006) 'Normative Properties', in T. Horgan and M. Timmons (eds) *Metaethics after Moore* (Oxford: Oxford University Press), 319–38.

Gibbard, A. (2008) *Reconciling Our Aims: In Search of Bases for Ethics* (Oxford: Oxford University Press).

Gibbard, A. (2010) 'Evolved Thinkers and Normative Concepts', MS to appear in R. Shafer-Landau (ed.) *Oxford Studies in Metaethics*, Volume 5 (Oxford: Oxford University Press).

Gilbert, M. (1989) *On Social Facts* (London; New York: Routledge).

Grice, H.P. (1957) 'Meaning', *The Philosophical Review* 66, 377–88.

Grice, H.P. (1989) *Studies in the Way of Words* (Cambridge, Mass.: Harvard University Press).

Grimm, S.R. (2006) 'Is Understanding a Species of Knowledge?', *British Journal for the Philosophy of Science* 57, 515–35.

Hale, R. (1993) 'Can There Be a Logic of Attitudes?', in J. Haldane and C. Wright (eds) *Reality, Representation, and Projection* (New York: Oxford University Press).

Hampton, J. (1998) *The Authority of Reason* (Cambridge: Cambridge University Press).

Hare, R.M. (1952) *The Language of Morals* (Oxford: Oxford University Press).

Harman, G. (1982) 'Conceptual Role Semantics', *Notre Dame Journal of Formal Logic* 28, 242–56.

Hart, H.L.A. (1961) *The Concept of Law* (Oxford: Clarendon Press).

Heuer, U. (2006) 'Explaining Reasons: Where Should the Buck Stop?', *Journal for Ethics and Social Philosophy* 1, 1–25. http://www.jesp.org

Heuer, U. (2010) 'Wrongness and Reasons', *Ethical Theory and Moral Practice* 13, 137–52.

Hieronymi, P. (2005) 'The Wrong Kind of Reason', *Journal of Philosophy* 102, 437–57.

Hills, A.E. (2009) 'Moral Testimony and Moral Epistemology', *Ethics* 120, 94–127.

Hills, A.E. (2010) The Beloved Self: Morality and the Challenge from Egoism (Oxford: Oxford University Press).

Holmes, R. (1985) *Acts of War: The Behaviour of Men in Battle* (New York: The Free Press).

Hopkins, R. (2007) 'What is wrong with moral testimony?', *Philosophy and Phenomenological Research* 74, 611–34.

Horgan, T. (1993) 'From Supervenience to Superdupervenience: Meeting the Demands of a Material World', *Mind* 102, 555–86.

Horgan, T. and M. Timmons (2006a) 'Cognitivist Expressivism', in T. Horgan and M. Timmons (eds) *Metaethics after Moore* (Oxford: Oxford University Press).

Horgan, T. and M. Timmons (2006b) 'Expressivism, Yes! Relativism, No!', in R. Shafer-Landau (ed.) *Oxford Studies in Metaethics*, Volume 2 (Oxford: Oxford University Press), 73–98.

Horgan, T. and M. Timmons (2007) 'Moorean Moral Phenomenology', in S. Nuccetelli and G. Seay (eds) *Themes from G.E. Moore* (Oxford: Oxford University Press).

Horgan, T. and M. Timmons (2009) 'Analytic Moral Functionalism Meets Moral Twin Earth', in I. Ravenscroft (ed.) *Minds, Ethics, and Conditionals* (Oxford: Oxford University Press).

Huemer, M. (2005) *Ethical Intuitionism* (Basingstoke: Palgrave Macmillan).

Hume, D. (1739/1975) L.A. Selby-Bigge (ed.) *A Treatise of Human Nature*, 2nd edition, revised by P.H. Nidditch (Oxford: Clarendon Press).

Hume, D. (1751/1998) T.L. Beauchamp (ed.) *An Enquiry Concerning the Principles of Morals* (Oxford: Oxford University Press).

Hussain, N. and N. Shah (2006) 'Misunderstanding Metaethics: Korsgaard's Rejection of Realism', in R. Shafer-Landau (ed.) *Oxford Studies in Metaethics*, Volume 1 (Oxford: Clarendon Press).

Jackson, F. (1998) *From Metaphysics to Ethics* (Oxford: Oxford University Press).

Jenkins, C. (2007) 'Epistemic Norms and Natural Facts', *American Philosophical Quarterly* 44, 259–72.

Johnson, R.N. (1999) 'Internal Reasons and the Conditional Fallacy', *The Philosophical Quarterly* 49, 53–71.

Johnson, R.N. (2003) 'Internal Reasons: Reply to Brady, Van Roojen and Gert', *The Philosophical Quarterly* 53, 573–80.

Johnston, M. (1989) 'Dispositional Theories of Value', *Proceedings of the Aristotelian Society*, Suppl. Vol. 63, 139–74.

Jones, K. (1999) 'Second-hand moral knowledge', *Journal of Philosophy* 96, 55–78.

Joyce, R. (2001) *The Myth of Morality* (Cambridge: Cambridge University Press).

Joyce, R. (2006) *The Evolution of Morality* (Cambridge, Mass.: MIT Press).

Joyce, R. (2010) 'Patterns of Objectification', in Joyce, R. and S. Kirchin (eds) *A World Without Values* (Dordrecht: Springer).

Joyce, R. (forthcoming) 'The Error in "The Error in the Error Theory"', *Australasian Journal of Philosophy*.

Kalderon, M.E. (2005) *Moral Fictionalism* (Oxford: Oxford University Press).

Kavka, G. (1978) 'Some Paradoxes of Deterrence', *Journal of Philosophy* 75, 285–302.

Kavka, G. (1983) 'The Toxin Puzzle', *Analysis* 43, 33–6.

Kelly, T. (2005) 'The Epistemic Significance of Disagreement', in J. Hawthorne and T. Gendler (eds) *Oxford Studies in Epistemology*, Volume 1 (Oxford: Oxford University Press).

Kelly, T. (forthcoming) 'Peer disagreement and Higher Order Evidence' in R. Feldman and T. Warfield (eds) *Disagreement* (Oxford: Oxford University Press).

Kitcher, P. (2002) 'Scientific Knowledge', in P. Moser (ed.) *The Oxford Handbook of Epistemology* (New York: Oxford University Press).

Kölbel, M. (2002) *Truth Without Objectivity* (New York: Routledge).

Kolodny, N. (2005) 'Why Be Rational?' *Mind* 114, 509–63.

Korsgaard, C. (1996) *The Sources of Normativity* (Cambridge: Cambridge University Press).

Korsgaard, C. (2003) 'Realism and Constructivism in Moral Philosophy', *Journal of Philosophical Research*, APA Centennial Supplement, 99–122.

Korsgaard, C. (2008) The Constitution of Agency: Essays on Practical Reason and Moral Psychology (Oxford: Oxford University Press).

Korsgaard, C. (2009) *Self-Constitution: Agency, Identity, and Integrity* (Oxford: Oxford University Press).

Kripke, S. (1982) *Wittgenstein on Rules and Private Language* (Cambridge, Mass.: Harvard University Press).

Kvanvig, J. (2003) *The Value of Knowledge and the Pursuit of Understanding* (Cambridge: Cambridge University Press).

Laden, A.S. (2009) 'The Trouble with Prudence', *Philosophical Explorations* 12, 19–40.

Lance, M. and M. Little (2006) 'Defending Moral Particularism', in J. Drier (ed.) *Contemporary Debates in Moral Theory* (Oxford: Blackwell), 305–21.

Lang, G. (2008) 'The Right Kind of Solution to the Wrong Kind of Reason Problem', *Utilitas* 20, 472–89.

Lavin, D. (2004) 'Practical Reason and the Possibility of Error', *Ethics* 114, 424–57.

Lawrence, G. (1995) 'The Rationality of Morality', in R. Hursthouse, G. Lawrence and W. Quinn (eds) *Virtues and Reasons* (Oxford: Clarendon Press), 89–147.

Lenman, J. (2003) 'Noncognitivism and Wishfulness', *Ethical Theory and Moral Practice* 6, 265–74.

Lewis, D. (1969) *Convention: a Philosophical Study* (Cambridge, Mass.: Harvard University Press).

Lewis, D. (1986). *On The Plurality of Worlds* (Oxford: Blackwell Publishers).

Lillehammer, H. (2007) *Companions in Guilt* (Basingstoke: Palgrave Macmillan).

Lipton, P. (2004) *Inference to the Best Explanation*, 2nd ed. (London: Routledge).

Loar, B. (2006) 'Language, Thought, and Meaning', in M. Devitt and R. Hanley (eds) *The Blackwell Guide to the Philosophy of Language* (Malden, Mass.: Blackwell Publishing).

Locke, J. (1690/2008) *An Essay Concerning Human Understanding*, P. Phemister (ed.) (Oxford: Oxford University Press).

McDowell, J. (1985) 'Values and Secondary Qualities', in T. Honderich (ed.) *Morality and Objectivity: A Tribute to J. L. Mackie* (Boston: Routledge and Kegan Paul), 110–29.

McKeever, S. and Ridge, M. (2005) 'What Does Holism Have to Do With Particularism?', *Ratio* 18, 93–103.

McKeever, S. and Ridge, M. (2006) *Principled Ethics: Generalism as a Regulative Ideal* (Oxford: Oxford University Press).

Mackie, J.L. (1977) *Ethics: Inventing Right and Wrong* (Harmondsworth: Penguin).

McLaughlin, B. and K. Bennett (2008) 'Supervenience', in E. Zalta (ed.) *The Stanford Encyclopedia of Philosophy* (Fall 2008 Edition). http://plato.stanford.edu/archives/fall2008/entries/supervenience/

McNaughton, D. and P. Rawling (2003) 'Naturalism and Normativity', *Proceedings of the Aristotelian Society*, Supp. Vol. 77, 23–45.

Markovits, J. (forthcoming) 'Why Be An Internalist About Reasons?', in R. Shafer-Landau (ed.) *Oxford Studies in Metaethics*, Volume 6 (Oxford: Oxford University Press).

Mele, A. (2003) *Motivation and Agency* (New York: Oxford University Press).

Merli, D.A. (2009) 'Possessing Moral Concepts', *Philosophia* 37, 535–56.

Miller, A. (2003) *An Introduction to Contemporary Metaethics* (Cambridge: Polity Press).

Moore, G.E. (1903) *Principia Ethica* (Cambridge: Cambridge University Press).

Moore, G.E. (1922) 'The Conception of Intrinsic Value', in his *Philosophical Studies* (London: Routledge & Kegan Paul), 253–75.

Nagel, T. (1970) *The Possibility of Altruism* (Oxford: Clarendon Press).

Nagel, T. (1979) 'Ethics Without Biology', in *Mortal Questions* (Cambridge: Cambridge University Press), 142–6.

Nagel, T. (1986) *The View from Nowhere* (Oxford: Oxford University Press).

Nichols, S. (2004) *Sentimental Rules* (Oxford: Oxford University Press).

Oddie, G. (2005) *Value, Reality, and Desire* (Oxford: Oxford University Press).

O'Leary-Hawthorne, J. and Price, H. (1996) 'How to Stand Up For Non-Cognitivists', *Australasian Journal of Philosophy* 74, 275–92.

Olson, J. (2004) 'Buck-Passing and the Wrong Kind of Reasons', *The Philosophical Quarterly* 54, 295–300.

Olson, J. (2007) 'Buck-Passing and the Consequentialism/Deontology Distinction', in T. Rønnow-Rasmussen, B. Petersson, J. Josefsson and D. Egonsson (eds) *Hommage à Wlodek. Philosophical Papers Dedicated to Wlodek Rabinowicz*, available at http://www.fil.lu.se/HommageaWlodek/site/papper/OlsonJonas.pdf

Olson, J. (2009) 'Reasons and the New Non-Naturalism', in S. Robertson, J. Skorupski and J. Timmermann (eds) *Spheres of Reasons* (Oxford: Oxford University Press).

Olson, J. (2010) 'The Freshman Objection to Expressivism and What to Make of It', *Ratio* 23, 87–101.

Olson, J. (forthcoming) 'Error Theory and Reasons for Belief', in A. Reisner and A. Steglich-Petersen (eds) *Reasons for Belief* (Cambridge: Cambridge University Press).

Parfit, D. (2001) 'Rationality and Reasons', in D. Egonsson, J. Josefsson, B. Peterson and T. Rönnow-Rasmussen (eds) *Exploring Practical Philosophy* (Aldershot: Ashgate), 17–39.

Parfit, D. (2006) 'Normativity', in R. Shafer-Landau (ed.) *Oxford Studies in Metaethics*, Volume 1 (Oxford: Oxford University Press), 325–80.

Parfit, D. (forthcoming, 2010) *On What Matters* (Oxford: Oxford University Press).

Pettit, P. (1990) 'The Reality of Rule-Following', *Mind* 99, 1–21.

Pettit, P. (1991) 'Realism and Response-Dependence', *Mind* 100, 587–626.

Pettit, P. (1998) 'Noumenalism and Response-Dependence', *Monist* 81, 112–32.

Pettit, P. (1999) 'A Theory of Normal and Ideal Conditions', *Philosophical Studies* 96, 21–44.

Pettit, P. (2002) *Rules, Reasons, and Norms* (New York: Oxford University Press).

Pigden, C. (2007) 'Nihilism, Nietzsche, and the Doppelganger Problem', *Ethical Theory & Moral Practice* 10, 441–56.

Plantinga, A. (forthcoming, 2010) 'Naturalism, Theism, Obligation and Supervenience.'

Posner, E.A. (1998) 'Symbols, Signals, and Social Norms in Politics and the Law', *Journal of Legal Studies* 27, 765–98.

Posner, E.A. (2000) *Law and Social Norms* (Cambridge, Mass.: Harvard University Press).

Price, H. (1988) *Facts and the Function of Truth* (New York: Blackwell).

Price, H. (1992) 'Metaphysical Pluralism', *Journal of Philosophy* 89, 387–409.

Price, H. (1997) 'Naturalism and the Fate of the M-worlds', *Proceedings of the Aristotelian Society*, Supp. Vol. 71, 247–67.

Price, H. (2003) 'Truth as Convenient Friction', *Journal of Philosophy* 100, 167–190.

Price, H. (2009) 'The Semantic Foundations of Metaphysics', in Ian Ravenscroft (ed.) *Minds, Ethics, and Conditionals: Themes from the Philosophy of Frank Jackson* (Oxford: Clarendon Press), 111–40.

Pritchard, D. (forthcoming) 'Knowledge, Understanding and Epistemic Value', in A. O'Hear (ed.) *Epistemology* (Cambridge: Cambridge University Press).

Pritchard, H.A. (1912/2002) 'Does Moral Philosophy Rest on a Mistake?', reprinted in his *Moral Writings* (J. MacAdam, ed.) (Oxford: Clarendon Press), 7–20.

Quine, W.V.O. (1970) *Philosophy of Logic* (Englewood Cliffs: Prentice Hall).

Quinn, W. (1993) 'Putting Rationality in its Place', in R.G. Frey and C.W. Morris (eds) *Value, Welfare, and Morality* (Cambridge: Cambridge University Press), 26–50.

Rabinowicz, W. and Toni Rønnow-Rasmussen (2004) 'The Strike of the Demon: On Fitting Pro-Attitudes and Value', *Ethics* 114, 391–423.

Rabinowicz, W. and Toni Rønnow-Rasmussen (2006) 'Buck-Passing and the Right Kind of Reasons', *Philosophical Quarterly* 56, 114–20.

Railton, P. (1986) 'Facts and Values', *Philosophical Topics* 24, 5–31.

Railton, P. (1989) 'Naturalism and Prescriptivity', *Social Philosophy and Policy* 95, 151–74.

Railton, P. (1997) 'On the Hypothetical and Non-Hypothetical in Reasoning about Belief and Action', in G. Cullity and B. Gaut (eds) *Ethics and Practical Reason* (Oxford: Clarendon Press), 53–79.

Raz, J. (1979) 'Kelsen's Theory of the Basic Norm', in *The Authority of Law* (Oxford: Oxford University Press).

Raz, J. (1999) *Engaging Reason* (Oxford: Clarendon Press).

Raz, J. (2001) *Value, Respect, and Attachment* (Cambridge: Cambridge University Press).

Raz, J. (2009) 'Reasons: practical and adaptive', in D. Sobel and S. Wall (eds) *Reasons for Actions* (Cambridge: Cambridge University Press), 37–57.

Ridge, M. (2004) 'How Children Learn the Meanings of Moral Words: Expressivist Semantics for Children', *Ethics* 114, 301–17.

Ridge, M. (2006) 'Ecumenical Expressivism: Finessing Frege', *Ethics* 116, 302–36.

Ridge, M. (2007) 'Ecumenical Expressivism: The Best of Both Worlds', in R. Shafer-Landau (ed.) *Oxford Studies in Metaethics*, Volume 2 (Oxford: Oxford University Press), 51–76.

Ridge, M. (2008) 'Moral Non-Naturalism', in E. Zalta (ed.) *Stanford Encyclopedia of Philosophy* http://plato.stanford.edu/archives/fall2008/entries/moral-non-naturalism.

Ridge, M. (2009) 'The Truth in Ecumenical Expressivism', in D. Sobel and S. Wall (eds) *Reasons for Action* (Cambridge: Cambridge University Press), 219–42.

Robertson, S.J. (2008) 'How to be an Error Theorist about Morality', *Polish Journal of Philosophy* 2, 107–25.

Robinson, L. (2006) 'Moral Holism, Moral Generalism, and Moral Dispositionalism', *Mind* 115, 331–60.

Rorty, R. (1995) 'Is Truth a Goal of Enquiry? Davidson Vs. Wright', *Philosophical Quarterly* 45, 281–300.

Rosati, C. (1995) 'Naturalism, Normativity, and the Open Question Argument', *Noûs* 29, 46–70.

Rosati, C. (2003) 'Agency and the Open Question Argument', *Ethics* 113, 490–527.

Rosenberg, J. (1974) *Linguistic Representation* (Dordrecht: D. Reidel Publishing Co.).

Ross, W.D. (1930) *The Right and the Good* (Oxford: Clarendon Press).

Russell, B. (1986) Collected Papers of Bertrand Russell, vol. 8, The Philosophy of Logical Atomism and Other Essays: 1914–1919, J.G. Slater (ed.) (London: Allen & Unwin).

Sayre-McCord, G. (1988) 'Moral Theory and Explanatory Impotence', in G. Sayre-McCord (ed.) *Essays on Moral Realism* (Ithaca: Cornell University Press).

Scanlon, T. (1998) *What We Owe To Each Other* (Cambridge, Mass.: Harvard University Press).

Scanlon, T. (2002) 'Reasons, Responsibility, and Reliance: Replies to Wallace, Dworkin and Deigh', *Ethics* 112, 507–28.

Scanlon, T. (2008) *Moral Dimensions* (Cambridge, Mass.: Harvard University Press).

Schiffer, S. (1972) *Meaning* (Oxford: Oxford University Press).

Schroeder, M. (2005) 'Cudworth and Normative Explanations', *Journal of Ethics and Social Philosophy* 1, 1–27.

Schroeder, M. (2007) *Slaves of the Passions* (Oxford: Oxford University Press).

Schroeder, M. (2008) *Being For: Evaluating the Semantic Program of Expressivism* (Oxford: Oxford University Press).

Schroeder, M. (2009a) 'Hybrid Expressivism: Virtues and Vices', *Ethics* 119, 257–309.

Schroeder, M. (2009b) 'Buck-Passers' Negative Thesis', *Philosophical Explorations* 12, 341–47.

Schroeder, M. (2009c) 'Means-Ends Coherence, Stringency, and Subjective Reasons', *Philosophical Studies* 143, 223–48.

Schroeder, M. (2010) *Noncognitivism in Ethics* (London: Routledge).

Schroeder, M. (forthcoming, 2010) 'Value and the Right Kind of Reasons', in R. Shafer-Landau (ed.) *Oxford Studies in Metaethics*, Volume 5 (Oxford: Oxford University Press).

Schroeder, M. (unpublished) 'Does Expressivism Have Subjectivist Consequences?'

Searle, J. (1962) 'Meaning and Speech Acts', *Philosophical Review* 71, 423–32.

Searle, J. (1979) *Expression and Meaning* (Cambridge: Cambridge University Press).

Sellars, W. (1969) 'Language as Thought and as Communication', *Philosophy and Phenomenological Research* 29, 506–27.

Sellars, W. (1974) 'Meaning as Functional Classification', *Synthese* 27, 417–37.

Setiya, K. (2003) 'Explaining Action', *Philosophical Review* 112: 339–93.
Setiya, K. (2007) *Reasons without Rationalism* (Princeton, NJ: Princeton University Press).
Shafer-Landau, R. (2003) *Moral Realism: A Defence* (Oxford: Oxford University Press).
Shafer-Landau, R. (2007) 'Moral and Theological Realism: The Explanatory Argument', *Journal of Moral Philosophy* 4, 311–29.
Shafer-Landau, R. (2009) 'A Defence of Categorical Reasons', *Proceedings of the Aristotelian Society* 109, 189–206.
Sinnott-Armstrong, W. (2006) *Moral Skepticisms* (New York: Oxford University Press).
Skorupski, J. (2006) 'Propositions about Reasons', *European Journal of Philosophy* 14, 26–48.
Skorupski, J. (2007) 'Buck-Passing about Goodness', in T. Rønnow-Rasmussen, B. Petersson, J. Josefsson and D. Egonsson (eds) *Hommage à Wlodek. Philosophical Papers Dedicated to Wlodek Rabinowicz*, available at http://www.fil.lu.se/hommageawlodek/site/papper/SkorupskiJohn.pdf
Smith, M. (1994a) *The Moral Problem* (Oxford: Blackwell Publishers).
Smith, M. (1994b) 'Why Expressivists About Value Should Love Minimalism About Truth', *Analysis* 54, 1–12.
Smith, M. (1995) 'Internal Reasons', *Philosophy and Phenomenological Research* 55, 109–31.
Smith, M. (2007) 'Book Symposium: In Defense of *Ethics and the A Priori*: A Reply to Enoch, Hieronymi, and Tannenbaum', *Philosophical Books* 48, 136–49.
Sobel, J.H. (2001) 'Blackburn's Problem: On Its Not Insignificant Residue', *Philosophy and Phenomenological Research* 62, 361–82.
Sobel, J.H. (MS) *Good and Gold: A Judgemental History of Metaethics from Moore through Mackie*. Available at http://www.utsc.utoronto.ca/~sobel/Gd_Gld
Southwood, N. (2008) 'Vindicating the normativity of rationality', *Ethics* 119, 9–30.
Southwood, N. and L. Eriksson (MS) 'Norms and Conventions.'
Stratton-Lake, P. (2000). *Kant, Duty, and Moral Worth* (London: Routledge).
Stratton-Lake, P. and B. Hooker (2006) 'Scanlon versus Moore on Goodness', in T. Horgan and M. Timmons (eds) *Metaethics after Moore* (Oxford: Clarendon Press), 149–68.
Street, S. (2006) 'A Darwinian Dilemma for Realist Theories of Value', *Philosophical Studies* 127, 109–66.
Street, S. (2008) 'Constructivism about Reasons', R. Shafer-Landau (ed.) *Oxford Studies in Metaethics*, Volume 3 (Oxford: Oxford University Press), 207–45.
Stevenson, C.L. (1937/1963) 'The Emotive Meaning of Ethical Terms', reprinted in his *Facts and Values* (New Haven: Yale University Press), 10–31.
Sturgeon, N. (1985) 'Moral Explanations', in D. Zimmerman and D. Copp (eds) *Morality, Reason, and Truth* (Totowa: Rowman & Littlefield).
Sturgeon, N. (1988) 'Moral Explanations', in G. Sayre-McCord (ed.) *Essays on Moral Realism* (Ithaca: Cornell University Press), 229–55.
Sturgeon, N.L. (2002) 'Ethical Intuitionism and Ethical Naturalism', in P. Stratton-Lake (ed.) *Ethical Intuitionism: Re-evaluations* (Oxford: Clarendon Press), 184–211.
Sturgeon, N. (2003) 'Moore on Ethical Naturalism', *Ethics* 113, 528–56.
Sturgeon, N. (2006) 'Ethical Naturalism', in D. Copp (ed.) *The Oxford Handbook of Ethical Theory* (Oxford: Oxford University Press), 91–121.
Sturgeon, N. (2009) 'Doubts About the Supervenience of the Ethical', in R. Shafer-Landau (ed.) *Oxford Studies in Metaethics*, Volume 4 (New York: Oxford University Press), 53–90.

Tännsjö, T. (2010) From Reasons to Norms: On the Basic Question in Ethics (Dordrecht: Springer Press).

Timmons, M. (1999) *Morality Without Foundations* (New York: Oxford University Press).

Ullmann-Margalit, E. (1977) *The Emergence of Norms* (Oxford: Clarendon Press).

Väyrynen, P. (2006) 'Resisting the Buck-Passing Account of Value', in R. Shafer-Landau (ed.) *Oxford Studies in Metaethics*, Volume 1 (Oxford: Oxford University Press), 295–324.

Väyrynen, P. (2009a) 'Normative Appeals to the Natural', *Philosophy and Phenomenological Research* 79, 279–314.

Väyrynen, P. (2009b) 'Objectionable Thick Concepts in Denials', *Philosophical Perspectives* 23, 439–69.

Velleman, J.D. (2000) *The Possibility of Practical Reason* (Oxford: Clarendon Press).

Velleman, J.D. (2009) *How We Get Along* (Cambridge: Cambridge University Press).

Verbeek, B. (2002) Instrumental Rationality and Moral Philosophy: An Essay on the Virtues of Cooperation (Dordrecht; Boston: Kluwer Academic Publishers).

Voss, T. (2001) 'Game Theoretical Perspectives on the Emergence of Social Norms', in M. Heidder and K.D. Opp (eds) *Social Norms* (New York: Russel Sage), 105–36.

Wallace, R.J. (2002) 'Scanlon's Contractualism', *Ethics* 112, 429–70.

Wallace, R.J. (forthcoming) 'Reasons, Values, and Agent-Relativity', *Dialectica*.

Weatherson, B. (2008) 'Intrinsic vs. Extrinsic Properties', in E. Zalta (ed.) *The Stanford Encyclopedia of Philosophy* (Fall 2008 Edition). http://plato.stanford.edu/archives/fall2008/entries/intrinsic-extrinsic.

Wedgwood, R. (2001) 'Conceptual Role Semantics for Moral Terms', *Philosophical Review* 110, 1–30.

Wedgwood, R. (2002) 'The Aim of Belief', *Philosophical Perspectives* 16, 267–97.

Wedgwood, R. (2004) 'The Metaethicist's Mistake', *Philosophical Perspectives* 18, 405–25.

Wedgwood, R. (2007) *The Nature of Normativity* (New York: Oxford University Press).

Wiggins, D. (1980) 'What Would Be a Substantial Theory of Truth?' in Z. van Straaten (ed.) *Philosophical Subjects: Essays Presented to P. F. Strawson* (Oxford: Oxford University Press), 189–221.

Wiggins, D. (1998) 'A Sensible Subjectivism?' in *Needs, Values, Truth*, 3rd ed. (New York: Oxford University Press), 185–214.

Williams, B. (1981a) 'Persons, Character, and Morality', reprinted in *Moral Luck* (Cambridge: Cambridge University Press), 1–19.

Williams, B. (1981b) 'Internal and External Reasons', reprinted in *Moral Luck* (Cambridge: Cambridge University Press), 101–13.

Williams, B. (1985) *Ethics and the Limits of Philosophy* (Cambridge, Mass.: Harvard University Press).

Williams, B. (1995) 'Internal Reasons and the Obscurity of Blame', reprinted in *Making Sense of Humanity* (Cambridge: Cambridge University Press), 35–45.

Williamson, T. (forthcoming) 'Past the Linguistic Turn?' in B. Leiter (ed.) *The Future for Philosophy* (Oxford: Oxford University Press).

Wittgenstein, L. (1922) *Tractatus Logico-Philosophicus* (London: Kegan Paul).

Wittgenstein, L. (1953) *Philosophical Investigations* (New York: Macmillan).

Woodward, J.B. (2003) *Making Things Happen: A Theory of Causal Explanation* (Oxford: Oxford University Press).

Wolterstorff, N. (1980) *Works and Worlds of Art* (Oxford: Oxford University Press).

Wright, C. (1991) 'Scepticism and Dreaming: Imploding the Demon', *Mind* 100: 87–116.

Wright, C. (1992) *Truth and Objectivity* (Cambridge, Mass.: Harvard University Press).
Wright, C. (1993) 'Realism: The Contemporary Debate – W(h)ither Now?' in J. Haldane and C. Wright (eds) *Reality, Representation and Projection* (Oxford: Oxford University Press), 63–84.
Young, H.P. (1998) *Individual Strategy and Social Structure* (Princeton, NJ: Princeton University Press).
Zagzebski, L. (2001) 'Recovering Understanding', in M. Steup (ed.) *Knowledge, Truth and Duty: Essays on Epistemic Justification, Responsibility and Virtue* (Oxford: Oxford University Press).
Zangwill, N. (1992) 'Quietism', *Midwest Studies in Philosophy* 17, 160–76.
Zangwill, N. (1998) 'Aesthetic/Sensory Dependence', *British Journal of Aesthetics* 38, 66–81.
Zimmerman, A. (2010) *Moral Epistemology* (London: Routledge).

Index

aesthetics, 264–7, 270, 275, 279–80, 282–4
   aesthetic knowledge, 270–5, 282–4
   aesthetic wisdom, 269, 282–4
agency, 208–33
anti-realism, 48, 85, 97, 100–1, 104, 120–3, 261
Argument from Queerness, 77, 92, 95
Ayer, A.J., 103, 126–8, 253

Barker, J., 272–3
Blackburn, S., 22, 103, 113, 126–7, 254

Chrisman, M., 234
constitutivism, 208–10, 212–19, 221–3, 226–30
constructivism, 90, 200–1, 275
Copp, D., 10, 26
Crisp, R., 166
Cuneo, T., 77

Dancy, J., 9, 265
default principles, 268–70, 279–81
descriptivism, 104–6
Dorr, C., 126–30, 132, 134–5, 138

Enoch, D., 126, 131–4, 137, 139
error theory, moral, 40, 62–83, 96
expressivism, 7–12, 14, 20–4, 32–4, 38, 40, 44, 47, 50, 55–9, 74, 90, 92, 97, 101, 103–30, 133, 138–9, 200–1

Ferrero, L., 219, 230–2
fictionalism, moral, 74, 85–102, 104–5, 107, 111, 118, 120, 122
Finlay, S., 63, 71–4, 76–7, 81–8
Frege-Geach problem, 92, 126, 129–30, 138

generalism, 266–7, 269–70, 275, 279, 281, 284
Gibbard, A., 7–16, 18–19, 21–5, 27–8, 31–5, 103, 108, 123–7

Hare, R.M., 103, 126–8
holism, 265–6, 268, 276
Hume, D., 97, 145
Humean, 98, 111, 159, 203
Humean Theory of Motivation, 145, 147

ideationalism, 103, 109–18, 120, 122
inferentialism, 114–23
internalism
   judgment, 119
   motivational, 63
   about reasons, 59, 141–2, 144, 146–52, 156, 159–63, 165, 180–1, 203, 208–9, 216–17, 229
intrinsic value, 187, 193
intrinsicality, 192–4

Jackson, F., 24
Johnson, R., 151–2, 159
Joyce, R., 63, 66–7, 72, 79–82, 87–100
judgment(s)
   aesthetic, 264–5, 274, 276
   moral/ethical, 9, 30, 32, 101, 127, 137, 162, 235, 238–41, 244, 248, 250–6, 260–1, 266–7, 276–7
   normative, 14–15, 22–3, 29, 31, 149, 162, 201, 235, 237–8, 240–5

Kalderon, M., 88, 90–2
Kavka, G., 153–4, 156
Korsgaard, C., 208–10, 213, 216–18, 229

Lenman, J., 126, 132, 134–7, 139

Mackie, J.L., 28, 63–4, 66–8, 77, 97
Mele, A., 145–6
Moore, G.E., 9–10, 92, 103, 187, 193, 274
moral epistemology, 31, 126, 129–30, 136–8, 249–53, 255, 258, 261, 275–6
moral understanding, 255–63
moral worth, 257–9, 261

naturalism, 36, 40, 51, 85, 100–1, 104, 107, 111, 116, 118, 120, 122
  ethical, 7–13, 21, 24–7, 30–2, 65, 85
  linguistic, 36–8, 40–1, 45
Naturalistic Fallacy, 103, 215
nihilism, 69, 107–8, 110, 112, 114, 197
non-cognitivism, 38, 49, 126–30, 135–9, 249, 252–5, 261
non-naturalism, 8, 11, 92, 104, 107, 118
  ethical, 7–11, 16, 20, 23–4, 26–9, 31, 65, 68, 118, 120, 122
normativity, 8–11, 16, 21, 28, 78, 167, 187–8, 190, 192, 208–9, 216, 220, 224, 229, 234, 236–8, 248

objectivity, 22, 46, 148, 159, 208–9, 217, 229
Open-Question Argument, 103, 228

Parfit, D., 175–6
particularism, 200, 264, 266–70, 275–6, 278–9, 283–4
Pettit, P., 37, 41–7, 50, 234
planning, 8, 12–16, 18–19, 21–2, 25, 27–8, 32, 127
Plantinga, A., 24
pragmatism, 37
Price, H., 37–41, 43–5, 47–50

Rabinowicz, W. & Rønnow-Rasmussen, T., 167, 169–70
Railton, P., 149
Raz, J., 173–4, 194
realism
  ethical/moral, 7, 10–13, 16, 19–24, 26–7, 31–2, 65–8, 97–8, 104, 121, 249, 251–5, 261
  normative, 7, 227
  quasi-, 7, 10–13, 20–4, 32, 39, 254
reasons
  categorical, 62–7, 71–3, 77–8
  and explanation, 148, 192
  external, 142–3, 147, 159
  hypothetical, 63, 77–8
  internal, 142, 148

normative, 40, 53, 141, 144, 146–9, 152, 158, 160, 186, 199–200, 227
relativism, 22–4, 26, 29, 71–4, 76–7
representationalism, 44, 103, 105–12, 114–18, 120, 122
response-dependence, 41–3, 46–50, 54
  global expressivist, 50–4, 58–9
Ridge, M., 52, 55–8, 127
rule-following, 42

Scanlon, T.M., 66, 166
Schroeder, M., 127, 189, 198, 229, 234
self-understanding, 212–17, 220–5, 227, 229
Smith, M., 52–4, 65, 127, 149, 151, 158–9
social norms, 234–41, 243–8
social practices, 235–45, 247–8
Stevenson, C.L., 103, 126–8
Stratton-Lake, P., 77
supervenience, 94, 137, 180, 189, 197, 268, 280

testimony, 89, 249–57, 259–60, 271, 273
thick and thin concepts, 195–6
truth, 31, 38–40, 47–8, 66–8, 86–9, 91, 95–8, 105, 116, 139, 173–7, 181, 197, 201, 253–4

value
  Buck-Passing account of, 166–70, 173–5, 177–81, 188
  Fitting-Attitude analysis of, 167–9, 179–80
  semantic, 43–4, 46
Väyrynen, P., 166
Velleman, J.D., 208–13, 215–18, 220–9

Williams, B., 141–5, 147–51, 158–60
Wishful-Thinking problem, 126–7, 129–32, 137–9
Wittgenstein, L., 37, 41–3, 53
Wrong-Kind-of-Reasons problem, 167, 169–73, 175, 178–80